中等职业教育课程改革教辅用书　中等职业学校对口升学考试用书

英语对口升学提升模拟测试

参考答案

主　编　郭洪湄　乔俊红
副主编　冯瑞金　冯变玲　高　馨
参　编　段春红　白　玉　宁惠兰

北京理工大学出版社
BEIJING INSTITUTE OF TECHNOLOGY PRESS

答案目录

基础模块(上册)Unit 1-Unit 3 阶段测试题一 ………………………………………………… 1
基础模块(上册)Unit 4-Unit 6 阶段测试题二 ………………………………………………… 5
基础模块(上册)Unit 7-Unit 9 阶段测试题三 ………………………………………………… 10
基础模块(上册)Unit 10-Unit 12 阶段测试题四 ……………………………………………… 15
基础模块(下册)Unit 1-Unit 3 阶段测试题五 ………………………………………………… 20
基础模块(下册)Unit 4-Unit 6 阶段测试题六 ………………………………………………… 24
基础模块(下册)Unit 7-Unit 9 阶段测试题七 ………………………………………………… 29
基础模块(下册)Unit 10-Unit 12 阶段测试题八 ……………………………………………… 34
拓展模块 Unit 1-Unit 3 阶段测试题九 ………………………………………………………… 39
拓展模块 Unit 4-Unit 6 阶段测试题十 ………………………………………………………… 44
拓展模块 Unit 7-Unit 9 阶段测试题十一 ……………………………………………………… 49
拓展模块 Unit 10-Unit 12 阶段测试题十二 …………………………………………………… 54
模拟测试卷一 …………………………………………………………………………………… 59
模拟测试卷二 …………………………………………………………………………………… 65
模拟测试卷三 …………………………………………………………………………………… 71
模拟测试卷四 …………………………………………………………………………………… 77
模拟测试卷五 …………………………………………………………………………………… 83
模拟测试卷六 …………………………………………………………………………………… 90
模拟测试卷七 …………………………………………………………………………………… 97
模拟测试卷八 …………………………………………………………………………………… 103
模拟测试卷九 …………………………………………………………………………………… 108
模拟测试卷十 …………………………………………………………………………………… 114
模拟测试卷十一 ………………………………………………………………………………… 121
模拟测试卷十二 ………………………………………………………………………………… 128

基础模块(上册)Unit 1-Unit 3 阶段测试题一

一、语音(本大题共 10 小题,每小题 1 分,共计 10 分)

从 A、B、C、D 四个选项中,选出画线部分发音不同的一项。

1.【D】D 选项的 ar 发[ə],在 B、C、D 中发[ɑː]。
2.【C】C 选项的 e 发[i],在 A、B、C 中发[e]。
3.【D】D 选项的 i 发[i],在 A、B、D 中发[ai]。
4.【B】B 选项的 a 发[ə],在 A、C、D 中发[æ]。
5.【A】A 选项的 ea 发[ei],在 A、C、D 中发[/iː/]。
6.【B】B 选项的 ed 发[id],在 A、C、D 中发[t]。
7.【A】A 选项的 th 发[θ],在 A、B、C 中发[ð]。
8.【D】D 选项的 n 发[n],在 B、C、D 中发[ŋ]。
9.【B】B 选项的 o 发[ə],在 B、C、D 中发[əu]。
10.【B】B 选项的 ear 发[iə],在 A、C、D 中发[ə]。

二、单项选择题(本大题共 30 小题,每小题 1 分,共计 30 分)

从 A、B、C、D 四个选项中,选出空白处的最佳选项。

11.【B】the way to…去……的路。
12.【B】enjoy doing 喜爱做…… be popular with 受……欢迎。
13.【D】in great joy 兴高采烈地。
14.【B】look forward to doing 期望做某事;would like,expect,want 后面都跟动词不定式。
15.【D】我希望在周末去当志愿者。你可以帮助打扫城市公园。cheer up 欢呼,使振奋;make up 编造;take up 占据,开始从事;clean up 扫除,清扫。
16.【B】hand 手,trip 旅行、出行,visit 拜访,foot 脚。"Kate,我要去购物,有什么需要给你买的吗?""是的,有。这将省我一次出行。"
17.【A】Thank you for…为……而感谢。
18.【B】后面是 five students,所以用 are。
19.【C】中心词为副词 fast,所以用 how。How+形容词/副词+主谓。
20.【A】形容词修饰不定代词要放在不定代词之后,且根据句意应选 A。
21.【B】由答语可知是对频率的提问,只能选 how often;how long 提问时长或长度;how much 对价钱或者数量提问;how soon 询问从现在起再过多长时间做某事。
22.【A】it 指上文提到的那份报纸。只剩下一份了。先生,您想要这份吗?
23.【A】no+名词表示全否定"没有"。
24.【C】由后面的 I'm really thirsty. 可知,任何一个都行,所以用 either。
25.【D】表示"带有,具有"带有或者具有某种特质。
26.【B】tell sb. to do sth. 告诉某人去做某事。
27.【D】由句意可知,两个男孩站在了他的前面,挡住了视线。

28. 【C】上课时，我跟不上老师的节奏，所以课后向同学求助。follow 跟随，在这里是听得懂、弄明白的意思。

29. 【B】five-star 五星级的。

30. 【A】room 表示房间是可数名词；表示空间是不可数名词。make room 表示让出……地方。

31. 【C】第一个空抽象名词具体化，表示具有某种特质的人或事，是可数名词。第二个空 experience 做经验讲时，是不可数名词。

32. 【C】leaf 的复数 leaves，所以选 C。

33. 【B】half an hour's 半个小时的。

34. 【D】a great deal of 修饰不可数名词 snow；a number of/many 修饰可数名词复数；a lot 副词。

35. 【C】work 是不可数名词，用 a great deal of 修饰。其余三个修饰可数名词复数。

36. 【A】exercise 锻炼 不可数名词；练习，可数名词。你应该出去多做运动，不要总是坐在桌前忙着做练习。

37. 【A】advice 不可数名词；learn well 学好，用副词。

38. 【A】interest 兴趣，direction 方向，habit 兴趣爱好，number 数字。根据 The Chinese Poetry Competition quickly rose to the top television rating ranks after it was presented on CCTV. 可知，收视率的增长说明了人们对传统文化的兴趣越来越高，选 A。

39. 【B】noise 做噪声讲是不可数名词。too much 修饰不可数名词。much too 修饰形容词。

40. 【A】how come? 怎么会呢？so what 那又怎样？No wonder 难怪。no problem 没问题。

三、完型填空（本大题共 15 小题，每小题 1 分，共计 15 分）

从 A、B、C、D 四个选项中，选出空白处的最佳选项。

41. 【A】考查名词及语境理解。A. inability 无能力；B. interest 兴趣；C. indication 指示；D. inspiration 启发；结合语境可知此处表示"它与学习挑战、无法与导师沟通有关"，由此可知答案选 A。

42. 【C】考查动词及语境理解。A. agree 同意；B. deal 交易；C. connect 联系；D. meet 遇见；根据前文 to connect with an instructor 可知，十年级时，我七节课中有六节不及格，因为我不了解老师的教学方法，故答案为 C。

43. 【D】考查动词及语境理解。A. feared 害怕；B. hated 恨；C. stayed 待在；D. repeated 重复；此处表示"结果，我重读十年级"，因此答案选 D。

44. 【D】考查形容词及语境理解。violent 疯狂的，bad 坏的，strange 奇怪的，陌生的，awesome 令人惊叹的。结合语境可知此处表示"费尔德女士明确表示我的行为是不允许的"，由此可知答案选 D。

45. 【D】考查副词及语境理解。luckily 幸好；regularly 定期地；immediately 立即；clearly 清楚地。此处表示"我们的谈话没有立即改变我的行为"，因此答案选 D。

46. 【A】考查名词及语境理解。scold 责骂；examination 考试；assistance 协助；explanation 解释，此处表示"上一学年我没有收到老师的任何帮助"，因此答案选 A。

47. 【B】考查名词及语境理解。plan 计划；system 系统；business 事务；career 生涯，职业。结合语境可知此处表示"她总是做我的事：办理入住手续，提供指导，支持我的成长"由此可知答案选 B。

48.【C】考查名词及语境理解。introduction 介绍；involvement 参与，插手；influence 影响；information 消息，结合语境可知此处表示"我不想让她插手"，因此选 C。

49.【A】考查形容词及语境理解。universal 普遍的；useful 有用的；unbearable 难以容忍的；unique 独特的，结合上下文可知此处表示"与费尔德女士在一起的这一年似乎让我难以忍受，这改变了我的思想和为"，由此可知答案选 A。

50.【C】考查连词及语境理解，结合语境可知这里表示转折，意为"但不幸的是，我的表现和对自己的期望需要很多年才能慢慢改变."，因此答案选 C。

51.【B】考查形容词及语境理解。spiritual 精神的；educational 教育的；professional 职业的；technical 技术上的，结合语境可知此处表示"我的教育之旅很艰难"，因此答案选 B。

52.【D】考查动词及语境理解。suggest 建议；keep 保持；consider 考虑，认为；avoid 避免。结合语境可知此处表示"我不断向前推进的部分原因是，我记得费尔德女士告诉我要做得更好，对自己有更高的期望。"，keep doing sth.，意为"不断做某事"，因此答案选 D。

53.【B】考查名词及语境理解。struggle 挣扎；application 申请书；performance 表演；research 研究，结合语境可知此处表示"经过多年的奋斗，我从一所著名的美国大学本科毕业"，因此答案选 B。

54.【B】考查形容词及语境理解。absent-minded 心不在焉的；hard-working 努力的；kind-hearted 好心的；at-risk 处于危险中的，可能遭受伤害的。根据语境可知此处表示"费尔德女士：谢谢你在那里，支持这个曾经处于危险中的年轻人"，因此答案选 B。

55.【A】考查动词及语境理解。share 分享；Compare 比较；agree 同意；combine 结合。结合语境可知此处表示"请知道，你教我的课程现在也通过我的工作与有风险的学生分享，帮助他们做得更好"，因此答案选 A。

四、阅读理解（本大题共15小题，每小题2分，共计30分）

从 A、B、C、D 四个选项中，选出符合题目要求的最佳选项。

A

56.【C】细节理解题，Everyone needs friends 任何人都需要朋友，由此可知交朋友是必须的。故选：C。

57.【B】细节理解题，It could be that we would even see them again 有的时候朋友离开了，但并不是永远也见不到，还是有机会再见的。故选：B。

58.【D】细节理解题，倒数第二段提到我们会以朋友的名字或者和朋友有关的信息去命名各种地方，比如图书馆、城镇等，但并没有提到坏的事情。故选：D。

59.【D】细节理解题，When we have friends, we will be very happy. Being happy helps you stay Well. Or it could be just knowning that someone cares. If someone cares about us, We take better care of ourselves. 有朋友之后我们会开心，最终会让我们更好的照顾自己。故选：D。

60.【B】主旨归纳题，文章首句提到 Everyone needs friends 所有人都需要朋友，下文也是围绕着这个论点展开。故选：B。

B

【文章大意】此题主要讲述关于大笑可以减缓压力的一篇故事。

61.【A】细节理解题。根据"The first Laughter Club was started in Mumbai, India"可知，第一个

62.【D】细节理解题。根据第二段"There are now more than 500 Laughter Clubs in India nd over 1,300 in the world"描述可知,现在在印度有 500 多个笑声俱乐部,世界上有 1 300 多个。所以选 D。

63.【C】细节理解题。根据"I was quite nervous at the beginning of the class"可知,我开始上课时很紧张,所以选 C。

64.【A】细节理解题。由文章最后一段"After ten minutes everybody in the room was laughing…"可知,所有人在 10 分钟后都开怀大笑了。故答案选 A,10 分钟之后。

65.【B】主旨大意题。根据"That's how thousands of people start their day at Laughter(笑声)Clubs around the world and many doctors now think that having a good laugh might be one of the best ways to stay healthy."可知,本文主要讲述了笑是保持健康的最好的方法之一。

C

66.【C】细节理解题。根据第一段最后一句"A recent study suggests music lessons can make children have better memories than their peers(同龄人). 最近的一项研究表明,音乐课可以让孩子比同龄人有更好的记忆力。"可知,你最好感谢父母花在音乐训练上的时间和金钱,因为音乐能帮助你提高记忆力。选 C。

67.【B】细节理解题。根据第四行"In one year, they took four tests in different times 一年里,他们在不同的时间做了四次测验,"可知,应该是一年时间,选 B。

68.【D】细节理解题。根据第五行 The results showed brain(大脑)development changes at least every four months. 结果显示大脑发育至少每四个月发生一次变化. 可知,应该是至少四个月,选 D。

69.【A】细节理解题。根据最后一段"People say music is the good medicine for a bro ken heart. 人们说音乐是治疗心碎的良药",可知,音乐可以让我们开心,选 A。

70.【B】主旨大意题。根据最后一句"We are sure to find more and more in the wonderful world of music. 我们一定会在美妙的音乐世界里发现更多的东西",可知,短文主要介绍音乐对我们有好处,选 B。

五、书面表达(15 分)

One possible version:

Dear Peter,

  I'm glad to receive your letter asking for my advice on how to learn Chinese well.

  Here are a few suggestions. First, it is important to take a Chinese course, as you'll be able to learn from the teacher and practice with your fellow students. Then, it also helps to watch TV and read books, newspapers and magazines in Chinese whenever possible.

  Besides, it should be a good idea to learn and sing Chinese songs, because by doing so you'll learn and remember Chinese words more easily. You can also make more Chinese friends. They will tell you a lot about China and help you learn Chinese.

  Try and write to me in Chinese next time. Best wishes.

Yours,
Li Hua

基础模块(上册)Unit 4-Unit 6 阶段测试题二

一、语音(本大题共 10 小题,每小题 1 分,共计 10 分)

从 A、B、C、D 四个选项中,选出画线部分发音不同的一项。

1.【A】A 选项的 s 发[z],在 B、C、D 中发[s]。
2.【D】D 选项的 oo 发[uː],在 A、B、C 中发[/u/]。
3.【C】C 选项的 ow 发[au],在 A、B、D 中发[əu]。
4.【B】B 选项的 or 发[ə],在 A、C、D 中发[ɔː]。
5.【B】B 选项的 u 发[ə],在 A、C、D 中发[ʌ]。
6.【B】B 选项的 e 发[i],在 A、C、D 中发[e]。
7.【D】D 选项的 o 发[ʌ],在 A、B、C 中发[əu]。
8.【A】A 选项的 ar 发[ɔː],在 B、C、D 中发[ɑː]。
9.【A】A 选项的 ou 发[au],在 B、C、D 中发[ʌ]。
10.【B】B 选项的 i 发[i],在 A、C、D 中发[ai]。

二、单项选择题(本大题共 30 小题,每小题 1 分,共计 30 分)

从 A、B、C、D 四个选项中,选出空白处的最佳选项。

11.【B】be happy with 对……很满意。农民对秋天的好收成很满意。pleasure 高兴,愉快;crazy 疯狂的,狂热的;fond 喜欢的,深情的。
12.【A】leave for 动身前往……
13.【B】be angry with 生……的气。我很生自己的气,竟犯了这样愚蠢的错误。
14.【C】quickly 迅速地;slowly 缓慢地;suddenly 突然,忽然;terribly 非常地,很厉害地。我忽然想起我把书落在家里了。
15.【D】gave sb. a lift 送某人一程,让某人搭便车。waited for 等待,等候。let sb. down 让某人失望;kicked sb. off 把某人开除。
16.【A】be busy with 忙于某事。
17.【D】in fact 事实上。
18.【A】in the north of China 在中国的北方。
19.【A】a way to do 干……的方法。
20.【A】a lot 副词,rain a lot 表示下雨多;a lot of=lots of 许多、大量,后面接名词。
21.【D】她唱得多动听啊!我从未听过比这更好的声音。a better voice=the best voice。
22.【A】enough 修饰副词,放在该词之后。fast 强调速度快;quickly 强调动作迅速、敏捷,表示动作需要在短时间内完成。
23.【A】It's time to do…该是做某事的时候了。
24.【D】第一空是泛指用不定冠词,organization 是元音音素开头的单词,用 an;第二空 the+形容词表示一类人。
25.【B】a most+形容词:其中的 most 相当于 very;the most+形容词是最高级用法。第五课是非常难的一课,但并不是本书中最难的一课。

26.【C】have the habit of…有……的习惯,the 表示特指;public places 是复数名词,表示泛指概念,前面不用冠词。

27.【A】in hospital 是"住院";in the hospital 是指"在医院",可能是在医院工作或是在照顾病人等。

28.【C】这位女士是做什么的?她是一名舞蹈演员兼时装设计师。a dancer and fashion designer。

29.【A】当我们和别人讲话时,应该尽可能地礼貌些。as…as possible 尽可能……第一个 as 后面的词在句中做表语,用形容词 polite。

30.【D】the+比较级;the+比较级"越……就越……"。

31.【C】work deep into the night 工作到深夜;修饰 move 用副词 deeply "深深地"。

32.【C】这里指"要成为一位像袁隆平一样的科学家",表示泛指,用不定冠词。

33.【A】由 He is always telling jokes 可知"吴老师是一个非常幽默的老师",所以答案选 A。A 幽默的,B 严肃的,C 认真的,D 英俊的。

34.【B】由后面的 enjoyed it a lot,可以推测出答案为 B。意思是电影很精彩,我们很开心。

35.【C】一个诚实的人既不说谎也不骗人。由"does not tell lies or cheat people"可知,应填"诚实的"。careless 粗心的,stupid 愚蠢的,honest 诚实的,humorous 幽默的。

36.【A】开车时要当心,尤其是像这样的暴风雨的天气。especially 尤其,特别;probably 可能,大概;nearly 几乎,差不多;hardly 几乎不。

37.【D】quickly 迅速地,suddenly 突然地,secretly 偷偷地,traditionally 传统上。句意为"赏月和吃月饼庆祝中秋节是中国的传统"所以选 D。

38.【D】由"hurt his back seriously"可知受伤很严重,所以没有帮助几乎下不了床。quickly 迅速地,easily 简单地,nearly 几乎,hardly 几乎不。

39.【A】根据句意及语境,这是购物交际用语,答语是想买东西。No, thanks. 不,谢谢。It doesn't matter. 没关系。Of course I can 当然了,我可以。故选 A。

40.【B】他人表示感谢回应时应用 You're welcome "不客气"。All right "好的";Good luck "祝你好运";Not too bad "还不错"。

三、完型填空(本大题共 15 小题,每小题 1 分,共计 15 分)

从 A、B、C、D 四个选项中,选出空白处的最佳选项。

41.【B】考查形容词。根据上下文结合设空处前面的 feeling 推断此处的句意是"他必须整体躺在床上,不能动弹。一整天他又伤心又难过",所以填形容词"伤心的",故答案是 B。

42.【C】考查名词。根据上下文结合设空处前面的 look out of the 推断此处的句意是"除了望着窗外,他无事可做",所以填名词"窗户"window,故答案是 C。

43.【D】考查名词。根据上下文结合推断此处的句意是"直到有一天他看到窗户里一个奇怪的形状",结合句意所以填名词"形状"shape,故答案是 D。

44.【D】考查介词。根据上下文结合推断此处的句意是"那只企鹅穿过开着的窗进来",表示从内部穿过所以填 through,故答案是 D。

45.【A】考查动词。根据上下文推断此处的句意是"然后转过身,迅速离开了",所以填 left,故答案是 A。

46.【B】考查形容词。根据上下文推断此处的句意是"哈利非常吃惊,他试图弄明白发生了什么",结合句意所以填形容词"吃惊的"surpriesd,故答案是B。

47.【A】考查代词。根据上下文推断此处的句意是"哈利非常吃惊,他试图弄明白发生了什么",所以填 what,故答案是A。

48.【D】考查名词。根据上下文结合 more and more crazy-looking 推断此处的句意是"但是过了一会儿,随着越来越多的造型古怪的角色出现在窗户外面",结合句意填名词"人物;角色"所以填 characters,故答案是D。

49.【B】考查动词。根据上下文结合 he couldn't help 推断此处的句意是"他禁不住大笑了起来并停不下来",can't help doing 表示"禁不住做某事",所以填 laughing,故答案是B。

50.【A】考查形容词。根据上下文结合 Those strange characters ended up putting joy back in his heart 推断此处的句意是"或者一只小狗戴着眼镜,用滑稽的方式表演着",设空处表示"滑稽的;有趣的"所以填 funny,故答案是A。

51.【B】考查动词。根据上下文结合 he was able to go back to school again 推断此处的句意是"不久以后,他的健康状况有了很大的改善",表示"改善;提高"所以填 improved,故答案是B。

52.【C】考查动词。根据上下文推断此处的句意是"他告诉了同学们他所有经历过的事情",表示动词"经历"所以填 experienced,故答案是C。

53.【A】考查代词。根据上下文推断此处的句意是"他发现有什么东西从他朋友的书包里面出来",设空处所在的句子是一个肯定句,所以填 something,故答案是A。

54.【D】考查副词。根据上下文结合 his friend had to show him what was in the bag 推断此处的句意是"他很坚持,最终他的朋友给他展示了书包里面的东西",表示"最后;最终"所以填 finally,故答案是D。

55.【A】考查短语。根据上下文推断此处的句意是"在书包里面,盛放着所有他的好朋友用来鼓励哈利振作起来的东西。"表示"使某人振作起来"所以填 cheer up,故答案是A。

四、阅读理解(本大题共15小题,每小题2分,共计30分)

从 A、B、C、D 四个选项中,选出符合题目要求的最佳选项。

A

56.【B】题意:据老师说,_____。考查细节理解题。A. Charles should be punished for the whistle 查尔斯应该因哨子而受到惩罚;B. John should be punished for the whistle 约翰应该因吹哨子而受到惩罚;C. both of them should be punished for the whistle 他们两个都因吹哨子应该受到惩罚;D. all the boys should be punished for the whistle 所有的男孩子都应该受到处罚。根据第一段 A teacher had been very annoyed by some of the boys whistling during school hours. At last he knew he would have to punish anyone who repeated the offence(过错). (有些学生在上课时吹口哨,老师很生气。最后他知道他将要惩罚那些重复的过错的孩子。)结合题意可知选 B。

57.【C】题意:查尔斯吹响了哨子,因为_____。考查细节理解题。A. nobody else did it 没有其他人做这件事;B. he was going to cough 他要咳嗽了;C. he rubbed out the wrong sum 他擦掉了错误的加法;D. he was used to whistling 他习惯吹口哨。根据第五段中 I was doing a long hard sum, and when I rubbed out another sum to make room for it, I rubbed out the difficult one by mistake. I spoiled it all, and before I knew what I had done, I had whistled out loud!

(刚刚我正在做一个又长又难的加法，我擦去另一个式子给它腾空时不小心把难的式子擦掉了。我把所有的搞砸了，当我意识到我在那之前，我已经吹了口哨!)结合题意可知选C。

58.【D】题意：约翰极力否认吹口哨，表明_____。考查细节理解题。A. he was afraid of being punished 他害怕受到惩罚；B. he knew who gave the whistle 他知道是谁给的哨子；C. his words had not been believed 他的话不被相信；D. he didn't give the whistle at all 他根本没吹口哨。根据第五段中第一句"Do not punish John, sir," he said to the teacher, "It was I who whistled."结合题意和语境可知选D。

59.【B】题意：事件的结果是_____。考查细节理解题。A. John had been wronged and punished 约翰受到了委屈和惩罚；B. Charles was praised for his courage 查尔斯因勇气而受到表扬；C. nobody cared about Charles's action 没人关心查尔斯的行动；D. the teacher made a more serious rule 老师制定了一个更严肃的规则。根据第五段中Taking the little boy's hand, the teacher said, "Charles, you have done right. No one can doubt that you have spoken the truth, and that you did not intend to whistle. I cannot punish you, my boy, after having acted so nobly."(老师抓住小孩的手说："查尔斯，你做得对。没有人能怀疑你说谎，而且你不是故意吹的口哨。我的孩子，在你表现这么好后，我不能惩罚你。")结合题意可知选B。

60.【B】题意：这篇文章最好的题目是_____。考查主旨理解题。A. Teacher's Mistake 老师的错误；B. True Courage 真正的勇气；C. Two Naughty Boys 两个调皮的男孩；D. A Sudden Whistle 一个突然的口哨。本文主要内容讲述了一个勇敢的男孩承认了自己的错误，最终受到了老师的表扬。结合题意和语境可知选B。

B

61.【D】细节理解题。根据第一段最后一句"No one had told them about the British custom(习惯)of lining up for a bus that the first person who arrives at the bus stop is the first person to get on the bus. 没有人告诉他们在英国排队等车的习惯是到达公交站牌的第一个人先上车。"可知，这三个外国人没按顺序上车，所以人们把他们推出去。故选D。

62.【B】细节理解题。根据文章第二段第二句"If you want to have a pleasant visit, find out as much as possible about the manners and customs of your host country. 如果你想有一个愉快的访问，应该尽可能多地找出你的东道国的风俗习惯"可知，如果你想在国外有一个愉快的旅行，应该先了解这个国家的礼仪和习俗。故选B。

63.【B】细节理解题。根据文章第二段"people there consider it impolite to use the left hand for passing food at table. 在印度，人们认为在餐桌上用左手来传递食物是不礼貌的"，故选B。

64.【A】细节理解题。根据文章第四段"In Europe it quite usual to cross your legs when you are sitting talking to someone even at an important meeting. 在欧洲，当你坐着和某个人交谈，其至在一个重要的会议上，跷二郎腿是很常见的"可知，在欧洲，在一个重要的会议上跷二郎腿是一个很平常的习惯，故选A。

65.【B】主旨大意题。根据"Learning the language of a country isn't enough. If you want to have a pleasant visit, find out as much as possible about the manners and customs of your host country. You will probably be surprised just how different they can be from your own." "学习一个国家的语言是不够的。如果你想有一次愉快的旅行，尽可能多地了解东道国的礼仪和习俗。你可能会惊讶于它们和你的习俗有多么不同。"可知，是要注意习俗礼节。所以B项

符合题意。故选：B。

C

66.【D】细节理解题。根据 It was a warm summer afternoon, went outside to play in the yard while they all sat around the kitchen table to talk. (那是一个温暖的夏日午后，他们一起出去院子里玩，围坐在餐桌旁聊天。) 可知，当其他人在厨房谈话时，作者院子里玩耍。故选 D。

67.【B】词义猜测题。根据 "No!" It was my grandmother's voice. I jumped back. That was the first time I can ever remember her yelling at me. ("不!"那是我祖母的声音。我跳了回去。那是我第一次记得她对我……) 可猜测出，下划线单词的意思应是"大喊"。故选 B。

68.【C】推理判断题。根据 Seeing the frightened look on my face, she smiled and showed me why she had yelled. (看到我脸上惊恐的表情，她微笑着告诉我她为什么大喊大叫。) 可推理出，作者在奶奶对他大喊大叫后感觉很害怕。故选 C。

69.【A】细节理解题。根据 If I pulled on it, I would have pulled the quilt apart and ruined (毁掉) hours of work. (如果我把它拉了，我会把被子拉开，毁掉工作时间。) 可知，如果作者把线扯了被子会被拉开。故选 A。

70.【B】推理判断题。根据 We are each a single piece of thread, but the other threads around us help hold everything together. That's our purpose — help and support the people around us. (我们每个人都是一根线，但我们周围的其他线有助于把一切联系在一起。这就是我们的目的——帮助和支持我们周围的人。) 可推理出，作者想告诉我们要帮助我们周围的人。故选 B。

五、书面表达(15分)

One possible version:

Dear Abby,

　　How nice to hear from you! In your letter you asked me how to keep healthy while the novel corona-virus (COVID-19) is spreading worldwide. I would like to give you some advice.

　　As you know, Good living and hygiene habits are of great importance to our health, especially during this serious situation.

　　Therefore, you must wear masks in public place and wash hands frequently after you get in touch with others. What's more, keeping good sleep is necessary for your growing body. So I advise you to have at least eight hours of sleep every day and not to stay up too late.

　　Also, after returning to school, you should take physical exercise regularly instead of studying in the classroom all the time to improve your immunity. Besides, keeping a healthy and balanced diet is very important. Don't forget we are what you eat. Only in this way can you keep healthy.

　　Wish you a good health!

Yours,
Li Hua

基础模块(上册)Unit 7-Unit 9 阶段测试题三

一、语音(本大题共10小题,每小题1分,共计10分)

从 A、B、C、D 四个选项中,选出画线部分发音不同的一项。

1. 【B】考查字母 i 的发音,在重读开音节中读[ai],在重读闭音节中读[i],在非重读音节中读[ə]或者[i]。i 在 A、C、D 中读[i],在 B 中读[ai]。

2. 【B】考查字母 e 的发音,在重读开音节中读[i:],在重读闭音节中读[e],在非重读音节中读[ə]或者[i]。e 在 A、C、D 中读[e],在 B 中读[i]。

3. 【D】考查字母 u 的发音,在重读开音节中读[ju:],在重读闭音节中读[ʌ],u 在 A、B、C 中读[ʌ],在 D 中读[u:]。

4. 【A】考查字母 ch 的发音,在一些单词中读[k],在一些单词中读[tʃ]。ch 在 B、C、D 中读[tʃ],在 A 中读[K]。

5. 【A】考查字母 ea 的发音,在重读音节中读[ei],在非重读音节中读[i:],ea 在 B、C、D 中读[i:],在 A 中读[ei]。

6. 【D】考查字母 oo 的发音,在一些重读音节中读[u:],在一些重读音节中读[u],在 Lood 中读[ʌ],oo 在 A、B、C 中读[u],在 D 中读[ʌ]。

7. 【A】考查字母 c 的发音,在 a, o, u 和辅音字母 l, r, t 及音节末尾读[k],在 e, i, y 中读[s],c 在 B、C、D 中读[k],在 A 中读[s]。

8. 【C】考查字母 ex 的发音,在重读音节中读[eks],在元音前的非重读音节中读[igz],在辅音前的非重读音节中读[iks]。ex 在 A、B、D 中读[iks],在 C 中读[igz]。

9. 【A】考查字母 a 的发音,在重读闭音节中读[æ],在 n, f, s, ph, th 前读[ɑ:],a 在 B、C、D 中读[æ],在 A 中读[ɑ]。

10. 【A】考查字母 are 的发音,parent 中 are 读[eərə],are 在 B、C、D 重读音节中读[eə]。

二、单项选择题(本大题共30小题,每小题1分,共计30分)

从 A、B、C、D 四个选项中,选出空白处的最佳选项。

11. 【C】题意:在老师的帮助下,我开始赶上我的同学。考查介词的固定搭配。with one's help 固定搭配,意为"在某人的帮助下";catch up with 固定搭配,意为"赶上",故选 C。

12. 【C】题意:努力学习,否则你会落后于其他同学。考查连词。根据题意,前后应为转折关系。or 可译为"否则,要不然"。

13. 【A】题意:假如你一个字也不认识,你可以查字典。固定搭配 look up… in the dictionary,查字典。

14. 【B】题意:我们学习教师的数量是118,四分之一是女老师。the number of…的数,a number of 很多。分数的表示法是:分子用基数词,分母用序数词,分子大于1时,分母加 s,three quarters 四分之三;根据句意"我们学校的教师人数是118人,其中四分之一是女教师"可知,要填"The number, one fourth"。

15. 【A】题意:布朗先生在一个晴朗的早上飞往昆明了。考查介词用法,具体在有形容词描述的早、中、晚用介词 on，所以为 A。

16.【C】题意：有一大群人在等开幕式开始。固定搭配 wait for 等待。

17.【C】题意：老师提出一个难问题，Jim 尽力想出一个好答案。考查动词短语的辨析。put up with 忍受，容忍；keep up with 紧跟，跟上；come up with 想出，提出（计划、想法等）；go through with 完成，把……进行到底。句意：老师问了一个难题，但汤姆设法想出了一个好答案。故选：C。

18.【A】题意：由于气温突变，这个小城市暴发流感。A 选项突发，暴发；B 选项 分裂，分手，打碎；C 选项破门而入，闯入；D 选项发生故障。故选 A。

19.【D】题意：让 Harry 也玩你的玩具。Clare，你必须学会与他人分享。support 支持，支撑；care 关心，喜欢，照顾；spare 抽出，留出；share 分享，共享。

20.【A】题意：整个社会应该关心儿童的健康和身心健康成长。根据句意，此空应表达"关心儿童的健康和身心健康成长"，根据固定短语"be concerned about：关心"，此空填"about"。

21.【D】题意：他说对于考试结果他一点也不失望，但是他脸上的表情泄露了他（的真实感受）。考查动词短语辨析。give away 意为：出卖，泄露。

22.【D】题意：Linda and Kitty will go to Greenery Theme Park，Linda 和 Kitty 下周日将去绿色主题公园，空格前有介词 by，结合选项，本题考查 by+反身代词，意思是某人自己，由于主语是两人，故用复数 themselves，答案是 D。

23.【B】题意：我们应该尊重那些为我们服务的人。考查短语 show respect to 向……表示敬意/尊重。句意：我们应该尊重为我们服务的人。人用 who。

24.【B】题意：当我们长大了，我们不能依靠我们的父母。rely on 表示依靠。in，for，with 通常不与 rely 连用；本文是表示依靠我们的父母，故选 B。

25.【B】题意：为什么不和你妹妹分享这个苹果呢？考查固定短语。share…with…意为与……分享……"，可知 B 符合题意。

26.【B】题意：昨天晚上八点钟托尼正在看电视。根据时间状语 at eight o'clock last night 可知用过去进行时，故选 B。

27.【C】题意：你能帮忙擦这些窗户吗？lend a hand 帮忙，帮助。据题意可知，故答案为 C。

28.【D】题意：他们中的一些人上课迟到了。A. 选项 much 许多，非常，修饰不可数名词。B. little 几乎没有，修饰不可数名词。C. a little 一点点，修饰不可数名词。D. a few 一些，修饰可数名词。由本句的动词 are 可知是可数的。

29.【B】题意：关于这件事情你最好问老师。You had better 后跟动词原形，故选择 B。

30.【C】题意：完成我的作业花费了一整天的时间。这道题考的是非谓语动词——不定式 to do 的用法，不是考时态。使用的句型是 It takes sb some time to do，这句话中 it 只是形式上的主语，真正的主语是不定式 to do，表示做某事要花某人多少时间。

31.【C】抽象名词具体化，在本句话中的意思是令我们大吃一惊。

32.【D】当宾语主语、表语主语、同位语与主语是同样对象时，用反身代词表示"本人、自己"。故选 D。

33.【D】大学、专业、系别前不用冠词。故选 D。

34.【B】far 可以修饰比较级。故选 B。

35.【B】In+时间段；after+时间点表示将来的某一时刻；since+过去的时间点，要用现在完成时态。故选 B。

36.【D】take 表示花费时，其主语多为形式主义 it。故选 D。

37.【A】could 用于否定句表示一种对结论非常有把握的推测，肯定不是……故选 A。

38.【C】And 连接的两个名词共有一个冠词的时候表示同一人或者事物，谓语动词用单数。故选 C。

39.【D】本题考查安慰的口语交际用语。振作起来，故选 D。

40.【B】指示代词 that 后不用冠词。二手的，故选 B。

三、完型填空（本大题共 15 小题，每小题 1 分，共计 15 分）

从前，有个富人非常爱他的儿子，他想尽力取悦他，所以他给买了一匹马骑，让他住在漂亮的房间里，画书、玩具和所有钱能买到的东西都给了他。但是一直以来，这个小男孩儿仍然不快乐，无论他走到哪里都皱着眉头，总想得到他没有的东西。这个人不知道该如何让他的儿子高兴。有一天，一个魔术师来到他跟前，对他说："我可以让你的儿子高兴，让他微笑，但是你必须为告诉他这个秘密付出巨大的代价。""好吧"，那人说，"不管你要什么，我都给你。"魔术师把那个男孩儿带到了一个秘密的房间，他在一张纸上写了一些东西。然后把他给了那个男孩儿。纸上写着："每天为某人做一件好事。"这个男孩儿听从了这个建议，成了最快乐的男孩儿之一。只有那些停止思考自己幸福的人才能真正幸福。

41.【B】当主句是过去时态，从句用相应的过去时 loved。

42.【C】try one's best to do 尽力，one's 表示所有格或形容词性物主代词。

43.【A】to do 不定时表示将要……题意是给了他一匹骑的马。

44.【C】everything 引起定语从句，连接词用 that。

45.【A】wherever 无论哪里，他无论在哪里都皱着眉头。

46.【C】make +n+adj，使……我能使他高兴。

47.【A】根据 a 可以判断需要一个单数名词，根据意思判断是魔术师。

48.【A】make +n+adj，使……我能使他高兴。

49.【A】and 前后连接的两个动词形式保持一致，前面是 can+动词原形，所以后面也应该是动词原形。

50.【B】but 表示转折，但是你必须付给我很多钱。

51.【A】根据本句中介词 for，可以知道后接动词的 ing 形式。

52.【A】根据句意无论你要什么，句子缺什么，所以选 what。

53.【A】give sth to sb. 给某人某物，根据句意把它给了这个男孩。

54.【A】根据句意，他听了魔术师的建议，follow advice 听从建议。

55.【A】stop doing 停止正在做的事情，stop to do 停下来去做另一件事情，根据题意，停止只考虑自己的幸福。

四、阅读理解（本大题共 15 小题，每小题 2 分，共计 30 分）

从 A、B、C、D 四个选项中，选出符合题目要求的最佳选项。

A

56.【A】细节理解题。根据 Cai Lun improved paper around 2000 years ago in China. 可知大约 2 000 年前，蔡伦在中国改进了造纸术。故选 A。

57. 【C】细节推断题。根据"With paper, we can make books and print newspapers. Sharing information is a lot easier with the help of paper."可知，有了纸，我们可以制作书籍和印刷报纸。有了纸，信息共享变得容易多了。选项A、B和D都是可以用纸来做的事情，只有选项C不是。故选C。

58. 【D】细节理解题。根据Many people called Turing the father of computer science. 可知，许多人称图灵为计算机科学之父。故选D。

59. 【B】细节理解题。根据"In the test, a human talked to two other people through a computer. One was a machine and the other was a person."可知，在测试中，一个人通过计算机与另外两个人交谈。一个是机器，另一个是人。故选B。

60. 【D】推理判断题。根据"People use paper every day. 人们每天用纸"，以及第五段中的"This idea is still used today. 这一思想至今仍在使用。"可推测，蔡伦的发明以及艾伦·图灵的主意现在仍然被人们使用，故选D。

B

翻译：世界上最大的射电望远镜于2017年9月25日中国完工。FAST是一个500米的望远镜。它也被称为天眼，有一个底盘，由30个足球场大小的地方组成，深藏于中国西南贵州省的群山中。这个巨大的盘子建在一个谷底。周围地区由无线电全覆盖，因为在5千米半径内没有城镇，25千米内只有一个乡村。FAST由4 450个面板组成。第二大射电望远镜在俄罗斯，较大的底盘能够接收较弱的信号。射电望远镜就像一只耳朵，从宇宙的噪声中挑选出有意义的无线电信息。在望远镜的帮助下，我们可以在遥远的空间接收到更弱和更多的无线电信息。它将帮助我们在银河系之外寻找智能生活，并探索宇宙的起源。"它的任何发现都将获得诺贝尔奖"，诺贝尔奖得主约瑟夫·泰勒说。FAST项目始于2011年。预计该望远镜将在未来10至20年内保持全球领先地位。

分析：

61. 【A】根据文章第一段中"The world's largest radio telescope was finished on Sept. 25 2017 in China"得到答案A。

62. 【B】根据文章第二段中…with a dish the sire of 30 foot ball grounds, deep in the mountains of southwest China's Guizhou Province. The giant dish is built on a howl-like valley, 推断出答案B。

63. 【D】根据文章第五段中 The radio telescope is like an ear listening to tell meaningful radio messages from white noise in the universe. 得到答案D。

64. 【A】根据文章第一段中"The world's largest radio telescope was finished on Sept. 25 2017 in China"，用排除法，得到答案A。

65. 【C】根据文章第一段中"The world's largest radio telescope was finished on Sept. 25 2017 in China"和最后一段中"The FAST project began in 2011."用2017-2011=6，得到答案C。

C

本文主要通过举例，说明在某些方面海豚与人类很相像。

66. 【B】细节理解题。根据Like humans, every dolphin has its own "name". The name is a special whistle. 可知，海豚使用特别的口哨作为名字。故选B。

67. 【C】词义猜测题。根据Dolphins and humans are similar in another way. 海豚和人类在另一方

面是相似的。此处的 both species 是上文的 dolphins 和 humans，而海豚和人类属于两个物种，故 species 意为"物种"。故选 C。

68.【B】细节理解题。根据"They get to eat some of the fish that escape from the net."可知，他们可以吃一些从网里逃出来的鱼。故选 B。

69.【B】推理判断题。根据文章最后一段可知，当鱼群要来时，海豚会向渔民发出信号，从而帮助渔民捕获更多的鱼，B 项与文意相符。故选 B。

70.【C】主旨大意题。由句子"But scientists say dolphin intelligence and human intelligence are similar in some ways. 但是科学家说海豚的智力和人类的智力在某些方面是相似的。"可知，这句话是本文的主旨句，下文主要是围绕海豚和人类的相似之处展开的。故选 C。

五、书面表达(15 分)

One possible version：

Hello, my classmates!

　　Pressure is a serious problem in today's world. Most students in our class are under too much pressure. Some students can't get on well with their classmates, while others may worry about their exams.

　　I'm always under pressure, too. My parents wanted me to be the student in class. They had me study all day. Even send me to all kinds of classes on weekends.

　　I had a talk with my parents and told them I had done my best. Finally, they understand me. In this way, I feel less stressed out so that I can concentrate more on my studies.

　　Less pressure makes better life. Thank you!

基础模块(上册)Unit 10-Unit 12 阶段测试题四

一、语音(本大题共 10 小题,每小题 1 分,共计 10 分)

从 A、B、C、D 四个选项中,选出画线部分发音不同的一项。

1. 【A】考查字母 ea 的发音,在重读音节中读[ei],在非重读音节中读[iː],ea 在 B、C、D 中读[iː],在 A 中读[ei]。

2. 【C】考查字母 a 的发音,在重读闭音节中读[æ],在 n、f、s、ph、th 前读[ɑː],a 在 A、B、D 中读[ei],在 C 中读[ɑ]。

3. 【C】考查字母 u 的发音,在重读开音节中读[juː],在重读闭音节中读[ʌ],u 在 A、B、D 中读[ʌ],在 C 中读[uː]。

4. 【B】考查字母 e 的发音,在重读开音节中读[iː],在重读闭音节中读[e],在非重读音节中读[ə]或者[i]。e 在 A、C、D 中读[e],在 B 中读[i]。

5. 【B】辅音字母 y 在 B 中读[j],在 A、C、D 中读[i]。

6. 【B】考查字母 i 的发音,在重读开音节中读[ai],在重读闭音节中读[i],在非重读音节中读[ə]或者[i]。i 在 A、C、D 中读[i],在 B 中读[ə]。

7. 【B】考查字母 e 的发音,在重读开音节中读[iː],在重读闭音节中读[e],在非重读音节中读[ə]或者[i]。e 在 A、C、D 中读[e],在 B 中读[i]。

8. 【D】考查字母 i 的发音,在重读开音节中读[ai],在重读闭音节中读[i],在非重读音节中读[ə]或者[i]。i 在 A、B、C 中读[i],在 D 中读[ai]。

9. 【D】考查字母 gh 的发音,在 ou 或者 au 之后读[f],在重读闭音节中读[e],在 ight 的组合中不发音。gh 在 A、B、C 中不发音,在 D 中读[f]。

10. 【C】考查字母 se 的发音,在一些单词中读[s],在一些单词中读[z]。se 在 A、B、D 中读[z],在 C 中读[s]。

二、单项选择题(本大题共 30 小题,每小题 1 分,共计 30 分)

从 A、B、C、D 四个选项中,选出空白处的最佳选项。

11. 【B】题意:一份研究表明,参加课后活动的学生比不参加的学生高兴。考查代词。ones 替代前面的复数名词,表泛指;those 代指时间或距离较远的人或事,或替代前面出现的同类名词,表特指,相当于 the+复数名词;these 代指时间或距离较近的,或下面要提到的人或事;them 是人称代词 they 的宾格,通常在句子中作宾语。此处代指前面名词 the students,是替代前面出现的同类名词,表特指,所以用 those。故选:B。

12. 【B】题意:我忙于我的工作。考查固定搭配 be busy with sth 忙于干某事。

13. 【B】题意:这家饭店极其受欢迎,所以你不得不等待座位。for 因为(表示因果关系);so 因此,所以(表示因果关系);or 或者,否则(表示并列关系);yet 然而(表示转折关系)。根据前后两句之间的逻辑关系应该是因果关系,可以排除 C 和 D;根据句子所表达的意思可排除 A,故答案选择 B。

14. 【A】题意:这个小学校的教学质量比那个大学校的教学质量好。that 指代同名异物,不可数名词，相当于 the+名词；one 一个，指代可数名词的单数；it 它；this 这个，近指代词；根据句中 than 可知，此句表示比较前后质量的对比，句子的代词要替代前面的不可数名词 the quality of education，所以要用 that，符合题意。故选 A。

15.【D】题意：许多青少年知道照顾老人们，经常在公共汽车上让座给老人。核心短语/词汇：care for 照顾。句子译文：很多青年人都照顾老人，他们经常在公共汽车上将他们的座位让给老人。解析：agree with 意为"同意"；worry about 意为"担忧"；laugh at 意为"嘲笑"；care for 意为"照顾"。根据句意为"很多青年人都照顾老人，他们经常在公共汽车上将他们的座位让给老人。"根据句意，本题应用 care for 表示"照顾"的意思。

16.【C】题意：在语言学习中培养读书的好习惯是有益的。develop 培养。

17.【B】题意：你选择哪个号码，小、中还是大？根据选项的意思 color 颜色；size 尺寸、尺码；price 价格；kind 种类。根据下文"small, medium or large 小号、中号还是大号"以及答语"Large, please 请给我大号的"可推知，上文询问的是选择的尺寸或尺码，故填 size，选 B。

18.【C】题意：收到她的来信我很惊奇，信不信由你，我们还是十年以前见过。Believe it or not 信不信由你。

19.【A】题意：下周六出去野餐怎么样？Why not 为什么不，后跟动词原形；How about 如何，后跟动名词；Would you like 你喜欢……吗？后跟动词不定式；Let's 让我们……，为陈述句，句末用句号。本题中 go 是动词原形，判断空格处用 why not。故选 A。

20.【B】题意：她出生在 2008 年 8 月 8 日的夜里。考查介词用法。此题学生会误选 A，具体某天的上午、下午及晚上都用介词 on。

21.【B】题意：在去年的运动会上，我比比尔跳得高。比较的对象是我和比尔。high 的比较级是 higher。A 是动词原形，C、D 都是最高级。故选 B。

22.【D】题意：坐火车时，尤其是上下车时，我们应该爱护自己的物品。本题考查动词短语。get up 起床，get into 进入，get out of 逃避，get off 下车。根据 get on 可知，此处表示上车和下车，故选 D。

23.【A】题意：在古代，不同的国家的人们用不同的方法写数字。根据题干，第一个空 in ancient times 在古代是固定用法，第二个空 in different ways 用不同的方式是固定用法。故选 A。

24.【B】题意：我希望这个城市的交通将变得越来越方便。easy，形容词，容易的；convenient，形容词，便利的；quickly，副词，快速地；better，形容词比较级，更好的；由"more"可知排除 D 项；由"the traffic in our city will become more"可知是交通便利，B 项正确。故选 B。

25.【C】题意：他想要和他的父母一起看电影。考查固定搭配。see 观看，动词原形；sees 第三人称单数形式；to see 不定式；seeing 动词 ing 形式。would like to do sth. 表示"想要做某事"，因此此空为动词不定式。故选 C。

26.【D】题意：下个月初，我们将有一次学校旅行。你确定吗？解析句意考查介词短语。on 在……上；about 关于；in 在……里；with 和；at 在……；to 朝。at the beginning of 意为"在……初；在……的开始"；be sure about 意为"对……有把握；确信"。两者都是固定搭配。故选 D。

27.【C】题意：假如你想得到这份工作，你需要两年的教学经验。经验 experience。

28.【D】题意：这幅画花费了我一个半小时的时间。spends 花费；costs 花费；needs 需要；takes 花费。根据句意，空格处表示"这幅画花费了我超过一个半小时的时间"，从句意上排除 C 选项。spend 的主语是人，所以排除 A 选项。cost 和 take 的主语是物，固定搭配是 sth. cost sb. +金钱；sth. take sb. +时间。所以空格处填动词 take，drawing the picture 作整体时，谓语动词用三单形式 takes。故选 D。

29.【A】题意：我们的学来的学生和其他人相处得很融洽。get on well with sb. 与某人相处融洽。

30.【B】题意：生活充满了起起落落。be full of 充满……

31.【C】题意：我妹妹的一个朋友住在这里。双重所有格所以选 C。

32.【B】题意：A、B 修饰不可数名词，C、D 修饰可数名词，由句意"不着急，我们还有时间"可知应选 B。

33.【D】题意：中国人讲汉语。表示某国人前用 the，表示学科语言前不用冠词。故选 D。

34.【C】题意：这消息太好了以至于我都觉得不是真的。too adj to do…表示"太……而不……"故选 C。

35.【C】题意：这是到某地的公交。表示"到……"，故选 C。

36.【D】题意：他太年轻了无法明辨是非。tell A from B 把和区分开，题意是：明辨是非。故选 D。

37.【A】题意：我告诉他什么时候想用我的电脑都可以用。can/could 表示允许可以。故选 A。

38.【B】题意：十年过去了。Ten years 通常被看作一个整体，谓语动词用单数形式。故选 B。

39.【D】题意：此处表示委婉的不同意。你最好不要抽烟。故选 D。

40.【C】题意：九除以三是三。除法的表示 divided by。故选 C。

三、完型填空(本大题共15小题，每小题1分，共计15分)

从 A、B、C、D 四个选项中，选出空白处的最佳选项。

翻译：乡村音乐在美国很流行。这是来自美国南部各州的一种传统音乐。起初，人们只在家庭聚会中演奏乡村音乐，当农村的人们搬到城镇找工作时，他们带着他们的音乐。随着乡村音乐的不断变化，它在整个美国流行起来。约翰·丹佛是 50 年前美国最著名的乡村歌手之一。他的歌《带我回家》《乡村道路》众所周知，人们至今仍在演奏。流行音乐是另一种音乐风格。流行音乐能让人感到快乐和舒适。流行音乐自 20 世纪 50 年代以来一直流行。在中国，周杰伦受到了众多不同年龄的粉丝的喜爱。他唱了许多关于我们生活的歌。其中之一就是《稻香》，它鼓励人们即使在生活困难的时候也不要放弃。

分析：

41.【A】单数作主语，谓语用单数，"乡村音乐受欢迎"是一件客观事实，用一般现在时，所以选 A。

42.【B】"来源于美国南部"，from 从……来，所以选 B。

43.【C】演奏音乐，用 play，所以选 C。

44.【A】move to sp. 搬到某地，所以选 A。

45.【D】look for 寻找，强调过程，"他们离开家去找工作"，所以答案选 D。

46.【D】take with sb 随身携带某物，所以选 D。

47.【B】with 表示伴随，"随着乡村音乐不断地变化"，所以答案选 B。

— 17 —

48.【D】one of+the+形最+名词复数，所以选 D。

49.【B】根据句子主语是 country roads，所以用代词 it 代替。

50.【B】another+名词，除去这一个的另外一个，"流行音乐是另一种音乐风格"，所以答案选 B。

51.【A】make sb. do sth. 让某人做，所以选 A。

52.【C】since 引导时间状语从句，主完成从过去，表示从 20 世纪 50 年代一直到现在都很流行，用现在完成时，所以选 C。

53.【A】根据题意大量的粉丝，用复数所以选 A。

54.【D】关于 DaoXiang 的定语从句，表物，先行词在从句中作主语，用 which/that 引导，非限定性定语从句，用 which 连接，所以选 D。

55.【B】encourage sb to do sth. 鼓励某人干某事。所以选择 B。

四、阅读理解（本大题共 15 小题，每小题 2 分，共计 30 分）

从 A、B、C、D 四个选项中，选出符合题目要求的最佳选项。

A

56.【B】细节理解题，根据 Ray Tomlinson is known as "the father of e-mail" 得知该题选 B。

57.【C】细节理解题，根据 In 1971, Ray created the first e-mail system 得知选 C。

58.【A】细节理解题，根据 "I used the '@' sign to show that the user was 'at' some other hosts rather than being local，我使用@标志表示用户在其他的主机而不是在当地"得知选 A．

59.【D】细节理解题，根据"Thanks Ray Tomlinson for inventing the email and putting the @ sign on the map."得知，感谢他是因为他发明了电子邮件并且在示意图上有@标志。

60.【D】主旨大意题。根据上下文排除。

B

61.【B】根据 She was kind to us before, but recently she had a chip on her shoulder. She often quarreled with my brother and me without any reason. 可知画线部分意为：很容易生气。

62.【C】根据 My mother got into trouble and didn't know how to deal with it. 及 He bought her a new smart phone and taught her how to use Wechat. 可知答案。

63.【A】根据 No matter where she went and whatever she did, she always used it. 可知答案。

64.【C】根据 To our surprise, we didn't find any pictures of her dumplings. 可知答案。

65.【B】根据"Oh, my God! I have to spend more money buying a new one!" cried my brother. 可知"我的智能手机在锅里煮了"这句话符合语境。

C

66.【B】细节理解题。题干定位：由题干中的 you can pay less at restaurants and shops 定位到第二段第二句。根据"Look for city tourism cards. With the card, you can pay less at restaurants and shops."可知，在饭店和商店，使用旅游卡会支付更少钱。故选 B。

67.【D】词义猜测题。根据"You might even get free tickets to top tourist attractions."可知，你甚至可能得到顶级旅游景点的免费门票。因此，tourist attractions 的意思是"旅游景点"。故选 D。

68.【C】细节理解题。根据第四段中的"It can help you save some money by choosing a hotel away from big tourist attractions."可知，为了省钱，应选择离大景区远一点的宾馆。故选 C。干扰排除项：A 项与第三段第一句"Don't get the best room."不符，故排除；B 项与第四段第二句"It can help you save some money by choosing a hotel away from big tourist attractions…"不一致，故排除。

69.【D】细节理解题。题干定位：由题干中的 breakfast and lunch in the hotel 定位到文章的最后一句。根据"I'd rather eat breakfast and lunch at the hotel and then spend much money on a delicious supper."可知，作者喜欢在宾馆吃早饭和午饭，然后在美味的晚餐上花许多钱。故选 D。

70.【A】主旨大意题。通读全文可知，文章主要介绍了旅游中省钱的方法。故选 A。

五、书面表达(15 分)

One possible version:

Dear Alice,

    I am glad to receive your letter. I will introduce my best friend to you. Her name is Lucy. She is 13 years old. Her birthday is on July 12th. She has parents and a brother. She likes blue and her favorite food is hamburgers. She likes English most, because she thinks that it is useful and interesting. She likes playing ping-pong, and she often plays it with me after school. I know you have a lot in common with her. I hope you can make friends with her.

    Looking forward to your early reply.

Yours,
Li Hua

基础模块(下册) Unit 1-Unit 3 阶段测试题五

一、语音(本大题共 10 小题,每小题 1 分,共计 10 分)

从 A、B、C、D 四个选项中,选出画线部分发音不同的一项。

1. 【D】解析:本题考查元音字母 a 的发音。A、B、C 均发 [æ],D 发 [eɪ],故选 D。
2. 【C】解析:本题考查元音字母 o 的发音。A、B、D 均发 [əʊ],C 发 [ɒ],故选 C。
3. 【A】解析:本题考查元音字母 e 的发音。B、C、D 均发 [ɪ],A 发 [e],故选 A。
4. 【B】解析:本题考查元音字母 i 的发音。A、C、D 均发 [ɪ],B 发 [aɪ],故选 B。
5. 【A】解析:本题考查辅音字母 y 的发音。B、C、D 均发 [ɪ],A 发 [aɪ],故选 A。
6. 【D】解析:本题考查字母组合 ex 的发音。A、B、C 均发 [ɪks],D 发 [eks],故选 D。
7. 【A】解析:本题考查元音字母 a 的发音。B、C、D 均发 [ə],A 发 [eɪ],故选 A。
8. 【B】解析:本题考查元音字母 o 的发音。A、C、D 均发 [ɒ],B 发 [ə],故选 B。
9. 【D】解析:本题考查元音字母 i 的发音。A、B、C 均发 [ɪ],D 发 [aɪ],故选 D。
10. 【D】解析:本题考查字母组合 ch 的发音。A、B、C 均发 [tʃ],D 发 [k],故选 D。

二、单项选择题(本大题共 30 小题,每小题 1 分,共计 30 分)

从 A、B、C、D 四个选项中,选出空白处的最佳选项。

11. 【A】解析:本题考查固定短语,be located in,故选 A。
12. 【A】解析:本题考查被动语态,使役动词 make 在被动语态中 to 还原出来,be made to do 故选 A。
13. 【C】解析:本题考查被动语态,被动语态结构是"be+动词过去分词",故选 C。
14. 【A】解析:本题考查固定短语,by hand 用手,以手工。故选 A。
15. 【B】解析:本题考查"数量+形容词(long, wide, high…)",表示某物的尺寸,故选 B。
16. 【A】解析:本题考查被动语态,出现 every day,故用一般现在时的被动语态,故选 A
17. 【B】解析:本题考查动词短语,interested in 对……感兴趣,afraid of 对……害怕,excited about 对……激动,worried about 对……担心,根据题意,故选 B。
18. 【A】解析:本题考查名词,选项 A. traffic 交通,选项 B. signal 信号,选项 C. alarm 警报,选项 D. smoke 烟、雾。根据题意故选 A。由于交通堵塞,故迟到。
19. 【B】解析:本题考查形容词,A. excited 激动的,B. sure 确定的,C. sad 伤心的,D. unhappy 不开心的,根据题意,安相当确定将会通过考试。故选 B。
20. 【C】解析:本题考查被动语态的固定句型,"it is said…"据说,被动结构,用过去分词形式,故选 C。
21. 【D】解析:本题考查动词不定式作主语,故选 D。
22. 【B】解析:本题考查动词不定式,根据题干,所填短语作 tell 的宾语,选项 C 和 D 是疑问句语序,而宾语从句用陈述句语序,故排除掉。选项 A 和 B 疑问词+不定式的结构,不定式中缺少动词 tell 的宾语;what 是代词,可作宾语;how 是副词,作状语。故选 B。
23. 【C】解析:本题考查不定式作后置定语,"so many things to do"如此多的事情要去做。

— 20 —

24.【A】解析：本题考查被动语态，make 在主动语态中省略掉不定式 to，make sb. do sth. 故选 A。

25.【C】解析：本题考查购物的情景对话，根据题意，故选 C。

26.【D】解析：本题考查不定式，动词不定式作定语修饰 person，故选 D。

27.【B】解析：本题考查固定搭配，ask sb. to do sth. 要求某人做某事，故选 B。

28.【D】解析：本题考查句式结构辨析，"why don't +主语+动词原形"和"why not 直接加动词原形"，故选 D。

29.【C】解析：本题考查介词，大地点前用 in，小地点前用 at，百货商店是小地点。

30.【A】解析：本题考查固定搭配，help sb. (to)do sth. to 可以省略，故选 A。

31.【C】解析：本题考查固定搭配，"at the beginning of 在……开始时"，故选 C。

32.【A】解析：本题考查固定搭配，in total，合计，总共，故选 A。

33.【A】解析：本题考查不定式做宾语，故选 A。

34.【C】解析：本题考查动词，need doing = need to be done 根据句意：卧室需要打扫。故选 C。

35.【A】解析：本题考查被动语态，make 在主动语态中省略掉不定式 to，make sb. do sth. 故选 A。

36.【B】解析：本题考查固定搭配，in cash 用现金，by credit 用信用卡，故选 B。

37.【A】解析：本题考查固定搭配，under a hard condition 在艰苦的条件下，故选 A。

38.【B】解析：本题考查固定搭配，区分短语：stop to do sth. 停下来去做另一件事，stop doing sth. 停止正在做的事，根据题意选 B。

39.【B】解析：本题考查固定搭配，be famous for 因……而闻名，故选 B。

40.【A】解析：本题考查固定搭配，put…into practice 付诸实践，故选 A。

三、完型填空(本大题共 15 小题，每小题 1 分，共计 15 分)

从 A、B、C、D 四个选项中，选出空白处的最佳选项。

41.【C】解析：根据前半句句意：有些人认为它就是为了练习语法"规则"。rule 规则，符合文意。root 根源；riddle 谜语；research 调查、研究，均不符合文意。

42.【A】解析：根据句意：语言是为了想法的"交换"。The exchange of ideas 意为"想法的交换"，of 表示所属关系，符合逻辑。

43.【A】解析：根据句意："学习"一种语言的方法就是尽可能经常地训练说。表示"学习一种语言的方法"使用 the way to learn a language，此处用法为动词不定式作后置定语。

44.【C】解析：根据句意：to drill as much as possible，是句子的真实主语，it 作形式主语。

45.【C】解析：根据句意：你在真实的环境中应用得越多，它将变得越自然。"the+比较级…the+比较级"表示"越……越……"，much 的比较级为 more。

46.【A】解析：句意：学习任何语言"花费"很多精力。take 花费，符合逻辑。其余三项分别表示：归还；起作用；提供，均不符合文意。

47.【D】解析：根据上文"Learning any language takes a lot of effort."可知，此处说不要"放弃"。give up 放弃，符合文意。give out 分发；give off 发出；give in 屈服，均不符合逻辑。

48.【B】解析：根据上文"Be patient and enjoy yourself…"可知，学习外语应该是"有趣的"。fun 有趣的，符合文意。necessary 必要的；easy 容易的；complete 完整的，均不符合文意。

49.【C】解析：think 意为"认为"；happen 意为"发生"；reward 意为"回报"；produce 意为"生产"。根据句意"你的努力有一天会得到上帝的回报的"可知答案为 C 项。

50.【D】解析：根据下文"Keep a small English dictionary with you"可知前句句意："经常地"使用字典和语法手册。constantly 经常地，符合文意。really 真实地；certainly 一定；differently 不同地，均不符合文意。

51.【A】解析：根据下文"When you see a new word, look it up."可知前句句意："总是"放一本小的英语字典在身边。at all times 总是，符合文意。at times 有时；at a time 一次；at no time 决不，均不符合文意。

52.【C】解析：在头脑中"思考"这个单词，使用它。think about，思考、考虑，符合文章的逻辑。look for 寻找；talk about 谈论；worry about 担心，均不符合逻辑。

53.【B】解析：句意是当你看到某物时，思考它对应的单词，"然后"在句子中思考这个单词。then 然后，符合文意。

54.【C】解析：句意：当你学习一个新的动词时，学习它的各种形式。when 当……时，符合逻辑。

55.【D】解析：句意是更多地了解语言背后的"文化"。culture 文化，符合文意。business 商业，生意；appointment 约定，约会；importance 重要性，均不符合文意。

四、阅读理解（本大题共 15 小题，每小题 2 分，共计 30 分）

从 A、B、C、D 四个选项中，选出符合题目要求的最佳选项。

A

56.【C】解析考查主旨大意题。根据文章最后一段"Poor Daisy. She didn't get a new blouse that day"可知，那天没有买到衣服。故答案为 C。

57.【D】解析：考查细节题。根据文章第五段"She was a size six last year."可知，去年尺码是 6，现在大些了。故答案为 D。

58.【C】解析：考查细节题。根据文章第七段"Daisy tried on several blouses."可知。故答案为 C。

59.【C】解析：考查细节题。根据文章第七段"Some were too big. Some were too small."不是太大就是太小。故答案为 C。

60.【C】解析：考查细节题。根据文章倒数第二段"That's much too expensive."可知，衣服太贵了没有买。故答案为 C Because that's too expensive.

B

61.【D】解析：细节理解题。从表格数字 6 行我们可以看到 Coffee shop，意思为咖啡店，所以如果你想喝一杯咖啡，你可以去第六层，故本题选 D。

62.【A】解析：细节理解题。从表格数字 1 行我们可以看到 Fruit, vegetables, meat，意思为水果、蔬菜和肉等，所以如果你想买水果和肉的话，你可以去第一层，故本题选 A。

63.【C】解析：细节理解题。从表格数字 3 行我们可以看到 Men's clothing，意思为男士服装，所以如果格林先生想去买一件衬衣的话，他可以去第三层，故本题选 C。

64.【C】解析：细节理解题。从表格数字 5 行我们可以看到 Children's pleasure ground/Game center，意思为儿童乐园和游戏中心，所以如果格林夫人的孩子想去玩，应该去第五层，

— 22 —

65.【C】解析：细节理解题。本表格的最后一行提到营业时间，平时是上午八点半到下午六点半，周末是上午九点到晚上九点，所以如果你想在晚上购物，你只有周末的晚上才可以去，故本题选C。

C

66.【A】解析：细节理解题。据If they are Germans, they'll arrive on time. 可知当德国人去开会时，他们会准时到，故选择A。

67.【C】解析：细节理解题。据If they are Americans, they'll probably be 15 minutes early. If they are Englishmen, they'll be 15 minutes late, and you should allow up to an hour for the Italians. 可知当开会时，美国人会早到15分钟，英国人则会迟到15分钟，但是意大利人，应该给他们留出一个小时的时间，所以意大利人开会时是最后到的，故选择C。

68.【B】解析：细节理解题。据The Japanese prefer not to work while eating, Lunch is a time for them to relax and get to know each other and they don't drink at lunchtime. 可知日本人在吃饭时不喜欢谈论工作，也不喝酒，因为他们觉得午餐是一个让他们放松、了解彼此的时间，故选择B。

69.【D】解析：细节理解题。据If they are Englishmen, they'll be 15 minutes late…the British are happy to have a business lunch and discuss business matters and have a drink during the meal…可知英国人开会会晚15分钟，他们在吃午餐期间也会讨论生意，故选择D。

70.【A】解析：主旨大意题。文中作者通过列举不同国家开会到达的时间不同，以及吃午餐时是否讨论工作，主要是要告诉我们他们的做事方式不同是因为不同国家有不同的文化差异，选择A。

五、书面表达(15分)

One possible version：

Dear Mike,

　　How are you. I'm glad to hear from you. I'd like to introduce my hometown—Taiyuan to you. It is very beautiful.

　　Taiyuan is the capital of Shanxi Province which is located in the west of Taihang Mountain and east of Yellow River. It has a long history and is famous for its places of interest, such as Jinci Temple, Taiyuan Museum. It has a population of 53.51 million. The whole city is clean and tidy. It is a livable city with mild climate. On both sides of the streets are tall buildings. The people there are friendly and hard working. Their life is modern and comfortable.

　　I love my hometown. I hope you can visit my hometown someday.

Yours,
Li Hua

基础模块(下册)Unit 4-Unit 6 阶段测试题六

一、语音(本大题共 10 小题,每小题 1 分,共计 10 分)

从 A、B、C、D 四个选项中,选出画线部分发音不同的一项。

1. 【D】解析:本题考查字母组合 th 的发音。A、B、C 均发[θ],D 发[ð],故选 D。
2. 【B】解析:本题考查字母组合 ou 的发音。A、C、D 均发[aʊ],B 发[ə],故选 B。
3. 【B】解析:本题考查辅音字母 c 的发音。A、C、D 均发[k],B 发[s],故选 B。
4. 【B】解析:本题考查元音字母 i 的发音。A、C、D 均发[ɪ],B 发[aɪ],故选 B。
5. 【D】解析:本题考查元音字母 e 的发音。A、B、C 均发[e],D 发[ɪ],故选 D。
6. 【B】解析:本题考查元音字母 o 的发音。A、C、D 均发[ɒ],B 发[əʊ],故选 B。
7. 【D】解析:本题考查元音字母 u 的发音。A、B、C 均发[ʌ],D 发[uː],故选 D。
8. 【A】解析:本题考查字母组合 ea 的发音。B、C、D 均发[e],A 发[eɪ],故选 A。
9. 【A】解析:本题考查元音字母 u 的发音。B、C、D 均发[ʌ],A 发[ə],故选 A。
10. 【C】解析:本题考查元音字母 i 的发音。A、B、D 均发[ɪ],C 发[aɪ],故选 C。

二、单项选择题(本大题共 30 小题,每小题 1 分,共计 30 分)

从 A、B、C、D 四个选项中,选出空白处的最佳选项。

11. 【C】解析:本题考查固定搭配"stay away from…缺席,离开",故选 C。
12. 【B】解析:本题考查固定搭配"spend…on sth. 花费……做某事",故选 B。
13. 【D】解析:本题考查固定搭配"take…out of 取出",还有条件句中 got 这个词用过去式,故选 D。
14. 【B】解析:本题考查固定搭配"not…any more 不再",故选 B。
15. 【B】解析:本题考查固定搭配 "take on 不安,烦恼""take care 当心",还有主语是 mother 为第三人称单数,故选 B。
16. 【A】解析:本题考查固定搭配"come to oneself 苏醒过来,恢复常态",还有主句中的谓语用 found 过去式,故选 A。
17. 【D】解析:本题考查固定搭配"fly up with the wind 随风飘起来",还有 and 后面的动词 came 用过去式,故选 D。
18. 【B】解析:本题考查固定搭配"keep silent 保持沉默",还有 but 后的 be 动词为 was,故选 B。
19. 【C】解析:本题考查固定搭配"at midnight 在午夜"故选 C。
20. 【B】解析:本题考查固定搭配"promise sb. to do sth. 答应某人做某事"故选 B。
21. 【A】解析:本题考查固定搭配 turn on 打开,turn off 关掉,turn down 调低,Turn up 调高,根据句意,故选 A。
22. 【A】解析:本题考查动词辨析。trust 信任,wake 叫醒,threaten 威胁,trouble 麻烦;根据句意,故选 A。
23. 【D】解析:本题考查动词辨析。run 跑,throw 扔,sleep 睡觉,lie 躺下;根据句意,故选 D。

24.【D】解析：本题考查副词辨析。sadly 伤心地，carefully 仔细地，greatly 非常，suddenly 突然地，根据句意故选 D。

25.【C】解析：本题考查固定搭配"get addicted to doing 上瘾，痴迷于"中 to 是介词，故选 C。

26.【D】解析：本题考查固定搭配"make good use of…好好利用"故选 D。

27.【A】解析：本题考查直接引语变间接引语，主语变成相应的人称代词，排除掉 B 和 D，时态用相应的过去式，故选 A。

28.【C】解析：本题考查直接引语变间接引语，用陈述句语序排除掉 A 和 B，主语变成相应的人称代词，故选 C。

29.【B】解析：本题考查不定式，it 作形式主语，不定式作真正的主语，故选 B。

30.【C】解析：本题考查固定搭配，"in sight and in sound 用图像和声音"故选 C。

31.【D】解析：本题考查定语从句，根据句意可知 all 是 tell you 的宾语，后面是定语从句，从句中缺少宾语，用 that 引导，也可以省略，故选 D。

32.【A】解析：本题考查定语从句，在定语从句中，先行词前有 no 修饰时，只能用关系代词 that 引导，故选 A。

33.【A】解析：本题考查宾语从句。从句中不缺成分，that 起连词作用，故选 A，这将是我最后一次过来帮你。

34.【C】解析：本题考查定语从句，因为题中"one of the three students"前有"the only"修饰，所以本题中定语从句的谓语动词用第三人称单数形式，故选 C。

35.【A】解析：本题考查定语从句，先行词 the place 指物，后面句子中缺少主语，所以关系代词在从句中作主语，应用 that 或 which，故选 A。

36.【C】解析：本题考查定语从句，根据 do you know the man 可知原句应该是 do you know the man whom/who I spoke to? 先行词在从句中充当宾语时可以省略，此处 who/whom 充当宾语，所以可省略，spoke 是不及物动词，介词 to 不能丢。故选 C。

37.【D】解析：本题考查定语从句，分析句子主句 this is the hotel in the city，定语从句为 where they stayed，stay 不及物动词，"待在某地方"，先行词 hotel 表示地点，用关系副词，故选 D。

38.【C】解析：本题考查定语从句，分析句子成分，先行词为 the year，定语从句中句子成分完整，不缺少成分，应该用关系副词，先行词指时间，故用关系副词 when/in which，故选 C。

39.【A】解析：本题考查定语从句，句意为这是我永远不能忘记的一天。the day 为先行词，指物，在从句中作宾语，故用 which 选 A。

40.【C】解析：本题考查定语从句，从句中的先行词为 factory，在定语从句中作 visit 的宾语，which 是关系代词，其他几个选项不能作定语从句的宾语，故选 C。

三、完型填空（本大题共 15 小题，每小题 1 分，共计 15 分）

从 A、B、C、D 四个选项中，选出空白处的最佳选项。

41.【D】解析：考查动词及语境理解。A. ended 结束；B. stayed 待在；C. stopped 停止；D. lasted 持续。根据空格前面的 she went to a birthday party which，以及后面的 until two o'clock in the morning. 可知，这里要填 lasted（持续），表示：她参加了一场持续到早晨 2 点钟的生日聚

会。故答案为 D。

42.【B】解析：考查形容词及语境理解。A. busy 忙碌的；B. quiet 安静的；C. noisy 嘈杂的；D. wide 宽的。根据前面的 two'clock in the morning. 以及空格后面的 alone 可知，这里要填 quiet，表示：阿加莎独自一人在安静的街道上行走。故答案为 B。

43.【C】解析：考查名词及语境理解。A. part 部分；B. block 街区；C. building 楼房；D. street 街道。根据常识可知，街道两边都是建筑物，所以这里要填 building，表示：突然，有一个带着刀的高个子男人从一栋黑暗的建筑物后面向她跑过来。故答案为 C。

44.【A】解析：考查名词及语境理解。A. morning 早晨；B. afternoon 下午；C. evening 晚上；D. night 夜晚。根据前面的 two o'clock in the morning. 可知，这里要填 morning，表示：这个男人向阿加莎打招呼，故选 A。

45.【A】解析：考查动词及语境理解。A. die 死；B. escape 逃离；C. fight 斗争；D. stay 待在。根据前面的 a tall man with a sharp knife in his right hand ran out at her 可知，这里要填 die，表示：我认为你不想死在这里。故答案为 A。

46.【D】解析：考查形容词及语境理解。A. funny 有趣的；B. safe 安全的；C. brave 勇敢的；D. bright 明智的。根据空格前面的 Agatha suddenly had a，以及后面的 idea，结合文章的内容可知，这里要填 bright，表示：突然阿加莎有一个聪明的想法。故答案为 D。

47.【C】解析：考查代词及语境理解。A. other 其他的；B. others 其他；C. the other 另一个（两者）；D. another 另一（泛指）。根据空格前面的 She tried to cover her necklace with the collar of her overcoat while she used，以及后面的 hand to take off both of her earrings 可知，这里要填 the other，表示：她试图(用一只手)掩盖她的大衣领子项链，而用另一只手去摘两只耳环。故答案为 C。

48.【B】解析：考查动词及语境理解。A. handed 递给；B. threw 扔；C passed 经过；D. put 放。根据空格前面的 then quickly，以及后面的 them on the ground 可知，这里要填 threw，表示：然后飞快地把它们扔在地上。故答案为 B。

49.【D】解析：考查动词及语境理解。A. own 拥有；B. keep 保持；C. have 有；D. protect 保护。根据前面的"她试图(用一只手)掩盖她的大衣领子项链"可知，这里要填 protect，表示：这个抢劫者认为那个女孩根本不喜欢耳环，只是想保护她的项链。故答案为 D。

50.【C】解析：考查形容词及语境理解。A. cheap 便宜的；B. expensive 昂贵的；C. more 更多；D. less 更少。根据前面的分析"只是想保护她的项链。"可知，这里要填 more，表示：它值更多钱。故答案为 C。

51.【D】解析：考查动词及语境理解。A. weigh 称重；B. take 带走；C. spend. 花费（人作主语）；D. cost 花费（物作主语）。根据空格前面的 It doesn't，以及后面的 much. Please let me wear it. 可知，这里要填 cost，表示：它不值很多钱。请让我戴着它。故答案为 D。

52.【C】解析：考查形容词及语境理解。A. afraid 害怕的；B. angry 生气的；C. silly 傻的；D. bad 坏的。根据空格前面的 I'm not that，以及后面的 Quick! 可知，这里要填 silly，表示：我不是那么愚蠢。(抢劫者不相信她的话)故答案为 C。

53.【A】解析：考查名词及语境理解。A. hands 双手；B. feet 脚；C. head 头；D. body 身体。根据空格前面的 With shaking，以及后面的 Agatha took off her necklace 可知，这里要填 hands，表示：随着手的晃动，阿加莎拿下她的项链。故答案为 A。

54.【D】解析：考查形容词及语境理解。A. much 许多；B. early 早的；C. carefully 小心的；

D. fast 快的。根据空格前面的 she picked up her earrings and ran as，以及后面的 as she could to one of her friends. 可知，这里要填 fast，表示：她捡起耳环，并且尽可能快地跑到她的朋友那里。故答案为 D。

55.【C】解析：考查副词及语境理解。A. really 确实；B. already 已经；C. only 仅仅；D. hardly, 几乎不。根据空格前面的 The earrings cost 480 pounds and the necklace the robber had taken away cost，以及后面的 six pounds. 可知，这里要填 only，表示：这耳环值 480 英镑，而抢劫者拿走的项链仅仅值 6 英镑。故答案为 C。

四、阅读理解（本大题共 15 小题，每小题 2 分，共计 30 分）

从 A、B、C、D 四个选项中，选出符合题目要求的最佳选项。

A

56.【B】解析：根据第一段中"So, I hope you'll let me give your readers some advice on smartphone etiquette."可知，作者写这封信的目的是希望《周日环球报》能让她给读者提出一些手机礼仪方面的建议。故选 B。

57.【C】解析：根据第一段最后一句可以推知本句句意为"我要陈述的第一点是吵闹声"，因此画线词 address 在句中的意思为"陈述"。故选 C。

58.【C】解析：根据第二段第二行 In fact, the microphones in smart phones are very sensitive(敏感的). So, you can be heard even if you speak quietly. 可知，智能电话是非常敏感的，不需要大声对话。

59.【D】解析：根据第三段中"I don't think it is polite to make calls in small space full of people. This makes others uncomfortable"可知，在挤满人的小空间里打电话会使别人感到不舒服。故选 D。

60.【D】解析：最后一段中讲到边开车边打电话是危险的，同样和朋友在一起时，我们应该放下手机，享受朋友的陪伴。由此可以推知，恰当地使用手机是重要的。故选 D。

B

61.【A】解析：细节理解题。根据第二段第二行句"He said it was easy for people to see yellow buses and the black letters on them in early morning or late afternoon. That would make children safer. 他说在清晨或傍晚人们很容易看到黄色的校车和黑色的字母。这会让孩子更安全。"可知黄色的校车更安全。故选 A。

62.【B】解析：细节理解题。根据倒数第二段第一行句"To make kids love their school, Japanese kindergartens and schools have colorful buses. The buses can easily make children want to take them and then, go to school. 为了使孩子喜欢他们的学校，日本幼儿园和学校有丰富多彩的校车，校车很容易带孩子去上学。"可知日本的孩子通过乘坐校车从而容易喜欢他们的学校。故选 B。

63.【D】解析：细节理解题。根据最后一段第一行句子"saves a lot of time for students to take a school bus. 学生乘校车节省了很多的时间。"可知中国学生乘校车上学节省了很多时间。故选 D。

64.【A】解析：主旨归纳题。根据整篇文章内容及其第一段句子"A school bus is one that is used to take children to and from school. 校车是用来带孩子上学的。"可知文章主要介绍了各个国家的校车。故选 A。

65. 【B】解析：细节理解题。根据文章最后一段的"It said that there will be 3,000 yellow school buses on the road by the end of this year in Chongqing."可知，中国的校车是黄色的，故选 B。

C

66. 【A】解析：细节理解题。根据短文中第二段"From April19 to 25, they are asking children all over the world to turn off their TVs for one week."知，从4月19日到4月25日是关掉电视周，这一周全世界的孩子都要关上电视。故选 A。

67. 【C】解析：细节理解题。根据短文中第二段"They hope children will find more interesting things to do. Maybe they can read some books, or learn to swim, or paint a picture."可知，在关掉电视的这一周里，人们希望孩子们能找到更多有趣的事情做，比如读书、学游泳、画画等。故选 C。

68. 【B】解析：推理判断题。根据短文中第五段"They say that if children watch lots of TV, they don't do well in school. Most children are getting overweight, Some kids become violent in real life"可知，看电视可以使孩子们变得超重、在学校里学习不好、在生活中变得暴力。故选 B。

69. 【C】解析：推理判断题。根据第二段"Since1995, about 24 million people in America have taken part in TV.-Turnoff Week."可知，A 说的是正确的；根据最后一段"If you want to learn more about this unusual week, you can go to this vebsite, www. tvturnof. org."可知，B 说的也是对的；根据倒数第四段 About 40% of America families watch TV at dinner time 可知五分之二的美国家庭在吃饭的时候看电视，即五分之三的家庭在吃饭的时候不看电视，故 D 说的也是对的；C 选项在短文中并没有说到，而且事实是很多孩子在 18 岁之前看很多暴力的电视。故 C 不对，故选 C。

70. 【B】解析：推测词义题。根据文章最后一段"If you want to learn more about this unusual week, you can go to this website：www. tvturnoff. org."可知，unusual 为不同寻常的，故选 B。

五、书面表达(15 分)

One possible version：

How to Make Good Use of the Internet

With the development of technology, internet play an important way in our life. More and more people need to use the Internet for their work. but how to make good use of the Internet is a question.

Firstly, we can use the Internet for study. Because there are almost all kinds of material provided and you can learn whatever interests you.

Secondly, we can search for the information we need on the internet.

Thirdly, it is easy for us to keep in touch with our friends through the Internet. We can also make new friends who share the same interests with us.

At last, we can enjoy ourselves on the Internet in many ways, such as listening to music and watching movies.

In a word, we can do a lot of things on the Internet. But we have to make the most of it in the right way.

基础模块(下册)Unit 7-Unit 9 阶段测试题七

一、语音(本大题共 10 小题,每小题 1 分,共计 10 分)

从 A、B、C、D 四个选项中,选出画线部分发音不同的一项。

1. 【A】考查元音字母组合 oo 的发音。在 A 选项中读/ʌ/,常见的还有 flood 一词。在 B、C、D 选项中读/u:/,所以选 A。

2. 【A】考查元音字母 u 的发音。在开音节中读/ju:/,在闭音节中读/ʌ/,在非重读音节中读/ə/,在 j,l,r,s 后读/u:/,在 B、C、D 选项中读/ʌ/,A 选项中读/u/,所以选 A。

3. 【C】考查元音字母组合 ea 的读音。在 C 选项中 ea 读/i:/,在 A、B、D 选项中读[e],所以答案为 C。

4. 【B】考查元音 o 的读音。在开音节中读/əu/,在闭音节中读/ɔ/,在非重读音节中读/ə/,在 m,n,v,th 前读/ʌ/,在 A、C、D 选项中读/ɔ/,B 选项中读/ə/,所以选 B。

5. 【C】考查元音字母 a 的读音。元音字母 a 在重读开音节中读/ei/,在重读闭音节中一般读[æ],有时候也可以读作/ə/;在非重读音节中,读作/ə/选项 A、B、D 为重读闭音节,在 C 选项中/ə/,所以选 C。

6. 【D】考查元音字母 e 的读音。在 A、B、C、选项中读/e/,在 D 选项中读/ə/,所以选 D。

7. 【C】考查元音字母 i 的读音,字母 i 在开音节中读/ai/,在闭音节或非重读音节中读/i/,A、B、D 选项中读/ai/,C 选项中读/i/,所以选 C。

8. 【C】考查辅音字母 s 的读音,A、B、D 选项中读/s/,C 选项中读/z/,所以选 C。

9. 【A】以字母组合 ex 开头的词,若 ex 后接一个元音字母且重音不落在第一个音节上,则 ex 的发音为/igz/。例如:exact, exam, example, exist。b. 以字母组合 ex 开头的词,若 ex 后接一个辅音字母,且重音不落在第一个音节上,则 ex 读/iks/。例:excuse, expect, exchange, except, experience, experiment, explain, expose, express, expression, expensive, extend, extraordinary。c. 以字母组合 ex 开头的词,无论 ex 后跟着什么字母,只要重音(包括次重音)落在第一个音节上,则 ex 的发音即为/eks/。例:exercise, expert(专家,能手),extra(额外的),exhibition。在 B、C、D 中读/igz/,A 选项中读/eks/,所以选 A。

10. 【B】考查字母组合 sion 的读音,在元音之后,读作/ʒn/,在辅音之后,读作/ʃn/。A、C、D 选项中读/ʒn/,B 选项中读/ʃn/,所以选 B。

二、单项选择题(本大题共 30 小题,每小题 1 分,共计 30 分)

从 A、B、C、D 四个选项中,选出空白处的最佳选项。

11. 【A】本题考查固定句型 It won't be long before…,意为"不久就……"所以选 A。

12. 【D】此题考查名词和固定搭配。第一个空 bad 为形容词,后跟名词,所以选 luck,luckily 为副词。第二个空为固定搭配,take a turn for the better"好转,变好",所以选 D。

13. 【D】此题考查修饰词。题中 time 为不可数名词,修饰不可数名词用 a great deal of,many 和 a number of 只能修饰可数名词复数,a lot 修饰名词要加 of,所以选 D。

14. 【B】此题考查动词固定搭配。第一个空 make sb. do,注意被动 sb. be made to do。第二个空 help sb. do，所以选 B。

15.【C】本题考查动词与介词的搭配。die off"相继死亡"；die of"因……而死"（死于内因，死因存在于人体自身）；die from"因……而死"（由外部原因导致的死亡）；die out"渐渐消灭"。根据文中的意思"死于外因"，故选 C。

16.【A】本题考查结果状语从句。so 是副词，与形容词或副词连用，其结构是：so+adj.（adv.）+that 从句。such 是形容词，它所修饰的名词可以是可数名词，也可以是不可数名词；名词前面可以带形容词，也可以不带。如果其后是单数可数名词，前面需加不定冠词 a 或 an。第一空 hot 为形容词，所以用 so，第二空修饰人用 V-ed 形式，所以选 A。

17.【C】此题考查动词短语。by means of"通过，借助于"，句意：我们通过外语了解了外国。所以选 C。

18.【C】此题考查非谓语动词。V-ing 形式作定语，接下来用 following，所以选 C。

19.【B】此题考查非谓语动词。介词 for 跟 V-ing，非谓语动词的否定式 not 都在非谓语动词之前。句意：你应该因你没有说实话向你姐姐道歉。所以选 B。

20.【D】本题考查情态动词表推测。时间是 last night，所以要用情态动词加完成时态表对过去事实的推测。句意"由于地面是湿的，所以昨晚肯定下雨了"。表肯定推测用 must have done，肯定下雨了，把握性很大，所以 D 选项符合句意。

21.【A】此题考查非谓语动词。主语 Brochures 和设计之间是被动关系，所以要用动词的过去分词 designed。D 选项因为时态不对故排除，如果把 they were designed 变为 they are designed 就对了。所以选 A。

22.【A】本题考查考查情态动词表祝愿。情态动词表祝愿的只有 may 一词，放在句首表祝愿。所以选 A。

23.【C】此题考查非谓语动词。Selected 过去分词作定语，顾客和选择之间关系为被动，所以选 C。

24.【A】本题考查考查情态动词。根据 No 和 You may do it tomorrow. 可知下面为否定回答，must 的含义是必须一定，其否定形式 mustn't 表示禁止的含义，在这里不是禁止的意思。must 的否定回答一般可借助于 needn' 和 don't have to 来构成，表示不必。故选 A。

25.【D】本题考查固定搭配。keep doing"一直做某事"，句意：当你离开时，你怎样保持机器一直运转。用 ing 表示一个持续的动作。所以选 D。

26.【D】本题考查非谓动词用法。分析句子结构可知，逗号之前是主句，逗号之后没有连接词应该是非谓语动词形式，主句的主语是 people 与所给动词 make 存在逻辑上的主动关系，应该用现在分词，故选 D。

27.【C】此题考查动词辨析。A. discover 发现，B. invent 发明，C. create 创造，D. find 找到，句意：就是这种我们想制造的氛围。所以选 C。

28.【D】此题考查动词短语辨析。句意：你最好学会自己处理不同种类的问题。A. give up 放弃；B. make up 编造；C. play with 和……玩耍；D. deal with 处理，对付。所以选 D。

29.【B】尽管 walk 用作名词时可以表示"散步"，但它是可数名词，指的是一次一次的具体的散步，而不表示抽象意义或泛指意义的"散步"，要表示此义，要用动名词 walking。所以选 B。

30.【B】no(没有)是形容词，常位于名词前，用来否定这个名词。有时用 no 否定名词时，可理解为这个名词的反义词，意思是"并非"。相当于 not a/an，或 not any。He is no fool. =

He is clever. 他很精明。（比较：He is not a fool. 他不是傻子。）所以选 B。

31.【B】考查独立主格结构。句意：由于老人带路，我们没有任何困难地找到了这个村庄。with 后有这样三种方式：①这个动作是主动的，+ing；②这个动作是被动的，+ed（过去分词）；③这个动作是将要做的，+to do。老人和带路为主动，所以用 leading。第二空 have no trouble in doing，所以选 B。

32.【A】此题考查固定搭配。Go wrong"出问题，出错"，either…or…"或者……或者……"，根据句意，所以此题选 A。

33.【A】本题考查固定搭配。What about 固定搭配为 What about doing，所以选 A。

34.【B】spend（in）doing 花费做某事，practicing doing 练习做某事。所以选 B。

35.【C】此题考查非谓语动词的完成时。从句中的动词发生在主句之前，故用完成时态。所以选 C。

36.【B】正确判断非谓语动词与其逻辑主语之间的关系是正确选择非谓语动词形式的保证，不管是作什么成分的非谓语动词都体现以下几个特点：如果非谓语动词与逻辑主语之间是主谓关系，则用现在分词；如果非谓语动词与逻辑主语之间是动宾关系，则用过去分词；如果表示将来，则用动词不定式。故选 B。

37.【C】从句谓语动词含 be 且主语与主句的主语一致可将从句主谓结构 sb. + be 省略。While we were watching television，省略 we were；又因为 hear sb./sth. do sth.。故选 C。

38.【A】动词不定式作结果状语表示意料之外、令人失望的结果，多与 only 连用，故选 A。

39.【D】表示对过去情况推测要用"情态动词+have done"；should have done 是虚拟语气，表示本来应该做的事却没做；might have done 表示推测"可能做过某事"，故选 D。

40.【B】had better+动词原形意思是"最好……"，故选 B。

三、完型填空（本大题共 15 小题，每小题 1 分，共计 15 分）

从 A、B、C、D 四个选项中，选出空白处的最佳选项。

41.【A】本题考查"不再"的表达。no more＝not anymore；no longer＝not any longer，文中已经出现了 not，所以排除 B 和 D。not any more 表示程度和次数上的不再，经常与短暂性动词连用；not any longer 表示在时间和距离上不再，常与延续性动词连用。文中抽烟表示次数，又是短暂性动词，故选 A。

42.【B】本题考查连词的用法。It won't be long before…固定搭配"用不了多久就……"，故选 B。

43.【C】本题考查动词的时态。句意为"对于一些人来说，抽烟已经成了一种日常习惯。"应该使用现在完成时，又因为 smoking 动名词作主语，谓语用单数，故选 C。

44.【C】本题考查引导名词性从句的引导词。文中缺少主语选择 what，故选 C。

45.【D】本题考查形容词词义辨析。根据文章内容，一些明星在电视上吸烟，使人们认为吸烟是酷的，而且是当今的一种时尚。那种想法是愚蠢和错误的。smart"聪明的"；wise"明智的"；exciting"令人兴奋的"；foolish"愚蠢的"，所以答案为 D。

46.【B】本题考查介词。have…effects on…固定搭配，意为"对……有……的影响"，所以选 B。

47.【B】本题考查对文章的逻辑理解。根据句意"每一支雪茄会缩短一个人的寿命"，short 是形容词"短的"，不能作谓语；shorten 是动词"缩短"，符合题意；strengthen"加强"的意

31

思，与文章的逻辑不符；lengthen 是"延长"的意思，也不符合题意。故选 B。

48.【C】本题考查词义的辨义。excuse 当名词时意为"借口"；cause 是"起因"，当动词使用 be caused by"由……引起"；reason 是"理由"。根据文章的意思"在多数情况下，他们的死亡是由癌症引起的"，根据主谓一致原则，deaths 做主语时谓语用复数，故选 C。

49.【A】本题考查动词辨析。attack"袭击"；protect"保护"；prevent"阻止"；stop"停止"。根据句意"当烟雾被吸入时，那些烟雾中的有毒物质就会袭击身体。可知答案是 A。

50.【D】本题考查词义辨析。根据句意"它们会使血压升高导致心脏病"。rise"升高"，不及物动词，用在这不合适；reduce"减少"，不符合题意；make 仅仅是个使役性动词；raise"举起，提高"，及物动词，所以选 D。

51.【C】本题考查动词与介词的搭配。die off"相继死亡"；die of"因……而死"（死于内因，死因存在于人体自身）；die from"因……而死"（由外部原因导致的死亡）；die out"渐渐消灭"。故选 C。

52.【A】本题考查并列连词。与 not only 相搭配的只有 but also，also 有时可以省略，故选 A。

53.【C】本题考查动词的固定搭配。题意"当一个人在抽烟时，周围的人也会被迫吸入烟雾。" be forced to do sth."被迫做某事"，固定搭配，故选 C。

54.【B】此题考查短语辨析。A. give in 让步、屈服；B. give up 放弃；C. give away 赠送；D. give out 发出，放出。根据题意：吸烟者应该立刻戒烟。所以选 B。

55.【D】此题考查修饰形容词比较级，题意：对于那些不吸烟的人来说，始终就不吸烟要比戒烟容易得多。easy 的比较级为 easier，much 在此修饰比较级，所以选 D。

四、阅读理解（本大题共 15 小题，每小题 2 分，共计 30 分）

从 A、B、C、D 四个选项中，选出符合题目要求的最佳选项。

A

56.【C】根据 Some middle schools in Australia have banned students from carrying mobile phone during school hours. 可知在澳大利亚学生在校期间，禁止携带手机。故选 C。

57.【C】根据 Several children have got mobile phones as Christmas gifts，送圣诞礼物的人主要有父母和朋友，故选 C。

58.【D】联系下文 during exams 可知是在考试中作弊，故选 D。

59.【D】根据 Some parents felt unhappy because they couldn't get in touch with their children 描述，可知选 D。

60.【A】根据"Many teachers said students should not have mobile phones at school，but if there was a good reason，they could leave their phones at school office"描述，可知选 A。

B

61.【B】细节理解题，根据文中语句"Often bags and clothes show the name of the company that made them."理解可知。

62.【A】细节理解题，根据文中语句"They are popular because when you see a logo，it is hard to forget that product or company."理解可知。

63.【C】细节理解题，根据文中语句"Advertisements often use funny situations as well. It is simple to remember it."理解可知。

64.【C】细节理解题，根据文中语句"All advertisements are designed to make people buy a product."理解可知。
65.【D】标题理解归纳题，根据文中语句理解可知。

C

66.【B】细节理解题。根据文中语句"You don't show your secret personality when you're awake because you can control your behaviour, but when you're asleep, your sleeping position shows the real you."理解可知选 B。
67.【C】细节理解题，根据文中第二段可知选 C。
68.【C】细节理解题，根据文中第三段可知选 C。
69.【A】细节理解题，根据文中第四段可知选 A。
70.【B】细节理解题，根据文中第四段可知选 B。

五、书面表达(15分)

One possible version：
Hello, Xiao li,

  I found an ad on the Internet. It says that in the east street there is an apartment furnished will be rented. There is a room, a kitchen, and a bathroom. Almost all the furniture is prepared. If you are interested in this apartment, you can call Jim at 56428176. you'd better call him after 6 p.m.

Wang Lin

基础模块(下册)Unit 10-Unit 12 阶段测试题八

一、语音(本大题共 10 小题,每小题 1 分,共计 10 分)

从 A、B、C、D 四个选项中,选出画线部分发音不同的一项。

1.【C】考查字母 y 的读音。字母 y 在词首时,读作/j/。字母 y 位于元音字母之后,与元音字母一起构成字母组合,读成元音,字母 y 不发音。字母 y 出现在词末,读成元音/i/。在开音节中,字母 y 读[ai],C 选项中读/i/,在 A、B、D 选项中读/ai/,所以选 C。

2.【A】考查元音字母 i 的读音。字母 i 在开音节中读/ai/,在闭音节中/非重读音节中读/i/,在 A 选项中读/ai/,B、C/D 选项中读/i/,所以选 A。

3.【B】考查元音字母 u 的发音。在开音节中读/ju:/,在闭音节中读/ʌ/,在非重读音节中读/ə/,在 j、l、r、s 后读/u:/,在 A、C、D 选项中读/ʌ/,B 选项中读/ə/,所以选 B。

4.【C】考查元音字母 a 的读音。元音字母 a 在重读开音节中读/ei/,在重读闭音节中一般读/æ/,有时候也可以读作/ə/;在非重读音节中,读作/ə/,选项 A、B、C 读/æ/,在 D 选项中读/ei/,所以选 C。

5.【B】考查字母组合 ch 的读音。字母组合 ch 一般读/tʃ/,但在源出希腊语的单词 ache、character、chemical、chemist、chemistry、school、stomach、technical、technique、technology 中,ch 发/k/。而在 moustache、machine、Chicago 中的 ch 读/ʃ/。在 B 选项中读/k/,A、C、D 选项中读/tʃ/,所以选 B。

6.【C】考查元音字母组合 ir 的读音。在 A、B、D、选项中读/ə/,在 D 选项中读/eə/,所以选 C。

7.【D】考查元音字母组合 ear 的读音。A、B、C 选项中读/iə/,D 选项中读/eə/,所以选 D。

8.【C】考查辅音字母 c 的读音,A、B、D 选项中读/k/,C 选项中读/s/,所以选 C。

9.【D】考查元音字母组合 e 的读音。A、B、C 选项中读/e/,D 选项中读/i/,所以选 D。

10.【A】考查元音 o 的读音。在开音节中读/əu/,在闭音节中读/ɔ/,在非重读音节中读/ə/,在 m、n、v、th 前读/ʌ/,在 B、C、D 选项中读/ɔ/,A 选项中读/ə/,所以选 A。

二、单项选择题(本大题共 30 小题,每小题 1 分,共计 30 分)

从 A、B、C、D 四个选项中,选出空白处的最佳选项。

11.【D】本题考查介词。Look after 照顾,照料;look up 向上看,查字典;look out 当心,小心;look for 寻找。句意:他正在寻找昨天丢了的钥匙。所以选 D。

12.【A】句意:找工作时第一考虑不是你能挣多少,而是你能为工作做什么。A. not…but 不是……而是。B. either…or 或者……或者 C. neither…nor 既不……也不 D. not only…but also 不仅……而且。所以选 A。

13.【A】考点:reason 作主语时,其后的表语从句要用 that 引导;disappointed"(人)感到失望的",disappointing 表示"(物)令人失望"。故选 A。

14.【B】此题考查非谓语动词。工作经历 work experiences 和包括之间为主动关系,用 V+ing 形式,所以选 B。

15. 【C】此题考查状语从句。句意：一旦写好了简历，你可以附上《求职附函》一起寄给你预期的雇主。A. Unless 除非；如果不。B. When 当……时候。C. Once 一旦。D. If 如果。所以选 C。

16. 【A】此题考查表语从句。从句 he used to be 缺成分，所以用 what。选 A。

17. 【A】the +姓氏的复数，表示一家人或一对夫妇，作主语时，谓语用复数。而短语 prefer…to…中的 to 是一个介词，后应接名词或动名词。故选 A。

18. 【C】由 that 引导的主语从句通常用形式主语 it 来代替；news 是不可数名词，前不能用不定冠词 a。故选 C。

19. 【B】此题考查短语辨析。used to 过去常常做某事，be/get used to doing 习惯于做某事，be/get used to do 被用来做某事。句意：去年 Lily 经常在晚饭后吃甜点，所以那个时候她很胖。选 B。

20. 【C】代词 it 指上文提到的同一物，one 指上文提到的同类中的另一个。故选 C。

21. 【D】句意：根据时间表，去伦敦的火车在晚上 7 点离开。A. Thanks to 幸亏；B. As for 关于，至于；C. With the help of 在……的帮助下；D. According to 根据。所以选 D。

22. 【A】句意：这个房子有点小；另外，它还太热了。in addition 后面接从句；in addition to 后面接名词、动词的 ing 形式，所以选 A。

23. 【A】根据主、从复合句时态一般要一致的原则，本题首先可排除 B、C，而主句主语含有 except 等时，其谓语的单复数取决于 except 前边的名词的单复数，故选 A。

24. 【B】it 作形式宾语的句型：动词 + it + when（if）从句。能用于此结构的动词常见的有 enjoy，hate，love，like，dislike，appreciate，prefer 等。故选 B。

25. 【D】考查 aware 的用法。Be aware of +名词；be aware that+句子。the danger 为名词。所以答案为 D。

26. 【B】介词宾语从句中缺宾语，that 引导名词性从句时不能作句子成分，how、when 均为连接副词，不能作宾语。故选 B。

27. 【A】句意：Florence 为士兵代笔给家人写信。on behalf of 代表；instead of 而不是；because of 因为，由于。所以选 A。

28. 【D】用动词不定式作真正主语/宾语的句型是：It + be + adj. for（of）sb. to do sth.。句型中介词 of 与 for 的区别是：of 表示前面的形容词是描述 sb 的性格、属性、特征等，可以说 sb is/are+形容词。此类形容词有：kind，good，nice，right，wrong，clever，careless，polite，foolish 等。介词 for 表示其前的形容词是描述 to do sth. 的属性，与 sb. 无直接关系。此类形容词有：difficult，easy，hard，important，dangerous，（im）possible 等。故选 D。

29. 【B】句意：他总是帮助别人，作为回报，他被别人所爱戴。in addition 此外，in return 作为回报，in response 作为回应，in case 以防、万一。所以选 B。

30. 【D】第一个空中的谓语要与前面的主语 we 一致，故用复数 have，此处的 each 为主语的同位语，不能决定谓语的数；第二个空中的谓语要与前面的主语 each 一致，故用单数 has。故选 D。

31. 【C】be known as 意为"作为……而著名"，其后的名词表示一个人的身份、职业等。be known for 意为"因……而著名"，其后所接内容表示某人或物的特点、特长等。be known to "为……所了解/知道"，其后接表示人的词语。所以选 C。

32. 【C】根据"不定代词作主语，谓语用单数"这一点，首先可以排除 A 答案。又由于 change

属于不及物动词，它没有被动语态，所以B也不正确。由since引出的一个含具体过去时间的句子，主句用现在完成时。故选C。

33.【B】if不能引导主语从句；whether...or 无论……还是……。故选B。

34.【B】it作形式主语的句型：It is+过去分词+that...用于这个句型的过去分词有：said, hoped, reported, announced, supposed等。故选B。

35.【B】句意：通过努力，无论我们在世界的哪个地方，我们都会起很大的作用。make a difference 有影响；起(重要)作用。所以选B。

36.【C】句意：你不喜欢他和我无关。考查名词性从句。分析句子可知这是一个主语从句 you don't like him，从句中不缺少句子成分，所以用that来引导，what, who引导主语从句，连接词在从句中都要作成分；whether引导意思是"是否"，所答案选C。

37.【A】why引导的从句作表语，同时why在从句中作原因状语。这里之所以选why，而不是when或where等，唯一的依据便是句子的逻辑含义及语境。故选A。

38.【B】宾语从句用陈述语序，排除A、C，从句中介词like缺宾语，how是连接副词，不能作宾语，故选B。

39.【A】考查主谓一致，"名词+as well as+名词"结构要求动词一般应与第一个名词一致。be to blame"受到责备"所以应填"are"，选A。

40.【C】考查主谓一致。第一个all是指人，谓语动词要用复数，第二个all泛指事情，此时all做主语，谓语动词要用单数的形式。句意：所有人都出席了，一切都准备好了。故选C。

三、完型填空(本大题共15小题，每小题1分，共计15分)

从A、B、C、D四个选项中，选出空白处的最佳选项。

41.【B】固定搭配 be named...after"根据……被命名"，故选B。

42.【A】本题考查谓语动词的形式。句意"她学习成绩优异"。excel"表现突出"；skill"技能"，不符合题意；C项和D项是形容词，在这里不能作谓语，故选A。

43.【D】本题考查动词辨析。句意为"这个决定使她的家人很……"。anger"愤怒"，please"使高兴"，satisfy"使满意"，upset"使烦恼"。根据语境，故选D。

44.【A】本题考查词组辨析。A."轻视，看不起"；B."向上看"；C."期盼，盼望"；D."照看，照顾"。根据句意"当时在英国的护士是被人们看不起的"可知，答案为A。

45.【C】本题考查词义辨析。injure尤指在事故中受伤；hurt指身体的疼痛或者感情上的伤害；wound指战争中受伤；damage指有形的破坏或者损害，一般指建筑。根据句意"在前线，许多英国士兵受伤了。"故选C。

46.【B】本题考查形容词辨析。A."害怕的"；B."可怕的，糟糕的"；C."令人恐惧的"；D."有趣的"。根据句意"对他们来说条件是糟糕的"。所以选择B。

47.【A】本题考查名词辨析。A."遭受的痛苦"；B"经历"；C."惩罚"；D."艰辛"根据句意"前线士兵们所遭受的痛苦的报道激起了民众的愤怒"，所以选A。

48.【A】本题考查固定搭配。in response"作为回应"，故选A。

49.【D】本题考查动词辨析。participate"参加"；appoint"任命"；tend"倾向"；help"帮助"。根据句意"起初，那些医生们认为这些女人们不会有帮助"可知，答案为D。

50.【B】本题考查动词的形式。该空为现在分词作状语表伴随。故选B。

51.【C】本题考查介词。around the clock"二十四小时",固定搭配,故选C。

52.【A】本题考查介词搭配。thanks to"幸亏,由于";thanks for"因……而感谢"。根据句意"多亏了她们的辛苦工作,许多受伤的士兵才存活下来"可知,答案为A。

53.【B】本题考查同义词辨析。because引导原因状语从句;because of后面跟名词,不能引导句子;for引导表原因的并列句,补充说明原因,放句末;as引导原因状语从句,常放于句首。该题后面只有一个名词短语her excellent work,所以选B。

54.【D】本题考查动词的形式。continue to do sth."继续做某事",故选D。

55.【A】本题考查同义词辨析。award"授予,给予";reward"回报";prize"奖品";gift"礼物"。根据句意"每年国际红十字会都会为全世界做出贡献的护士们授予南丁格尔奖",故答案为A。

四、阅读理解(本大题共15小题,每小题2分,共计30分)

从A、B、C、D四个选项中,选出符合题目要求的最佳选项。

A

56.【B】细节理解题。根据短文的开头标题下面Wed:May 11,10:00am-12:30am可知,这个谈话将会从10点到12点半,持续两个半小时,故应选B。

57.【B】细节理解题。根据短文第二段中"smart phones are used to send people medical information, disease-treatment information and other information to some places short of care workers."可知,智能手机可以给人们提供很多医疗信息,因此B选项与原文的意思一致,选B。

58.【A】词义猜测题。根据画线单词所在的句子"Smart phones are often used to watch the movements and habits of animals in danger, helping with their protection."可知,智能手机可以用来观察濒危动物的移动和习性,帮助保护他们。这里的their指代的就是这些濒危的动物,故应选A。

59.【C】细节理解题。根据短文的最后"Free talks but only ticket holders are allowed in"可知,C选项不对。根据短文最后可知Dr. Levi Tbile and Dr. Erin Lasiter是两个演讲者,故A正确;根据短文第四段中"Smart phone video cameras allow people to record news events."可知B正确;根据短文的最后一句话"A light lunch reception will follow in the Goldstein Library."可知,D选项是正确的。

60.【D】主旨大意题。根据短文第一段中"Mobile communication technology has become an important part of life and has changed the world in many important ways."可知,移动电话在很多方面改变了我们这个世界,文章中从几个方面讲述了智能手机对我们的生活带来的影响。故应选D。

B

61.【D】根据第一段中"Collecting coins from all over the world can make you learn about different cultures."可知答案。故选D。

62.【C】根据第四段中"If you have very dear coins you can store them in special boxes. Maybe this is the easiest way to store your coins."可知答案。故选C。

63.【B】根据第三段中"You'll want to get a good magnifier(放大镜)to see your coins clearly. You'll also need to get a good book about coins."以及第四段中"Another way is to buy albums(相册)

— 37 —

where you can store your coins. "可知答案。故选 B。

64. 【D】根据原文"Also you'll need a place to store your coins. "可知画线单词的含义为"存储"。故选 D。

65. 【A】文章主要讲了一些关于收集硬币的建议。故选 A。

C

66. 【C】推理判断题。题意：作者通过李红的故事想要给我们展示什么？根据短文内容：李红把剩下的食物带回家而被解雇后，许多人站在她一边，批评食物浪费。由此可以看出，许多中国人不同意浪费食物的行为。故选 C。

67. 【D】细节理解题。题意：从第三自然段里，我们可以知道什么？由本段中的"Six million children die of hunger every year. "可知，每年有六百万孩子死于饥饿。故选 D。

68. 【C】推理判断题。题意：根据短文内容，我们不应该浪费食物是因为什么？A. there is enough food to feed all the people. 有足够多的食物供所有人吃。根据短文，世界上没有人们吃的足够的食物。错。B. six million children die of hunger every day. 每天有六百万孩子死于饥饿。根据短文第三段可知，每年死于饥饿的孩子是六百万。错；C. food comes from very hard work. 食物来自辛苦的劳动。D. Chinese are hospitable and generous. 中国人热情慷慨。这不是不能浪费的原因。错。故选 C。

69. 【A】细节理解题。题意：下面哪一个是节约食物的好方式？根据短文倒数第三段的内容，把剩下的带回家可以节省食物。故选 A。

70. 【B】主旨大意题。题意：短文的中心思想是什么？A. Many people die of hunger. 许多人死于饥饿。B. Don't waste food. 不要浪费食物。C. Don't be picky about food. 不要太挑食。D. Eat all the food you order. 吃下你所点的所有食物。本文分析了世界上的粮食短缺问题，告诉我们不要浪费粮食，要养成节约粮食的好习惯。故选 B。

五、书面表达(15 分)

One possible version：

Dear manager,

  My name is Li Hua. I am interested in working as a waiter in your restaurant. I had a part time job in a cafe last summer, so I think I will be able to adapt to the position very soon. I am free on weekends. As a college student, I do very well in English, so I will be able to communicate with your foreign customers. I am looking forward to an interview with you.

Yours,
Li Hua

拓展模块 Unit 1–Unit 3 阶段测试题九

一、语音(本大题共 10 小题,每小题 1 分,共计 10 分)

从 A、B、C、D 四个选项中,选出画线部分发音不同的一项。

1. 【C】解析:本题考查字母组合 ea 的发音。A、B、D 均发[iː],C 发[e],故选 C。
2. 【B】解析:本题考查元音字母 u 的发音。A、C、D 均发[juː],B 发[uː],故选 B。
3. 【A】解析:本题考查元音字母 a 的发音。B、C、D 均发[eɪ],A 发[ɑː],故选 A。
4. 【D】解析:本题考查元音字母 o 的发音。A、B、C 均发[ɒ],D 发[ʌ],故选 D。
5. 【A】解析:本题考查元音字母 a 的发音。B、C、D 均发[æ],A 发[ɒ],故选 A。
6. 【A】解析:本题考查元音字母 e 的发音。B、C、D 均发[e],A 发[ɪ],故选 A。
7. 【A】解析:本题考查字母组合 gh 的发音。B、C、D 均发[f],A 发[/],故选 A。
8. 【D】解析:本题考查元音字母 o 的发音。A、B、C 均发[əʊ],D 发[uː],故选 D。
9. 【B】解析:本题考查字母组合 ch 的发音。A、C、D 均发[tʃ],B 发[k],故选 B。
10. 【D】解析:本题考查元音字母 a 的发音。A、B、C 均发[eɪ],D 发[æ],故选 D。

二、单项选择题(本大题共 30 小题,每小题 1 分,共计 30 分)

从 A、B、C、D 四个选项中,选出空白处的最佳选项。

11. 【B】解析:本题考查固定搭配"be tolerant of 对……宽容,体谅",故选 B。
12. 【B】解析:本题考查分词作定语,现在分词表示进行,过去分词表示完成。美国是发达国家,故用过去分词,选 B。
13. 【C】解析:本题考查分词作表语,过去分词表示完成,已经破了,故选 C。
14. 【A】解析:本题考查分词作状语,逻辑主语是 Bill,被问到,故选 A。
15. 【B】解析:本题考查分词作宾语补助语,有被动含义,故选 B。
16. 【B】解析:本题考查分词作表语,表示主语的状态,故选 B。
17. 【D】解析:本题考查分词作表语,表明主语的状态,故选 D。
18. 【C】解析:本题考查分词作宾语补助语,使役动词 have 后面常接过去分词,表示动作一般由他人完成。故选 C。
19. 【C】解析:本题考查词组"succeed in doing 成功做某事",故选 C。
20. 【B】解析:本题考查让步状语从句,"now that 既然",故选 B。
21. 【D】解析:本题考查 some 和 any 用法。一般情况下,在否定句和一般疑问句中用 any,但是在想得到对方肯定回答时,就可以用 some 代替 any,故选 D。
22. 【D】解析:本题考查 whether 和 if 用法。whether 和 if 都可以引导宾语从句,表示是否,但是 whether 引导的宾语从句可以和连词 or,or not 连用,而 If 不能。根据句意,故选 D。
23. 【A】解析:本题考查词组辨析。A. at least 至少;B. at once 立刻;C. at times 有时,偶尔;D. at noon 在中午。根据句意,故选 A。
24. 【B】解析:本题考查词组辨析。根据句意 by means of 借助于,故选 B。
25. 【B】解析:本题考查词汇辨析。A. Wherever 无论哪儿;B. Whenever 无论什么时候;

C. Whoever 无论谁；D. However 无论怎样。根据句意，故选 B。

26.【A】解析：本题考查让步状语从句。though 尽管，根据语境和上下文，故选 A。

27.【A】解析：本题考查词组辨析。根据语境和上下文，所有的妇女都想要自由控制体重。keep down 控制，故选 A。

28.【C】解析：本题考查 so \ such…that 句型，句中 day 是可数名词单数，所以要用不定冠词修饰，相关语法提示：such a \ an+形容词+名词单数+that 从句；so+形容词+a \ an+名词单数+that 从句，故选 C。

29.【B】解析：本题考查过去分词做后置定语，故选 B。

30.【B】解析：本题考查分词作状语，现在分词表示主动进行，过去分词表示被动完成，根据句意，故选 B。

31.【B】解析：本题考查分词，现在分词表示主动进行，过去分词表示被动完成，根据句意地面被落叶覆盖，故选 B。

32.【A】解析：本题考查分词，根据句意尽管被告知了好多次了，他还是不明白。用分词的完成被动式。故选 A。

33.【B】解析：本题考查分词，根据句意，所填单词在句子中作方式或者伴随状语，和句子主语是主动关系，故选 B。

34.【C】解析：本题考查分词，根据句意表示主动进行，故选 C。

35.【A】解析：本题考查固定搭配，have trouble (in) doing，故选 A。

36.【D】解析：本题考查固定搭配，be busy (in) doing 忙于某事，故选 D。

37.【C】解析：本题考查分词作表语，表示主语的状态，故选 C。

38.【D】解析：本题考查分词，现在分词表示主动进行，学习语言和人是主动关系，故用现在分词，作定语，第二空 forget 和 use the foreign，同时进行，用现在分词表示伴随状语。故选 D。

39.【D】解析：本题考查固定搭配，"对于生活的态度 attitude towards life"，故选 D。

40.【B】解析：本题第一空考查分词作状语，表示主动进行，用现在分词，第二空停下来去做另一件事，故选 B。

三、完型填空（本大题共 15 小题，每小题 1 分，共计 15 分）

从 A、B、C、D 四个选项中，选出空白处的最佳选项。

41.【C】解析：考查动词。A. take 带走，B. bring 带来，C. carry 携带，D. give 给；根据上文 When you write a letter or make a telephone call 可知，本句是指你说的话里带有各种信息。carry 可以接抽象名词，译为传播、承载。这里的 message 是信息的意思，是抽象名词，故选 C。

42.【D】解析：考查介词。A. by 通过；B. with 和，与；C. use 使用；D. without 没有。根据上下文 Do you think you can communicate _____ words? 可知与前面的 with 成对比，前面讲到用语言交流，接下来讲到不用语言交流。应说如果没有了语言，你还能表达你的意思吗？故选 D。

43.【B】解析：考查介词。A. in 在、里；B. on 在……上；C. at 在，D. over 越过。根据下文 your face shows you are happy and friendly. 可知，On the face 指在脸上，固定用法，故选 B。

44.【A】解析：考查词义辨析。Others 泛指别人；B. the others 特指另一部分人；C. other 别的，后面要加名词复数；D. the other 特指另一个。根据上下文"Tears in your eyes tell that you are sad."可知，你的眼泪告诉其他人你很难过，故选 A。

45.【C】解析：考查动词短语。A. put on 穿上；B. put out 熄灭；C. put up 举起；D. put down 放下。根据下文"the teacher knows you want to say something or ask questions. 老师知道你想说什么或问问题。"可知，当你举手的时候，老师就知道你有话要说，或者要问问题。故选 C。

46.【B】解析：考查连词。A. when 当……时；B. or 或者；C. but 但是；D. if 如果。根据上文"When you put up your hand in class. 当你在课堂上举手的时候。"可知，Or 表示选择关系，当你举手的时候，老师就知道你有话要说，或者要问问题。故选 B。

47.【C】解析：考查细节理解。根据上文的 You nod 说明你点头是想说是。点头表示是，这是常识。故选 C。

48.【D】解析：考查固定词组。根据上文 For example, a sign at the bus stop helps you to know which bus, 可知乘坐公交车 take the bus。本句把它转换成疑问词加上不定式的形式。故选 D。

49.【C】解析：考查疑问词。A. which 哪一个；B. where 哪；C. how 怎样；D. what 什么。根据上文"A sign on the wall of your school helps you to find the library. 你学校的墙上有一个标志，可以帮助你找到图书馆。"可知，门上的标牌告诉我们如何进出。使用 how，表示方式。故选 C。

50.【D】解析：考查时态。根据 ever noticed 说明使用现在完成时，结构为 have/has done. 表示曾经，强调到目前为止。可知你是否注意到在你的周围有很多的标牌，你从女性标牌上也得到了很多的信息。故选 D。

51.【A】解析：考查介词。A. from 从；B. of ……的；C. about 关于；D. for 为了。根据上文"Have you ever noticed that there are a lot of signs around you. 你是否注意到在你的周围有很多的标牌。"可知，应说你从那些标牌上也得到了很多的信息。故选 A。

52.【D】解析：考查固定结构。A. with 和，与；B. by 通过；C. without 没有；D. in 在……里。根据上下文 People can communicate _____ many other ways. 可知，In this way 用这种方法，用很多其他的方法，人们可以传达情感。故选 D。

53.【B】解析：考查冠词。A. the 表示特指；B. an 表示泛指，用于元音音素开头的单词前；C. a, 表示泛指，用在辅音音素开头的单词前；D. some 一些。根据下文的 artist 可知，是元音音素开头的单词，故选 B。

54.【D】解析：考查动词。根据上下文"Books…to tell you about all wonderful things in the world and also about people and their ideas."可知，Books 与 write 之间构成被动的关系，一般现在时的被动语态，结构为 be+done，主语是 books 复数。故选 D。

55.【A】解析：考查宾语从句。A. what 什么；B. which 哪一个；C. that 那；D. who 谁。根据上下文 They all help us to know…is going on in the world. 可知 What 引导起一个宾语从句，并在句中做主语。故选 A。

四、阅读理解（本大题共15小题，每小题2分，共计30分）

从 A、B、C、D 四个选项中，选出符合题目要求的最佳选项。

41

A

56. 【C】解析：细节理解题。短文中没有提到这位农夫为什么去坐牢。故选：C。

57. 【B】解析：细节理解题。根据"I am worried about our farm,"she wrote. 句意："我很担心我们的农场，"她写道。可知，担心农场。故选：B。

58. 【A】解析：细节理解题。根据 Don't dig the fields. 句意：不要挖土地。可知，农民告诉他妻子先不要挖土地。故选：A。

59. 【D】解析：细节理解题。根据"Don't dig the fields. This is where my gold(金子)is. Don't plant potatoes until I come home."句意：不要挖土地。这里有我的金子。直到我回家才能种植土豆。结合选项，可知，他们都想去挖到金子。故选：D。

60. 【A】解析：细节理解题。根据"They have dug our field."The farmer wrote to his wife at once. "Now you can plant our potatoes,"he wrote. 他们挖了我们的田。农夫立刻写信给他的妻子："现在你可以种我们的土豆了，"他写道。可知，农夫想了一个主意，说他家田里有金子，这些监狱看守想得到金子，于是他们的田被看守们翻了，因此农夫告诉他妻子可以种土豆了。故选：A。

B

61. 【C】解析：细节理解题。由文章第一段内容可知，如果你拜访一个法国家庭，不要急于脱掉外套，这会使主人感到很紧张。A 外套会使房间脏的；B 你会感冒；C 那会使主人紧张；D 那会给主人带来坏的运气；故选 C。

62. 【B】解析：细节理解题。由第二段最后一句可知，即使你有最好的礼仪，在法国也不会被接受。A 帮助你很多；B 不被接受；C 是相同的；D 最坏的礼仪；故选 B。

63. 【C】解析：细节理解题。由文章第三段内容可知，如果你给主人送花，是不礼貌的，因为主人必须得忙着找花瓶。A 在法国，花意味着坏运气；B 在法国，没有人喜欢花；C 因为主人必须得忙着找花瓶；故选 C。

64. 【A】解析：细节理解题。由文章第四段最后一句可知，however, offer a box of chocolate which the hostess will pass after dinner with coffee. 然而，主人在饭后发巧克力。故选 A。

65. 【D】解析：细节理解题。由文章最后一段"guests must never get up and leave the table—not to go to the bathroom, not to help the hostess in the kitchen, and not to serve or clear. 客人一旦落座，不能离开饭桌，不能去卫生间，不能去厨房帮忙等"。可知故选 D。

C

66. 【A】解析：细节理解题。由文章第一段可知 It was brought to Britain in 1994 from America. 带女儿上班日是由美国传至英国的。故选 A。

67. 【C】解析：细节理解题。由文章第一段可知，On that day, thousands of girls take a day off school and go with one of their parents to their work places. 在那一天，女孩们会跟他们的父亲或母亲一起到工作的地方。故选 C。

68. 【D】解析：细节理解题。由文章第一段 By doing this, it can teach girls more about the society where they live. 可知这个活动可以教她更多关于她们生活的有关社会的东西。由文章第二段后面 This helped her understand her mother's work better. 这个活动可以让他们能够更好地了解父母的工作。She said that this made her feel more confident about her future. 这个活动可以让女孩感觉对未来更有信心。故选 D。

69.【C】解析：细节理解题。由文章第一段 By doing this, it can teach girls more about the society where they live. 可知这个活动可以教她们更多关于她们生活的有关社会的东西。由文章第二段后面"This helped her understand her mother's work better. 这个活动可以让他们能够更好地了解父母的工作。She said that this made her feel more confident about her future. 这个活动可以让女孩感觉对未来更有信心。"可知，女孩们喜欢这个节日的原因是能得到很多益处，并不是不愿意去上学。故选 C。

70.【B】解析：细节理解题。由文章第二段的后面"She said that this made her feel more confident about her future. 这个活动可以让女孩感觉对未来更有信心。"，以及文章第四段"Experts think that girls with more self-confidence are more likely to be successful than common girls."可知，在他们的将来，自信心对女孩们来说是最重要的。故选 B。

五、书面表达(15 分)

One possible version:

Dear Jack,

  My birthday is coming. I am going to have a birthday party at Sunshine Restaurant. I would like to invite you to come to my birthday party. The party will be on Tuesday, October 20th at 4:00p. m. We will play games, eat delicious food and watch some good movies. My father is going to tell us a funny story.

  Can you come to my birthday party? Please reply to me if you come by Monday, October 19th.

Yours,
Susan

拓展模块 Unit 4-Unit 6 阶段测试题十

一、语音(本大题共 10 小题,每小题 1 分,共计 10 分)

从 A、B、C、D 四个选项中,选出画线部分发音不同的一项。

1. 【D】解析:本题考查元音字母 o 的发音。A、B、C 均发[ə],D 发[ɒ],故选 D。
2. 【D】解析:本题考查元音字母 i 的发音。A、B、C 均发[ɪ],D 发[aɪ],故选 D。
3. 【B】解析:本题考查元音字母 e 的发音。A、C、D 均发[e],B 发[iː],故选 B。
4. 【C】解析:本题考查元音字母 a 的发音。A、B、D 均发[eɪ],C 发[ə],故选 C。
5. 【A】解析:本题考查组合字母 oo 的发音。B、C、D 均发[uː],A 发[ʌ],故选 A。
6. 【B】解析:本题考查辅音字母 s 的发音。A、C、D 均发[s],B 发[z],故选 B。
7. 【C】解析:本题考查辅音字母 ch 的发音。A、B、D 均发[tʃ],C 发[k],故选 C。
8. 【C】解析:本题考查元音字母 o 的发音。A、B、D 均发[ɒ],C 发[ʌ],故选 C。
9. 【A】解析:本题考查辅音字母 t 的发音。B、C、D 均发[t],A 发[tʃ],故选 A。
10. 【B】解析:本题考查辅音字母 h 的发音。A、C、D 均发[h],B 发[/],故选 B。

二、单项选择题(本大题共 30 小题,每小题 1 分,共计 30 分)

从 A、B、C、D 四个选项中,选出空白处的最佳选项。

11. 【D】解析:本题考查固定搭配"be associated with 由……联想到",故选 D。
12. 【D】解析:本题考查固定搭配"习惯于做某事 be used to doing sth.""过去常常做某事 used to do sth."。故选 D。
13. 【B】解析:本题考查固定搭配"被当场捉住 be caught red-handed",故选 B。
14. 【A】解析:本题考查颜色的联想固定搭配,绿色总能给人生的希望,故选 A。
15. 【C】解析:本题考查过去分词作定语,"他们爱的人 their loved one",故选 C。
16. 【B】解析:本题考查固定搭配"提醒某人某事 warn sb. of sth."故选 B。
17. 【B】解析:本题考查固定搭配"火冒三丈 see red",故选 B。
18. 【C】解析:本题考查固定搭配"提醒某人某事 remind sb. of sth.",故选 C。
19. 【B】解析:本题考查固定搭配"情绪不高 in low spirits","情绪很好 in high spirits",故选 B。
20. 【A】解析:本题考查固定搭配"正相反 on the contrary""总的来说 on the whole""信不信由你 believe it or not""同时 at the same time"故选 A。
21. 【C】解析:本题考查倒装句,把 neither, nor 放在句首时,表示前面否定的内容也适用于另一人或者物。其句型是:neither(nor)+be(have, 助动词或者情态动词)+主语,故选 C。
22. 【B】解析:本题考查倒装句,only 所修饰的副词、介词短语或者状语从句放在句首时,用倒装语序,故选 B。
23. 【A】解析:本题考查倒装句,含有否定意义的副词或者连词放到句首时用倒装,如 hardly, never, not, seldom, little 等。故选 A。
24. 【A】解析:本题考查倒装句,含有否定意义的副词或者连词放到句首时用倒装,如

25.【B】解析：本题考查倒装句，含有否定意义的副词或者连词放到句首时用倒装，如 hardly, never, not, seldom, little 等。再根据后面的时态 be 动词用 was，故选 B。

26.【B】解析：本题考查倒装句，第一空，表示同一个人、同一件事，用部分倒装；第二空用完全倒装，把副词 so 放在句首，表示前面所说的情况也适用于另一个人或物，其句型是：so+be(have, 助动词或情态动词)+主语，故选 B。

27.【B】解析：本题考查倒装句，如果表示同一个人、同一件事时，用部分倒装，既主语在中间，谓语在最后。故选 B。

28.【C】解析：本题考查倒装句，含有否定意义的副词或者连词放到句首时用部分倒装，如 hardly, never, not, seldom, little 等。故选 C。

29.【D】解析：本题考查倒装句，含有否定意义的副词或者连词放到句首时用部分倒装，如 hardly, never, not, seldom, little 等。故选 D。

30.【C】解析：本题考查倒装句，含有否定意义的副词或者连词放到句首时用部分倒装，如 hardly, never, not, seldom, little 等，hardly 和 when 搭配表示，一怎么样就怎么样。故选 C。

31.【D】解析：本题考查辨别词性，根据句意，请接受我真诚的道歉，用形容词，故选 D。

32.【C】解析：本题考查辨别词性，根据句意"我表示道歉因为我的态度太差了"。态度 attitude，故选 C。

33.【B】解析：本题考查固定搭配，对于道歉的应答语，我们应该说没关系，故选 B。

34.【D】解析：本题考查定语从句的时态，用现在完成时，表示对现在造成的影响和结果。故选 D。

35.【B】解析：本题考查固定搭配，"对什么感到不好意思 be/feel ashamed of"，故选 B。

36.【C】解析：本题考查固定搭配，"面对面 face-to-face"，根据句意故选 C。

37.【D】解析：本题考查代词用法，much"许多，大量"；all"所有，一切"；"neither""两者都不"；none"一个也没有"，侧重数量概念，后面常跟 of 短语。本题是 as 引导的原因状物从句，因为骑自行车不会有乘坐公交车的麻烦，侧重于"一个麻烦也没有"，所以 none 符合要求，故选 D。

38.【A】解析：本题考查固定搭配，"熟悉，通晓 be familiar with"，故选 A。

39.【C】解析：本题考查代词，根据句意："——先生，我能帮您挑选牛仔裤吗？——是的，我想试穿那些蓝色的牛仔裤。"根据 those blue 可知用复数，代词 ones 代替 jeans，故选 C。

40.【C】解析：本题考查代词词义辨析：all 三个以上都；no 没有；none 是三个以上都不，与 of 短语连用；any 一些，常用于否定句和一般疑问句中。根据前文表示我们不能在饭店里吃饭，又因 none of 为固定用法，所以第一个空选用 none，在这里表示表示没有一个人；同时此句为否定句，所以第二个空要选用 any。故选 C。

三、完型填空(本大题共 15 小题，每小题 1 分，共计 15 分)

从 A、B、C、D 四个选项中，选出空白处的最佳选项。

41.【B】解析：根据下文"红色用于危险的标志"。故选 B。

42.【C】解析：根据下文"如停车标志和消防车"。故选 C。

43.【B】解析：leaves 秋天树叶。故选 B。

44. 【A】解析：lively 橙色，是活泼的颜色。故选 A。

45. 【C】解析：sunlight 黄色，是阳光的颜色。故选 C。

46. 【B】解析：绿色，是春天草的颜色。故选 B。

47. 【C】解析：A. speak 说话；B. say 说；C. talk about 谈论。根据句子意思是指人们谈论的话题。故选 C。

48. 【B】解析：上文中提到"黄色是阳光的颜色"绿色是春天草的颜色，而且没有提到白色。故选 B。

49. 【C】解析：A. calm 平静；B. sleepy 睡意绵绵；C. active 活跃的；根据句子意思是在有暖色和很多光的地方，人们通常想要活动一下。故选 C。

50. 【D】解析：固定搭配，others 别的人，故选 D。

51. 【A】解析：black 黑色；B. red 红色；C. green 绿色。故选 A。

52. 【B】解析：A. go around 四处走动；B. go by 时间流逝；C. go along 沿着。故选 B。

53. 【B】解析：way 方式，故选 B。

54. 【C】解析：A. factory 工厂；B. classroom 教室；C. restaurant 饭店。故选 C。

55. 【B】解析：那么冷色更适合办公室。故选 B。

四、阅读理解（本大题共15小题，每小题2分，共计30分）

从 A、B、C、D 四个选项中，选出符合题目要求的最佳选项。

A

56. 【C】解析：细节理解题。根据第一段 Happiness is for everyone. 可知，幸福是给所有人的。故选 C。

57. 【A】解析：细节理解题。根据第二段 when you do something wrong, people around you will help you to correct it. 当您做错事时，周围的人会帮助您进行纠正。可知，当您做错事时，您可以纠正它。故选 A。

58. 【C】解析：细节理解题。根据第二段 When you are in trouble at school, your friends will help you; when you study hard at your lessons, your parents are always taking good care of your life and your health; when you get success, your friends will say congratulations to you; when you do something wrong, people around you will help you to correct it. And when you do something good to others, you will feel happy, too. 当你在学校遇到麻烦时，你的朋友会为您提供帮助；当你认真学习时，你的父母总是会照顾你的生活和健康；当你获得成功时，朋友们会向你表示祝贺；何时你做错了什么，你周围的人会帮你纠正它。当你做对别人有益的事情时，你也会感到高兴。可知，A、B 均正确，故选 C。

59. 【B】解析：细节理解题。根据第三段 Happiness is not the same as money. It is a feeling of your heart. When you are poor, you can also say you are very happy, because you have something else that can't be bought with money. 幸福和金钱不一样。这是你内心的感觉。当你贫穷的时候，你也可以说你很幸福，因为你还有其他一些用钱买不到的东西。可知，我们说"幸福与金钱不一样"，因为金钱并不总是带来幸福。故选 B。

60. 【C】解析：主旨大意题。根据第一段的第一句 Happiness is for everyone. 和最后一段的第一句 Happiness is not the same as money. 可以得出答案为 C。

46

B

61. 【C】解析：细节理解题。根据 Some people have very good memories and they can easily learn many things by heart，可知有些人有很好的记忆力，他们可以很容易地记住许多事情。故选C。

62. 【C】解析：细节理解题。根据题干：什么样的人不能轻松记住事情。由第一段可知，回忆是记住东西的关键，所以选C。

63. 【B】解析：细节理解题。题干一个好的记忆帮助人们，由第二段 A good memory is a great help in learning a language 可知轻松学习语言，选B。

64. 【A】解析：细节理解题。题干一些孩子和他们父母居住在外国。所以 They can learn two languages as early as. 选A。

65. 【C】解析：细节理解题。题干，什么可以帮助人们改善记忆。由最后一段 we want to…可知需要大量练习，故选C。

C

66. 【A】解析：细节理解题。推理判断题。根据文章"Surtsey was born in 1963. Scientists saw the birth of this is land. It began at 7.30 a.m. on 14th November. A fishing boat was near Iceland."（Surtsey出生于1963年。科学家们见证了这个岛的诞生。它始于11月14日上午7时30分。一艘渔船在冰岛附近。）可推知，Surtsey是在冰岛附近。故选A。

67. 【A】解析：细节理解题。根据文章"Scientists flew there to watch."（科学家们飞到那里观看。）和"Surtsey grew and grew. Then it stopped in June1967. It was 175 meters high and 2 kilometers long."（Surtsey越来越大。然后在1967年停止变大。它高达175米，长约2 000米）可知，科学家飞去那里是为了观看岛屿的诞生。故选A。

68. 【C】解析：细节理解题。根据文章"It began at 7.30a.m. on 14th November."（它始于11月14日上午7时30分。）和"It was 10 meters high the next day and 60 meters high on 18th November. Scientists flew there to watch."（第二天有10米高，11月18日有60米高。科学家们飞到那里观看。）可知，火山爆发后四天科学家飞往了那里。故选C。

69. 【A】解析：细节理解题。根据文章"It began at 7.30 a.m. on 14th November. A fishing boat was near Iceland. The boat moved under the captain's feet. He noticed a strange smell. He saw some black smoke. A volcano（火山）was breaking out. Red-hot rocks, fire and smoke were rushing up from the bottom（底部）of the sea. The island grew quickly."（它始于11月14日上午7时30分。一艘渔船在冰岛附近。船在船长脚下移动。他注意到一种奇怪的气味。他看到一些黑烟。一座火山正在喷发。炽热的岩石、火和烟从海底涌上来。这个岛发展得很快。）可知，d. A fishing boat was near Iceland. 排在第一个；a. The captain found the boat was moving. 排在第二个；c. Fire, smoke and rocks were seen rushing up. 排在第三个；b. A new island appeared in the sea. 排在第四个；e. The island grew quickly 排在最后。正确的语序是：d-a-c-b-e。故选A。

70. 【B】解析：标题归纳题。根据文章第一句"Surtsey was born in 1963. Scientists saw the birth of this island"（Surtsey出生于1963年。科学家们见证了这个岛的诞生。）可知，文章主要讲述了一个岛屿的诞生。故本文的最佳标题可以是"一个新岛屿"。故选B。

五、书面表达(15分)

One possible version:

  Nowadays, people in many big cities are complaining about the heavy traffic. It has seriously influenced people's daily life and economic development. To solve the problem, some pieces of advice are put forward.

  Some people suggest that more streets and roads should be built. In this way, the traffic density can be reduced, so it can speed up the flow of buses and cars. But the new roads and streets will be filled with many cars and buses soon.

  Some people advise to limit the number of bikes and cars. This can decrease the traffic flow. But on the other hand, this will affect the consumption and make buses more crowded.

  In my opinion, the number of private cars should be put under control. And at the same time, buses should have their own special routes which cannot be used by other vehicles. Besides, underground train and city train should be developed quickly.

拓展模块 Unit 7—Unit 9 阶段测试题十一

一、语音(本大题共 10 小题,每小题 1 分,共计 10 分)

从 A、B、C、D 四个选项中,选出画线部分发音不同的一项。

1.【C】考查字母 a 的发音,字母 a 在 C 中读[ei],在 A、B、D 中读[aː]。
2.【D】考查字母组合 re 的发音,在 A、B、C 中读[re],在 D 中读[ri]。
3.【D】考查字母组合 th 的发音,在一些单词中读[ð],在一些单词中读[θ];th 在 A、B、C 中读[ð],在 D 中读[θ]。
4.【C】考查字母 a 的发音,字母 a 在 A、B、D 中读[ei],在重读闭音节中读[æ]。
5.【C】考查字母 i 的发音,在非重读音节中读[i],在 A、B、D 中读[ai]。
6.【A】考查字母 o 的发音,o 在 s、t、l、d 前读[əU],在重读闭音节中读[ɔ],在重读开音节中读[əu]。
7.【D】考查字母 u 的发音,在一些重读音节中读[ʌ],在一些重读音节中读[juː],u 在 A、B、C 中读[ʌ],在 D 中读[juː]。
8.【A】考查字母 g 的发音,在 B、C、D 中读[g],在 A 中读[jʒ]。
9.【C】考查字母 n 的发音,在 A、B、D 中读[ŋ],在 C 中读[n]。
10.【C】考查字母组合 ou 的发音,在一些重读音节中读[ʌ],在 C 中读[ʌ],ou 在 A、B、D 中读[au]。

二、单项选择题(本大题共 30 小题,每小题 1 分,共计 30 分)

从 A、B、C、D 四个选项中,选出空白处的最佳选项。

11.【D】题意:他的家庭对他有良好的影响。本题考查固定搭配 have an influence on sb/sth.,表示"对某人或某事有影响"。
12.【B】题意:这部电影无聊得令人难以置信。本题考查固定搭配 to a…degree,表示:"在……程度上""到……程度"。
13.【D】题意:美国流行音乐在 20 世纪得到迅速发展。本题考查动词辨析。A. transmit 表示:"传送,传输",B. produce 表示"生产,产生",C. expose 表示"揭露,揭发",D. accelerate 表示"加速"。
14.【A】题意:由于天很晚了,我们很快就回来了。本题考查 as 用作从属连词,表示原因或理由时,意思是"由于""因为",其语气比 because 弱得多,表示原因已为人们所知。
15.【C】题意:午饭过后,他们又继续交谈了三个小时。本题考查 go on 表示"继续",go on doing sth. 继续做原来做的事。go on to do 做了一件事后,接着做另一件事。
16.【D】题意:她承诺在医院照顾她的母亲。本题考查 promise to do sth. 表示"承诺去做某事",但还没有做。promise doing sth. 表示"承诺做某事",已经在做。
17.【B】题意:保持安静是会议的必备要求。本题考查名词辨析。A. idea 表示"想法",B. demand 表示"要求",C. question 表示"问题",D. meaning 表示"意义"。
18.【C】题意:被称作"网虫"的人是指那些沉迷网络的人。本题考查动词短语辨析。refer to…

as 称……为，called 称……为，be known as 被认为是……，be known for 因……而闻名。此处与先行词 the people 是被动语态。

19.【A】题意：他宁可到农村去工作。本题考查固定句式 would rather do sth. 表示："宁愿""最好"。

20.【C】题意："——现在很晚了。我想和你说再见。——希望你玩开心了。明天见。"客人要走，英美人不留客。选项B"没关系"，用于回应道歉。选项D"我会想念你的"，这里使用不恰当。

21.【B】题意：——露西期中考试没通过。——真遗憾！难怪她情绪低落。本题考查动词短语辨析。get over 克服，度过。get through 穿过（强调贯穿），通过（考试），熬过。get across 穿过（强调横穿），使……被理解。get round 走动，消息传开。

22.【B】题意：在寒冬，哈尔滨的气温通常整日在零度以下。本题考查介词。above"多于"，below"少于"，二者主要用于表示温度、高度等有纵向标准可比的情况。

23.【D】题意：他们每人有一本字典。each 不能与 of 搭配使用；all 或 both 与 of 搭配作主语，谓语动词用复数形式；each of 作主语，谓语动词用单数形式。

24.【C】题意：假如不下雨，我就会去。本题考查连词。providing 假设，假如。Although 尽管。unless 除非。because 因为，由于。

25.【C】题意：我们希望你可以在这里多待一段时间。本题考查固定句式 expect sb to do sth. 希望某人做某事。

26.【A】题意：很难用语言传递含义，但是你会明白我们在视频中所谈论的事情。本题考查介词短语辨析。in words 用语言，in need 需要，in detail 详细地，in order 按顺序。

27.【B】题意：你可以通过实践获得知识。本题考查动词辨析。calculate 计算；obtain（尤指经努力）获得，赢得，push 推，移动；multiply 乘。

28.【A】题意：他匀速驾驶。本题考查形近词辨析。constant"不变的，经常的"，content"满意的"，conscious"有意识的"，continue"持续，继续做"。

29.【D】题意：聚会的消费将与被邀请的人数成正比。本题考查固定搭配。be proportional to "和……成比例"。respond to 回应，响应。the same as 和……一样。

30.【C】题意：对于他来说解出这个数学问题很难。本题考查固定搭配。work out 得出，计算出。count out 数（钱）。

31.【D】题意："八除以二等于四。"本题考查考查数学运算。plus 加，minus 减，times 乘以，divided by 除以。

32.【D】题意："我的手表无法工作了，我必须现在去修一修。"本题考查：have sth. done 找人做某事。have sth. to do 自己有事要做。eg：I have some clothes to wash。立刻；马上 right now；at once；immediately。

33.【A】题意："我认为他没有去过猴子岛，是吗?"本题考查：He has ever been to…他曾经到过。He has gone to …他正在去……的途中。Island (n)岛屿。本句考查完成时态的反义疑问句。

34.【A】题意："我害怕这个衬衫对于我弟弟来说太大了。"本题考查：这个衬衫太大了。(汉语中我们可以说：这个衣服比较大。但是此时的比较，没有英语中比较级含义，是"very"的含义。比较级只用在有可比较的情形。)

35.【C】题意："自从他离家已经两周多了。"本题考查：It has been… since…自从……已经……

36.【D】题意:"我们不知道想见你的那个女人是谁。"本题考查:定语从句,从句中缺成分,缺主语,所以选who。

37.【B】题意:"——我必须在一小时内完成这些工作吗?——不,你不需要。"考点分析: Must 的疑问句,如果是否定回答用 no,you need not。

38.【C】题意:"——你想跟我们一起去吗?——如果玛丽去,我也去。"本题考查:So + 助动词+主语:某人也一样做……(so 在此中无意思)eg: You are so great, so is your son. 你如此伟大,你的儿子也一样。So+主+助动词:于是,我做……(so,于是……正常的句子)eg: It is very cold, so I wear a heavy coat. 天气很冷,所以我穿了厚衣服。

39.【B】题意:"当他们看到浦东有如此多的高大建筑时,情不自禁地叫喊道:'太棒了!'"本题考查: couldn't help doing…情不自禁做……(只此一种搭配)。

40.【C】题意:"——停止讲话,让我们开始上课吧。——好的,我们将停下来听你讲。"考点分析: stop/remember/forget/regret doing 停止/记得/忘记/遗憾……做过(正在做)的事情。stop/remember/forget/regret to do 停止/记得/忘记/遗憾……没有做过的事情。(仔细体会 to 的未做的含义)

三、完型填空(本大题共15小题,每小题1分,共计15分)

从 A、B、C、D 四个选项中,选出空白处的最佳选项。

41.【A】考查动词。A. laughing"笑"; B. crying"哭"; C. speaking"说"; D. joking"开玩笑"。作者和父亲优雅地一圈圈跳舞,笑着点头和别的舞者打招呼。故选 A。

42.【A】考查动词。A. refused"拒绝"; B. hated"憎恨"; C. used"使用"; D. hid"隐藏"。当时作者和父亲是舞池中跳得最好的,作者拒绝和他跳舞的那些年过去了。下文"Don't touch me! I am sick and ___8___ of dancing with you!"可知以前拒绝和父亲跳舞。故选 A。

43.【C】考查形容词。A. happy"高兴的"; B. hard"困难的"; C. early"早期的"; D. unhappy"不高兴的"。此处指作者又想起了以前的那些事。根据下文"One night when I was fifteen,"可知选 C。

44.【C】考查名词。A. head"头"; B. hands"手"; C. arms"胳膊"; D. face"脸"。根据"when I was almost three"可知当时作者才三岁,父亲是把作者搂进胳膊里抱着跳舞。故选 C。

45.【D】考查动词。A. covered"覆盖"; B. settled"定居"; C. stopped"停止"; D. lost"迷失,失去"。此处指作者陷入痛苦中,lost in…固定短语,"迷失于……",故选 D。

46.【B】考查名词。A. feelings"感情"; B. unhappiness"苦恼"; C. pains"疼痛"; D. regret"遗憾"。此处指父亲希望通过跳舞摆脱苦恼,与下文"Let's get the unhappiness on the run."呼应,故选 B。

47.【D】考查动词。A. ran"跑"; B. waved"挥动"; C. walked"走"; D. jumped"跳"。此处指作者从椅子上跳起来,朝着父亲喊不让他碰。根据当时情境,选 D。

48.【A】考查形容词。A. tired"疲劳的,厌烦的"; B. concerned"关心的"; C. uninterested"不感兴趣的"; D. frightened"害怕的"。作者告诉父亲自己厌倦了和父亲一起跳舞,be tired of 固定短语,"对……厌烦",故选 A。

49.【B】考查名词。A. disappointment"失望"; B. hurt 痛苦; C. attitude"态度"; D. anger"生气"。作者告诉父亲厌倦了和他跳舞后,父亲脸上露出痛苦的表情。根据常识选 B。

50.【C】考查副词。A. formally"正式地"; B. incorrectly"不正确地"; C. loudly"大声地";

D. hardly"几乎不"。作者说的伤害父亲的话已经收不回来，所以跑回房间大哭。故选 C。

51.【C】考查名词。A. control"控制"；B. floor"地板"；C. life"生活"；D. field"田野，领域"。父亲在作者上高中和大学时一直等着作者，此处指这段时间作者从他的生活中跳了出来。指这段时间没有和父亲一起跳过舞。故选 C。

52.【D】考查名词。A. speed"速度"；B. heart"心"；C. body"身体"；D. health"健康"。此处指父亲的健康从心脏病得到好转。故选 D。

53.【A】考查动词。A. joined"参加"；B. left"离开"；C. started"开始"；D. trained"训练"。母亲写信说他们参加了一个跳舞俱乐部。加入某个组织成为成员用 join。故选 A。

54.【B】考查动词。A. loving"爱"；B. remembering"回忆"；C. worrying"担心"；D. dancing"跳舞"。父亲喜欢跳舞，作者的眼里充满了回忆。指回忆父亲当年跳舞的事，故选 B。

55.【C】考查名词。A. answer"回答"；B. change"改变"；C. apology"道歉"；D. praise"表扬"。作者知道父亲一直等着道歉，但作者找不到合适的词。故选 C。

四、阅读理解（本大题共 15 小题，每小题 2 分，共计 30 分）

从 A、B、C、D 四个选项中，选出符合题目要求的最佳选项。

A

56.【B】第一段的最后一句"He found that they were about two inches too long."。

57.【A】年轻人提出缩短裤子的要求，这个要求是向在场的妈妈和他的两个姐妹提出的。

58.【C】因当时妈妈和姐妹俩都忙于干活，所以当时都没有回答他的话。

59.【D】从第四段的原句(Later on, after supper, the elder sister remembered her brother's trousers)中我们可知是晚饭后去把裤子缩短了。

60.【C】通读全文，知道有三人把裤子各缩短了两英寸，那么总共缩短了六英寸。

B

61.【A】从整篇文章我们知道，在学习英语翻译句子时，我们不能逐字逐词译成母语，这样做是不明智的，结果是译成错误的句子。

62.【C】从文章中的第二段的这一句中 It's important to master the rules for word order in the study of English, too. 可知 C 项为正确答案。

63.【C】从文章所举的两组例子和原句 Sometimes when the order of words in an English sentence is changed, the meaning of the sentence changes. 说明了作者的这一观点：有时，不同的词序会有不同的意思。

64.【B】She only likes apples. only 在这句中修饰动词 likes，意为"她只喜欢苹果，而不喜欢吃其他水果"。Only she likes apples. only 在此句中修饰主语 she，意为"只有她喜欢苹果，而其他人就不一定喜欢吃苹果了"。所以正确答案是 B。

65.【D】从整篇文章可以看出其大意是"怎样学习英语"，把它作为标题应该是最佳的。

C

66.【D】"Like the earth, a comet goes round the sun, but…"是判断本题的根据。

67.【C】根据"…is water frozen into pieces of ice and mixed with iron and rock dust and perhaps a few big pieces of rock."这句话即能得出答案。

68.【D】由第五段的首句"Many people perhaps have seen a comet."可知。

— 52 —

69. 【C】"Some comets move out of our sight and never come back. Others keep coming back at regular times."一句是答案的出处。
70. 【C】哈雷彗星每七十六年才能看到一次。再结合"…the last time it came close to the sun and the earth was in the year 1986."这句话的意思，即可得到答案。

五、书面表达(15分)

One possible version：

  What should we do to keep healthy? First, we should have more healthy food. We should eat more vegetables and less meat. We had better not have the fast food such as the potato chips, hamburgers and so on.

  Second, we should have good eating habits. For example, we had better wash our hands before meals so that the germs can't get into our bodies through the mouths.

  Third, we must do more sports to keep fit. We can play football, basketball, table tennis and so on.

  Finally, we should go to bed early. Getting enough sleep is necessary for our health. We must try our best to have healthy bodies. Just remember, good health is more important than wealth.

拓展模块 Unit 10-Unit 12 阶段测试题十二

一、语音(本大题共 10 小题,每小题 1 分,共计 10 分)

从 A、B、C、D 四个选项中,选出画线部分发音不同的一项。

1. 【A】考查字母 o 的发音,o 在 s、t、l、d 前[əU],在 B、C、D 中读[əU],在非重读音节读[ə]。
2. 【D】考查字母组合 er 的发音,在一些重读音节中读[ɜ:],在非重读音节读[ə]。
3. 【D】考查字母 s 的发音,s 在 A、B、C 读[S],在 D 中读[Z]。
4. 【C】考查字母 u 的发音,在 A、B、D 读[ʌ],在开音节中读[ju:]。
5. 【B】考查字母 a 的发音,字母 a 在 B 中读[ei],在重读闭音节中读[æ]。
6. 【C】考查字母 o 的发音,o 在非重读音节读[ə],在闭音节中读[ɔ]。
7. 【D】考查字母组合 ou 的发音,在 A、B、C 中 ou 发[u:]的音,D 中 ou 读[ɔ:]。
8. 【B】考查字母组合 ear 的发音,在 A、C、D 中 ear 发[eə]的音,在 B 中读[ɜ:]。
9. 【A】考查字母组合 ow 的发音,ow 在 A 中读[au],在非重读音节中读[əU]。
10. 【A】考查字母组合 tion 的发音,tion 在 A 中读[TʃəN],在 B、C、D 中读[ʃN]。

二、单项选择题(本大题共 30 小题,每小题 1 分,共计 30 分)

从 A、B、C、D 四个选项中,选出空白处的最佳选项。

11. 【C】题意:"李雷真好,把落水的男孩救起来了。"本题考查强调句 It's kind of sb to do sth. 表示某人好、很善良。通常侧重指品质。
12. 【B】题意:"你如果不早起就会迟到。"本题考查强调句连词辨析。but 但是,if 如果,and 和,or 或者。
13. 【D】题意:"——这个月你们要去哪里?——我们也许去北京,但是还没确定。"本题考查情态动词辨析。must 必须,mustn't 禁止,needn't 不需要,might 也许。
14. 【A】题意:"两座山之间矗立着一座塔。"本题考查完全倒装。其正常语序应是:A tower lies between the two mountains.
15. 【D】题意:"——爸爸,我在演讲比赛中得了第一名。——祝贺你!"本题考查情态情景交际。Not at all 一点也不,用于回答感谢,别客气。Good luck 祝你好运。Good idea 好主意。Congratulations 祝贺你,祝贺的话语。
16. 【B】题意:"老师说这本字典可以帮助他提高成绩。"本题考查 help to do sth 表示"帮助,援助"。
17. 【A】题意:"汤姆和迈克踢足球踢的很好。我们希望他俩可以加入我们的队伍。"本题考查 both 作形容词。both 指两个人或物。而 all 指三个以上的人或物,在句中直接修饰名词。
18. 【B】题意:"尽量保护自己的皮肤以免被太阳晒伤。"本题考查 protect...from... 表示:保护……以免受(伤害)。同时,皮肤与晒伤之间是被动关系,故选 B。
19. 【B】题意:"我们应该关注我们的地球。"本题考查 pay attention to 表示:关心,关注。此处 to 为介词,后跟 V-ing 形式。故选 B。

20.【A】题意："直到信末她才提到她的计划。"本题考查强调句 It is/was +被强调部分+that+句子其他成分。

21.【D】题意：鲍勃既可以说英语，又可以说法语。本题考查 also，as well 用于肯定句，also 常用于 be 动词之后、行为动词之前，as well 用于句末，neither，either 用于否定句中。

22.【B】题意：很难预料何时我们的城市才会出现大量的无人驾驶汽车。本题考查动词辨析，addict 使上瘾，predict 预料，indict 控告、起诉，contradict 反驳、否认。

23.【A】题意：我们不同意您的观点，不过，谢谢您提出来。本题考查 nevertheless，既可作连词也可作副词，表示"然而"；since 自从，as 和……一样，till 直到……

24.【B】题意：你提前订票了吗？本题考查动词短语辨析。on time 按时，in advance 提前，in a row 连续地，time after time 一次又一次。

25.【D】题意：——真是一件好外套，你穿起来很漂亮。——谢谢你，我昨天买的，但是我不在意颜色。本题考查动词短语辨析。afraid of 害怕，concentrate on 集中注意力在……，worry about 担心、担忧，concern about 关心、在意。

26.【C】题意：除了洗盘子，她还能做什么？本题考查常混介词。beside 在……旁边，except 除了……之外，besides 除……之外(还有)，expect 期望。

27.【A】题意：他们承认他是最好的歌手之一。本题考查固定搭配。recognize…as…承认是……

28.【C】题意：邀请她了，但她没来。本题考查固定搭配。show off 炫耀，show through 流露、显露，show up 出现，show around 参观、巡视。

29.【B】题意：争吵是没有用的。本题考查固定句式。It's no use dong sth. 做……是没有用的。

30.【A】题意：看！那幅画多漂亮呀！本题考查感叹句。that picture is 是句子的主语+be 动词，用括号括起来，beautiful 是形容词。

31.【D】题意："假如我已经看过这部电影，我就跟你讲了。"本题考查虚拟语气。条件从句的谓语用过去完成式 had done，主句的谓语用 would/should/could/might+have done，表示与过去事实相反的虚拟语气。

32.【C】题意："我希望你能再次尝试。"本题考查 wish 后接宾语从句的虚拟语气。表示将来不大可能实现的愿望。构成：主语+wish(that)+从句主语+would/could+动词原形。

33.【D】题意："——多谢你丰盛的晚餐。——我很高兴你喜欢它。"本题考查情景交际。Don't say that. 别那么说。It's nothing. 没什么。I don't think so. 我认为不是这样。英美人不这样回答别人的感谢。

34.【A】题意："如果你按时吃药，你的身体很快就会恢复。"本题考查固定搭配。take the medicine 吃药。

35.【B】题意："这首歌使我想起了与同学相伴的时光。"本题考查固定搭配。remind sb of…使某人想起……

36.【B】题意："——这蛋糕看起来很漂亮。——是的，它尝起来更美味。"本题考查 look/taste (系动词)+adj. (作表语)。

37.【C】题意："这些漂亮的纸花被用来装饰整个商店。"本题考查固定句式辨析。be used to do sth. 被用来做某事。used to do sth. 过去常常做某事。be used to doing sth. 习惯于做某事。根据题意，paper flowers 与 store 是被动关系，所以应该用 be used to do sth. (被用来做某事)这一结构。

38.【A】题意:"——你多久才能回来?我感到有点无助。——一个小时之后。"本题考查对"in+一段时间"(在一段时间之后)提问,要用 how soon;how often 对频率进行提问;how far 对距离进行提问;how long 对时间段进行提问。

39.【A】题意:"他坚持要我出国留学。"本题考查宾语从句中的虚拟语气。insist 表示:"坚决要求"时,用虚拟语气,从句的谓语动词用"should+动词原形",should 可省略。

40.【C】题意:"我真的什么也看不见,他的头挡住了我的视线。"本题考查介词词组。on the way 在途中;by the way 顺便说,顺便问一下;in the way 挡道,碍事;out of the way 不碍事。

三、完型填空(本大题共15小题,每小题1分,共计15分)

从 A、B、C、D 四个选项中,选出空白处的最佳选项。

41.【B】考查形容词。A. wise"明智的";B. ashamed"羞愧的";C. cautious"谨慎的";D. numb"麻木的"。作为作家,作者羞于承认对书籍的热爱已经被一个坐不住的大脑所取代。故选 B。

42.【A】考查动词。A. determined"下决心";B. happened"碰巧";C. seemed"似乎";D. hesitated"犹豫"。作者下定决心在网络毁掉自己之前回归读书。故选 A。

43.【D】考查名词。A. standard"标准";B. choice"选择";C. expectation"期待";D. task"任务"。作者给自己制订了读书计划,这似乎是不可能完成的任务。故选 D。

44.【C】考查形容词。A. intelligent"聪明的";B. diligent"勤勉的";C. average"普通的,正常的";D. gifted"有天赋的"。一本400页的书要花普通人大约8个小时。average person 固定短语,"普通人"。故选 C。

45.【B】考查动词。A. received"获得";B. made"做到";C. refused"拒绝";D. got"得到"。作者认为这尽管是一个挑战,但他还是无论如何做到了。make it 固定短语,"做或完成某事"。故选 B。

46.【D】考查名词。A. delay"耽搁";B. hesitation"犹豫";C. permission"许可";D. disturbance"打扰"。作者每天能不受打扰地读书一两个小时。故选 D。

47.【B】考查动词。A. avoid"避免";B. practice"实践,练习";C. admit"承认";D. imagine"想象"。我们远离电子设备的时间花得越多,我们就会变得越平静、越专注。故选 B。

48.【A】考查形容词。A. calmer"更安静";B. stronger"更强";C. tougher"更艰苦";D. luckier"更幸运"。读书能使我们平静和专注。故选 A。

49.【C】考查副词。A. hardly"几乎不";B. violently"激烈地";C. easily"容易地";D. difficultly"困难地"。作者能非常容易地让自己回归读书。故选 C。

50.【C】考查动词。A. expressing"表达";B. possessing"占有";C. accepting"接受";D. resisting"抵制"。这里指抵制住去碰触电脑屏幕的冲动。故选 D。

51.【C】考查动词。A. required"需要";B. suggested"建议";C. meant"意味着";D. differed"不同于"。对作者来说,找到安静的时间意味着找到时间来阅读。故选 C。

52.【B】考查形容词。A. critical"关键的";B. delightful"开心的";C. special"特别的";D. busy"繁忙的"。拿起书本对作者来说是一个开心的时刻。故选 B。

53.【C】考查名词。A. wallet"钱包";B. book"书";C. phone"电话";D. pen"笔"。作者已经抵制住手机等带来的网络诱惑了。故选 C。

54. 【D】考查名词。A. program "节目"；B. menu "菜单"；C. option "选项"；D. break "休息"。作者每时每刻都在阅读，在电车上，在晚上，在午休时。故选 D。

55. 【A】考查动词短语。A. slow down "减速"；B. speed up "加速"；C. cheer up "振奋"；D. feel down "沮丧，消沉"。读书是一种强大的慢下来做自己的方式。故选 A。

四、阅读理解（本大题共 15 小题，每小题 2 分，共计 30 分）

从 A、B、C、D 四个选项中，选出符合题目要求的最佳选项。

A

56. 【A】"Sit down and stay where you are."和"Give them a signal by shouting or whistling three times."是解答本小题的关键句子。

57. 【D】该题的答案源自"Keep up shouting or whistling always three times together. When people hear you, they will know that you are not just making noise for fun."一句中。

58. 【C】"They give you two shouts, two whistles, or two gun-shots. When someone gives you a signal, it is an answer to a call for help."是答案的出处。

59. 【D】根据"Don't just walk away. Pick off small branches and drop them as you walk so that you can find your way back."可知"当你离开原地去找水喝时，不要径直走开，要在路上留下标记，以便能找到回到原地方的路。"

60. 【B】由文章末句"The most important thing to do when you are lost is—stay in one place."和开头的"…this is what you should do."可不难得出答案。

B

61. 【B】第一段的最后一句 He found that they were about two inches too long。

62. 【A】年轻人提出缩短裤子的要求，这个要求是向在场的妈妈和他的两个姐妹提出的。

63. 【C】因当时妈妈和姐妹俩都忙于干活，所以当时都没有回答他的话。

64. 【D】从第四段的原句(Later on, after supper, the elder sister remembered her brother's trousers)中我们可知是晚饭后去把裤子缩短了。

65. 【C】通读全文，知道有三人把裤子各缩短了两英寸，那么总共缩短了六英寸。

C

66. 【A】细节理解题。短文说明了美国 the Botanical Museum of Harvard University 收藏玻璃花的目的、收藏品的丰富、精致的细节等内容，所以用 An Extensive Collection of Glass Flowers 作标题最合适。

67. 【C】推理判断题。根据第二段的"The intention was to have the collection represent at least one member of each flower family native to the United States."可知收藏的目的把美国所有的花都复制一种。

68. 【B】推理判断题。根据它前后的内容：目的是使收藏能代表美国的每一类花，尽管还没有完成，只能是收藏还没有完成。

69. 【C】细节理解题。信息来自第二段的内容，C 项的内容在第二段中没有提及，其他各项的内容都有相关的说明。

70. 【D】推理判断题。根据第二段的"Every detail of these is accurately reproduced in color and structure."可知这些玻璃花的每一个细节都制作得很精致，都是真实的再现。

五、书面表达(15分)

One possible version:

  I think reading is important in the whole life for people. There are many benefits of reading.

  Firstly, reading increases our knowledge and we can learn the world affairs without going out. Secondly, reading is a good way to improve reading and writing skills. Before you learn to write you must know how others write. Thirdly, reading can broaden our knowledge and horizon which is important to job hunting in the future. Finally, reading helps us become self-cultivation that would be beneficial to our whole life.

  Therefore start to reading no matter how old you are and what you are doing. Then you may find the great charm and benefits of reading.

模拟测试卷一

第一部分 共答题(所有考生作答,共70分)

一、语音(本大题共10小题,每小题1分,共计10分)

1.【D】考查字母 e 的发音,在重读开音节中读[iː],在重读闭音节中读[e],在非重读音节中读[ə]或者[i]。e 在 A、B、C 中读[e],在 D 中读[i]。

2.【B】考查字母 c 的发音,在 a, o, u 和辅音字母 l, r, t 及音节末尾读[k],在 e, i, y 中读[s],A、C、D 中读[k],在 B 中读[s]。

3.【D】考查字母 oo 的发音,在一些重读音节中读[uː],在一些重读音节中读[u],oo 在 A、B、C 中读[u],在 D 中读[uː]。

4.【A】考查字母 th 的发音,在一些单词中读[ð],在一些单词中读[θ],th 在 B、C、D 中读[ð],在 A 中读[θ]。

5.【A】考查字母 ou 的发音,在一些重读音节中读[ʌ],在一些重读音节中读[u],ou 在 B、C、D 中读[ʌ],在 A 中读[u]。

6.【C】考查字母 ex 的发音,在重读音节中读[eks],在元音前的非重读音节中读[igz],在辅音前的非重读音节中读[iks]。ex 在 A、B、D 中读[iks],在 C 中读[igz]。

7.【B】考查字母 ea 的发音,在重读音节中读[ei],在非重读音节中读[iː],ea 在 A、C、D 中读[iː],在 B 中读[ei]。

8.【A】考查字母 er 的发音,在重读音节中读[əː],在非重读音节中读[ə],er 在 B、C、D 中读[ə],在 A 中读[əː]。

9.【B】考查字母 n 的发音,在多数情况下发[n],在[g]和[k]前发[ŋ],A、C、D 中读[ŋ],在 B 中读[n]。

10.【B】考查字母 a 的发音,在重读闭音节中读[æ],在 n, f, s, ph, th 前读[ɑː],a 在 A、C、D 中读[ei],在 B 中读[ə]。

二、单项选择题(本大题共25小题,每小题1分,共计25分)

11.【C】题意:假如你买便宜的东西,你就能省钱。before 意为"在……以前";unless 意为"除非";if 意为"如果"引导条件状语从句;until 意为"直到……才",根据"buy cheaper things"以及"save money"可知,如果买便宜的东西,就可以节约点钱。故选 C。

12.【A】题意:我正在寻找一个带浴室的公寓。be looking for 寻找,所以选 A。

13.【B】题意:我正在给我的妈妈找生日礼物,但是我没有找到任何合适的。此处考查不定代词+形容词的用法。因为前面的 couldn't 为否定词,故此处需要用不定代词 anything。

14.【B】题意:我们很容易受"prefer...to..."的影响而误选 A。根据上下文,"我"想要的是"加牛奶的咖啡"。

15.【D】题意:——你想要一些酒吗?——不,谢谢。我现在不想喝东西。would like to do sth. 想做某事;feel like doing sth. 想做某事。

16.【D】题意：小男孩害怕考试。be afraid to do sth. 害怕干某事。

17.【B】题意：对李明来说，在即将到来的演讲比赛中赢得一等奖是可能的。A. beat 击败；B. win 赢得；C. make 制作；D. receive 收到。根据空后的"the first prize（一等奖）"可知，这里指"赢得"一等奖。

18.【B】题意：张华真勇敢！how 引导的感叹句的句型是：How+形容词+主语+谓语+其他！what 引导的感叹句的句型是：What(+a/an)+名词+主语+谓语+其他！根据题目中所给的单词，形容词是 brave，主语是 Zhang Hua，谓语是 is，应用 how 来引导，故选择 B。

19.【C】题意："the+比较级，the+比较级"是一个固定句型，表示"越……越……"。

20.【B】题意：G 和 B 都是我的邻居，此处应该是名词性物主代词。

21.【B】题意：努力学习你才会赶上其他同学。此题考查固定句型结构：祈使句+and/or+主语+will+动词原形。由句意，空处填"这样"，A. but 但是；B. and 这样；C. or 或者；D. so 所以。选 B。

22.【C】题意：虽然我们学英语学了三年，但学新单词仍有困难。have problem/trouble/difficulty (in) doing sth. 表示"做……有困难"，故选 C。考查非谓语动词。

23.【D】题意：现在人们有了更多空余时间，广场舞变得越来越受欢迎。comfortable 舒服的，difficult 困难的，different 不同的，popular 受欢迎的。由句意，应该选 popular。本题主要先理解句意，掌握形容词的比较级 more and more+多音节的形容词/副词 表示越来越……的用法。

24.【A】题意：别迟到，没有人愿意一直等。would like 后接动词不定式结构，故排除 B、D。动词不定式由"to+动词原形"构成。being 是动词的 v+ing 形式。keep 后的动词用 v+ing 形式，故答案是 A。waiting 是动词的 v+ing 形式，to wait 是动词不定式结构。

25.【D】题意：我们越努力，我们获得的快乐就越多。解析：句意为"我们越努力，我们获得的快乐就越多。"the+比较级…，the+比较级…越……越……

26.【D】题意：他非常累，他不想做任何事情。

27.【A】题意：后半句的含义是他从自行车上摔了下来，那么前半句的含义为他失去了平衡意思才符合，balance 表示平衡的意思，lose one's balance"失去平衡"，B 力气、力量；C 权力、力量；D 方法，故本题选 A。

28.【A】题意：一个苹果从树上掉下来砸在他的头上。泛指的单数名词 apple 前应该用不定冠词 an，而在句型 hit sb. in/on the face/head 中，head, nose, face, eye 等表示身体部位的名词前要用定冠词 the。所以 A 选项符合。

29.【A】题意：会议室大到可以容纳 600 人。考查短语 enough to do sth. 的用法，A. large enough"足够大"，符合短语用法；B. very large"非常大"，不符合句意；C. so large"那么大"，不符合题意；D. too large"太大"，不符合题意。

30.【C】题意：这幅画让我想起了我快乐的童年时光。remind sb. of…是个固定用法，意思是"……使某人想起……"。

31.【A】题意：我们被迫等了两个小时。固定搭配 be made to do sth 被迫干某事。

32.【B】题意：有小车的人们的数量在增长。主谓一致。分析句子可 who _____ cars 是一个定语从句，修饰先行词 teachers，因为 teachers 是复数形式，所以定语从句的谓语动词用 own；the number 在句中做主语，所以谓语动词用单数形式，故答案选 B。

33.【C】题意：有雨水和阳光才会有彩虹。It takes sth. to do sth.

60

34. 【B】题意：多久你才回来？根据答句"in ten minutes"，可知这是 in+时间段，表示在十分钟之后，一般用于将来时。how long 提问时间段，一般用 for+时间段回答；how soon 多久之后，一般用 in+时间段回答；how often 提问频率，用频率副词回答；how far 提问距离。所以 B 选项是正确的。

35. 【B】他从我身边走过，没有注意到我。take notice of 固定搭配。

三、完形填空(本大题共 15 小题，每小题 1 分，共计 15 分)

36. 【A】由第二空后面的 the beautiful flowers 可以推出该空应填 flowers。

37. 【C】本文以老人花园里的野花为题材，因此该空应填 garden。

38. 【D】该空表示"如果"，因此应填 if。

39. 【A】由下文 You can't see these flowers. 可以推出该空表示"瞎的"，因此应填 blind。

40. 【C】由 You can't see these flowers. 可以推出该空表示"为什么"，因此应填 Why。

41. 【B】下文介绍老人每天照料花的原因，因此该空应填 reasons。

42. 【A】该空表示"尽管"，因此应填 although 引导让步状语从句。

43. 【C】由上文的 First，Second 可以推出该空表示第三，因此应填 Third。

44. 【B】由下文 Me？可以推出该空应填 you。

45. 【A】由语境逻辑可知，老人不认识年轻人是一个事实，因此该空应填 true。

46. 【D】花是天使是人人都知道的事实，因此该空应填 knows。

47. 【C】老人精心护理花的工作开阔了我们的眼界，愉悦了我们的心。

48. 【D】老人的工作也使自己的生活更愉快。

49. 【B】由第 13 空后面的 deaf 可以推出该空表示"听"，因此应填 hear。

50. 【D】但是他的音乐已经鼓励了数百万人勇敢地面对困难。

四、阅读理解(本大题共 10 小题，每小题 2 分，共计 20 分)

A

51. 【B】推理判断题。根据文中语句 If you know someone is coming up behind you to attack, turn toward the person with your hands up in front of your body and loudly say "stop" before walking away. 如果你知道背后有人攻击你……理解可知，attack 的意思是"攻击"，故选 B。

52. 【C】细节理解题。根据文中语句 Your friend may ask you to join in a fight. Learn to say no. 理解可知，学会拒绝，故选 C。

53. 【A】细节理解题。根据文中语句 Fights at school sometimes happen. But how can you keep away from a fight? Here's something you can do. 理解可知，此文主要是让学生如何避免打架，故选 A。

54. 【C】理解归纳题。由文中语句 In the school, everyone involved（卷入）in a fight will be punished, no matter who started it. 理解可知，作者是以严肃的语气来说明这个问题的。

55. 【B】推理判断题。排除法。这篇文章可能选自报纸。

B

56. 【B】根据文中的句子"Two weeks after the Second World War（战争）began, Peter wanted to join the army，"可知是"二战"期间。

57. 【C】根据文中的句子"he was only 16 years old,"可知，他16岁了。
58. 【B】根据But Peter's brother Bill had joined the army a few days before，可知是战士。
59. 【A】根据文中的句子 so when he saw Peter's papers, he was surprised 可知，是A。
60. 【D】根据上下文推测可知是检查。

第二部分 （文科类职业模块考生作答，共15分）

五、单项选择题（本大题共5小题，每小题1分，共5分）

61. 【A】考查交际用语。上句意思是"托尼说他能修好我的自行车。但我有点怀疑"，可以看出说话人对托尼修理自行车的能力有点怀疑。答语后半句为"他很擅长做这种事情（修自行车）"，可以看出这是对第一个说话者的安慰，故应用"Don't worry"，而干扰项"I couldn't agree more"的意思是"我非常同意"，显然不符合语境。故选A。

62. 【D】考查语言交际。A项：Change it, please 这是一种汉语的表达，不符合英语习惯；B项：Never mind 没关系；C项：With pleasure 很乐意；D项：Help yourself 请自便。根据句意。D项符合题意。

63. 【C】I've never found a better job. 的实际意思是"这是我所找到的最好的一份工作"，对于此句话，对方最佳的回答应是表示祝贺。

64. 【D】So what 那又怎么样；It cannot be better 再好不过了；Good idea 好主意；I cannot agree more 我非常赞同。根据语境，D项正确。故选D。

65. 【A】A. no way 没门；not possible 不可能；no chance 没有机会；not at all 一点也不，根据句意和各个选项的含义可知答案。故选A。

六、阅读理解（本大题共5小题，每小题2分，共10分）

66. 【D】细节理解题。根据第一段句子"He took very good care of this cow and one day when it was ill, he was very worried. He telephoned the vet. 他细心地照顾这头牛，有一天它病了的时候，他很着急。他打电话给兽医。"可知，一定是给动物看病的医生。故选D。

67. 【A】细节理解题。根据第一段句子"He took very good care of this cow and one day when it was ill, he was very worried. He telephoned the vet. 他细心地照顾这头牛，有一天它病了的时候，他很着急。他打电话给兽医。"可知，他的牛生病了。故选A。

68. 【A】细节理解题。根据第二段句子 He took a bottle out of his box, put two pills into his hand and said,"The pills should make her better". 他从他的盒子里拿出一个瓶子，在他的手上放了两粒药片，说，"给她这些药就好了。"可知是两片药。故选A。

69. 【B】细节理解题。根据第三段句子 The vet gave him a tube（管子）and said,"Put this tube in her mouth, then put the pills in the tube and blow." 兽医给了他一个管子说："把这个管子放到她嘴里，然后把药片放在管子里，然后吹气。"可知，告诉他怎样让牛吃这些药丸。故选B。

70. 【A】细节判断题。根据第五段句子"How's your cow?"the vet asked."No change,"the farmer said,"and I'm feeling very strange myself.""Oh?"the vet said,"Why?""I did what you said,"the farmer answered."I put the tube in the cow's mouth and then put two pills down it.""And?"the vet asked."The cow blew first,"the farmer said. 你的牛怎么样？兽医问。"没有改变，"农

62

夫说,"我自己觉得非常奇怪。""哦?"兽医说,"为什么?""我照你说的做,"农夫回答,"我把试管放在牛的嘴里,然后把药放进去。""然后呢?"医生问。"牛先吹的,"农夫说。可知农夫自己吃了药片,故选 A。

第三部分 (工科类职业模块考生作答,共15分)

七、单项选择题(本大题共5小题,每小题1分,共5分)

71.【A】翻译:27 的立方根加上 8 的立方根等于 5。A 项表示 5;B 项表示 36;C 项表示 6;D 项表示 18。根据 27 的立方根等于 3,8 的立方根等于 2,3 加上 2 等于 5,故答案为 A。

72.【C】翻译:立方米是容量或者体积的基本单位。A 项意为"牛顿(力的基本单位)",B 项意为"平方米",C 项意为"立方米",D 项意为"公吨",而容量或者体积的基本单位是立方米,故选 C。

73.【A】翻译:重量的基本单位是千克。A 项 kilogram(千克,公斤);B 项 gram(克);C 项 milligram(毫克);D 项 metric ton(公吨)。题目问的是重量的基本单位,注意基本单位并不代表最小的单位,重量的基本单位是千克,所以选 A。

74.【D】(100.4−32)÷1.8=68.4÷1.8=38(摄氏度)。

75.【D】length 是长度。句意是螺丝刀 25cm 长,故选 D。

八、阅读理解(本大题共5小题,每小题2分,共10分)

76.【D】细节理解题。根据 It seems strange that nearly 3/4 of the earth is covered with water while we say we are short of water. Why? Because about 97% of water on the earth is sea water which we can't drink or use for watering plants directly. 可知,奇怪的是,当我们说我们缺水的时候,地球近四分之三的地方都被水覆盖了。为什么?因为地球上大约 97% 的水是海水,我们不能直接饮用或用来浇灌植物。所以,这个世界之所以干渴是因为地球上约 97% 的水不能饮用或直接用来浇灌植物。故选 D。

77.【A】细节理解题。根据 Because about 97% of water on the earth is sea water which we can't drink or use for watering plants directly. Man can only drink and use the 3% of the water that comes from rivers and lakes. 可知,因为地球上大约 97% 的水是海水,我们不能直接饮用或用来浇灌植物。人类只能饮用和使用来自河流和湖泊的 3% 的水。所以,地球上约 3% 的水存在于河流和湖泊中是正确的。故选 A。

78.【C】细节理解题。根据 Today, in most large cities water is used only once. 可知大多数城市用水只使用一次。

79.【D】细节理解题。根据 There is a lot of water in the sea. All that needs to be done is to get the salt out of the sea water. This is expensive. Scientists are trying to find a cheaper way to do it. 可知,海里有很多水。我们所要做的就是把海水中的盐去掉。这是昂贵的。科学家们正试图找到一种更便宜的方法。所以为了避免严重缺水,试着找一种更便宜的方法把海水中的盐取出来是最重要的。故选 D。

80.【C】最佳标题。根据 The world is not hungry, but it is thirsty. 可知,世界不饿,但很渴。所以这篇文章的标题是饥渴的世界。故选 C。

非选择题

九、书面表达(15)

  I'm a student from Class 10, Grade 7. Let me tell you something about my school life. It's very interesting. Classes begin at 7:50 am. I have five classes in the morning. In the afternoon, I have three classes. We study many subjects. They are English, art, history, biology and some other subjects. My favorite subject is English. It's easy and interesting. I like P. E. and music, too. Our P. E. teacher is very funny. But I don't like history at all. I think it's difficult and boring.

  After school, I like playing soccer on the playground with my classmates. Sometimes I go swimming. Every Tuesday and Thursday, I go to the library.

  I like my school life a lot.

模拟测试卷二

第一部分 共答题(所有考生作答,共70分)

一、语音(本大题共10小题,每小题1分,共计10分)

1. 【B】考查字母 gh 的发音,在 ou 或者 au 之后读[f],在重读闭音节中读[e],在 ight 的组合中不发音。gh 在 A、C、D 中不发音,在 B 中读[f]。
2. 【B】考查字母 tion 的发音,一般情况发[ʃn],前有字母 s 读[tʃn]。tion 在 A、C、D 中读[ʃn],在 B 中读[tʃn]。
3. 【D】考查字母 ow 的发音,在重读开音节中读[au],在重读音节和非重读音节中读[əu],在 e 在 A、B、C 中读[əu],在 D 中读[au]。
4. 【B】考查字母 u 的发音,在重读开音节中读[juː],在重读闭音节中读[ʌ],u 在 A、C、D 中读[uː],在 B 中读[ʌ]。
5. 【C】考查字母 ea 的发音,在重读音节中读[ei],在非重读音节中读[iː],ea 在 A、B、D 中读[iə],在 C 中读[iː]。
6. 【A】考查字母 th 的发音,在一些单词中读[ð],在一些单词中读[θ],th 在 B、C、D 中读[θ],在 A 中读[ð]。
7. 【C】考查字母 i 的发音,在重读开音节中读[ai],在重读闭音节中读[i],在非重读音节中读[ə]或者[i]。i 在 A、B、D 中读[ai],在 C 中读[i]。
8. 【C】考查字母 a 的发音,在重读闭音节中读[æ],在 n, f, s, ph, th 前读[aː],a 在 A、B、D 中读[ə],在 C 中读[æ]。
9. 【B】考查字母 g 的发音,在多数情况下发[g],在 e, i, y 前读[dʒ],a 在 A、C、D 中读[g],在 B 中读[dʒ]。
10. 【D】考查字母 h 的发音,在多数情况下发[h],部分情况不发音。h 在 A、B、C 中不发音,在 D 中读[h]。

二、单项选择题(本大题共25小题,每小题1分,共计25分)

11. 【B】improvement 提高,agreement 同意,doubt 怀疑,sentiment 观点。当有人对你提出的建议、计划或者见解说 Yes,你就得到了他们的同意。
12. 【B】practical,实际的,实用的;certain,确定的,肯定的;funny,有趣的,搞笑的。"毫无疑问,地球围绕太阳转。"It's certain that……表示"毫无疑问",答案选 B。
13. 【C】prevent 阻止,防止;control 控制,管理;solve 解决,解答。Puzzle 是"谜语,难题"的意思,与之搭配的动词应该是"solve 解决",答案选 C。
14. 【A】run over,溢出;act out,把……付诸行动;dry up,干涸。"宝贝,走慢一点,否则杯子里的水会溢出来。"答案选 A。
15. 【A】句子中出现了 the healthy lifestyle 和 she 两个主语,说明有从句。she is used to 是修饰 lifestyle 的定语从句,可以删去不看。由于真正的主语 lifestyle 是三单,所以选择 A。

16.【C】die of 死于内因,die from 死于外因,hunger 属于内因,所以选 of;research 可以作为名词或动词,用法均为 research into sth.。

17.【B】题意:去机场前别忘了带上护照。本题考查连词的辨析。A. 在……之后;B. 在……之前;C. 当……的时候,与……同时;D. 直到……为止。可知本句说的是去机场前别忘了带上护照。所以事情还未做,这里用 forget to do sth.,表示忘记做某事,后面跟 to 引导的不定式,此动作是在去机场前,此空应填 before,故选 B。

18.【B】你知道我在纽约的朋友多久会收到我的邮件吗?根据从句部分的 will be received(将被收到),结合句意可知,这里要填 how soon(从句部分通常要用一般将来时),表示问:你知道我在纽约的朋友多久会收到我的邮件吗?A. how long(多久,对时间长度提问;多长,对物体长度提问);C. how often(多久一次,对时间频率提问,句子要用一般现在时);D. how far(多远,对路程提问)都不符合要求。故选 B。

19.【A】——你想让我告诉你操作新相机的方法吗?——你真善良。本题考查日常交际用语。A. 你真善良;B. 是的,我想;C. 没问题;D. 一点也不。根据题干 Would you like me to show you the way to operate the new camera? 你想让我告诉你操作新相机的方法吗?可知,应该说你真善良。故选 A。

20.【D】——我们今晚出去吃饭吧。——对不起,恐怕今天我不行。本题考查情景交际。A. 我经常在周末去听音乐会;B. 非常感谢你的支持;C. 让自己待在家里;D. 今晚我们出去吃晚饭吧。根据下句 Sorry, but I cannot make it today. 对不起,恐怕今天我不行。可知,选项 D 比较合适,故选 D。

21.【D】此题形式会误选 B。但瞬间性动词不能与一段时间 for twenty minutes 连用。

22.【A】此题极易误选 B、C、D。英语中名词单数可以修饰名词,如:an apple tree—two apple trees. 但注意 a man teacher—two men teachers。

23.【A】此题容易误选 B。class, family, team 等单词如果表示整体谓语就用单数,表示个体就用复数,从语境及其后面的代词 them 可以看出,class 表示个体,故选择 A。

24.【B】选择 B。此题容易误选 C、D。在英语中数词中间用连字符号加名词单数,构成符合名词,在句中只能作定语,如果选择 C,需要把逗号放 s 后面。

25.【B】选 B。此题最容易误选 A。room 在句中是空间而非房间。句意:角落里没有摆桌子的空间了。

26.【A】选 A。此题容易误选 C、D。根据句意:如果我们创造一个没有污染的世界,那么我们就拥有一个蓝色的天空。

27.【B】选择 B。此题容易误选 A。其实不是对前面的句子进行反问,而是对 he likes running 进行反问。

28.【D】此题非常难,选 D。下周任何一天都可以再次见面。Any 在肯定句中意思是"任何的"。下周有七天容易排除 A、B。如果把 next week 改为 next Monday or Tuesday,则必须选择 A。

29.【C】三个以上另外一个用 another,other 一般情况下修饰名词复数,the other 表示两个中的另外一个,any other 任何别的。句意:罗伯特去了另一个城市,一周后回来。

30.【B】考查学生对 teach sb. sth. 的掌握情况。此题容易误选 C。误选 C 的学生是看见后面有名词 math,思维定式名词前面必须用形容词性物主代词。

31.【A】此题容易误选 D。街道只有两边,排除 B、C。both 后面接复数,on either side of the street 等于 on the both sides of。如果选择 D，side 必须用复数形式。

32.【B】此题容易误选 A、C 人口多少用 What，相当于 How，many people are there in the city？

33.【B】此题极容易选错，误认为是 A。但 two thousand 后面直接接名词复数，不能有冠词 the，句意是：歌迷中大约有 2 000 人在那里等，想看看这位伟大的歌星。

34.【C】介词的考查。句意：Mr. Green，这是你的信。学生容易误选 A。

35.【A】此题学生容易受思维定式 not… until…的影响误选 D。since 用于现在完成时，如果此题是一般过去时就选择 D。

三、完形填空（本大题共 15 小题，每小题 1 分，共计 15 分）

翻译：树木是地球上最古老的"公民"之一。他们保持我们的空气清洁，减少噪声污染，改善水质，提供食物和建筑材料。在一到三岁时，幼树学会如何保护自己。大多数幼树都有很大的深绿色叶子，这样它们就能捕捉到足够的阳光，并将其转化为食物和能量。当树木有 4 年的树龄时，它们就开始生长得非常快，变得足够强壮，能够在以后的生活中面对挑战。15 岁时，树木变成了年轻人。直到这棵树 20 到 25 岁，它才成为真正的成年人。逐渐地，树开始变老甚至死亡。当一棵树变成空心的或它的一部分死亡了，它给小动物提供了一个家，也是许多其他动物的食物来源。在许多方面，树的生命与我们自己的生活经历是相似的。当我们看着一棵树的生命时，我们了解到，生命的每一个阶段都会带来自己的快乐和挑战。享受生命中的每一分钟，照顾好树木吧！

分析：

36.【A】keep+n+adj 保持……，所以选 A。

37.【C】provide 提供"改进水的质量，提供食物和创造建筑材料"，所以选 C。

38.【C】"能保护他们自己"，反身代词的用法，所以选 C。

39.【B】so that 为了，以便于。"大多数年轻树木都有茂密的叶子以便于捕捉到足够的阳光，并将其转化为食物和能量"，所以答案选 B。

40.【D】change…into 把……转换成……

41.【B】begin to do sth. 开始干某事。

42.【D】become 是系动词，后接形容词，enough 修饰形容词后置，所以选 D。

43.【A】at the age of 在……岁时，所以答案选 A。

44.【C】强调句型：It is not until…that 直到……才，所以答案选 C。

45.【C】根据题意是树长得越来越大。

46.【A】根据上下文知道是食物的资源。

47.【B】other+名词的复数，别的、其他的，所以答案选 B。

48.【B】根据上下文联系需要相似的。

49.【A】look at 看，强调动作，"当我们看树的生命的时候"，所以答案选 A。

50.【D】learn about 了解、学习关于，所以选 D。

四、阅读理解（本大题共 10 小题，每小题 2 分，共计 20 分）

A

51.【A】根据 Many of us in China enjoy adding chilies to our food but did you know that this spicy （辣的）vegetable could also be dangerous？A 34-year-old US man recently ended up in hospital after eating a Carolina Reaper, the spiciest chilies people have known so far. After taking just a single bite of one, the man suffered from serious headaches in the following days reported BBC News. 可知吃辣椒有时也很危险。故选 A。

52.【C】根据 The human body is influenced by natural chemicals that produce a sense of happiness 可知人们喜欢吃辣椒，他能得到一种个人享受。故选 C。

53.【D】根据 Scientists found that the death rate of those who eat spicy food once or twice a week is 10 percent lower than those who eat it less than once a week. The death rate is 14 percent lower for those who eat spicy foods is to seven times a week. This encourages people to eat more spicy food to improve health and bring less death risk at an early age. 可知正确地吃辣的食物可以改善人们的健康。故选 D。

54.【B】根据文章介绍了关于辣椒的一些情况，一种让人又爱又恨的蔬菜。可知选 B。

55.【C】根据上下文理解是辛辣的。

B

56.【B】细节理解题。根据 It stops as soon as it sees a stop light，可知，它每次看到红绿灯都会停下来。故选 B。

57.【A】细节理解题。根据 If you feel lonely, you can talk with me. I'm talented at singing, writing poems and telling stories. I want to be your friend. 可知，聊天机器人可以聊天，可以唱歌，写诗和讲故事，也可以成为你的朋友。结合所给选项，只有 A 选项不可以做。故选 A。

58.【B】细节理解题。根据 This beautiful painting was at an auction（拍卖）in 2020. The painting is worth about 3,000,000 yuan，可知，这幅油画在 2020 年的一次拍卖会上价值约 300,000 元。故选 B。

59.【D】推理判断题。根据 AI（人工智能）makes our lives easier and better. 可知，人工智能使我们的生活更好更简单，所以 A 选项错误。根据 It has 14 seats and doesn't need a driver. 可知，无人驾驶公交车不需要司机，所以 B 选项错误。根据 I speak like a 17-year-old girl. 可知，Xiaobing 像一个 17 岁的女孩一样说话，所以 C 选项错误。根据 It can work 24 hours and doesn't make any mistakes. 可知，人工智能主播可以工作 24 小时，并不犯任何错误，所以 D 选项正确。故选 D。

60.【C】推理判断题。根据 AI（人工智能）makes our lives easier and better. Let's see the amazing AI. 可知，本文介绍了四种人工智能产品，结合所给选项，这篇文章我们最可能会在报纸上看到。故选 C。

第二部分 （文科类职业模块考生作答，共 15 分）

五、单项选择题(本大题共 5 小题，每小题 1 分，共 5 分)

61.【A】题意：考查常用日常交际用语。根据题干：—I'm going to Hawaii with my aunt this month for my holiday. ——我要和我的姑姑这个月去夏威夷度假。Have a good time 译为玩得开心，Best wishes to them 向他们致以最良好的祝愿，Thank you very much 译为非常感谢，It's OK 译为没关系、没问题。故结合我要和我的姑姑这个月去夏威夷度假，选择 A 符合语境。

62.【C】A 是不用谢的意思。比如，你感谢某人帮了一个忙"thank you for helping me…"，对方可以说不用谢"you are welcome"；而题目是别人帮比尔拿东西，这个话不应该是比尔说；答案 B 是"没问题"的意思，比如你想请别人帮个忙"could you help me with the homework？"对方如果想帮忙的话就会说"no problem"；答案 C 是"来杯咖啡吧"，符合题意；答案 D 是"没关系"，比如你向对方道歉"I'm sorry that I broke your glasses"，对方可以说"it doesn't matter"。故选 C。

63.【B】联系上下文语境，根据 They are delicious（它们很美味），可知前者说喜欢吃奶油蛋糕，后者也觉得美味；又知 Good luck 意为祝你好运，常用于对别人的祝福；Me, too 意为我也是，用于对上文的赞同，自己也如此；I hope so 意为我希望如此，用于对前者说法的看法；You're kidding 意为你在开玩笑吗，用于对前者说法的不赞同。所以此处应用 Me, too。故选 B。

64.【B】考查日常交际用语。A. Never mind. 没关系；B. What a pity! 真遗憾；C. My pleasure. 不客气；D. No problem. 没问题。根据句中答语 I'm looking forward to it 可知热切盼望的旅行被取消，肯定会感到遗憾。故选 B。

65.【D】联系上下文语境，回应上文的鼓励应该表示感谢。

六、阅读理解（本大题共 5 小题，每小题 2 分，共 10 分）

文章大意：本文主要介绍在假期根据自己的年龄和兴趣，找到适合自己的工作。

66.【C】细节理解题。由 If you're 13 to 15…. And you can't work before 7 a.m. or after 7p.m. 可知十四岁的儿童不能晚上工作，故选 C。

67.【C】细节理解题。由 If you're 16 or 17. The lowest wage for 16-17 years old teenagers should be no less than 7 dollars per hour. 16~17岁青少年的最低工资应不低于每小时 7 美元。可知结合题干，两个小时就应该14 美元，故选 C。

68.【D】细节理解题。由 If you're 13 to 15. It seems that you can't work almost anywhere, but you're probably allowed to clean your neighbors' cars or walk their dogs. 可知想要为邻居清洗车，至少十三岁。故选 D。

69.【B】细节理解题。由 It can be pretty hard work, but it pays really well. 可知累但报酬很好，故选 B。

70.【B】细节理解题。由 If you're mad about football, you can choose to work in a sports shop or help out at a local football club. No matter how much you are paid, you are doing what you like. 可知青少年可以根据自己的兴趣选择工作。故选 B。

第三部分 （工科类职业模块考生作答，共 15 分）

七、单项选择题（本大题共 5 小题，每小题 1 分，共 5 分）

71.【B】根据 About of the engineers，可知本部分考查分数的表达法是：分子用基数词，分母用序数词，分子超过 1，序数词要加 s，所以九分之二表示成 two-ninths。表示在几十岁时，一般用 in the+数字（整十）的复数，要将后缀 ty 变成 ties。故选 B。

72.【C】倍数的表达方法。倍数+as+形容词/副词原级+as；倍数+形容词或副词的比较级+than；倍数+the+size/length/weight/height/width…+of。

73.【C】题意：64 的立方根减 3 等于 1。

— 69 —

74. 【B】摄氏温标(℃)和华氏温标(℉)之间的换算关系为：F=C×1.8+32；C=(F-32)÷1.8，当 F 等于 50 时，C=(50-32)÷1.8=10。

75. 【B】最小的数。

八、阅读理解(本大题共 5 小题，每小题 2 分，共 10 分)

短文大意：本文讲述了斯密斯夫妇有两个儿女。一个是凯文，另一个是珍妮。由于比较忙，所以他们彼此留言。本材料就是他们之间的留言。

76. 【C】细节理解题。根据 To Jenny, It's your turn to walk our pet dog Teddy and play with him after school. 珍妮，轮到你今天放学后遛咱们的宠物狗泰迪。故选 C。

77. 【A】细节理解题。根据 6:45 pm, To all, Has anyone found my tennis shoes? I'm doing my homework in my bedroom, Kevin. 可知，时间 6:45，有谁见到我的网球鞋，我在卧室做作业。故答案选 A。

78. 【B】细节理解题。根据 I saw your shoes this morning. They smelt terrible so I put them outside the back door. Good night, dear! Mum. 可知，我在今天早上看到你的鞋，太难闻了，于是我就把它们放在了后门的外面。可知可以在后门外找到球鞋。故选 B。

79. 【C】细节理解题。根据 To Kevin, Mr, King rang, telling there is no football practice today, and he asked you to get ready for the football match tomorrow. 致凯文，王先生打电话，说今天不进行足球训练，他让你准备一下明天的足球比赛，可知明天凯文要参加足球比赛。故选 C。

80. 【B】细节推断题。根据 To Kevin, Mr, King rang, telling there is no football practice today, and he asked you to get ready for the football match tomorrow. 致凯文，王先生打电话，说今天不进行足球训练，他让你准备一下明天的足球比赛。可知王先生可能是一位足球教练。故选 B。

非选择题

九、书面表达(15 分)

  There are four people in my family. My grandmother, my father, my mother and I. My grandmother has short white hair. She looks very nice. My father has short black hair and small eyes. He looks very fat, so I often call him "fat man". He works at a factory. My mother is a teacher. My mother has long black hair. She likes sports and traveling, so I often go on sports with my mother. On holidays, my family often go to travel. I study at a vocational School. We are very happy.

模拟测试卷三

第一部分 共答题(所有考生作答,共70分)

一、语音(本大题共10小题,每小题1分,共计10分)

1.【A】本题考查辅音字母 h 的发音。B、C、D 都不发音,只有 A 读[h],所以答案为 A。

2.【C】本题考查字母组合 ea 的发音,A、B、D 选项发[e],C 选项发[iː],所以答案为 C。

3.【C】本题考查字母 a 的发音,A、B、D 选项均发[ei],C 选项发[aː],所以答案为 C。

4.【D】本题考查字母组合 ea 的发音,A、B、C 选项均发[iː],D 选项发[ei],所以答案为 D。

5.【B】本题考查字母 y 的发音,A、C、D 均发[i],B 选项发[ai],所以答案为 B。

6.【B】本题考查辅音字母 n 的发音。A、C、D 都读[n],B 读[ŋ],所以答案为 B。

7.【A】考查元音字母 i 的读音,字母 i 在开音节中读[ai],在闭音节或非重读音节中读[i],B、C、D 选项中读[ai],A 选项中读[i],所以选 A。

8.【D】考查元音字母组合 or 的读音,在重读音节中读[ɔː],在非重读音节中读[ə],在选项 A、B、C 中读[ɔː],选项 D 中读[ə],所以选 D。

9.【A】考查辅音字母组合 th 的读音。一般情况下,th 在词首、词尾读[θ],在词中或代词、冠词、介词中读[ð],在 B、C、D 选项中 th 在词中,在 A 选项中在词尾,所以选 A。

10.【B】考查字母组合 ch 的读音。字母组合 ch 一般读/tʃ/,但在源出希腊语的单词 ache、character、chemical、chemist、chemistry、school、stomach、technical、technique、technology 中,ch 发/k/。而在 moustache、machine、Chicago 中的 ch 读/ʃ/。在 B 选项中读/k/,A、C、D 选项中读/tʃ/,所以选 B。

二、单项选择题(本大题共25小题,每小题1分,共计25分)

11.【C】句意:那些外国客人在机场受到了热烈的欢迎,他们中大多数是政府官员。考查非限定语从句。分析句子结构可知这是一个定语从句,先行词 The foreign guests 在从句中作介词 of 的宾语,排除 B 项,且 A、D 项缺少连词,也应排除,只有 C 项正确。

12.【A】本题考查代词辨析。句意为:看了 Wendy's 的菜单,我发现很多都和麦当劳的菜品类似。由语境可知,此处用 those 来指代前文提到的 the items。ones 指代不带定冠词的复数形式的名词;any 指代任何一样物品,通常是单数形式的名词;all 则表示所有东西,与语境不符。所以答案为 A。

13.【B】本题考查形容词的用法。bored 意为"无聊的,感到厌烦的",表示人多主观感受;boring 意为"令人讨厌的",表示事物本身的性质。故选 B。

14.【D】本题考查动词短语。根据句意可知皮特在炫耀他得了一等奖。A 选项为"发光,发热",B 选项为"推迟",C 选项为"推迟",D 选项"炫耀",故选 D。

15.【B】本题考查固定搭配。come into effect 意为"生效",句意为"这项新的法律会在通过之日起生效",所以答案为 B。

16.【A】本题考查比较级结构。Of 指在具体的两者当中，且明确的两者之间比较用比较级，前面需要加 the 表示特指；第二空不定冠词和最高级连用表非常。故选 A。

17.【D】名词 advice 为不可数名词，不能用不定冠词。用感叹词 what，故选 D。

18.【B】本题考查特殊句型的倒装。句意：直到他渡过了真正的艰难时期，他才意识到爱对我们的家庭很重要。Not until 置于句首主句半倒装，排除 C 和 D。分析句子由从句的 went through 可知，选 B。

19.【D】本题考查虚拟语气。句意：眼科医生建议小孩子在 6 个月大的时候应该接受第一次视力检查。根据题干中的 suggest"建议"后接宾语从句时，从句中的谓语动词为 should+动词原形，其中 should 可省略。但要注意如果 suggest 意为"暗示时，表明"时，不用虚拟语气。故选 D。

20.【C】本题考查词义辨析，thanks to 幸亏、由于，后经常跟好事情，故选 C。

21.【A】本题考查形容词辨析。句意：学生人数的不断增加使有限的电脑不够每个学生使用。available"可利用的"，affordable"负担得起的"，helpful"有帮助的"，acceptable"可接受的"。根据句意选 A。

22.【A】本题考查主谓一致。由 together with 连接的两个并列主语遵循就远原则，和前面保持一致。the trainer 为第三人称单数，故选 A。

23.【D】本题考查短语辨析。break out 爆发；break up 破碎，分手；break into 闯入；break down 机器故障，身体垮了，车抛锚了。所以选 D。

24.【C】本题考查名词。A、B、D 三项均只能修饰不可数名词的复数形式。a great deal of 修饰不可数名词。work 是不可数名词，所以答案为 C。

25.【D】本题考查宾语从句和状语从句。第一空为宾语从句，从句中有时间状语 tomorrow，故第一空为 will rain。第二空考的知识点为由 if 引导的时间状语从句，即主将从现，故选 D。

26.【D】本题考查情态动词。回答 must 提出的问句，肯定回答用 must，否定回答用 needn't 或 don't have to，且情态动词后应用动词原形，故选 D。

27.【B】本题考查虚拟语气。wish+宾语从句，当表示与过去事实相反时，需使用过去完成时，故选 B。

28.【C】本题考查 since 的用法。since+时间点，主句的时态应用现在完成时，并且要用延续性动词，所以答案选 C。

29.【C】本题考查固定搭配，can't help doing sth. 意为"禁不住做某事"，此处句意为：这是一场如此有趣的表演，以至于人们忍不住笑了一次又一次。故选 C。

30.【D】本题考查 with 的复合结构。动词不定式 to settle 作为 difficult problems 的定语，表示现在或将来要解决的难题；过去分词 settle 作定语表示已解决的难题；现在分词的被动式 being settled 作定语表示正在解决的难题。故选 D。

31.【A】本题考查介词，根据句意：我妈妈经常说，要像向日葵一样挺起胸膛，为自己感到骄傲。be proud of，固定搭配，"为……骄傲"，故选 A。

32.【B】本题考查时态和被动语态。句意：——为什么你要离职？——我再也不能忍受了。我总是被要求加班。第一空因为有副词 always，故第一空填一般现在时 am。第二空根据句意为被动语态，故选 B。

33.【B】本题考查时态。句意：这是我们第二次成功地举行这样重要的聚会。It was the +序数词+time+that 从句，从句中用过去完成时，如果是 It is the +序数词+time+that 从句，从句中用现在完成时，所以选 B。

34. 【C】本题考查表语从句。句意：每个人都是不一样的，这就是使我们的世界更好的东西。如果表语从句缺少主宾表，用 what 连接主语从句，如果不缺成分，用 that 连接，引导表语从句的 that 在从句中不做成分，只起到连接的作用，这里的表语从句缺少主语，用 what 连接。选 C。

35. 【D】本题考查目的状语从句。so...that...的常用搭配，so 是副词，只能修饰形容词或副词；或是与表示"多，少"的 many/much，few/little 连用，形成固定搭配。so+形容词/副词+that..；so+形容词+a/an+单数名词+that...；so+many/few+复数名词+that...；so+much/little+不可数名词+that...；题中 so ... that...引导目的状语从句，句意：那儿有很多人，我没能找到她。故选 D。

三、完形填空（本大题共 15 小题，每小题 1 分，共计 15 分）

36. 【D】动词辨析。A 打破；B 走近；C 建立；D 成对；根据 All the girls in her class were with a best friend or in groups. 她班上的所有女孩应该是和好友成对或小组，故答案是 D。

37. 【A】副词辨析。A 独自；B 再次；C 高兴地；D 快速地；根据后面 instead of playing with anyone 没和任何人玩，应该是独自地走。故答案是 A。

38. 【C】连词辨析。A 和；B 所以；C 但是；D 因为；根据她想玩跷跷板，那是你和朋友需要做的事，表转折关系。故答案是 C。

39. 【B】词动辨析。A 决定；B 希望；C 解释；D 建议；根据 Also, she liked to swing(荡秋千) and someone would push her to get her started. 而且，她喜欢荡秋千，有人会推她开始，应该是希望有人推她，故答案是 B。

40. 【D】代词辨析。A 我的；B 你的；C 他的；D 她的；根据前面 Mrs Gibbs 应该是用她的胳膊搂着 Amy，故答案是 D。

41. 【D】动词辨析。A 写；B 学习；C 同意；D 玩；根据语境，应该是问为什么没有和别的小朋友玩，故答案是 D。

42. 【A】名词辨析。A 朋友；B 同学；C 姐妹；D 父或母；根据上文 Amy did not have any friends and felt sad. 可知没有朋友，故答案是 A。

43. 【B】名词辨析。A 计划；B 方法；C 课；D 原因；根据语境，应该是 Amy，交朋友的方法就是做朋友，故答案是 B。

44. 【B】动词辨析。A 转；B 看；C 跳；D 坐；根据下句 There are three classes of third-graders out here during this break time. 在这个休息时间有一个三年级的班，应该是看看操场四周，故答案是 B。

45. 【C】动词辨析。A 停止；B 隐藏；C 发现；D 引导；根据 someone who is alone and then go to ask them to play，应该找一个和你一样孤独的人，故答案是 C。

46. 【A】形容词辨析。A 害怕；B 骄傲；C 高兴；D 惊奇；根据后面 she would be refused 她会被拒绝应该是害怕，故答案是 A。

47. 【C】名词辨析。A 兴趣；B 技巧；C 勇气；D 注意；根据 She worked up her and walked to the girl 及上文害怕被拒绝，这里应该是鼓起勇气，故答案是 C。

48. 【C】名词辨析。A 跷跷板；B 椅子；C 秋千；D 自行车；根据 As they took turns pushing each other on the _____ 前面说轮流推对方，应该是玩秋千，故答案是 C。

49. 【A】动词辨析。A 需要；B 选择；C 分享；D 相信；根据前面 Her family had just moved from Japan 她的家人刚从日本搬来，所以应该是她也需要朋友，故答案是 A。

50. 【D】副词辨析。A 小心地；B 安静地；C 简单地；D 开心地；根据 Paired up with each other, they played so _____ 他们是一对一对，应该是开心地玩，故答案是 D。

四、阅读理解(本大题共 10 小题，每小题 2 分，共计 20 分)

A

51. 【B】细节理解题。据第一段句子 On February 9th, 2013, Sarah Darling was walking along the street when she met a homeless man named Billy Ray Harris. 2013 年 2 月 9 日，萨拉·达林在街上走着，遇到了一个叫比利·雷·哈里斯的流浪汉。第二段句子 Sarah didn't realize that she had given Billy not only all her change but also her diamond ring that she had put in her change purse earlier until the following morning. 莎拉没有意识到，她不仅给了比利她所有的零钱，而且她还把她放在零钱钱包里的钻戒也给了比利，直到第二天早上她才意识到，可知应该是 2013 年 2 月 10 日。故选 B。

52. 【C】细节判断题。据倒数第二段句子 Billy is living with a person who is generous 可知，A 选项在文章中提到了；根据倒数第二段句子 Thanks to the news report, he got together again with his older brother 可知，B 选项提到了；根据倒数第二段句 Thanks to the news report 多亏了新闻报道可知，D 选项也提到了。根据第二段句子 Sarah didn't realize that she given Billy not only all her change but also her diamond ring that she had put in her change purse earlier until the following morning. 可知 C 选项这句话不符合文意，这个钻石戒指是 Sarah 的，并不是 Billy 买的。故选 C。

53. 【D】细节推理题。根据第三段句子 So on February 18, he set up a special page to raise money for him in just four days, Billy received over ＄85,000 and there seems to be no end yet. 可知，这里的 that 代指的应该是前文中所提到的事情，这里应该指的是当 Billy 归还了戒指之后，在 Billy 的努力下，人们为他捐了很多钱。故选 D。

54. 【C】主旨归纳题。根据整篇文章内容可知，这篇短文讲述的是一个诚实的流浪汉归还了 Sarah 无意间给他的一枚戒指，而他的这份善良也给他自己带来了回报。他不仅从人们那里得到了很多捐款，而且找到了他失散多年的哥哥。故这篇短文的标题应该是无家可归的人返回钻石戒指。故选 C。

55. 【A】细节理解题。根据最后一句 All the good luck is just because Billy did the right thing—returning something that didn't belong to him. 可知比利归还了戒指，并因此受到一笔很大的捐款，还找到了自己失散多年的兄弟，因此帮助别人就是帮助自己，选 A。

B

56. 【C】细节理解题。根据 60 percent for junior high students 故选 C。

57. 【B】细节理解题。根据 Parents might have tried to do something to fix it, such as having their children get massages(按摩) take medicine or even get surgery. 故选 B。

58. 【A】细节理解题。根据 The notice bans businesses from using words like "recovery(恢复)" and "myopia cure" in their advertisements. 故选 A。

59. 【B】细节理解题。根据 The plan limits(限制) not only the time children play video games but

also the production video games. 故选 B。

60.【C】细节理解题。通读全文可知政府和人们都在挽救孩子们的视力，故选 C。

第二部分 （文科类职业模块考生作答，共 15 分）

五、单项选择题（本大题共 5 小题，每小题 1 分，共计 5 分）

61.【D】根据 Thank you for the delicious dinner 可知，此处应为主人回应客人的感谢。A 不要那样说，B 没什么，C 我不认为它很好，D 我很高兴你喜欢它。只有 D 符合语境，故答案为 D I'm glad you enjoyed it.

62.【A】A 项意为"节约用水"，B、C、D 项都是交通标识，所以答案为 A。

63.【A】你能帮我关一下窗户吗？愿意效劳。With pleasure 用来回答"请求帮助的"，意为愿意效劳。My pleasure 用来回答"谢谢"，意为没关系，我的荣幸。故选 A。

64.【D】本题考查情景交际，句意："我怎么才能到达最过近的公园。""沿着这条街然后左转。"A 选项意为"那里的花是漂亮的"；B 选项意为"这个公园非常大"；C 选项意为"离这里不远"；只有 D 选项为问路的答语，故选 D。

65.【C】A. 别客气，B. 好吧，C. 放轻松，D. 不错。根据句子意思我总是感到很糟糕、很孤独，我该怎么办？放轻松，和你的朋友聊天，并注意自己的健康。故选 C。

六、阅读理解（本大题共 5 小题，每小题 2 分，共计 10 分）

66.【A】细节理解题。根据文章 The invention of paper meant that more people could be educated 可知，纸的发明，意味着越来越多的人能够受到教育，故选 A。

67.【C】细节理解题。根据文章 Paper was not made in southern Europe until about the year 1100. 可知，直到 1100 年，西方国家才制作纸。故选 C。

68.【D】细节理解题。根据文章 Finland makes the best paper in the world. 可知，芬兰生产的纸是世界上最好的。故选 D。

69.【C】词义猜测题。根据句意：没有东西比这更温暖的了。联系文章内容主要是说纸的用途，故选 C 纸是最暖和的。

70.【D】主旨大意题。纵观全文本文主要谈论的是纸的用途，故选 D。

第三部分 （工科类职业模块考生作答，共 15 分）

七、单项选择题（本大题共 5 小题，每小题 1 分，共计 5 分）

71.【C】a two-month holiday 意为两个月的假期。故选 C。

72.【D】本题考查看图识安全标识。A. Fire extinguishers safety signs 灭火器安全标识 B. Construction warning signs 施工警告标志 C. Chemicals safety signs 化学品安全标志 D. Electrical warning signs 电气警告标志，答案选 D。

73.【A】本题考查倍数。倍数结构为：倍数+as+adj/adv 原级+as；倍数+adj/adv 比较级+than；倍数+the+n. +of, 故选 A。

74.【B】second 翻译为秒，秒是时间的基本单位，故选 B。

75.【A】the cube root of sixty-four 64 的立方根为 4，the square of three 3 的平方根为 9。Times 为

乘，故选 A。

八、阅读理解(本大题共 5 小题，每小题 2 分，共计 10 分)

76.【B】细节理解题。根据 So how did Polo make the trip? He rode a camel. 那么，波罗是如何旅行的呢？他骑着骆驼。可知他骑着骆驼，故选 B。

77.【A】词义猜测题。根据 They can go for several days without water. They can survive a long time without food, too. 它们可以在没有水的情况下生存几天。它们也可以在没有食物的情况下_____很长时间。结合选项可知 survive 意为"live"，故选 A。

78.【D】细节理解题。根据 They have a thick coat 和 They have long eyelashes and an extra eyelid. 可知能帮助骆驼应对沙漠生活是①和④，故选 D。

79.【C】细节理解题。根据 They also have very large feet. These help camels walk on sand. Camels can run on sand, too.（它们也有很大的脚。这有助于骆驼在沙滩上行走。骆驼也可以在沙滩上奔跑。）可知骆驼可以用大脚在沙滩上跑得很快。故选 C。

80.【D】主旨大意题。通读可知，本文主要从骆驼的习性、品种、用处等方面描写了骆驼，所以本文最好的标题就是，骆驼——沙漠之舟。故选 D。

九、书面表达(15 分)

One possible version:

Saying No to Smoking

　　Some people has the daily habit of smoking. They think that smoking makes them feel happy and helps them relax. They think it is cool and a fashion of the day because some famous actors show smoking on TV. In fact, smoking is bad for their health. Nowadays, many cities have made laws to stop smoking in public areas in China. It won't be very long before smoking is not allowed anywhere in public areas.

　　First, smoking can cause many diseases such as lung cancer, mouth cancer and tooth disease. A smoker usually lives a shorter life than a non-smoker. Second, smoking is harmful not only to smoker but also to non-smokers, because people around are forced to breathe in the smoke when a person smokes. So we must do something to keep away from smoking. If someone offers us a cigarette, we should refuse it. And if anyone smokes nearby, we should try to stop him.

　　From now on, everyone should follow the law and say no to smoking.

模拟测试卷四

第一部分 共答题(所有考生作答,共70分)

一、语音(本大题共10小题,每小题1分,共计10分)

从A、B、C、D四个选项中,选出画线部分发音不同的一项。

1.【C】本题考查字母组合ay的发音,A、B、D选项发[ei],C选项发[i],故选C。
2.【A】本题考查字母组合tion的发音。B、C、D都读[ʃn],只有A读[tʃən],所以答案为A。
3.【A】本题考查辅音字母s的发音。B、C、D选项发[z],A选项发[s],故选A。
4.【D】本题考查辅音字母b的发音。A、B、C选项都不发音,D选项发[b],故选D。
5.【D】本题考查字母组合ed的发音,A、B、C均发[id],D选项发[t],所以答案为D。
6.【D】本题考查元音字母u的发音,A、B、C选项均发[ʌ],D选项发[u],所以答案为D。
7.【C】本题考查字母组合ear的发音,A、B、D选项发[iə],C选项发[ə:],故选C。
8.【C】本题考查元音字母a的发音,A、B、D选项发[ə],C选项发[æ],所以答案为C。
9.【D】本题考查元音字母o的发音,A、B、C都读[ʌ],只有D读[əu],所以答案为D。
10.【A】考查元音字母组ow的读音。字母组合ow通常读[au],ow常常出现在词尾。字母组合ow还可读[əu],在部分单词中,他们还可读/u:/和/ʌ/,在A选项中读[əu],B、C、D选项中读[au],所以选A。

二、单项选择题(本大题共25小题,每小题1分,共计25分)

从A、B、C、D四个选项中,选出空白处的最佳选项。

11.【D】本题考查定冠词the的用法。The Great Wall长城是专有名词,由普通名词构成的专有名词前要加the,第二个空为形容词最高级,形容词最高级前要用the。故选D。
12.【B】that不能引导非限制性定语从句,所以排除A。in which相当于where,而这里缺主语,所以C、D排除。正确答案是B,which指物,这里指代前面的hotel,同时which在定语从句中充当句子的主语。故选B。
13.【D】句意:亲爱的同学们,请仔细地阅读每一个句子。你越仔细,犯的错误越少。The+比较级,the+比较级,表示越……越……。前一句用形容词,下句提到的错误mistake是可数名词,用few修饰。故选D。
14.【B】句意:关童从长江救出一位老太太,他表现出多么非凡的勇气啊!本题考查的感叹句,由于courage是不可数名词,因此用感叹词What,how引导感叹句时应该与形容词副词连用,故不符合题意。故选B。
15.【D】本题考查短语辨析。give up放弃;give off发出(光、热);give out用光,用尽,筋疲力尽;give away分发,赠送,泄露,出卖。句意为"他说他对期末考试的成绩并不失望,但他脸上的表情出卖了他"。只有D符合语境,所以答案为D。
16.【C】本题考查名词辨析。句意为:你今晚要和Jade外出吗?那是我的事,请管好你自己的事。business 意为"事务"。所以答案为 C。

17.【C】本题考查 there be 句型的用法。根据句中 tomorrow evening 可知用一般将来时。There be 句型的一般将来时有两种形式：1. There will be…2. The is/are going to be…故选 C。

18.【C】本题考查情态动词的用法。根据答语可知答话的人提了一个建议——你应该关注别人对你的评价，should 可以用来向别人提建议，故选 C。

19.【D】本题考查固定句型。Sb. find it +adj to do sth.，意为"某人发现做某事如何"，it 在这里作形式宾语，真正的宾语为不定式。故选 D。

20.【B】本题考查地点状语从句。题意为：在战争后，一个新的图书馆建立在曾经有一个游泳池的地方。where 表地点，在……地方，所以答案为 B。

21.【D】本题考查动词辨析。句意：无论你多么有钱，它都比不上一个健康的身体。Match "与……相匹敌"和"和……不相上下"，所以答案为 D。

22.【A】本题考查非谓语动词。see 和句子的主语 he 之间是主动关系，所以答案为 A。

23.【C】本题考查固定搭配及状语从句。scarcely…when 意为"一……就……"，其位于句首时句子要倒装，且 scarcely 后用过去完成时，when 后用一般过去时。所以答案为 C。

24.【D】本题考查介词 except 与 besides 的辨析。except 意为"除……之外"；besides 意为"除……之外，还有"。根据句意：除了英语，你还知道其他的外语吗？所以选 besides。

25.【C】句意：为了得到"黑色星期五"的低价，购物者在清晨排队。本文考查动词不定式表目的；in order that/so that 表目的时后接状语从句，通常可以换用，但是 so that 不放在句首；in order to/so as to 属于动词不定式表目的，通常可以换用，但是 so as to 不放在句首；题干中需要不定式，故答案是 C。

26.【B】本题考察强调句的用法。强调句型结构：it is/was+被强调部分 that…句意：正是在昨天下午的 5 点，警察遇到了他。所以选 B。

27.【A】本题考查不定代词。句意：——你更喜欢哪件衣服？两件都不喜欢。他们又贵又不时尚。neither 两者都不身表示否定：either"（两者之中）任何一个"：none"没有一个，无人（指三者或三者以上）"：both 两者都"。根据句意可知选 A。

28【C】本题考查虚拟语气。句意：——你认为乔治通过驾驶考试了没？——没有。如果通过的话，他昨天就会开车来学校了。由句子中的 yesterday 知对一般过去时虚拟，填空处为主句，对主句虚拟为 would/should/could/might + have done，故选 C。

29.【A】本题考查独立主格结构中的过去分词，句意：把所有的因素考虑在内，我们决定把这项工作给李伟，他是一位具有丰富经验的人。根据主语的逻辑关系推知用独立主格结构中的"名词+过去分词"，此处"因素"与"考虑"是动宾关系。故选 A。

30.【D】本题考查反义疑问句。句意：他很难保持清醒，因为他是如此的劳累，是不是？前文 hardly 表示否定含义，后附加部分用肯定。前有情态动词 can，后附加疑问句 can he。故选 D。

31.【B】本题考查主谓一致。except 遵循"就前原则"，本题主语为 No one，不定代词作主语，谓语动词用第三人称单数。故选 B。

32.【B】本题考查固定结构。prefer to do…rather than do…，故选 B。

33.【C】本题考查介词，at the foot of…在……的底部，为固定短语，故选 C。

34.【C】本题考查名词性从句。主语是 the reason 表语从句用连词 that。切记本题不可以选 because。故选 C。

35.【C】考查宾语从句。句意为："你能告诉我，他是怎样在没有任何援助的情况下修好这台收音机的吗？"分析题干，所给选项充当动词 tell 的宾语，是宾语从句，要用引导词引出，后面从句要用陈述句语序，即主语+谓语，故排除 A、B 选项；D 选项：mend 后面的宾语是 the radio，宾语从句中不缺主语和宾语，用 what 的话，what 在句子中不属于任何句子成分，因此 D 是错误的连接副词 how"怎样"，在从句中作状语，所以选 C。

三、完形填空（本大题共 15 小题，每小题 1 分，共计 15 分）

从 A、B、C、D 四个选项中，选出空白处的最佳选项。

36.【C】根据上句句意可知，到剧院看音乐会，要找座位。表示"座位"应用 seats。

37.【A】根据句意可知，他妈妈看到朋友，走过去打招呼。Greet sb."给某人打招呼"，所以选 A。

38.【B】根据句意可知：他认为这是一个很好的机会去探索这个音乐大厅。所以选 B。

39.【D】根据上文句意可知，他起身，四处逛逛。表示"起身"应用 rose。

40.【A】考察介词。Through 从中间穿过，across 从表面穿过，over 从上方穿过，文中穿过一扇门，所以用 A。

41.【B】根据上文"这个小孩与他母亲一起来看音乐会"可知，此句指的是"当大厅灯光变暗时，音乐会将开始了"。表示"音乐会"应用 concert。

42.【B】根据上一段句意"她儿子起身，四处逛逛"可知，此句指的是"母亲回到了座位上，发现她儿子不见了"。表示"不见了，丢失了"应用 missing。

43.【A】考查 so/such...that...句型，如此……以至于……Worried 为形容词，所以用 so，选 A。

44.【D】根据上句句意"音乐会开始了，灯光聚焦在舞台上完美的钢琴上"可知，母亲看到她的小男孩坐在钢琴旁她当然惊讶了。表示"惊讶"应用 surprised。

45.【C】根据句意可知，那个男孩当时在钢琴旁就像他在家练习弹奏钢琴曲 Twinkle, Twinkle Little Star 一样。表示"像……"，应用 as。

46.【C】根据下文"这位伟大的钢琴家与这位小男孩共同演奏了那首钢琴曲"可知，此句指的是"那一刻，这位伟大的钢琴家来了，迅速走向钢琴，并在男孩的耳边低声说：'不要停下来。继续弹。'"表示"低声说"应用 whispered。

47.【A】根据上下文可知在弹钢琴肯定用手，所以选 A。

48.【D】根据下句句意"这位老钢琴家和年轻的初学者将一种令人恐惧的状况变成了一种奇妙的创作体验"可知，上句指的是"他们一起弹钢琴很开心"。表示"开心地"应用 happily。

49.【D】根据上文"他们开心地一起弹钢琴"可知，此句指的是"观众们站起来，为他俩喝彩"。表示"为某人喝彩"应用 cheer for sb。

50.【B】句意：艺术家的成就和魅力不仅取决于他的完美技巧，还取决于他的优秀品质。not only...but(also)...意为"不仅……而且……"。

四、阅读理解（本大题共 10 小题，每小题 2 分，共计 20 分）

从 A、B、C、D 四个选项中，选出符合题目要求的最佳选项。

A

51.【D】题干意思是：在什么情况下我们必须出示健康码？A 项，在办公室上网。B 项，为我们买的东西付钱。C 项，待在家里。D 项进出公共场所。根据第一段第二行"The health code works as an electronic credential for people to show they have a healthy body when they need to get in and out of the public area. (健康码是电子证明,当人们需要进出公共区域时,他们可以用它来证明自己有一个健康的身体。)可知进出公共场所时我们必须出示健康码。故选 D。

52.【A】题干意思是:画线词"characteristics"的意思是什么?根据四个表格的标题"Quick and safe"(快速安全)和"Cost-free"(免费的)和"Convenient"(方便的)以及"Environmentally friendly"(环保的)可知本文介绍了健康码的特点,画线词"characteristics"的意思是"特点"。故选 A。

53.【B】题干意思是:哪种健康码持有者不被允许四处走动? A 项,绿色和黄色的健康码持有者。B 项黄色和红色的健康码持有者。C 项,只有红色的健康码持有者。根据文中"A green code holder with normal body temperature is allowed to enter and leave pubic places and take public transportation vehicles such as buses, trains and planes. But yellow and red code holders are not"故选 B。

54.【D】题干意思是:健康码可以如何帮助保护环境? A 项,通过卖更多的手机。B 项,通过获得更多的信息。C 项,通过少用手机。D 项,通过少用纸。根据文中"Everything is done on the mobile phone without using any paper thus saving many resources"故选 D。

55.【A】题干意思是:本文的目的是什么? A 项,告诉我们健康码的优点。B 项,理解为什么我们不喜欢支付宝。C 项,通过手机使用健康码。根据四个标题可知本文的目的是告诉我们健康码的优点。故选 A。

B

56.【C】细节理解题。根据文章第一段的最后一句"Something that looks cool may not be good for your health. 得出的判断",it (drinking cold things) may do some harm to ones health. 故答案为 C。

57.【D】细节理解题。根据文章第三段中"These drinks are typically aimed at young people, students, busy people and sports players."可以判断,并没有特别指出 women and girls。故答案为 D。

58.【C】细节理解题。根据文章的最后一段 Teenagers should be discouraged from consuming drinks with a lot of caffeine in them, 得出判断。故答案为 C。

59.【D】细节理解题。根据文章第四段"Makers sometimes say their drinks make you better at sports and can keep you awake. But be careful not to drink too much. Caffeine raises your heartbeat."可知。故答案为 D。

60.【B】主旨大意题。合文章的大意,energy drinks 因为含有 caffeine, 所以在带给人们清爽的同时,也包含着对身体不利的一方面。故答案为 B。

第二部分 (文科类职业模块考生作答,共 15 分)

五、单项选择题(本大题共 5 小题,每小题 1 分,共计 5 分)

从 A、B、C、D 四个选项中,选出空白处的最佳选项。

61.【C】本题考查情景交际。A 项,Go ahead"去吧;干吧";B 项,Cheers"干杯";C 项,Congratulations"祝贺你";D 项,Come on"加油;拜托"。分析题干意思,第一说话人说

"我得到了我想要的在公共图书馆的工作",第二说话人表示祝贺,应该用"祝贺你(Congratulations)"。其他三项均不符合题意。故正确答案为C。

62.【A】本题考查情景交际。A项,"我能为你做点什么?";B项,"正如我所料";C项,"情况怎么样呢?";D项,"给你"。根据题干句意"嗨,我能请你帮个忙吗?""当然可以"可知只有A项符合语境,所以答案为A。

63.【A】本题考查情景交际。句意:"你是谁""我Jack。"本题考查打电话用语,答语用 This is … speaking,故选A。

64.【D】本题考查标志。"我能在这里停车吗?""不,你不能,标语写着禁止停车。"A为"危险";B选项意为"禁止左拐";C选项意为"禁止拍照";D选项意为"禁止停车";故选D。

65.【C】本题考查情景交际。句意:"爸爸,如果我买一个钱包作为妈妈的生日礼物,你觉得怎么样?""再好不过了。"A选项意为"别麻烦了";B选项意为"看情况吧";C选项意为"再好不过了";D选项意为"就这么办吧"。根据语境,故选C。

六、阅读理解(本大题共5小题,每小题2分,共计10分)

从A、B、C、D四个选项中,选出符合题目要求的最佳选项。

66.【C】本题为细节理解题。可以用排除法,A由倒数第三段 Cohen's interviewed 193 adults every day for two weeks;B由倒数第三段 stay alone in a room for six days;D由倒数第三段 the people were given colds by doctors,所以选C。

67.【D】本题为细节理解题,由第三段 positive feelings may reduce the danger of illness 可以知道答案,所以选D。

68.【D】本题为细节理解题。由第四段第一句话 Cohen found that people who were cheerful and lively caught coughs and colds less often. 可以知道答案,所以选D。

69.【C】本题推理题,本文主要说明一项研究:心情好的人很少得病,是一篇报道性文章,所以选C。

70.【A】本题考查文章标题归纳。纵观全文理解可知,本篇文章主要内容"心情好的人很少得病",可以推出答案,所以选A。

第三部分 (工科类职业模块考生作答,共15分)

七、单项选择题(本大题共5小题,每小题1分,共计5分)

从A、B、C、D四个选项中,选出空白处的最佳选项

71.【B】本题考查数词,年代的表达法为" in the 年代 s's/s",在某人多少岁时表达法为"in one's+整十数的复数",故选B。

72.【A】句意:每天有数百万人通过电子邮件传递信息。考查数词的用法。million 前有具体数字或 several 等词时,要用单数形式。many 一般不与 million 等数词连用,表示"数百万"英语为 millions of。

73.【D】A注意事项:戴安全帽;B警告:高压;C.消防水管;D.注意:限制区域。故选D。

74.【C】F=(℃×1.8)+32,选C。

75.【B】本题考查分数表达法。"子基母序",分子大于1,分母加s,所以答案为B。

81

八、阅读理解(本大题共 5 小题,每小题 2 分,共计 10 分)

从 A、B、C、D 四个选项中,选出符合题目要求的最佳选项。

76.【D】问题是"如果 Harry 只上 4 节舞蹈课,他应该多少美元。"根据 DANCE & MUSIC 中的"￥15 each class"可知,四节舞蹈课的费用为 15×4=60 美元。故选 D。

77.【B】根据 A GREEN CITY 中的 Help make the city greener by planting trees(通过植树帮助城市变得更绿)以及 Time:10-11:30am. every Saturday. Place:Foxdale Park(时间:每周六上午 10-11:30。地方:Foxdale 公园)可知,在周六上午,Foxdale 公园的人们可以植树。故选 B。

78.【C】根据 SWEET THINGS 中的"learn to make cakes with Anne(和安妮一起学习做蛋糕)"以及"Place:Sunnyside Kitchen(地方:Sunnyside 厨房)"可知,人们可以在 Sunnyside 厨房制作蛋糕。故选 C。

79.【C】根据 A GREEN CITY 中的 Help make the city greener by planting trees(通过植树有让城市变得更绿)以及 Time:10-11:30a. m. every Saturday Place:Foxdale Park(时间:每周六上午 10-11:30。地方:Foxdale 公园)可知,人们在每个周六都可以在 Foxdale 公园让城市变得更绿。故选 C。

80.【A】通读全文可知,本文介绍了三则不同类型的广告,而广告最有可能在报纸上出现,故选 A。

九、书面表达(15 分)

My Hobby

  I have many hobbies, such as reading, skating, and watching TV. But reading is my favorite hobby.

  I like reading for three reasons. First of all, books introduce me to a new world, which is colourful and without time and space limit. Secondly, reading can better myself by showing me a new horizon. In the past years, most of my knowledge has been obtained from books. I have learned from many people by reading about their ideas on politics, life and society. Thirdly, reading bridge the gap between my dream and my goal. In order to succeed in my career in the future, I must keep reading, thinking and practising.

模拟测试卷五

第一部分　共答题(所有考生作答，共70分)

一、语音(本大题共10小题，每小题1分，共计10分)

从A、B、C、D四个选项中，选出画线部分发音不同的一项。

1.【D】本题考察元音字母a在重读开音节中读[ei]，在重读闭音节中读[æ]发音规律。basic，awake，plane都是元音字母a的开音节[ei]，drag是元音字母a的重读闭音节[æ]。

2.【D】元音字母e在dessert，design，effect非重读音节中的读音是[i]，exercise是字母e的重读闭音节[e]。

3.【C】oo字母组合的发音规律是：在[k]，[d]之前读[u]，但food，mood中读[u:]；其他音前读[u:]，但foot例外读[u]，因此，good，foot，took中oo读音是[u]，flood中oo读音是[ʌ]。

4.【B】元音字母u在guard中不发音，其他三个是元音字母u在重读开音节中的读音是[ju:]。

5.【C】au字母组合在audience，August，cause中读[ɔ:]，在laugh中读[a:]。

6.【C】ow字母组合在now中读[au]，在know，narrow，owe中读[əu]。

7.【A】辅音字母c在perfect，project，product中读[k]，在once中读[s]。

8.【D】-es在[tʃ]后读[iz]，在元音或浊辅音后读[z]。

9.【A】al在重读音节词首读[ɔ:l]，在重读音节词中读[ɔ:]。

10.【A】b一般读[b]，但在comb中不发音。

二、单项选择题(本大题共25小题，每小题1分，共计25分)

从A、B、C、D四个选项中，选出空白处的最佳选项。

11.【A】句意：没有面包我们不能制作三明治。bread 面包；onions 洋葱；yogurt 酸奶；tomatoes 西红柿。制作三明治需要面包，其他东西都是可以没有的。因此根据名单应该选A。

12.【B】本题考查形容词、副词及其固定短语的用法。句意：尽可能地仔细写，尽量别出错。固定短语as...as possible 尽可能……，副词修饰动词，所以选B。

13.【B】句意：我们怎样在自然灾害之后，帮助一个受害者？Who 谁；How 怎样；Where 在哪儿；When 何时。根据句意，故选B。

14.【B】句意：——你觉得你的初中生活怎么样？——我认为是丰富多彩的，虽然我总是很忙。if 表示如果；though 表示虽然；while 表示当……时候；until 表示直到……才，根据语境，我认为是丰富多彩的，虽然我总是很忙，故选B。

15.【C】句意：在5月或10月纽约是个参观的好地方。根据句意及题干分析具体到月要用介词in，故选C。

16.【A】句意：我能和你谈话吗？不会很长时间的。根据上下文可知，说话人在请求听话人允许不长时间的一个交谈，所以选择A。表示"能不能，可以不可以"。

— 83 —

17.【D】句意：——我长大后想要成为一名教师。——努力学习，你的梦想将会实现。or 或者，否则；but 但是；though 虽然；and 和。根据"work hard"和"your dream will come true."可知前后两者是顺承关系，用 and，此处构成结构：祈使句，and+陈述句，故选 D。

18.【B】句意：汤姆在昨天的班会上提出了一个有趣的问题。rise 升起，不及物动词。raise 提出，及物动词。此空后接宾语 an interesting question，应填及物动词 raise。结合 in yesterday's class meeting 可知，句子用一般过去时，动词用过去式，故选 B。

19.【C】句意：我一整晚一直尝试去给妈妈打电话，但我似乎打不通。get in 进入；get off 下车；get through 通过，打通电话；get along 进展。根据 trying to phone 可知是打电话相关的话题，故选 C。

20.【A】句意：Tim Cook 每周都给他的母亲打电话，即使他正在环球旅行。while 引导时间状语从句时，强调主从动作同时发生，从句中常用进行时态。本题主句是一般过去时态，故从句中用过去进行时态。故选 A。

21.【A】句意：在学校，一些学生很活跃而一些却很害羞，然而他都可能彼此成为好朋友。两个分句是两种情况的对比，这是 while 作为并列连词的用法。

22.【B】句意：我不得不把车停到路边，因为如果我们把它留在这儿我们将会被罚款。根据 fine，动词，罚款；形容词，好的。结合语境，应是罚款，主语是 we 与动词 fine 之间是被动关系，用被动语态，又因 if 引导的条件状语从句中，时态是主将从现，空格处正是主句，用一般将来时，即是用一般将来时的被动语态，构成：will + be+ 动词的过去分词，故选 B。

23.【C】句意：老师知道如何处理你今天带到学校的手机。how to deal with sth. 怎样处理某事，后面有宾语 the mobile phone。what he will do with 是正确用法，故 A 不正确有。所以选 C。

24.【B】句意：——你看起来很累，为什么不停下来休息一下？——好吧，但我得再多工作几分钟。Why not do sth.？为什么不做某事，是一个固定句型。

25.【B】句意：比尔建议早起床，这样我们可以在海边看日出。suggest doing sth. 建议做某事。

26.【B】句意：——你养的金鱼多么可爱啊！——是的，它们都是我的好朋友。goldfish 单复数同形。

27.【A】句意：——听，铃声响了。——让我们去教室。英语中由 here 和 there 表示地点状语的词放在句首，当句子的主语是名词时一般采用倒装结构，谓语动词与后面的名词保持一致。A. 铃声响了。B 有个铃铛。其他两项是错误结构。

28.【A】句意：直到我告诉他，他才知道这件事。根据语义可知本句为 not...until...句型的强调句，句型为：It is/was not until +被强调部分+that+其他部分。when/while/as 不是强调句型结构的连词。

29.【D】句意：山顶上有一座老人曾经住过的庙宇。on the top of the hill 方位介词短语位于句首，句子完全倒装。因此谓语动词要和主语调换位置；the old man once lived 修饰先行词 a temple，且定语从句缺少状语成分，因此用 where 作引导词。

30.【B】句意：我很高兴我找到了和我工作时一样的现代电脑。such, as, the same 引导限制性定语从句时，后只能用 as 作关系词。

31.【C】句意：我不确定我是否要去参加汤姆的生日聚会。我可能改去听音乐会。whether 和 if 引导宾语从句，表示"是否"，但与 or not 连用时，只能用 whether。instead of 代替，介词短语，后跟名词、动名词等作宾语。instead 代替，副词，第二空后没有宾语，故应用 instead。

32.【A】句意：我不认为他说的话是正确的。don't think 后跟 that 引导的宾语从句，从句里又包含了一个主语从句。主语从句的从句部分缺少宾语，用连词 what。

33.【B】句意：如果我年轻时努力学习，我就会进入大学，过上不同的生活。if 引导的虚拟语气句型，对过去情况的虚拟，从句用 had + done，主句用 would/should/might/could have done。根据句意，work hard 是假设条件，用过去完成时 had worked hard，enter a university 是假设的结果，would have entered。

34.【D】句意：——这些苹果多少钱？——五美元够了。第一个空根据后面的主语 apples，可知是复数名词，用复数 are；第二个空的主语是 five dollars，表示金钱、重量、距离等做主语时，谓语动词用单数。

35.【B】句意：他问约翰会不会游泳。直接引语变间接引语，直接引语如果是一般疑问句，间接引语应改为由 whether 或 if 引导的宾语从句，时态由一般现在时变为一般过去时，因为是问句，因此转换用 ask。

三、完型填空（本大题共 15 小题，每小题 1 分，共计 15 分）

从 A、B、C、D 四个选项中，选出空白处的最佳选项。
解析：本文通过描述作者的经历，建议我们伤心时，可以通过喝杯茶来改变一下心情。

36.【B】句意：这是他们生活中离不开的东西。with 和；without 无，没有；beside 在……旁边；through 穿过。根据"Tea to some people in eastern countries is like air or water."可知，这是他们生活中离不开的东西。故选 B。

37.【D】句意：当我 22 岁时，我体验了来自邻居的深厚和温暖的善良。mother's 妈妈的；teacher's 老师的；friend's 朋友的；neighbor's 邻居的。根据下文"My neighbor…"可知，此处应该是邻居的。故选 D。

38.【A】句意：我深爱的奶奶去世后我很难过。after 在……之后；but 但是；before 在……之前；and 和。根据"I was very sad…my loved grandma died."可知，奶奶去世后我很难过。故选 A。

39.【C】句意：一天晚上，我的邻居邀请我去她家喝茶。taught 教；needed 需要；invited 邀请；agreed 同意。根据"to have tea at her home"可知，此处指"邀请我去她家喝茶"。故选 C。

40.【A】句意：她向我讲述了她的故事。told 告诉；talked 谈话；said 说；spoke 讲。根据"…me all about her life story"可知，此处指"讲述她的故事"。故选 A。

41.【C】句意：她来美国是因为她失去了丈夫。gave 给；helped 帮助；lost 失去；left 离开。根据下文"her sad feeling was gone"可知，她应该是失去了丈夫。故选 C。

42.【D】句意：她建议我制订一个如何前进的计划。fire 火；idea 观点；life 生活；plan 计划。make a plan"制订计划"。故选 D。

43.【D】句意：我们在凌晨两点结束了晚上的茶点。started 开始；drank 喝；made 做；ended 结束。根据"at 2 a.m."可知，是在凌晨两点结束的。故选 D。

44.【B】句意：这真是一杯暖心又难忘的茶。badly 差地；really 真正地；even 甚至；never 从不。根据"a heartwarming and unforgettable cup of tea"可知，这真是一杯暖心又难忘的茶。

45.【A】句意:在最后一节课上,一位年轻的女士带来了她的茶具——一个可爱的盒子,里面有日本茶所需的所有东西,以感谢我。last 最后的;first 第一;different 不同的;same 相同的。根据"one young woman brought her tea set…"可知,这是在最后一节课上发生的事。故选 A。

46.【D】句意:她静静地跪在我的茶几旁,把绿茶粉倒进碗里。prepared 准备;painted 绘画;planted 种植;poured 倒。根据"…green tea powder into a bowl"可知,此处指把绿茶粉倒进碗里。故选 D。

47.【A】句意:她静静地用双手捧着给我喝,甜甜地笑着。smiling 笑;whispering 低语;answering 回答;crying 哭。根据"sweetly"可知,应该是甜甜地笑着。故选 A。

48.【B】句意:我对她美丽的礼物和善良的心感到惊讶。excited 兴奋的;surprised 惊讶的;angry 生气的;sad 难过的。根据"at the beauty of her gift and at her kind heart"可知,作者对此感到惊讶。故选 B。

49.【B】句意:那可不仅仅是一杯茶! more 更多的;more than 多于;less than 少于;less 更少的。作者认为这份礼物已经远远超出了它的价值,这不仅仅是一杯茶。故选 B。

50.【C】句意:当你感到不安的时候,为什么不喝一杯茶,享受它给你带来的快乐和平静呢? where 哪里;when 什么时候;how 怎样;why 为什么。根据"happy"和"calm"是形容词可知,此处应该用 how 连接。故选 C。

四、阅读理解(本大题共 10 小题,每小题 2 分,共计 20 分)

从 A、B、C、D 四个选项中,选出符合题目要求的最佳选项。

A

解析:本文是一篇记叙文。主要讲述画家尚新周通过画作来记录农村的变化。

51.【C】细节理解题。根据文章第二段"Thanks to my experience in Duomai Village, I can make the paintings much lovelier"可知,多亏了在农村的经历,他才可以使他的画更加可爱。故选 C。

52.【D】词义猜测题。根据"people's hard times to better conditions and happy lives."可知,人民的生活从艰难到更好、更幸福的方向发展,因此他的画展示了与贫困作斗争的进程。故选 D。

53.【B】细节理解题。根据文章"he put his paintings about the local life on the Internet to help villagers sell their products. To make the nightlife there richer, he sold paintings to buy streetlights,"可知,他通过画作帮助农民卖产品,通过卖画来买路灯。故选 B。

54.【A】细节理解题。根据"I want to record the changes of the poor areas and create more works about people"可知,他是为了记录贫困地区的变化以及创造更多关于劳动人民的创作。故选 A。

55.【C】主旨大意题。根据文章第一段"With the development of China, many traditional ink paintings(水墨画)show the changes in southern Chinese villages."可知,很多水墨画反映了中国南方农村地区的变化。故选 C。

B

解析:本文是一篇说明文,文章对海洋塑料污染问题进行分析并提出一些解决方案。

56.【D】细节理解题。根据第三段"Some areas, such as the Mediterranean, East China and Yellow Seas, already have dangerous levels of plastic."可知,地中海、中国东部和黄海等一些地区的塑料含量已经达到了危险水平。故选 D。

57.【C】词句猜测题。根据第四段"The writers reported that almost every kind of ocean animal has been affected by plastic pollution."可知,几乎每种海洋动物都受到了塑料污染的影响。affect 表示影响,故选 C。

58.【D】细节理解题。根据"Heike Vesper is with the World Wildlife Fund. She said people can help reduce plastic pollution by changing their behavior."可知,Heike Vesper 认为人们可以通过改变自己的行为来帮助减少塑料污染。故选 D。

59.【C】推理判断题。通读全文可知,本文主要讲述了海洋塑料污染问题。推知可在报纸的环境板块读到此篇文章。故选 C。

60.【A】主旨大意题。通读全文可知,当前海洋塑料污染已达到令人担忧的水平,本文对海洋塑料污染问题进行了分析并提出一些解决方案。故选 A。

第二部分 （文科类职业模块考生作答,共 15 分）

五、单项选择题(本大题共 5 小题,每小题 1 分,共计 5 分)

从 A、B、C、D 四个选项中,选出空白处的最佳选项。

61.【C】句意:——你好,我是吉姆。我可以和汤姆讲话吗? ——请稍等,他在书房里。Go ahead 去吧;That's all right 没关系;Hold the line, please 请稍等,别挂电话;Hurry up 快点。根据 He is in the study 他在书房里,可知应说"请稍等",因此 C 选项符合语境。

62.【B】句意:——我能为您点餐吗? ——当然,我想要一碗米饭和一瓶啤酒。May I have the bill 可以结账了吗;May I take your order 你要点什么菜;Could you please help me 你能帮我一下吗;May I help you 我能帮你吗。根据答语 Sure. I'd like a bowl of rice and a bottle of beer 可知,上述问的是点餐。

63.【C】句意:——你好,本。有什么问题吗? ——我肚子疼得厉害,我感觉很糟糕。Can you help me 你能帮助我吗;How do you do 你好吗;What seems to be the problem 有什么问题吗;How long have you felt like this 你有这样的感觉多久了。根据语境可知,此处是医生在询问他有什么问题。

64.【B】句意:——我们明天早上 8 点在公园门口见面好吗? ——我赶不到。9 点可以吗? It's not a big deal 没什么大不了;I can't make it 我做不到;I can't agree more 我很同意;It's a good idea 这是个好主意。根据语境可知是时间上有问题,8 点赶不到要调到 9 点,故选 B。

65.【B】句意:下面哪一个含义是"小心头。天花板太低了。没有多少空间了。"WARNING: NO TRESPASSING 警告:不得擅自闯入;CAUTION: LOW HEADROOM 警告:低头;CAUTION: DEEP WATER 警告:深水;CAUTION: MIND YOUR HEAD 警告:小心你的头。

六、阅读理解(本大题共 5 小题,每小题 2 分,共计 10 分)

从 A、B、C、D 四个选项中,选出符合题目要求的最佳选项。

解析:本文主要讲述了中西方不同的饮水习惯,可能与历史、文化和科学有关。

66.【D】细节理解题。根据"However, most Chinese people think the Americans' habit of drinking ice water is also strange and even unhealthy."可知，然而，大多数中国人认为美国人喝冰水的习惯是奇怪的，甚至是不健康的。故选 D。

67.【A】细节理解题。根据"Chinese doctors are encouraging more people to take on the habit of drinking hot water, especially for women."可知，中国医生鼓励更多的人养成喝热水的习惯，尤其是女性。故选 A。

68.【C】词句猜测题。根据"Finally, the man received the hot water but felt cold stares from every corner of the cafe."可知，最后，这个人收到了热水，但从咖啡馆的每个角落他都能感到冰冷的目光，说明餐厅里的其他人都认为这个男人的要求很奇怪。故选 C。

69.【C】推理判断题。根据第四段内容可知，是为了表明在英国喝热水是不常见的。故选 C。

70.【C】推理判断题。根据全文内容可知，不同的饮水习惯与历史、文化和科学有关，也就是可能与不同的国家有关。故选 C。

第三部分 （工科类职业模块考生作答，共 15 分）

七、单项选择题(本大题共 5 小题，每小题 1 分，共计 5 分)

从 A、B、C、D 四个选项中，选出空白处的最佳选项。

71.【D】句意：2 的立方减去 64 的立方根等于 4。

72.【C】句意：米是长度的基本单位。

73.【C】句意：孔深 100 毫米。

74.【D】句意：1000 升等于 1,000,000 立方厘米。1 liter＝1,000ml＝1,000cm。

75.【A】句意："A set of strict and complete supervisory system"意思是"一套严格和完善的监管制度"。

八、阅读理解(本大题共 5 小题，每小题 2 分，共计 10 分)

从 A、B、C、D 四个选项中，选出符合题目要求的最佳选项。

解析：本文主要内容是作者通过给时间算账告诉我们，我们工作的时间不多，时间很重要，不能浪费时间。

76.【B】题意：我们一年睡多少天？考查细节理解题。A. 365 天 B. 122 天；C. 8 天；D. 52 天。根据第一段第二句 We sleep 8 hours a day, so we have 122 days for sleeping.（我们一天睡 8 个小时，所以我们有 122 天时间用于睡眠。）可知我们一年睡 122 天，结合题意和选项可知选 B。

77.【D】题意：在＿＿＿＿我们花费了 15 天。考查细节理解题。A. rest 休息；B. the coffee break 喝咖啡时间；C. lunch 午饭；D. breakfast and supper 早饭和晚饭。根据第 1 段第 7 句 It takes us about one hour to have breakfast and supper. This comes to 15 days over a year.（我们大约花一个小时吃早饭和晚饭。一年有 15 天。）可知，在早饭和晚饭上一年要用 15 天。所以本题选 D。

78.【B】题意：下列哪一项是正确的？考查细节理解题。A. Each weekend has one day 每个周末都有一天；根据第一段第 2 行第三句 Each weekend is two days 可知 A 是错误的；C. We get 3 days' holidays at Easter. 根据第 2 段第 2 行第二句 We have to remember that we get 2 days' holiday at Easter(复活节），可知 C 是错误的；D. The coffee break takes us one hour. 根

据第 2 段第 4 行 and half an hour's coffee break 可知 D 是错误的；B. We have 61 days for free time. 根据第 2 段第四句 Four free hours each evening takes up 61 days 可知 B 是正确的，结合题意可知选 B。

79.【D】题意：根据文章，这个词 That 是指_____。考查细节理解题。A. time for work 工作时间；B. time for sleep 睡觉时间；C. time for holiday 假期时间；D. time for lunch and coffee break 午餐时间和咖啡休息时间。根据上文和此句 But then we have one and a half hours' lunch every day, and half an hour's coffee break. That comes to 30 days a year. 的意思"但是我们每天有一个半小时的午餐，还有半个小时的咖啡休息时间。那一年达到 30 天。"可知 that 指代的午餐和咖啡休息时间。结合题意可知选 D。

80.【B】题意：这篇文章的大意是_____。考查主旨理解题。A. we should know the numbers. 我们应该知道这些数字；B. time is important and we'd better not waste it. 时间很重要，我们最好不要浪费时间；C. we need more holidays. 我们需要更多的假期；D. a few days for work is enough 工作几天就够了。本文主要内容是作者通过给时间算账告诉我们工作的时间不多，时间很重要，不能浪费时间。结合题意和语境可知选 B。

点睛：本文通过算账的形式告诉我们，时间很重要，不能浪费时间。由于文中出现的数字较多，不易把握，所以在阅读时尽量减慢速度，注意体会作者的意图。当然本题的题目并不是很难，主要考查学生的细节理解能力，首先正确理解题意，再细读短文，到文中找出答案。像第 81、82、83、84 题都可以在文中找到答案，第 85 小题是主旨理解题，通过通读课文，体会作者的意图，可知本文的中心思想。

九、书面表达(15 分)

One possible version：

　　As we all know, the environment around us is getting worse and worse.

　　In some places, we can't see fish swimming around in the rivers or trees on the hills. Some people even have no clean water to drink. So I think we must do something to protect our environment. For example, we can go to school on foot or by bike and can use shopping baskets instead of plastic bags when shopping. And in our daily life, we should use both sides of the paper.

　　By doing small things like these, there will be less pollution and our life will be better. Let's work together to make our earth more beautiful.

模拟测试卷六

一、语音(本大题共 10 小题,每小题 1 分,共计 10 分)

从 A、B、C、D 四个选项中,选出画线部分发音不同的一项。

1. 【D】本题考察元音字母 a 在重读开音节中读[ei],在重读闭音节中读[æ]发音规律。age, page, danger 都是元音字母 a 的开音节[ei], fact 是元音字母 a 的重读闭音节[æ]。

2. 【C】元音字母 e 在 elect 非重读音节中的读音是[i], debt, deck, fetch 是字母 e 的重读闭音节[e]。

3. 【D】元音字母 i 在 engine, exit 非重读音节和 fill 重读闭音节中的读音是[i], idea 是字母 i 的重读开音节[ai]。

4. 【A】ew 在 few 中读[juː], 在 flew, brew, jewelry 中读[uː]。

5. 【B】ie 在 quiet 中读[aɪə], 在 piece, relieve, thief 中读[iː]。

6. 【A】our 在 courage 中读[ʌr], 在 four, pour, your 中读[ɔːr]。

7. 【D】y 在 cry 中读[ai], 在 ability, angry, apology 中读[i]。

8. 【C】ch 在 machine 中读[ʃ], 在 each, hatch, lunch 中读[tʃ]。

9. 【C】x 在 exact 中读[gz], 在 mix, next, except 中读[ks]。

10. 【A】ere 在 here 中读[ɪə], 在 interest, reference, difference 中读[rə]。

二、单项选择题(本大题共 25 小题,每小题 1 分,共计 25 分)

从 A、B、C、D 四个选项中,选出空白处的最佳选项。

11. 【B】句意:——她是谁?——她是王太太。a woman 一位妇女;Mrs Wang 王太太;a driver 一位司机;a worker 一位工人。根据 Who is she? 可知此处询问她是谁,故回答是什么人,故选 B。

12. 【D】句意:生活是可改变的。没有人知道未来可能发生什么。should 应该,表示责任与义务;need 需要,必须;have to 必须,强调客观愿望;might 可以,可能,表示"可能"的肯定推测。根据句意,表示"未来可能发生什么";故选 D。

13. 【B】句意:假期之后,我比以前更胖了。根据 very 修饰形容词或副词的原级;a little 可以修饰形容词或副词的比较级;a few +可数名词的复数;more 是 many 和 much 的比较级,故答案为 B。

14. 【A】句意:他们通常在家看卡通片而不是做户外活动。考查 instead of 的用法,instead of sth./doing sth. 意为"代替,而不是……"。故选 A。

15. 【D】句意:学校在博物馆的东边,离博物馆有五千米。in 表示一个属于另一个,在范围内;on 表示两者互不相属,接壤;to 表示两者互不相属,中间有事物隔开。由句意可知,两地相距五千米,说明中间有隔开,用介词 to,具体的距离后面用 away,不用 far,故选 D。

16. 【D】句意:再见,John,有时间再来。我会的。will 表示意愿。

17. 【A】句意:我的胳膊仍然很疼,所以我要去看医生。so 因此,所以;for 为了,因为;but

但是，表示转折；or 或者，否则；根据句意可知，这两句话是因果关系，故选 A。

18．【C】句意：欢迎来到我们的餐厅，我们将为您提供美味的食物。provide sb. with sth. = provide sth. for sb. 意为"给某人提供某物"；give sth. to sb. = give sb. sth. 意为"给某人某物"；根据 you…delicious food，可知用 provide sb. with sth.，故选 C。

19．【B】句意：李丽一到北京你能打电话给我吗？根据语境可知，这里由 as soon as 引导的时间状语从句，主句表示一个即将发生的动作，从句应用一般现在时，结合选项可知应选 B。

20．【C】句意：——对不起，先生，我们什么时候可以在游泳池游泳？——直到下个月修好才可以。此句是 until 引导的时间状语从句，要用一般现在时表将来，主语 it (the pool) 是动作 repair 的承受者，所以用被动语态，一般现在时被动语态的构成是：主语+is/are+动词的过去分词，故选 C。

21．【C】句意：我是在上海遇到我的同学的。强调句型：It is/was +被强调的部分+that (who) +剩余部分。被强调的部分是人用 who，地点用 that。

22．【C】句意：昨天在公园里我们玩的多么高兴呀！have a good time 固定搭配，感叹句结构：What+ (a/an) +形容词+名词 (+主谓)!

23．【A】句意：——我要一杯加肉桂的卡布奇诺和一块芝士蛋糕。——对不起，我没听懂你的话。你刚才订的什么？根据 I'm sorry 可知是一般现在时，否定句表达"没有听懂"用助动词的否定 don't 和动词原型 catch。根据 just now 可知疑问句是一般过去时，将助动词 did 放在主语 you 前，主语后接动词原型 order。

24．【A】句意：我今天胃痛，我不想吃任何东西。feel like 想要做，后接动名词；would like 想要，后接动词不定式；want to 想要，后接动词原型。

25．【B】句意：由于不知道医院在哪儿，他找了一位路人问路。现在分词 knowing 与句子主语 he 是主动关系，做原因状语。

26．【C】句意：假期期间，很多人被吸引到成都，因为它有悠久的历史和美丽的风景。先行词 Chengdu 指物，在从句中作主语，用关系代词 that 或 which。

27．【B】句意：Mary 想成为一名秘书，那就是她想成的样子。考察表语从句的引导词，代职业的疑问代词是 what，用来引导表语从句时，依然用 what，因此引导表语从句的引导词用 what。

28．【A】句意：为了参加大学入学考试，她建议他读什么书？suggest 表示"建议"，后接从句用 that sb. should do 结构，should 可以省略。特殊疑问句的结构是特殊疑问词+be 动词 (助动词) +主语+其他。

29．【C】句意：这里有一些书给你，汤姆。主语 some books，be 动词用 are。

30．【B】句意：三分之二的信息是由德国人翻译成德语的。分数的表达：分子是基数词，分母是序数词，当分子大于 1 时，分线用序数词的复数形式。三分之二的表达是：two thirds。分数作主语时，谓语与 of 后的名词的单复数保持一致，information 是不可数名词，be 动词用 is，German 复数形式是 Germans。

31．【C】句意：——虽然前线只剩下三个士兵，但他们还在继续战斗。——他们多么勇敢呀！though 尽管；because 因为；though 引导让步状语从句，不能与 but 连用。because 引导原因状语从句，不能与 so 连用。

32．【C】句意：后悔你过去的错误是没有用的。句型：It is no use doing sth. 做某事是没有用的。it 是形式主语，doing sth. 是真正的主语。

33. 【B】句意：在春节正月里，你最好不要剪头发。had better not do sth. 最好不做某事。

34. 【B】句意：现代奥运会的格言是：更快，更高，更强。

35. 【B】句意：不要在医院吵闹，好吗？陈述部分是否定的祈使句，反义疑问句部分要用 will you。

三、完型填空（本大题共 15 小题，每小题 1 分，共计 15 分）

从 A、B、C、D 四个选项中，选出空白处的最佳选项。

解析：本文主要介绍了狗对人类和环境的帮助。

36. 【C】句意：它们也拯救处于危险中的人。half 一半；the river 河流；danger 危险；the rain 雨。根据"They work with the police and help fight against bad men."可知，他们也拯救处于危险中的人，danger 符合语境，in danger"在危险中"，固定搭配。故选 C。

37. 【B】句意：作为导盲犬，它们照顾盲人。look for 寻找；look after 照顾；look up 查阅；look like 看起来像。根据"As guide dogs,"可知，狗会照顾盲人。故选 B。

38. 【D】句意：在一些医院，一些病人太虚弱了，所以狗甚至可以为他们开门、开灯或关灯。turn into 变成；turn up 出现；turn to 转向；turn on 打开。根据"…or off the lights"可知，此处指"开灯"，用 turn on。故选 D。

39. 【A】句意：他们是让生病的人感到温暖的友好的帮手。friendly 友好的；friends 朋友（复数）；friend 朋友（单数）；friend's 朋友的。此空修饰名词 helpers 要用形容词 friendly。故选 A。

40. 【A】句意：他们是让生病的人感到温暖的友好的帮手。warm 温暖的；cool 凉爽的；sad 难过的；scary 恐怖的。根据"They are…helpers"可知，狗会让生病的人感到温暖。故选 A。

41. 【C】句意：但是你知道人们是如何训练狗来帮助保护植物和动物的吗？blind 盲的；police 警察；plants 植物；dogs 狗。根据语境可知，C 是正确选项。

42. 【B】句意：狗用鼻子找出树上的有害昆虫。mouths 嘴；noses 鼻子；eyes 眼睛；heads 头。根据常识和下文"With dog's sniffing"可知，此处应该是 noses。故选 B。

43. 【D】句意：例如，每年 5 月，一种昆虫以白蜡树的枝干和树根为食，杀死了白蜡树。eat 动词原形；ate 动词过去式；eatting 格式错误；eating 动名词/现在分词。空格前 by 为介词，后面跟动名词形式 eating。故选 D。

44. 【A】句意：当虫卵长成昆虫时，它们开始吃树木的一部分。of 属于……的；at 在；to 朝；with 和。分析句子可知，part 和 the tree 为所属关系，用介词 of 表示"树木的一部分"。故选 A。

45. 【B】句意：昆虫的卵很小以至于人们很难看见它们。often 经常；hardly 几乎不；sometimes 有时；usually 通常。根据"But the eggs of the insects are so small"可知，人们几乎看不见它们。hardly 符合题意。故选 B。

46. 【A】句意：利用狗的嗅觉，科学家们就能找到虫卵并采取行动。eggs 卵、禽蛋；insects 昆虫；trees 树；people 人们。根据"the eggs of the insects are so small"可知，用狗的嗅觉，科学家们就能找到虫卵并采取行动。故选 A。

47. 【C】句意：每年，有些人为了得到他们需要的东西而捕杀动物，从鱼翅到虎皮。help 帮助；protect 保护；kill 杀死；eat 吃。根据"from shark's fin to the tiger's skin"可知，鱼翅和虎皮是把动物杀死后得到的。故选C。

48.【D】句意：狗的特殊气味帮助警察发现产品并阻止销售。policewomen 女警察；polices 表达有误；policeman 警察；police 警察。空前有定冠词the，用police。the police 表示"警察，警方"。故选D。

49.【B】句意：狗的特殊气味帮助警察发现产品并阻止销售。get 得到；stop 停止；need 需要；where 哪里。根据"Dogs special smelling helps the …find out products"可推测这样可以阻止销售，stop 符合语境。故选B。

50.【A】句意：狗不仅成为人类最好的朋友，也是环境最好的朋友。also 也，放于句中；always 总是；either 也，放于否定句句末；too 也，放于肯定句句末。根据"…not only man's best friends"再结合but 可知，此处是also。not only…but also 为固定搭配，表示"不但……而且……"。故选A。

四、阅读理解（本大题共10小题，每小题2分，共计20分）

从A、B、C、D四个选项中，选出符合题目要求的最佳选项。

A

解析：本文是一篇记叙文。本文主要讲述了滑旱冰这项体育运动是怎样被Hoseph Merlin 发明的。

51.【A】细节理解题。根据"Merlin's work was making instruments."可知 Merlin 的工作是制作乐器。故选A。

52.【D】细节理解题。根据"Merlin was a man with many ideas and many dreams. People called him a dreamer."可知人们叫 Merlin 梦想家是因为 Merlin 有许多不同的想法。故选D。

53.【B】细节理解题。根据"He wanted to find a way to make a wonderful entrance at the party."可知梅林想到用轮子溜冰是因为他想在聚会中找一个很棒的入场方式。故选B。

54.【A】细节理解题。根据"There was just one problem. Merlin had no way to stop his roller skating."可知他进入房间后的问题是没有办法让他的旱冰鞋停下来。故选A。

55.【C】主旨大意题。这个故事讲述的是 Merlin 乐于发明制造，有很多的点子，后来他为了在一次聚会中出场更引人注意，从而发明了溜旱冰这项运动的故事。故选C。

B

解析：文章大意：本文介绍了几个中学生的英语学习方法，告诉我们对于中学生来说，光靠刻苦是不够的，还要注意学习方法。

56.【B】细节理解题。根据第二段中"They don't have effective learning methods. This is the main reason of their difficulties…"可知他们没有有效的学习方法。故选B。

57.【C】细节理解题。根据第二段中"She is a well-known English teacher in Beijing No. 4 High School."可知她是北京四中的一名老师。故选C。

58.【B】词义猜测题。根据第二段中的"They try their best at something but can't make it."可知，前后句是转折关系，他们尽力了，却没成功，所以"make it"有获得成功的意思。故选B。

59.【B】细节理解题。根据第三段中的"The more you use new words, the better you can remember them"可知，使用新单词越多，越能更好地记住它们。故选B。

60.【D】细节理解题。根据最后一段中的"I like English novels like The Old Man and Sea…In this way, I can remember more words, and make my reading and writing better."可知 A、B、C 与文章内容不符。故选 D。

第二部分 （文科类职业模块考生作答，共 15 分）

五、单项选择题（本大题共 5 小题，每小题 1 分，共计 5 分）

从 A、B、C、D 四个选项中，选出空白处的最佳选项。

61.【A】句意：下面哪一个意思是"勿踏草坪"。Please Keep Off Grass 勿踏草坪；STOP 停/禁止通行；CLEAN OUT 大甩卖；STAY CLEAR 请勿靠近。

62.【B】句意：——艾米，我还没去过宽厚里，你呢？——我也是，我们这个周末去那里吧。Me, too 我也是，表示肯定；Me neither 我也是，表示否定；I agree 我同意；I'd love to 我很乐意。根据语境可知，应该是艾米也没有去过。

63.【C】句意：——明天早上六点在这里见面怎么样？——对不起，我做不到，七点可能吗？A 是当然，你说了算；B 是当然，没问题；C 是对不起，我做不到；D 是对不起，我现在没空；根据 Will seven be OK 七点可以吗，可知，6 点不可以。

64.【A】句意：——别忘了保持至少一米的安全距离！——谢谢，我会的。Thanks, I will 谢谢，我会的；No, I can't do it 不，我不会的；Not at all 一点也不；I don't think so 我不这么认为。根据语境可知此处是回应对方的提醒。

65.【D】句意：——抱歉，已经 6 点钟了。我得下班去参加一个重要的晚宴。——好的，今天就到这儿吧。It couldn't be better 那再好不过了；You really have me there. 你真的说服我了；Take your time. 慢慢来；Let's call it a day. 今天就到这儿吧。根据语境可知，已经到了下班时间了，对方有重要的晚宴要参加，因此应结束一天的工作了。

六、阅读理解（本大题共 5 小题，每小题 2 分，共计 10 分）

从 A、B、C、D 四个选项中，选出符合题目要求的最佳选项。
解析：本文介绍了参观英美家庭的一些礼仪。

66.【C】细节理解题。根据"It is not very common that one would be invited to a British person's home."可知，很少有人会被邀请到英国人家里做客，即不太经常。故选 C。

67.【D】细节理解题。根据"If you are invited, don't ask to see more than the downstairs that your British host invites you into."可知，如果你被邀请，除了主人带你参观的楼层，不要要求去参观楼下以外的房间。故选 D。

68.【B】细节理解题。根据"To the American, most of them want their home to be a place where they can entertain（款待）and share their lives with their friends."可知，在美国，大部分人还是想把家变成一个款待朋友的地方，因此别人到家里的时候，他们会很开心。故选 B。

69.【B】词义猜测题。根据"Both British and American people will engage in quite a bit of talk and a drink or two before meals."英国人和美国人在饭前会谈一些话，或小酌一杯。可推测出，engage in 意为"参与"。故选 B。

70.【A】主旨大意题。通读全文可知，本文介绍了参观英美家庭的一些礼仪。A 选项"拜访英国人和美国人的一些礼节"符合。故选 A。

第三部分 （工科类职业模块考生作答，共 15 分）

七、单项选择题(本大题共 5 小题，每小题 1 分，共计 5 分)

从 A、B、C、D 四个选项中，选出空白处的最佳选项。

71.【D】句意："在美国，紧急呼救号码是……"常识题。

72.【A】句意："1.8 公吨等于……"1kg＝1,000g＝1,000,000mg；1t＝1,000kg；cm 厘米。

73.【A】句意："national specialty safety organization"意思是"国家专业安全机构"。

74.【A】句意："100 摄氏度跟……华氏度一样温暖。"根据公式：℉＝（℃×1.8）+32 可计算出答案。

75.【B】句意：16 除以 4 等于多少。

八、阅读理解(本大题共 5 小题，每小题 2 分，共计 10 分)

从 A、B、C、D 四个选项中，选出符合题目要求的最佳选项。

解析：本文讲述青少年床上的电子产品会影响到他们的睡眠，导致垃圾睡眠。

76.【B】主旨大意题。根据第一段"junk sleep"及"there are many electronic products in teenagers' bedrooms. They are influencing teenagers' sleep badly"，可知文章主要介绍了垃圾睡眠。故选 B。

77.【C】推理判断题。根据第二段"The survey was done among 1,000 British kids from 12 to 16. It found that 50% of them got just 4 to 7 hours' sleep every day"可知，有 1,000 个孩子参与调查，其中 50%的孩子每天只睡 4 到 7 小时，可知只睡四到七个小时的人数是 1,000×50%＝500 人。故选 C。

78.【A】推理判断题。根据第四段"We call it 'junk sleep'. It means you don't get enough sleep and the quality of the sleep is bad, too"可知，垃圾睡眠指睡眠质量不好，垃圾食品指的是质量不好的食品，可推断两者质量都不好。故选 A。

79.【C】推理判断题。根据最后一段"parents should help their children keep away from electronic products, and teenagers should spend less time on the electronic products"父母应该帮助孩子远离电子产品，青少年花费在电子产品上的时间应该更少。可知，青少年花费在电子产品上的时间太多了。故选 C。

80.【D】推理判断题。根据最后一段"parents should help their children keep away from electronic products, and teenagers should spend less time on the electronic products"可知，电子产品影响青少年的睡眠，解决问题的最好的办法是花更少的时间在电子产品上。故选 D。

九、书面表达(15 分)

One possible version：

　　Early summer is the season of disease, and prevention is very important in advance. So how do we do that?

First, try not to go out. You'd better wear masks when you go out. Second, it is very necessary to develop good habits, such as healthy diet, washing your hands and doing some exercise and so on. Third, we shouldn't stay up all night, or you'll get flu easily. We must pay attention to rest in our daily life. Last but not least, it is also very useful to keep happy and relaxed.

I think we should pay more attention to our health, not to be afraid of disease, but to prevent them actively, If we do so, we will stay away from disease.

模拟测试卷七

第一部分 共答题(所有考生作答,共70分)

一、语音(本大题共10小题,每小题1分,共计10分)

从 A、B、C、D 四个选项中,选出画线部分发音不同的一项。

1.【B】考查字母 a 的发音,在开音节中读[ei],在闭音节中读[æ],a 在 A、C、D 中读[æ],在 B 中读[ei]。

2.【C】考查字母 u 的发音,在辅音字母 l, j, r, s 后面读[uː],在闭音节中读[ʌ],在 A、B、D 中读[ʌ],在 C 中读[uː]。

3.【D】考查字母 o 的发音,在闭音节中读[ɔ],在非重读音节中读[ə],o 在 A、B、C 中读[ɔ],在 D 中读[ə]。

4.【A】考查字母组合 al 的发音,在 f, m 前读[aː],在一些重读音节中读[ɔː],al 在 B、C、D 中读[ɔː],在 A 中读[aː]。

5.【C】考查字母组合 ea 的发音,在一些重读音节中读[iː],ea 在 A、B、D 中读[iː],在 C 中读[e]。

6.【D】考查字母组合 oo 的音,oo 在 A、B、C 中读[u],在 D 中读[uː]。

7.【D】考查字母组合 our 的发音,在重读音节中读[ɔː],our 在 A、B、C 中读[ɔː],在 D 中读[auə]。

8.【B】考查字母组合 ie 的发音,在重读音节中读[ai],ie 在 B 中读[ai],在 A、C、D 中读[aiə]。

9.【C】考查字母组合 gh 的发音,gh 在 A、B、D 中不发音,在 C 中读[f]。

10.【D】考查字母 y 的发音,在非重读闭音节中读[i],在 t, f 后读[ai],y 在 A、B、C 中读[ai],在 D 中读[i]。

二、单项选择题(本大题共25小题,每小题1分,共计25分)

从 A、B、C、D 四个选项中,选出空白处的最佳选项。

11.【B】题意:我妈妈劝我再试一次。考查固定句型 persuade sb to do 劝说某人做某事。

12.【C】题意:此国家的这个区域盛产煤矿。考查短语 be rich in…在……盛产……。

13.【D】题意:我们可以通过更多练习来提高数学成绩。考查介词,通过……的方式,用介词 by。

14.【D】题意:这里有许多中文书,每一本都很好读。Both 表示两者之间,all 三者或三者以上,every 后必须加名词,不可单独用,each 可单独用,后跟 of。

15.【D】题意:在夏天有很多雨。A great deal of 修饰不可数名词。rain 不可数。

16.【A】题意:莉莉和我不仅仅是工作伙伴,还是好朋友。more than 不仅仅是。

17.【A】would rather…than…宁愿,而不愿……

18.【D】倒装结构,把 were 提前。表示与将来事实相反的虚拟语气。

19.【B】倒装结构，把 had 提前。表示与将来事实相反的虚拟语气。
20.【B】题意：我希望我知道世界上的所有事。表示与现在事实相反的愿望，主语+wish+从句主语+动词过去式。
21.【D】我希望这个实验是成功的。表示与现在事实相反的愿望，主语+wish+从句主语+动词过去式，be 一律用 were。
22.【A】他不是有钱人，但他希望自己是。he were 说明是虚拟语气，只有 wish 用于虚拟语气。
23.【D】考查宾语从句。你能猜出这时候他正在干什么吗？at this moment 就在这时，at that moment 就在那时，at moment 立刻、马上。
24.【A】考点：1）对于此类题"根据实际情况回答"。如本句问戒烟，戒了就用 yes；没有就用 no. 不要和汉语习惯混淆。You have not had dinner, have you? 你还没有吃晚饭，是吗？Yes, I had 是的，我吃过了；NO, I haven't 不，我没有吃。2）No more 不再（用于句中）Not …any more（not 标准否定句；any more 用于句尾）He smokes no more now = he doesn't smoke any more。
25.【B】题意：——你多久上一次历史课？——每隔一天，周一，周三，周五。从"Monday, Wednesday, Friday"可知是每隔一天。故选 B。
26.【B】题意：——这蛋糕看起来很漂亮。——是的，它尝起来更美味。look/taste（系动词）+ adj.（作表语）。
27.【D】你应该戒掉坏习惯，而不是沉溺其中。get rid of 戒掉（不良习惯）。
28.【C】考点分析：1）有连字符的名词全部用单数。2）see sb. doing sth. 看见某人正在做某事。
29.【D】考点分析：1）take 拿走；bring 带来；2）carry 随身携带；fetch 派人去取。
30.【B】考点分析：1）keep 是中招重点词汇之一。2）keep sb doing sth. 使某人一直做某事（用持续性动词）。3）keep on 保持；维持。4）keep sb./sth. adj 使某人/某事保持某种状态。
31.【B】考点分析：1）not（需掌握各种否定句）…until…直到……才……2）I am afraid not. 恐怕不行。
32.【C】考点分析：回答 must 开头的疑问句，用 needn't（基础题）。
33.【A】考点分析：固定搭配 sb named/called …叫……名字的人。
34.【C】考点分析：how 引导的一系列特殊疑问词（必考题）how soon；how far，how often；how long；how many；how much；how. 关于 how 的用法：1）How+形容词+句子！（感叹句）It is hot. 天气热；How hot it is! 天太热了 2）特殊疑问词（表方式或程度）How did you reach there? I got to there by bus.
35.【D】考点分析：介词+宾格 except（prep）除……之外。

三、完形填空（本大题共 15 小题，每小题 1 分，共计 15 分）

从 A、B、C、D 四个选项中，选出空白处的最佳选项。

36.【B】考查形容词。句意：我妻子会在她工作的地方附近看到一个无家可归的人。A. sick "生病的"；B. homeless"无家可归的"；C. generous "大方的"；D. energetic "精力充沛的"。根据下文"We were a step away from being homeless ourselves then"可知，此处指一个无家可归的人。故选 B。
37.【C】考查形容词。句意：那是圣诞节的前一周，她说她想给他买一件新外套，因为他的外套很破旧。A. loose"宽松的"；B. large"大的"；C. shabby"破旧的"；D. tight"紧的"。根据上文"she said she wanted to purchase a new coat for him because his coat was"可知因为他的外套很破旧所以想给他买新的。故选C。

38.【A】考查名词。句意：我们没有很多钱。A. money"金钱"；B. power"力量"；C. time"时间"；D. trouble"麻烦"。根据下文"We are really a step away from being homeless in rags most months"可知作者他们也没有很多钱。故选A。

39.【D】考查动词。句意：在大多数的月份里，我们离无家可归只有一步之遥，但我们会尽我们所能去帮助他们。A. recover"恢复"；B. bargain"讨价还价"；C. escape"逃跑"；D. help"帮助"。根据下文"We talked and found a way to get some money together"可知作者尽自己所能去帮助别人。故选D。

40.【A】考查动词。句意：我们谈了谈，想办法凑点钱给他买件外套。A. buy"购买"；B. make"制造"；C. show"展示"；D. lend"借"。根据上文"get some money together to"可知凑钱给他买了件外套。故选A。

41.【D】考查动词。句意：我坚持认为既然我们要给他一件外套，我们应该看看他还需要什么。A. commanded"命令"；B. warned"警告"；C. regretted"后悔"；D. insisted"坚持"。根据下文"since we were giving a coat to him, we should look at what else he might"可知作者坚持认为，既然我们要给他一件外套，我们应该看看他还需要什么。故选D。

42.【B】考查动词。句意：我坚持认为既然我们要给他一件外套，我们应该看看他还需要什么。A. ignore"忽略"；B. need"需要"；C. dislike"不喜欢"；D. store"商店"。根据上下文既然我们要给他一件外套，我们应该看看他还需要什么。故选B。

43.【A】考查名词。句意：我们决定在背包里装一些日常用品——牙刷、肥皂、衣服、帽子、手套和一些食物。A. backpack"背包"；B. room"房间"；C. suitcase"手提箱"；D. car"汽车"。根据下文"a toothbrush, soap, clothes, a hat, gloves and some food."可知是在背包里装一些日用品。故选A。

44.【C】考查形容词。句意：我们决定在背包里装一些日常用品——牙刷、肥皂、衣服、帽子、手套和一些食物。A. left"左边的"；B. external"外部的"；C. daily"日常的"；D. cheap"便宜的"。根据下文"a toothbrush, soap, clothes, a hat, gloves and some food."可知都是日用品。故选C。

45.【B】考查名词。句意：我们已经很多年没有钱来交换生日或圣诞节的礼物了。A. principles"原则"；B. gifts"礼物"；C. opinions"观点"；D. congratulations"恭喜"。根据下文"for birthdays or Christmas"可知是交换礼物。故选B。

46.【C】考查动词短语。句意：圣诞节有人想起你，感觉真好。A. rely on"依赖"；B. turn to"求助于"；C. think of"想起"；D. stand for"代表"。因为送出的背包，作者和妻子在圣诞节会有人想起自己。故选C。

47.【A】考查形容词。句意：当朋友问我"你圣诞节得到了什么"时，我总是有点尴尬。A. embarrassed"尴尬的"；B. contradictory"矛盾的"；C. pleased"高兴的"；D. content"满意的"。根据上文可知作者已经很多年没有交换礼物了，因此别人问起会尴尬。故选A。

48.【D】考查动词。句意：这总是让我的妻子感到难过，因为她没有钱给我任何东西，我也有同样的感觉。A. expect"期待"；B. reject"拒绝"；C. wait"等待"；D. afford"付的起"。根据下文"to give me anything"可知妻子买不起礼物。故选D。

49.【B】考查动词。句意：所以我会撒谎说她给我买了这个或那个。A. admit"承认"；B. lie "撒谎"；C. debate"辩论"；D. disagree"不同意"。根据下文"she bought me this thing or that"可知是在撒谎。故选 B。

50.【C】考查动词。句意：但那一年，我们可以说，我们向别人赠送了一些东西，而事实也确实如此。A. compared"比较"；B. exposed"暴露"；C. presented"赠送"；D. sold"出售"。根据上文可知作者和妻子那一年送给了别人东西。故选 C。

四、阅读理解（本大题共 10 小题，每小题 2 分，共计 20 分）

从 A、B、C、D 四个选项中，选出符合题目要求的最佳选项。

A

51.【C】推断题。根据 I kept the speed less than 100 kilometres per hour. 我把速度保持在每小时 100 千米以下。可知是开车，即 by car，故选 C。

52.【B】细节题。根据后句 because none of us could swim. 因为我们都不会游泳，所以买了一些救生圈，故选 B。

53.【D】细节题。根据"But my daughter was fascinated by the sand. She played with the sand with all her attention, which made us laugh. 但是我的女儿被沙子迷住了。她全神贯注地玩着沙子，这使我们笑了起来。"可知，女儿正在玩沙子，故选 D。

54.【D】细节题。根据"Of course, we had some seafood there too. 当然，我们也吃了一些海鲜。"可知，是吃了海鲜，故选 D。

55.【A】主旨题。根据全文可知主要讲了作者去北戴河旅行，故选 A。

B

56.【C】细节题。根据 Wang Yuan was born November 8th, 2000 in Chongqing. 可知王源出生在 2000 年 11 月 8 日，故选 C。

57.【B】细节题。根据 His English name is Roy. 可知英语名字是 Roy，故选 B。

58.【D】细节题。根据 He is good at singing, dancing and playing the piano. 可知他擅长唱歌、跳舞和弹钢琴，故选 D。

59.【D】细节题。根据 In January, 2017, Wang Yuan made a speech on good quality education（优质教育）in English at the United Nations in front of 500 people from around the world. 可知他在 2017 年在联合国家演讲，故选 D。

60.【A】细节题。根据 we should learn from Wang Yuan, and put our hearts into what we are doing to make a difference in our daily lives. 可知我们应该向王源学习，全心全意投入我们正在做的事情，并且在我们的日常生活中起作用，即努力工作会产生作用，故选 A。

第二部分 （文科类职业模块考生作答，共 15 分）

五、单项选择题（本大题共 5 小题，每小题 1 分，共计 5 分）

从 A、B、C、D 四个选项中，选出空白处的最佳选项。

61.【B】——人们应该停止使用汽车，改用交通工具。——确实，现在太拥挤了。

62.【A】——因为你住的如此远，要不要搭便车。——多谢，这真是再好不过了。

63. 【D】——你最好不要吃太多盐。对你的健康有害。——谢谢你的建议。
64. 【C】——你怎么能那么说呢？——很抱歉，我不是故意要伤害你的。
65. 【B】——请不要在这里吸烟。——对不起，我不会了。

六、阅读理解（本大题共5小题，每小题2分，共计10分）

从A、B、C、D四个选项中，选出符合题目要求的最佳选项。

66. 【D】细节题。根据 four year old Henry Davies…可知，Henry 4岁了，故选D。
67. 【A】细节题。根据 The next thing she remembers is fainting down on the floor 可知，亨利的母亲晕倒在地板上，故选A。
68. 【B】推理题。根据"Henry has a storybook, Ambulance Crew, on what to do in an emergency. 亨利有一本故事书《救护人员》，讲述在紧急情况下该怎么做。"可知，Henry 是通过读书知道救他母亲的知识，故选B。
69. 【A】词义辨析题。根据 He calmly dialed 999 他平静地拨打了999，可知999是个紧急应变机构，故 emergency services 是紧急应变机构的意思，故选A。
70. 【D】细节题。根据 His father, Iran, 35. 可知他的父亲29岁是错的，故选D。

第三部分 （工科类职业模块考生作答，共15分）

七、单项选择题（本大题共5小题，每小题1分，共计5分）

从A、B、C、D四个选项中，选出空白处的最佳选项。

71. 【B】hectare（公顷）是面积单位，不是容积和体积。
72. 【C】我们通常说的36.5度，等于多少华氏度？算式：36.5乘以1.8加32得到97.7。
73. 【C】4的平方减4等于12。
74. 【A】在中国，紧急呼叫号码是110，属于常识考查。
75. 【A】1.5公吨等于多少？1 t＝1,000 kg。

八、阅读理解（本大题共5小题，每小题2分，共10分）

从A、B、C、D四个选项中，选出符合题目要求的最佳选项。

76. 【C】细节理解题。根据最后一自然段最后一句可知，建立国家保健中心的最初目的是为农村居民提供免费的基本健康护理，而不是针对所有人，所以前两项错误。
77. 【C】细节理解题。根据第4自然段"The NHS is the biggest employer in Europe…"可知。从第二自然段第一句可以看出国家保健中心由中央政府直接负责，但由地方当局管理，所以A项错误。
78. 【B】细节理解题。根据最后一自然段话"and encouraging GPs to compete for patients"可知政府鼓励全科医生之间相互竞争，而不是让他们进行竞赛，看谁的医术高明。
79. 【D】猜测词义题。前面提到医生开药方及给病人治疗牙病需要收费，再结合 but 一词可推断儿童、孕妇等可享受免费治疗。
80. 【D】细节理解题。根据最后一自然段最后一句可知。

非选择题

九、书面表达(15分)

　　The increase of private cars has brought more and more serious air pollution and traffic jams in our city, especially in the rush hour.

　　So I think it's time to promote the green travel at present. In my opinion, first, we'd better not travel by car unless it's necessary. Second, people should be encouraged to choose the public transport. They can take a bus or the light rail. They can even go by underground. These ways of travel can save energy and reduce air pollution. They can also improve the traffic condition. Third, we should choose to walk or ride a bicycle if we don't go far away. Travelling on foot or by bike provide us with a chance to make us stronger and healthier.

　　In a word, I believe that we can improve the environment as well as our traffic condition if we all choose the green travel.

模拟测试卷八

第一部分 共答题(所有考生作答,共70分)

一、语音(本大题共10小题,每小题1分,共计10分)

从 A、B、C、D 四个选项中,选出画线部分发音不同的一项。

1. 【A】考查字母组合 th 的发音,在 B、C、D 中读[θ],在 A 中读[ð]。
2. 【C】考查字母 e 的发音,在闭音节中读[e],在 C 中读[i]。
3. 【B】考查字母组合 or 的发音,在一些重读音节中读[ɔː],在/w/后读[ɜː]。
4. 【C】考查字母组合 ch 的发音,在 A、B、D 中读[tʃ],在 C 中读[ʃ]。
5. 【A】考查字母 u 的发音,在一些重读音节中读[ʌ],在一些重读音节中读[u],u 在 B、C、D 中读[ʌ],在 A 中读[u]。
6. 【B】考查字母组合 wh 的发音,wh 在 A、C、D 中读[w],在 B 中读不发音。
7. 【B】考查字母组合 oa,ow 的发音,在 A、C、D 中读[əʊ],在 B 中读[aʊ]。
8. 【D】考查字母 o 的发音,o 在 s,t,l,d 前[əʊ],在 m,n,v,th 前读[ʌ]。
9. 【B】考查字母 h 的发音,在 A、C、D 中发[h],在 B 中不发音。
10. 【D】考查字母组合 ou 的发音,在 A、B、C 中 ou 发/aʊ/的音,D 中 ou 发/ʌ/的音。

二、单项选择题(本大题共25小题,每小题1分,共计25分)

从 A、B、C、D 四个选项中,选出空白处的最佳选项。

11. 【C】考点分析:1)Either...or...或者 a 或者 B(两者)。2)Neither...nor...既不是 a 也不是 B(两者)。3)Not only...but also 既是 a 又是 B。
12. 【D】考点分析:1) begin doing sth./begin to do sth. 2) at the age of ... = when sb is ... years old。
13. 【A】考点分析:固定搭配 the job is to do ...某人的工作是……
14. 【B】考点分析:1)介词+ving 所以排除 a,D;2)by 通过……方式 with 本身就有"戴"的意思,意思重复,就像 enter 不能和 into 连用:protect our environment from pollution。
15. 【A】考点分析:some,any 的区别。somewhere else 其他的某地,anywhere else 其他的任何地方。
16. 【C】考点分析:the other + ns = the others(复数);another 另一个,后加可数名词单数;Others 其他的,后跟谓语动词复数形式;one...the other...(两者)一个,另一个。
17. 【B】考点分析:考定语从句(定语从句可还原成两个简单句):all the students like the teachers, the teachers make their lessons interesting.
18. 【B】考点分析:because 与 because of 的区别(单选和完型常考题):because +从句,because of+单词。
19. 【A】考点分析:1)tell sb not to do ...(不定式的否定,基础语法知识)。2)bring 与 take 的区别,bring 带;take 拿走。

20.【D】考点分析：sometime 某个时候，sometimes 有时，some times 几次，some time 一段时间。

21.【A】考点分析：考同义词的词性区别。1) can，情态动词：He can do that。2) be able to 动词词组。He will be able to do that.

22.【C】本题考查 sth. costs...：某物值……sth be worth 钱：某物值……sb. pay 钱 for 物：某人为某物花费……；sb spend 钱 on...某人在……花费……

23.【B】考点分析：常考题 so 的用法。常与 have，be，do 或情态动词引导的倒装句连用，放于句首，"同样，也一样"。

24.【A】考点分析：常考题(特殊动词其后配 ving/to do 的不同含义)。remember doing 记得过去已做过的事，remember to do...记住将要做某事。forget doing 已经做过，却忘了，forget to do ...因没有记住而忘了。

25.【B】考点分析：It is ... for sb to do sth. 强调句。

26.【D】考点分析：考感叹句，感叹句有两种：How adj +陈述句！How cloudy it is！What n+陈述句！What a cloudy day it is！

27.【A】考点分析：1) thousands of 成千上万的（大约的概念）thousand 一千。2) 类似词：hundreds of ... millions of...

28.【C】考点分析：考对句子的理解：没有他，我不可能做出来。without（prep）+ 宾格（没有）。work out 算出。

29.【C】考点分析：how to do ...如何做某事。

30.【C】考点分析：happen to sb。

31.【A】考点分析：第一个是宾语从句；第二个是状语从句(主将从现)。

32.【C】考点分析：考时态（一般过去时）。

33.【B】考点分析：一般过去时被动语态：主+ was/were+ ved。

34.【B】考点分析：船上没有空间了（常考题，要求背此题）。room（n）空间，不可数；不要和汉语习惯"没有位置了"混淆。

35.【D】考点分析：考时态（现在完成）；这些外国人在南京已经待了两天了。(reach; arrive in; get to 都是瞬间词，不能和一段时间联用)。

三、完形填空(本大题共15小题，每小题1分，共计15分)

从 A、B、C、D 四个选项中，选出空白处的最佳选项。

36.【A】考查名词。句意：我尝试了不同的饮食方式，但是没有效果。A. diets"饮食"；B. drinks"饮料"；C. fruits"水果"；D. dishes"餐具"。故选 A。

37.【D】考查名词。A. height"身高"；B. ability"能力"；C. wisdom"聪明"；D. weight"体重"。根据上文可知，尝试了不同的饮食方式，但是没有效果，可知此处作者想表达的意思：对于自己的体重什么也做不了，故选 D。

38.【C】考查副词。A. temporarily"临时地"；B. recently"最近地"；C. seriously"严重地，严重地"；D. secretly"秘密地"。根据下文可知，"我"的体重严重地影响到了"我"。故选 C。

39.【B】考查形容词。句意："我"不想带着这额外的体重度过余生。A. ideal"理想的"；B. extra"额外的"；C. normal"正常的"；D. low"低的"。故选 B。

40.【A】考查动词。句意："我"参加了一个研讨会，在那我们被要求去创建一个可以触摸世界的项目。A. attended"参加";B. organized"组织";C. recommended"推荐,介绍";D. mentioned"提到"。故选 A。

41.【B】考查名词。A. folk"民族";B. success"成功";C. adventure"冒险";D. science"科学"。根据研讨会领导讲的故事的内容"she had not only lost 125 pounds, but also raised $25,000 for homeless children"她不仅体重减少 125 磅,而且为无家可归的孩子筹集了 25 000 美元,所以这应该是一个成功的故事,故选 B。

42.【C】考查形容词。A. Surprised"惊讶的";B. Amused"愉快的";C. Influenced"有影响的";D. Disturbed"扰乱的"。根据下文作者创建了一个项目,可知作者被研讨会领导人的故事所影响,故选 C。

43.【A】考查名词。A. project"项目";B. business"商业";C. system"系统";D. custom"习惯"。根据上文,"we were asked to create a project",出现过 project,可推测应该是我创建了"我们痊愈,世界痊愈"的项目,故选 A。

44.【D】考查介词短语。句意:我的目标是减掉 150 磅,筹集 50,000 美元,支持 30 年前创立的"结束饥饿"的运动。A. in search of"寻找";B. in need of"需要";C. in place of"代替";D. in support of"支持"。故选 D。

45.【D】考查动词。句意:治愈我和治愈世界的联合在我看来是完美的解决办法。A. scared"使害怕";B. considered"考虑";C. confused"困惑";D. struck"打击"。strike me as 意为"我认为,在我看来…"。故选 D。

46.【A】考查状语从句。A. As"当……时";B. Until"直到";C. If"如果";D. Unless"除非"。根据下文,应该是当我开始我自己的体重计划,故选 A。

47.【B】考查动词短语。句意:我害怕我像之前一样陷入困难,打击自己。A. get over"克服,恢复";B. run into"遭遇,陷入";C. look for"寻找";D. put aside"放在一边"。故选 B。

48.【A】考查形容词。句意:A. regularly"定期的,有规律的";B. limitlessly"无限制地";C. suddenly"突然地";D. randomly"随便地"。故选 A。

49.【B】考查动词。句意:一年后,我实现了目标——减掉 150 磅,并且筹集了 50,000 美金。A. set"布置,树立";B. reached"到达";C. missed"错过,想念";D. dropped"落下"。reach one's goal 固定短语,"实现某人的目标",故选 B。

50.【C】考查形容词。A. stressful 有压力的,B. painful 痛苦的,C. meaningful 有意义的,D. peaceful 和平的。这里 something 指作者自己创建的项目,是有意义的事,故选 C。

四、阅读理解(本大题共 10 小题,每小题 2 分,共计 20 分)

从 A、B、C、D 四个选项中,选出符合题目要求的最佳选项。

A

51.【B】细节理解题。解析:从第一段可知。

52.【A】推理判断题。解析:从第一句"Parents have to do much less for their children today than they used to do, and home become much less of a workshop."和下文所述可知,过去日常生活所需大部分都由自己做,"家"就如 a workshop 一样。

53.【D】词义猜测题。解析:从"When mother works, economic advantages…"可判断出。

54.【C】推理判断题。解析:由"…in many towns they have a fairly wide choice of employment and so do girls. The young wage-earner often earns good money…"可知答案。

55.【A】细节理解题。解析：见第二段"With mother earning and his older children drawing substantial wages father is seldom the dominant figure that he still was at the beginning of the century."。

B

56.【C】推理判断。根据第一段 Worrying about our problems can affect how we do at school. 可知作者是一个学生。不是店主、医生或牙医。故选 C。

57.【A】主旨大意。根据文章第一段 People all have problems. If we don't deal with these problems, we can easily become unhappy. 可知是讨论如何处理问题，故选 A。

58.【C】根据 Sometimes people can stay angry for years about a small problem. Time goes by, and good friendship may be lost 可知为小事长时间生气会失去好朋友。故选 C。

59.【B】根据 Sometimes they have disagreements, and decide not to talk to each other. 可知小孩不说话是因为他们有分歧。故选 B。

60.【B】归纳总结。根据最后一句话 This is an important lesson for us to learn. 可知长时间生气不好，所以要学会遗忘。故选 B。

第二部分 （文科类职业模块考生作答，共15分）

五、单项选择题（本大题共5小题，每小题1分，共计5分）

从 A、B、C、D 四个选项中，选出空白处的最佳选项。

61.【B】我想让你认识一下我的新朋友，莉莉。初次见面寒暄用 how do you do.。

62.【A】回答别人的感谢时，常说 you're welcome/Not at all/It's my pleasure.。

63.【C】在比赛中获得一等奖，表示祝贺。

64.【B】当某人即将做某事时，祝福好运。

65.【A】当某人外出旅行时，送行时要祝福。

六、阅读理解（本大题共5小题，每小题2分，共计10分）

从 A、B、C、D 四个选项中，选出符合题目要求的最佳选项

66.【C】细节题。根据 Many of the students seem bored. 可知许多学生对早晨已经厌倦了，故选 C。

67.【B】推断题。根据前后句可知一所学校在做早操，而另一所学校在和着流行音乐跳舞，所以 meanwhile 意思是同时，故选 B。

68.【B】细节题。根据 Since 1951, morning calisthenics(健身操)have been a part of Chinese life. 可知自从1951年，健身操已经成为中国人生活的一部分，所以已经有60多年的历史了，故选 B。

69.【A】细节题。根据 The school in Xiangyang wanted to make morning exercises more fun, so it looked to a group of people who seemed to really enjoy exercising damas(大妈)！可知大部分人认为跳舞是有趣的，故选 A。

70.【D】主旨题。根据全文可知主要讲了学生们应该像大妈一样跳舞锻炼，而不是仅仅做健身操。故选 D。

第三部分 (工科类职业模块考生作答,共15分)

七、单项选择题(本大题共5小题,每小题1分,共计5分)

从A、B、C、D四个选项中,选出空白处的最佳选项。

71.【D】10的4次方是10,000即ten thousand。

72.【B】我妹妹买地图付了平常价格的三倍。表示倍数基数词+times,A比B大(小)几倍:倍数+the 名词。

73.【A】这名新生在二班。Class 2=the second class。基数词表达中,第一个字母大写。

74.【A】九点四十的读法为nine forty。

75.【D】27的立方根乘以5等于多少。

八、阅读理解(本大题共5小题,每小题2分,共计10分)

从A、B、C、D四个选项中,选出符合题目要求的最佳选项。

76.【B】细节题。根据Animal bites(咬伤):Wash the bite area with soap and water. 可知动物咬伤时用肥皂和水清洗,故选B。

77.【C】细节题。根据Broken bones(骨头):Don't move the hurt body part while waiting for the doctor to arrive. 和Fainting(昏厥):Don't move the body if you think there might be wounds from the fall 可知当骨折和昏厥时不要移动伤者,故选C。

78.【D】细节题。根据Pinch(捏)the lower part of the nose for at least 10 minutes. 可知当流鼻血时捏鼻子更低的部分至少10分钟,而不是整个鼻子,故选D。

79.【B】推断题。根据全文可知讲了意外伤害的急救,所以可能来自健康部分,即health,故选B。

80.【A】主旨题。根据全文可知主要讲了四种意外伤害的急救知识,故选A。

非选择题

九、书面表达(15分)

  Science and technology play an important role in people's daily lives. If you compare the life of people today with that in the past, it is easy to see that science and technology have done a great deal to improve the quality of people's lives. For example, computers have become our good friends: with the help of computers, people all over the world are able to share whatever information on the net, which shortens the distance between them. With the invention of radio and TV, people now can stay at home to get themselves informed about both domestic and international news.

  But as a coin has two sides, technology can also have an negative influence upon people's lives. Now technology crimes are very common. What's more, the nuclear bomb threatens our human existence. So I think we must pay enough attention to the misuse of technology.

  In spite of its disadvantages, we should admit that technology is very useful. Without science and technology, man's life would not be as convenient as today.

模拟测试卷九

一、语音(本大题共 10 小题,每小题 1 分,共计 10 分)

从 A、B、C、D 四个选项中,选出画线部分发音不同的一项。

1. 【C】元音字母 a 在 st 前读[ɑː],其他三个是元音字母 a 在重读开音节中的读音[ei]。
2. 【A】元音字母 e 在 respond, request, replace 非重读音节中的读音是[i],region 是字母 e 的重读开音节[iː]。
3. 【A】ie 在 science, variety, diet 中读[aɪə],在 field 中读[iː]。
4. 【B】ear 在 heart 中读[ɑː],在 fear, near, year 中读[ɪə(r)]。
5. 【D】gu 在 language 中读[gw],在 dialogue, guard, figure 中不发此音。
6. 【C】o 在 hotel, devote, comb 中读[əʊ],在 cost 中读[ɒ]。
7. 【B】oo 字母组合的发音规律是:在[k],[d]之前读[u],但 food, mood 中读[uː];其他音前读[uː],但 foot 例外读[u]。
8. 【B】h 一般读[h],但在 yeah 中不发音。
9. 【D】s 在 indoors 中读[z],在 horse, host, increase 中读[s]。
10. 【C】th 在 northern 中读[ð],在 method, month, northward 中读[θ]。

二、单项选择题(本大题共 25 小题,每小题 1 分,共计 25 分)

从 A、B、C、D 四个选项中,选出空白处的最佳选项。

11. 【D】句意:你第二次犯了同样的错误,在单词"government"中少写了一个字母"n"。for a second time 再次;字母"n"的发音为[en],故用 an。
12. 【A】句意:——这两个电脑游戏你更喜欢哪个?——事实上,这两个我都不喜欢。both 表示"两者都"是肯定意思;none 表示"三者或三者以上都不",是否定意思。either"两者中任何一个",neither"两者都不"。根据 two computer games 和 I didn't like 可知是两者都不喜欢,didn't 是否定形式,用 either,故选 A。
13. 【B】dollar 前数词为 10,因此 dollar 应为复数,故选 B。
14. 【C】句意:早餐令人生厌,他每天通常吃同样的东西。never 从不,绝不;every 每个;usually 通常;sometimes 有时,因为经常吃,所以吃厌了。故选 C。
15. 【C】句意:李雷,你怎样提高你的发音?我通过在收音机上听中央电视台的新闻的方式学习。前空指"以……方式",用介词 by;后空"通过电台",用介词 on,故选 C。
16. 【A】句意:我不需要一双新鞋,我需要买一件新衬衫。need 作实义动词时,表示"需要",固定短语 need sth."需要某物",其否定形式为 don't need sth."不需要某物",根据 I need to buy a new shirt instead 可知不需要鞋子,B 选项是情态动词,不符合,故选 A。
17. 【B】句意:已经宣布这条路将于明天关闭进行维修。题干中 that the road will be closed tomorrow for repairs 主语从句,It 作形式主语,从句动词用"will+动词原型"表示将来,由此推断出空白处谓语动词应用现在的某种时态,在所给四个选项中,只有 B 项正确。
18. 【A】句意:我们学校的学生喜欢午饭后看书,除非下雨,他们大多数都坐在草地上。本

— 108 —

题前后两句话之间没有连接词，不是并列句，是一个长句，第二个句子中的 seated 一词明显为表示"就座"意义的非谓语动词，故应该是 most of them 作 seated 非谓语动词的逻辑主语，即非谓语动词的独立主格结构。

19.【A】句意：和我们学习相关的事当然需要认真对待。The matter related to our study，这里是过去分词作后置定语；require doing = require to be done。

20.【A】句意：Jennifer 没有参与这项研究，这让她的妈妈很担心。involved 参与；responded 回答；inspired 激励；persuaded 说服。根据句意及所给句子可知，此处是固定短语 be involved in 参与。

21.【B】句意：这个年轻的妈妈看到孩子掉到了地上，把她吓得心提到了嗓子眼。分析句子可知，逗号前后没有连词，故排除 A、D；用 and 连接两个句子，且在此用 that 作主语，指代上文中的这件事；which 表示"哪一个"，不合语境，故答案选 B。

22.【C】句意：汤姆的、指针是金子制成的手表非常昂贵。句中包含定语从句，先行词是 watch 和 hands 的关系是手表的指针，故用关系代词 whose。

23.【C】句意：李白是中国的一位伟大的诗人，他的出生地是众所周知的，但有些人不愿接受这一事实。分析句子结构可知，a great Chinese poet 做 Li Bai 的同位语，is 前面是主语从句，比较选项中有 where 符合句意，where 在从句中作地点状语，故选 C。

24.【B】句意：如果你错过这次机会，可能要等多年后才会再有。it be + 时间段 + before…表示"要过多久才会……"。

25.【B】句意：请不要打电话到我的办公室，除非是真的有必要。before 在……以前；unless 除非，引导条件状语从句；although 尽管；till 直到……为止。

26.【B】句意：父亲说："对客人一定要有礼貌。"引号中是一个表强调的祈使句，祈使句的强调是在动词前加 Do，be polite 有礼貌。

27.【C】句意：前天，我爸除了几副眼镜什么也没有买。分析句子可知，设空处是谓语动词，由 the day before yesterday 判断为一般过去时，but 意为"除了"时适用就远原则，即谓语动词根据 nothing 来确定，nothing 是第三人称单数，且此处是被动语态，be 应用 was。

28.【D】句意：就是在年轻的时候他接受的训练让他成为一名好的工程师。第一空是定语从句，关系代词 which 指代先行词 the training 作为句中动词 had 的宾语，指在年轻的时候所接受的训练；第二空的 that 与句首的 it was 构成强调句型。

29.【D】句意：尽管她尝试了，Sue 不能打开门。as 引导的让步状语从句，应将状语、表语、谓语提前构成形式上的倒装。

30.【A】句意：男孩在街上骑车，但他妈妈叫他不要这么做。不定式的内容如果前面出现了，为避免重复，可以省略后面的 do，只保留不定式符号 to。

31.【A】句意：这是她第一次目睹这么大的雨。It was the first time that…为固定句型，that 引导的从句中使用过去完成时。

32.【C】句意：我的很多同学不喜欢熬夜做作业，是吗？一般来说反意问句是前肯后否，但是 dislike 虽然意思是不喜欢，但是前半句仍然是肯定句式，所以用 don't they，不用 do they。

33.【C】句意：我们都知道琥珀屋是俄国人的。此句 it 作形式主语，that the Amber Room belings to the Russians 作真正的主语。

34.【B】句意：强烈建议机器每年进行一次检查。It is strongly recommended that…强烈建议……，从句用 should+动词原形的虚拟语气，should 可以省略，主语 the machine 与 check

之间为被动关系,所以用被动语态。

35.【C】句意:被拒绝了太多次,让他觉得自己毫无价值。value 价值;invaluable 无价的;valueless 没有价值的,没用的;valuable 有价值的。

三、完形填空(本大题共 15 小题,每小题 1 分,共计 15 分)

从 A、B、C、D 四个选项中,选出空白处的最佳选项。
解析:文章大意:本文是一篇记叙文。一个秋天的晚上,一个勇敢的男孩在回家的路上发现水库的大坝上有一个小洞,由于知道大坝决堤的危险,他一晚上都用手指堵着这个洞。第二天早上一个农民发现后叫来了其他村民把洞堵上,把他送回了家,每个人都为这个男孩感到骄傲。

36.【C】句意:秋季的一天……spring 春天;summer 夏天;autumn 秋天;winter 冬天,根据第二段的第一句"in autumn"可知是在秋天,故选 C。

37.【C】句意:然后,Hans 决定回家。clean 打扫;find out 找到;return to 返回;draw 画画,根据第二段中"On his way home"可知此处指他要返回家,故选 C。

38.【D】句意:水库的水位在秋天通常会升高。dirtier 更脏;colder 更冷;quieter 更安静;higher 更高,根据第三段"Then the dam could break and the whole Harlem would be covered by the water"可知水大,说明水位高,故选 D。

39.【A】句意:Hans,要小心点。careful 小心的;kind 热心的;clever 聪明的;helpful 有帮助的。根据"Be"及语境可知是老人嘱咐 Hans 在路上要小心些,故选 A。

40.【B】句意:突然,天变黑了,开始下起了大雨。Surely 当然;Suddenly 突然;Finally 最终;Normally 正常地,根据"the sky got dark and heavy rain began to fall"可知是突然大雨倾盆而下,故选 B。

41.【C】句意:Hans 感到害怕,开始跑起来。jump 跳;wait 等待;run 跑;work 更脏,根据"Hans felt afraid and started to…"可知,Hans 害怕的跑起来,故选 C。

42.【B】句意:然后注意到水坝里有一个小洞。made 制造;noticed 注意到;dug 挖;felt 感觉,根据"He looked around carefully"可知,应该是注意到大坝上有一个洞,只有 notice 符合句意,故选 B。

43.【A】句意:Hans 感到害怕,因为他知道会发生什么。because 因为;even if 即使;before 在……之前;so that 以至于,根据"he knew what could happen"是他害怕的原因,故选 A。

44.【D】句意:这个洞变得越来越大。rain 雨;dam 水坝;finger 手指;hole 洞,根据前文"a very small hole in the dam"可知水坝上有个洞,推出这个洞越来越大,故选 D。

45.【C】句意:他把手指伸进洞里,这样水就不会流出来了。unless 除非;when 当……时;so 因此;but 但是,空格前后句是因果关系,前是因后是果,故选 C。

46.【D】句意:Hans 大喊。regretted 遗憾;expected 期待;imagined 想象;shouted 大喊,根据"Please, someone, help me"可知这是他大喊救命的声音,故选 D。

47.【A】句意:但他不能离开大坝。leave 离开;believe 相信;see 看到;build 建造,根据"All night long, Hails waited and waited",推出他不能离开大坝,故选 A。

48.【C】句意:我想让水停下来。rabbits 兔子;people 人;water 水;river 河,根据"I am trying to stop the"可知他在堵住这个洞,想阻止水蔓延,故选 C。

49.【B】句意:他们迅速修好了这个洞。discovered 发现;repaired 修理;developed 发展;

110

protected 保护，根据"The farmer called some other people and they quickly"可知，在其他人的帮助下，他们修好了这个洞，故选 B。

50.【A】句意：每个人都为那个勇敢的男孩感到骄傲。brave 勇敢的；patient 耐心的；active 活跃的；cute 可爱的，根据"Everyone was very proud of that"可知，Hans 堵住水坝洞口，说明他是勇敢的男孩，故选 A。

四、阅读理解（本大题共 10 小题，每小题 2 分，共计 20 分）

从 A、B、C、D 四个选项中，选出符合题目要求的最佳选项。

A

解析：本文介绍了中国数字化的发展，数字化给中国人民的生活带来非常大的便利，中国也在促进 5G 通信技术的发展。

51.【B】细节理解题。根据第二段第二句"People take less cash（现金）with them because most of the stores and hotels accept WeChat Pay and Alipay."可知，由于大多数商店和酒店接受微信支付和支付宝支付，所以人们随身携带的现金较少了。由此说明用手机在线支付更方便（比使用现金方便）。故选 B。

52.【D】推理判断题。根据原文第三段第二句"You can shop…finger taps."可知，你可以利用手机购物、旅行、交流、娱乐，所有的活动只需用手指点击几下。文中没有提到利用手机能做饭。由此判断通过使用手机，你可以做很多事情除了烹饪美味的东西。故选 D。

53.【C】词义猜测题。根据第三段内容"You can shop, travel, communicate, have fun by using a mobile phone, and all of these tasks can be completed with a few finger taps"可知，有了手机可以做很多事情。由此推测没有了手机，人们的生活不可能是"有趣的""令人惊奇的""刺激的"，只能是"无聊的"，符合语境。故选 C。

54.【A】细节理解题。根据第五段内容"At the two sessions…long distance calls would be canceled."可知，在两会上，李克强总理指出，2017 年移动的速度网络将会提高，成本将会大大降低。国内漫游费和长途电话费将被取消。由此说明，使用手机的成本更低了。故选 A。

55.【D】推理判断题。根据最后一段"In 2020, China's 5G network is in service. It helps China's mobile telecommunication overtake（反超）the international community's"可知，在 2020 年，中国的 5G 网络投入使用。它帮助中国的移动通信反超国际社会。由此推断选项 D"中国的 5G 网络已经投入使用。"正确。故选 D。

B

解析：本文讲述了 Gibb 为了参加只允许男性选手参加的波士顿马拉松，进行了刻苦训练，并且通过伪装成功参加了比赛，并且超过了大多数男选手，成为第一位参加波士顿马拉松的女性。

56.【B】推理判断题。根据"It has a 125-year history."可知，马拉松有着 125 年的历史，今年是 2022 年，所以是始于 1897 年，故选 B。

57.【D】词句猜测题。分析"She wore her brother's shorts and a shirt to disguise that she was a woman."可知，她穿着她哥哥的短裤和衬衫来伪装她是一个女人。所以 disguise 的意思是"伪装"，与"掩盖"意思相近，故选 D。

111

58.【C】细节理解题。根据"That year she took part in the Boston Marathon and finished faster than most of the men."可知，她跑得比大多数男子都快，故选C。

59.【C】细节理解题。根据"For nearly two years, Gibb trained hard to prepare for the race."可知，她训练了将近两年，故选C。

60.【D】主旨大意题。本文向我们介绍第一个参加波士顿马拉松的女性Gibb，故选D。

第二部分 （文科类职业模块考生作答，共15分）

五、单项选择题（本大题共5小题，每小题1分，共计5分）

从A、B、C、D四个选项中，选出空白处的最佳选项。

61.【D】句意：——你好，你是谁？——我是William。That's Jane 那是Jane；I'm Mike 我是Mike；This is William speaking 我是William。根据Who's that speaking可知此处是打电话用语，可用This is...speaking。

62.【C】句意：——我没找到去邮局的路。——怎么会呢？我今天早上告诉你了。no problem 没问题；Not really 真的没有；How come? 怎么会呢？That's for sure 那是肯定的。根据语境可知，空格所填内容应该为"怎么会呢？"。

63.【D】句意：——这些天我感觉不舒服。医生，我有什么问题吗？——别担心，没什么严重的。Don't mention it 别客气；You are kind 你太好了；No problem 没问题；Don't worry 别担心。根据语境可知，对方身体没什么大问题，医生告诉他不用担心。

64.【B】句意：——出去吃饭吗？我请客。——听起来很不错，可是我要写作业。

65.【A】句意：_____意思是你可以在这里掉头。A 可以在这里掉头；B 单行线；C 不准在这里掉头；D 停／禁止通行。

六、阅读理解（本大题共5小题，每小题2分，共计10分）

从A、B、C、D四个选项中，选出符合题目要求的最佳选项。

【解析】本文主要介绍了英国人的名字构成。

66.【C】细节理解题。根据"Most English people have a first name, a middle name and the family name"可知大部分英国人的名字有三部分：名字、中间名和姓。故选C。

67.【D】细节理解题。根据"Green is my family name. My parents gave me both of my other names"可知父母给孩子取名字和中间名。故选D。

68.【A】细节理解题。根据"They use Mr., Mrs. or Miss with the family name but never with the first name."可知他们把Mr.、Mrs.或Miss与姓氏一起使用。故选A。

69.【D】细节理解题。根据"That's because it is shorter and easier than（比）James."可知人们叫他Jim是因为它更短更容易叫。故选D。

70.【B】最佳标题题。本文主要介绍了英国人的名字构成，故以选项B"英国人的名字"为标题更合适。故选B。

第三部分 （工科类职业模块考生作答，共15分）

七、单项选择题（本大题共5小题，每小题1分，共计5分）

从A.B、C、D四个选项中，选出空白处的最佳选项。

71. 【D】句意:"……不是面积单位。"square millimeter 平方毫米;hectare 公顷;square kilometer 平方千米;centimeter(cm)厘米是长度(length)单位。

72. 【B】句意:DANGER:BURIED CABLE 意思是"危险:地下埋有电缆"。WARNING:MEN WORKING ABOVE 警示:上方有人干活;DANGER:BURIED CABLE 危险:地下埋有电缆;CAUTION:OPEN PIT 小心深坑;EMERGENCY:911,FIRE RESCUE POLICE 紧急呼叫:911,火灾救援警察。

73. 【A】句意:53.273 读作 fifty-three point two hundred and seventy-three。

74. 【A】句意:Rated power 意思是"额定功率"。

75. 【C】句意:125 的立方根加上 3 的平方等于 14。

八、阅读理解(本大题共 5 小题,每小题 2 分,共计 10 分)

从 A、B、C、D 四个选项中,选出符合题目要求的最佳选项。
解析:本文主要介绍了在中国政府的领导下西藏发生的变化。

76. 【B】细节理解题。根据"In old Tibet, about 5 percent of the population owned almost all of the land, forests, mountains and rivers."可知在旧西藏百分之五的人口拥有这片土地。故选 B。

77. 【A】细节理解题。根据"Thanks to the leadership of the Chinese government, Tibet is catching up with other parts of the country."可知西藏会赶上中国其他地区是因为中国政府的领导。故选 A。

78. 【A】细节理解题。根据"It has also made great progress in improving its environment, spending 81.4 billion yuan on the area by the end of last year."可知截至去年年底,西藏在环境保护方面投入了 814 亿元。故选 A。

79. 【C】细节理解题。根据"By the end of 2019, all poor people in Tibet had shaken off poverty for the first time in history."可知到 2019 年底西藏贫困人口全部摆脱贫困。故选 C。

80. 【D】推理判断题。根据"People's life has risen from 35.5 years in 1951 to 71.1 years in 2019."可知人们的寿命从 1951 年的 35.5 岁提高到 2019 年的 71.1 岁,由此推出 2019 年人们的寿命比 1951 年长了 35.6 年。故选 D。

九、书面表达(15 分)

One possible version:

Dear Steve,

Knowing that you are interested in the traditional Chinese festival, which is called Dragon Boat Festival. I am writing to introduce it to you.

The Dragon Boat Festival falls on the fifth day of the fifth lunar month in honor of the great poet, Qu Yuan. On that day, we often eat rice-dumplings and drink a special wine. Besides, what should be stressed is the dragon-boat racing, which is very interesting and exciting. people gather on the both sides of the river to watch the participants spare no effort to make for the finishing line.

The Dragon Boat Festival is coming. Would you like to join us to spend it?

Yours,
Li Hua

模拟测试卷十

一、语音(本大题共 10 小题,每小题 1 分,共计 10 分)

从 A、B、C、D 四个选项中,选出画线部分发音不同的一项。

1.【D】元音字母 e 在 depend 非重读音节中的读音是[i],medal,lecture,helicopter 是字母 e 的重读开音节[e]。

2.【A】元音字母 u 在 public,result,rubber 中重读闭音节读音[ʌ],其 pollute 中读[uː]。

3.【A】元音字母 o 在 remove 中读[uː],在 slope,stone,stove 中读[əʊ]。

4.【C】or 在 sorry 中读[ɒ],在 sort,sport,storm 中读[ɔː]。

5.【B】ow 在 toward 中读[əw],在 tomorrow,unknown,widow 中读[əʊ]。

6.【D】wh 在 who 中读[h],在 wheat,wheel,whistle 中读[w]。

7.【C】c 在 cellar 中读[s],在 bicycle,broadcast,cart 中读[k]。

8.【D】b 在 blame 中读[b],在 climb,comb,debt 中不发音。

9.【B】ch 在 headache 中读[k],在 coach,kitchen,match 中读[tʃ]。

10.【B】s 在清辅音后读[s],在浊辅音或元音后读[z]。

二、单项选择题(本大题共 25 小题,每小题 1 分,共计 25 分)

从 A、B、C、D 四个选项中,选出空白处的最佳选项。

11.【A】句意:世界读书日是 4 月 23 日。这是由英国在 1995 年创建的一个特殊的日子,根据时间状语 April 23,可知这是具体到了某一天,应用时间介词 on,根据 special 的首字母发音/s/,可知这是辅音,故用 a,故选 A。

12.【D】句意:你应该诚实,在考试中不要抄袭别人的答案。anybody else 其他人,else 放在不定代词后面,其所有格在 else 后加 's。所以选 D。

13.【D】句意:——你觉得她教英语怎么样?——很棒!我们学校没有人比她教得更好了。根据句意用比较级,worse 意为"更糟糕",better 意为"更好",故选 D。

14.【B】句意:这个地区三分之二被树木覆盖。分数的构成:分子用基数词,分母用序数词,分子大于一,分母加-s。分数作主语,谓语动词的单复数根据分数后面的名词而定。area 是不可数名词,故选 B。

15.【A】句意:为了纪念这个英雄,他们在镇中心修建了一个雕像。in memory of 意为"为了纪念",in memory 意为"在记忆里",from memory 意为"凭记忆",with memory 意为"带着记忆"。

16.【C】句意:河上没有桥,所以我们乘船过河。across 介词,穿过;cross 动词,穿过。根据第一个空所在的句子有 be 动词 is,所以空缺处用介词 across,表示"横跨河流",排除 A 和 B,第二个空所在的句子缺少谓语动词,所以用 cross,排除 D,故选 C。

17.【C】句意:他的英语口语很好,因为他来自澳大利亚,一个讲英语的国家。spoken English 英语口语,形容词 spoken 作定语;English-speaking country 讲英语的国家,复合形容词 English-speaking 作定语。故选 C。

18.【D】句意：这个可怜的女孩因为近来一直咳嗽不得不去看医生。根据时间状语 lately 和动作一直在进行，要用现在完成进行时，结构为 have/has been doing，故选 D。

19.【A】句意：在任何不安全的环境中，只按一下按钮，一个训练有素的工作人员就会带给你所需的帮助。句型：祈使句+and/or+表将来的陈述句。所以此处是祈使句部分，用动词原型。

20.【A】句意：因为对英语感兴趣，他加入一家俱乐部练习说好英语。interested 表示"感兴趣的"，主语是人，interested in "对……感兴趣"；practice doing sth. 练习做某事，故选 A。

21.【B】句意：没有公交车来，我们不得不走回家了。there be 表示"存在……有……"。独立主格形式为 n. +v-ed 表示被动关系；n+v-ing 表示主动关系。we had to walk home 是一个完整的句子，且与"_____ no but"主语不同，需要用独立主格形式，there 与 bus 为主动关系，故选 B。

22.【B】句意：我将于今年六月毕业于北京大学，获得硕士学位。come up with 提出，想出；graduate from 从……毕业；根据句意可知应用动词短语 graduate from，是谓语动词，根据空前的助动词 will，可知应用一般将来时。

23.【B】句意：我的电话坏了，你能告诉我有关新冠的最新消息吗？lately 最近，近来；latest 最近的，最新的；later 后来，较晚；later 后者，稍后。此处形容词作定语。

24.【C】句意：这就是那个他在会议上解释的工作粗心的原因吗？_____ at the meeting for his carelessness in his work 是限制性定语从句，先行词是 the reason，指事物，且有 the only 修饰且在从句中作宾语，只能用关系代词 that，也可省略，故选 C。

25.【D】句意：这就是你在信中所说的我们要住的酒店吗？此题会让人误认为是定语从句，you said 是插入语，从句中缺少地点状语，不缺少主语或宾语，因此用 where，此句子结构为由 where 引导的地点状语从句作表语。

26.【A】句意：他说他两星期前看望了他初中的老师们。before 一般用在过去完成时，且 before 置于时间段后。

27.【D】句意：这是一本很有趣的书。不管花多少钱要把它买下来。这里考查状语从句，however much＝no matter how much 无论多少钱。

28.【A】句意：委员会由 20 个成员组成，都是医学专家。the committee "委员会"，是一个整体概念，谓语动词用单数，故填 is；who _____ experts in medicine 是一个非限制性定语从句，先行词 members，在从句中作主语，谓语动词用复数，故填 are。

29.【D】句意：你在一个错误的地方等，大巴车就在宾馆接了游客。本句中强调句型：It is/was + that/who+其他成分。强调地点状语 at the hotel，其中的 it is 和 that 是可以省略的，因为被强调的成分并不表示人，所以不用 who。

30.【C】句意：北京提供这么多有趣的地方，以至于游客还没看完就没时间了。so…that…句型的倒装用法：so/such 放在句首时，后面用部分倒装，即将 be 动词、助动词、情态动词提到主语前。

31.【A】句意：如果没有现代的电信业，要想得到世界各地的消息，我们就不得不等几个星期。本题是一个表示与现在相反的 if 引导的虚拟条件句，if 从句中使用 did/were，主句中使用"情态动词(would/could/should/might)+动词原型"；而 if 虚拟条件句发生省略和倒装的条件是：从句谓语部分含有 were/had/should，若满足该条件，可将 if 省去，将 were/had/should 提于句首，发生部分倒装。

32. 【A】句意：——Della 怎么了？——噢，她父母不允许她去参加那个聚会，但是她还是想去。原句是 she still hopes to go to the party. 因此选择 A，是动词不定式的省略。

33. 【D】句意：——今晚出去散步如何？——听起来不错。此处指这个主意听起来不错，主语是单数，动词也用单数。

34. 【A】句意：我认为他昨天晚上不可能做出这傻事，是不是？I don't think 是主句，he could have done such a stupid thing last night 为宾语从句，作动词 think 的宾语，当主句主语为第一人称，且谓语动词为 think，变反义疑问句时，否定要还原；could have done 是表示猜测的，其反义疑问句应该按照表推测的情态动词之后的句子 he didn't do such a stupid thing last night 来变。

35. 【B】句意：——洞庭湖是中国最大的湖吗？——不，它是中国第二大湖。large 是一个形容词，意思是大的。这里考查的是句型 the second+形容词最高级，表示第二大……，of……中，表示同类范围。

三、完型填空（本大题共 15 小题，每小题 1 分，共计 15 分）

从 A、B、C、D 四个选项中，选出空白处的最佳选项。

解析：文章讲述了一个小男孩想一次性把一把坚果从罐子里拿出来，结果手被卡在了罐子瓶口。在妈妈的建议下，丢弃了几个才把手拿出来。这个故事告诉我们，人不能太贪婪，否则可能适得其反。

36. 【C】句意：我肯定如果我妈妈在这里，她一定会给我的。while 当……时；because 因为；if 如果；whether 是否。根据"I'm sure my mother will give them to me"与"she is here."可知，两句之间是条件关系，应用 if 引导条件状语从句，故选 C。

37. 【D】句意：于是他把手伸进罐子里。put into 把……放进；took out 拿出；push into 推进；reached into 把手伸进。根据"I want some to eat now."可知，男孩把手伸进罐子里拿坚果，故选 D。

38. 【A】句意：由于他很饿，他尽可能多地抓了一些。many 很多，修饰复数名词；much 很多，修饰不可数名词；some 一些；few 几乎没有。根据"As he was very hungry"可知，男孩抓了尽可能多的坚果，空格修饰 nuts，应用 many 修饰，故选 A。

39. 【A】句意：但当他想把手拉出来时，发现罐子口太小了。hand 手；head 头；mouth 嘴巴；legs 腿。根据"His hand was held fast."可知，是想把手拉出来，故选 A。

40. 【B】句意：但当他想把手拉出来时，发现罐子口太小了。big 大的；small 小的；large 大的；tiny 极小的，侧重极小的东西。根据"His hand was held fast."及常识可知，罐子的口太小了所以抓了坚果的手取不出来，故选 B。

41. 【B】句意：他的手被罐子卡住了，但他不想丢下任何他从罐子里抓的坚果。to drop 动词不定式；drop 动词原形；dropping 是动名词形式或者动词的现在分词形式；dropped 动词的过去式或者过去分词。根据 want to，可知是动词结构 want to do 想做某事，故选 B。

42. 【A】句意：他试了一次又一次，但始终拿不出整把坚果。tried 尝试；did 做；thought 认为；threw 扔。根据"again and again, but he couldn't get the whole handful out all the time."可知，男孩一次又一次地尝试把手拿出来，故选 A。

43. 【C】句意：最后他哭了起来。Recently 最近；Luckily 幸运地是；Finally 最后；Simply 简直。根据"He...again and again, but he couldn't get the whole handful out all the time."可知，

他已经尝试了很多次了，但是都没有成功，所以最后他哭了，故选 C。

44.【C】句意：我不能把这一把坚果从罐子里拿出来。in 在……里；off 离开；out of 从……出来；into 到……里面。take…out of…"把……从……取出"，故选 C。

45.【D】句意：只要拿两三个，你就可以毫不费力地把手拿出来了。to give 给，动词不定式；giving 给，动名词；to get 得到，不定式；getting 得到，动名词。根据"your hand out"可知，此处指的是容易把手拿出来，英语表达为 get your hand out，此处是 have trouble（in）doing sth. 的结构，所以应用动名词形式，故选 D。

46.【A】句意：那太容易了! easy 容易的；difficult 困难的；interesting 有趣的；boring 无聊的。根据"'Well, don't be so greedy,' his mother replied. 'Just take two or three, and you'll have no trouble…your hand out.'"可知，在妈妈的指导下，男孩的手很容易地从罐子里拿出来了，故选 A。

47.【A】句意：男孩一边把手从罐子上拉出来一边说。the jar 罐子；the room 房间；his mother 他的妈妈；his neck 他的脖子。根据"I can't take this handful of nuts…the jar"可知，手被卡在罐子里，此处说的是手从罐子里拿出来了，故选 A。

48.【B】句意：我本来应该自己想到的。itself 它自己；myself 我自己；yourself 你自己；herself 她自己。根据"'How…that was!' said the boy as he moved his hand off…'"可知，男孩认为自己应该想到的，引用男孩的原话用 myself，故选 B。

49.【B】句意：如果我们想一次完成一件事，也许事情会走向相反的方向。right 正确的；opposite 相反的；possible 可能的；same 相同的。根据 if we want to finish a thing in one time 如果我们想一次性完成一件事，可知这样做可能会"适得其反"，故选 B。

50.【B】句意：这是最好的成功之道。answer 回答；way 方法；information 信息；example 例子。根据"Do things step by step!"以及"Only like that can we go further."可知，这里说的是循序渐进地做事情才是成功的最佳方法，故选 B。

四、阅读理解（本大题共 10 小题，每小题 2 分，共计 20 分）

从 A、B、C、D 四个选项中，选出符合题目要求的最佳选项。

A

解析：本文是一篇记叙文。主要记叙了河北省的一个贫困村——沙石峪在中国共产党脱贫攻坚的正确领导下，在全体村民的共同努力下，发生了翻天覆地的变化的故事。

51.【A】细节理解题。根据文中"In the ancient Chinese story, Yu Gong could move mountains with his strong will and hard work, why can't we?"可知，张贵顺用愚公的故事来激励村民是因为愚公意志坚强，工作努力。故选 A。

52.【B】细节理解题。根据文中"Led by the Communist Party of China（中国共产党），the villagers carried water and soil to their village from faraway places to improve their land."可知，从 1966 年到 1971 年，村民们把水和土壤运到他们的村庄改善土地来改善他们的生活状况。故选 B。

53.【A】推理判断题。根据文中"Led by the Communist Party of China（中国共产党），the villagers carried water and soil to their village from faraway places to improve their land. From 1966 to. 1971, they reclaimed（开垦）lots of land and greatly improved their life."和"and villagers started grape cultivation, which soon became a main industry in Shashiyu."可推理出，

沙石峪的村民是很勤奋的。故选 A。

54.【D】推理判断题。根据文中"In 2009, the city-level government invested over 1 million yuan ($152,723) to change the village's exhibition hall into a museum in memory of development efforts made by earlier generations. After 10 years, the village was called 'National Forest Village'."可推理出，沙石峪在2019年被称为"国家森林村"。故选 D。

55.【B】推理判断题。短文主要记叙了河北省的一个贫困村——沙石峪在中国共产党脱贫攻坚的正确领导下，在全体村民的共同努力下，发生了翻天覆地的变化的故事，这是一篇新闻报道，故推理出，你可能在报纸上读到这篇文章。故选 B。

B

解析：本文报道了中国的植树造林在应对全球气候变化中起到的重大作用。

56.【C】推理判断题。根据"A recent study in the journal *Nature* shows that the amount of carbon dioxide absorbed by new forests in two parts of China is more than we thought"可知，《自然》杂志最近的一项研究表明，中国现在的二氧化碳排放量减少了，故选 C。

57.【A】细节理解题。根据"A carbon sink is a natural area like a forest or ocean that absorbs more carbon dioxide than it emits. Carbon sinks help to reduce the amount of CO_2 in the atmosphere"，可知碳汇吸收的二氧化碳要比排放的多，故选 A。

58.【B】细节理解题。根据"China's goal is to peak its CO_2 emissions before 2030 and reach carbon neutrality by 2060, Xinhua reported"，可知中国将在2030年后降低二氧化碳排放量，故选 B。

59.【D】细节理解题。根据"A recent study in the journal Nature shows that the amount of carbon dioxide absorbed by new forests in two parts of China is more than we thought. These areas are in the northeastern Heilongjiang and Jilin provinces and the southwestern Yunnan and Guizhou provinces and Guangxi Zhuang autonomous region. They make up about 35 percent of China's land-based carbon sinks"，可知是说这两个地区森林吸收的二氧化碳量约占中国陆地碳汇的35%，而不是中国35%的土地受到了二氧化碳排放的影响；"35 percent of China's land has been affected by CO_2 emission"陈述错误，故选 D。

60.【C】推理判断题。通读全文，结合"Climate change is a global challenge. One way to fight it is by reducing the amount of carbon dioxide in the air. New research shows that trees planted in China have helped in this fight"，可知植树造林有利于实现减少碳排放的目标，所以未来会种植更多的树木，故选 C。

第二部分 （文科类职业模块考生作答，共15分）

五、单项选择题（本大题共5小题，每小题1分，共计5分）

从 A、B、C、D 四个选项中，选出空白处的最佳选项。

61.【B】句意：——你好，我能为你做什么？——我只是看看，谢谢。May I speak to Alice 我可以和爱丽丝说话吗；What can I do for you 我能为你做什么；May I take your order 您点什么菜；Could you tell me your name 你能告诉我你的名字吗。根据 i'm just looking, thanks 可知此处是指自己仅仅是看看，这是一个购物场景，所以对方应该说"我能为你做什么？"。

62.【C】句意：——你去年去黄山的旅行怎么样？——真的非常好，我希望再去那里。We drove there 我们开车去那；It took me two hours 花费了我两个小时；It was really great 真的非常好；People there were friendly 那里的人们很友好。根据语境可知，询问对旅行的评价。

63. 【B】句意：——这是一次奇妙的旅行。那么，你最喜欢哪个城市，杭州、苏州还是扬州？——很难说，他们都有优点和缺点。No problem 没问题；It is hard to say 很难说；Enjoy yourself 玩得高兴！You must be joking 你一定在开玩笑。根据语境可知，应该是很难说。

64. 【B】句意：——火车要开动了，我得走了。——保重！我会非常想念你的。Let it go 任它去；Take care 保重；Come on 快点；Don't mention it 别客气。根据语境可知告别时要让对方保重。

65. 【C】句意：——这双鞋20美元。——好的，我买了。You're welcome 别客气；Here you are 给你；I'take them 我买了；Yes, you are right 是的，你说得对。根据对方介绍的价格，结合上文的肯定回答OK，可知决定买这双鞋。

六、阅读理解(本大题共5小题，每小题2分，共计10分)

从A、B、C、D四个选项中，选出符合题目要求的最佳选项。
解析：本文是一篇说明文，主要介绍了世界各地新年的食物。

66. 【A】细节理解题。根据第二段"They are the symbol of happiness and richness for a family."可知，它们是一个家庭幸福和富裕的象征。故选A。

67. 【D】细节理解题。根据第三段"And when it is twelve o'clock at night and the New Year begins, people will eat twelve grapes."可知，当晚上十二点的时候，新年开始了，人们会吃十二颗葡萄。结合选项可知，D选项描述的是人们会吃二十个葡萄，与文章内容不符。故选D。

68. 【B】细节理解题。根据第三段"In Spain, families like to get together, listen to music and play games. And when it is twelve o'clock at night and the New Year begins, people will eat twelve grapes."可知，西班牙庆祝新年的方式是在晚上十二点的时候，吃十二颗葡萄。故选B。

69. 【A】细节理解题。根据第四段"They mean tuanyuan."可知，中国人喜欢吃饺子，是因为它们意味着团圆。故选A。

70. 【B】主旨大意题。通读全文可知，文章第一段引出不同国家新年食物的话题，第二段描述了美国新年食物——鲱鱼；第三段描述了西班牙新年食物——葡萄；第四段描述了中国新年食物——饺子；最后一段做总结。可见本文主要讲述了不同国家的新年食物。故选B。

第三部分 （工科类职业模块考生作答，共15分）

七、单项选择题(本大题共5小题，每小题1分，共计5分)

从A、B、C、D四个选项中，选出空白处的最佳选项。

71. 【B】句意：3的3次方减5等于22。

72. 【A】句意：零下5摄氏度写作_____。

73. 【B】句意：公顷不是容量或体积的单位。milliliter 毫升；hectare 公顷；cubic centimeter 立方厘米；cubic meter 立方米。

74. 【A】句意：_____清楚地标记出故障的机器、正在修理的或者已经停止使用的机器。Bold signs 醒目标志；Construction warning signs 建筑警告标志；Chemicals safety signs 化学品安全标志；Electrical equipment warning signs 电气设备警告标志。

75.【A】句意：作为雇主或雇员，基本安全的重要性怎么强调都不为过。overstressed 过分强调；overworked 过分劳累的；overnight 整晚的；overtime 在规定时间之外。

八、阅读理解（本大题共 5 小题，每小题 2 分，共计 10 分）

从 A、B、C、D 四个选项中，选出符合题目要求的最佳选项。

解析：研究发现，过度使用电子产品会影响人们的睡眠、学习和工作，因此美国从 2010 起设立了一个全国断网日，在每年3月份的第二个周五。对于这个断网日不同的人有不同的观点。

76.【D】细节理解题。根据短文第一段的最后一句话 But studies have found that overuse of electronics can affect our sleep, our study and work. 可知，过度使用电子产品会影响我们的睡眠、学习和工作。由此可知应选 D。

77.【D】细节理解题。根据短文第二段中 To help people take a break from their always-on lifestyles, America set the National Day of Unplugging in 2010 to encourage people to put away their electronics for 24 hours, which is on the second Friday of March every year. 可知，设立全国断网日是为了帮助人们远离一直以来的生活方式，即对电子产品的依赖，故 D 选项是正确的。

78.【B】词义猜测题。根据画线单词所在的上下文语境可知，这一段介绍的是人们对全国断网日的反面观点，再根据所在的这句话 Another shared his grief at not being able to look at his phone during bus and train rides, calling the day "the longest time of my life". 可知，他觉得断网的这一天是最长的一天，所以 grief 应该是一个贬义的意思，结合语境可知应选 B。

79.【D】细节理解题。根据短文第四段中 "My friend and I has dinner in the evening, and we both discussed about how much more present we felt — how we could hear what each other was saying," one participant wrote. 可知，这个实验的参与者体会到了与朋友面对面交流的快乐，由此可知 D 选项是正确的。

80.【A】主旨大意题。这篇短文讲述了为了使人们远离对电子产品的依赖，美国设立了一个全国断网日，对此参与者们发表了自己的看法，虽然有支持的，也有反对的，但文章的重点是放在了支持者们身上。因此 A 选项"回归真实生活"这个题目能够点明文章主旨，故应选 A。

九、书面表达（15 分）

One possible version：

Dear Sir/Madam,

　　I've learned that the English Association of our school is now in need of some volunteers to receive foreign middle school students visiting our school. I'm writing to apply to join it, thinking that I'm well qualified for the job.

　　For one thing, I have developed fluency in spoken English. I have no difficulty communicating with them. What's more, I have accumulated related experience by working part-time in a travel agency, accompanying some foreign tourists. And I treasure this as a good chance to broaden my perspective as well as improve my spoken English.

　　Looking forward to your reply at your convenience.

Yours,
Li Hua

模拟测试卷十一

一、语音(本大题共 10 小题,每小题 1 分,共计 10 分)

从 A、B、C、D 四个选项中,选出画线部分发音不同的一项。

1.【C】u 在单词 sugar 中读[u],在 study、subway、sun 中读[ʌ]。
2.【B】ow 在 flow 中读[əʊ],在 cow、down、town 中读[aʊ]。
3.【B】ui 在 guide 中读[aɪ],在 fruit、juice、suit 中读[uː]。
4.【D】o 在 prove 中读[uː],在 stove、stone、smoke 中读[əʊ]。
5.【A】ea 在 sweat 中读[e],在 steal、speak、steam 中读[iː]。
6.【A】qu 在 cheque 中读[k],在 frequently、quarter、queen 中读[kw]。
7.【D】o 在 son 中读[ʌ],在 fond、honor、hot 中读[ɒ]。
8.【C】s 在 peasant 中读[z],在 house、just、mouse 中读[s]。
9.【B】er 在 serious 中读[ɪər],在 player、shipper、whoever 中读[ə(r)]。
10.【C】gh 在 cough 中读[f],在 although、daughter、delight 中不发音。

二、单项选择题(本大题共 25 小题,每小题 1 分,共计 25 分)

从 A、B、C、D 四个选项中,选出空白处的最佳选项。

11.【B】句意:——她的音乐会取得了巨大的成功。——我认为它一定会对一个有才能的新人产生巨大的影响。第一空:表示"成功的事"时,success 是可数名词,此处用不定冠词表泛指;第二空:固定短语 make a difference,"起作用,有影响"。故选 B。

12.【A】句意:月饼在中国文化中是团圆和幸福的象征。A. symbol"象征";B. signal"信号";C. "标记";D: symptom"症状"。月饼象征团圆、幸福。故选 A。

13.【C】句意:我哥哥而不是我父母喜欢新能源汽车。并非所有人都对这一趋势持积极态度。A. Both"两者都";B. All"三者及以上都";C. Not all"并非所有";D. Not any"都不是"。根据"My brother rather than my parents"可知此处表示"并不是所有人",故选 C。

14.【B】句意:将来,机器人也许会自己思考,就像人们用大脑思考并自己行动一样。think for oneself 独立思考;act for oneself 自己行动。故选 B。

15.【D】句意:在会议上,老人提出一些好的建议,大家都同意。came about 发生;came up 过来;came out 出版;came up with 提出。

16.【D】句意:这项法律可追溯到 17 世纪,至今仍在使用。date back to 固定短语,"追溯到",为不及物动词短语,在句中作定语,应用现在分词形式,故选 D。

17.【B】句意:Mary 应该接受他给她的工作,但她没有。ought to have done = should have done "本应该做却未做"。根据后面的 but she didn't 可知这是一个与过去事实相反的虚拟语气,故选 B。

18.【D】句意:舞台上每一个害怕的学生需要来自老师和父母的帮助。frightening 令人害怕的,用于形容物或事;frightened 感到害怕的,形容人。根据名词 students 可知,句子表达的是"感到害怕的学生"用形容词 frightened。need 需要;need to (do)需要做某事,根据 help

121

from their teachers 可知 help 是名词,用动词 need sth. 的结构。"each + 可数名词单数"表单数意义,作主语时,谓语动词用单数,表达"需要帮助"动词用第三人称单数形式 needs,故选 D。

19.【A】句意:这条河已经遭受了如此严重的污染,所以现在清理它可能已经太晚了。结合语境和时间状语 already 判断此处应用现在完成时,主语 the river 是第三人称单数,助动词用 has,故选 A。

20.【C】句意:——那么,程序是怎样的?——在管理者做出最终决定之前,所有的申请者都要被面试。applicant 申请人和 interview 面试/采访之间是被动关系,且根据问句可知,整个过程还尚未开始,D 项是现在进行时,意为正在发生,因此选 C。

21.【D】句意:天生一幅优美的歌喉,所以她被鼓励去申请声乐节目。句子是并列句,so 前应该是个句子,要有主谓语。

22.【B】句意:虽然台风正在路上,人们仍然期待着不要取消由那个流行歌手举办的户外音乐会, looking forward not to…希望不要……,to 是介词,后接名词、代词、动名词。

23.【D】句意:我还记得我母亲和我过去常常在晚上坐的那个起居室。分析句子结构可知,空处用关系词引导定语从句,先行词是 sitting-room,指物,关系词在定语从句中作地点状语,所以空处需用关系副词 where 引导定语从句。

24.【A】句意:任何有狗作宠物的人会告诉你狗对一个家庭意味着什么。anyone 作先行词,指人,后面是定语从句,从句缺少引导词和主语,故第一空填 who;tell 后面是宾语从句,从句缺少引导词和宾语,根据句意第二空填 what。

25.【A】句意:我非常喜欢听音乐,因为它能让我放松,使我不去想其他的事情,前后是因果关系。

26.【D】句意:计算机是多么重要的工具啊!感叹句:How +adj. +a/an+单数可数名词。

27.【C】句意:正如你能看见的,道路上汽车的数量这些天一直在增长。keep doing 一直做, the number of……的数量,作主语谓语用单数。

28.【A】句意:如果你有一份工作,一定要全身心投入,最终你会成功的。在动词前面加 do/did/does 表示强调,意为"务必,一定",本题的 do 放在祈使句的动词 devote 之前,表示强调。

29.【D】句意:如果我早知道日程安排,可能会省去一些麻烦。根据题干中 might have saved 可知主句是对过去的虚拟,从句应从 if had known 与主句保持一致。if 虚拟条件句中含有 had 时,可将 if 省去,同时将 had 提前构成倒装结构。

30.【A】句意:关于空气污染我们得采取一些措施了,是不是?此句为反义疑问句,根据前肯后否的原则,不定代词指物时用 it,可知选 A。

31.【C】句意:——对不起,我弄丢了你的笔记。——没关系。You're welcome 不用谢。That's right 对的;That's all right 没关系;Not at all 别客气。

32.【D】句意:你可能觉得所有的训练都是浪费时间,但是我有 100%的把握你以后会感激它的。should 应该;need 需要;shall 将会;may(不确定)可能。

33.【A】句意:我不喜欢数学,因为它对我来说很难。根据句意需要选一个表示因果关系的连词,because 因为;but 但是;in 在……里面;and 和,又。

34.【D】句意:——即将到来的周末你有什么计划?——这里将会举行马戏表演,如果你去那儿,我也去。这类句子就答时态要与上句保持一致,本题描述未来时间里要做的事情,在 if 从句中用一般现在时，在主句中用一般将来时，表示"某人也……"，用倒装结构 so+助动词+主语。主句用将来时态，所以助动词用 will，故答案为 D。

35.【C】句意：那个水果店离我家 200 米，在公交站旁边。第一空根据固定搭配 be+数词+metres+away from 离……远，可知应用介词短语 away from；第二空根据固定搭配 be next to…在……旁边，可知应用介词短语 be next to…。

三、完型填空（本大题共 15 小题，每小题 1 分，共计 15 分）

从 A、B、C、D 四个选项中，选出空白处的最佳选项。

【解析】本文介绍了作者在喧嚣的广场看见一位女士在那里演奏钢琴，并演唱关于爱、自信和坚持努力的歌曲。原来她是想要通过音乐让那些悲伤的人高兴起来。得知她在这里演奏的原因后，作者不再悲伤，认为没有什么困难能阻止我们前进。

36.【D】句意：一天，当我正走在大街上，我听见钢琴声和唱歌声在人们的吵闹声中升起。driving 开车；riding 骑，乘；running 跑；walking 散步。根据后文的"I walked more slowly to…where it was coming from."可知是走在大街上，故选 D。

37.【A】句意：我更慢地走过去，弄明白它来自哪里。find out 查明；send out 发送；take out 拿出；get out 出去。根据"where it was coming from."可知我想要查明那个声音来自哪里，故选 A。

38.【B】句意：她正在唱关于爱、自信和坚持努力的歌曲。dressing 给……穿衣；believing 相信；hurting 受伤；losing 失去。根据"keeping on trying."可知此处表示鼓励大家坚持努力，因此此处表示相信自己，believe yourself"相信你自己"，故选 B。

39.【D】句意：我安静地站在那里，看着她在这么拥挤的广场上演奏。nervously 紧张地；rudely 粗鲁地；angrily 生气地；quietly 安静地。根据"watching her playing"可知观看别人表演，应是安静地看，故选 D。

40.【A】句意：我认为她在这么多人面前表演，一定足够勇敢。brave 勇敢的；shy 害羞的；bored 无聊的；honest 诚实的。根据"to perform in front of so many people."可知在很多人面前表演，应是非常勇敢。故选 A。

41.【C】句意：我走过去告诉她，她的音乐听起来多么好。advice 建议；idea 主意；music 音乐；interest 兴趣。根据前文的"Then I saw a young lady sitting at a piano. She was singing songs about love…yourself and keeping on trying."可知此处指的是那位女士演奏的音乐，故选 C。

42.【B】句意：我最近经历困难时期，但是你让我再次充满了希望。or 或者；but 但是；so 所以；and 而且。前半句表示我遇到了困难，后半句表示有希望，前后表示转折关系，故用连词 but，故选 B。

43.【C】句意：你为什么如此悲伤？dirty 脏的；busy 忙的；sad 悲伤的；lazy 懒惰的。根据前文的"I was feeling a little blue because my mother had lost her job."可知我母亲失业了，我感到悲伤，故选 C。

44.【A】句意：你注意到你走路的方式了吗？way 方式；time 时间；reason 原因；station 车站。根据后文的"if your head is down, you might not see it. You should…more and lift your head up."可知低头走路就看不见它，抬头走路，看见的更多，这是在说走路的方式，故选 A。

45.【A】句意：不要悲伤，因为机会来自不同的方面。opportunity 机会；health 健康；pain 疼；

— 123 —

life 生活。根据"if your head is down, you might not see it. You should…more and lift your head up."可知抬起头来才能看见它，因此此处表示要自信，就会看见机会，故选 A。

46.【C】句意：你应该多微笑，抬起你的头。complain 抱怨；rest 休息；smile 微笑；pay 支付。根据"Don't be upset,"可知不要悲伤，因此要微笑，故选 C。

47.【D】句意：我看着她，对她鼓励我的方式感到惊讶。like 像；after 在……之后；for 为了；at 在。此处他们正在交谈，因此是我看着她，look at"看着"，故选 D。

48.【B】句意：我带着微笑问她："你为什么在这里弹钢琴?"How 如何；Why 为什么；When 何时；Where 哪里。此处询问原因，故用疑问词 why，故选 B。

49.【D】句意：她解释说她看见世界上很多人不高兴。dreamed 梦想；hoped 希望；guessed 猜；explained 解释。根据前文的"…are you playing the piano here?"可知我问她问题，所以她进行解释，故选 D。

50.【B】句意：她尝试通过演奏音乐让他们高兴起来。us 我们；them 他们；me 我；her 她。此处代指"a lot of unhappy people in the world"世界上很多不高兴的人，故用代词 them，故选 B。

四、阅读理解（本大题共 10 小题，每小题 2 分，共计 20 分)

从 A、B、C、D 四个选项中，选出符合题目要求的最佳选项。

A

解析：本文主要讲述了作者的妈妈跟一位孤单的老人保持了近一年的通话，这位老妇人总是喊作者的妈妈为 Donna，并跟妈妈讲述她的过去，一年后电话突然中止了，妈妈因此还感到难过，妈妈这一个小小的善举或许给这位孤单的老妇人带来了很大的帮助。

51.【D】细节理解题。根据"Sometimes she'd talk about memories of Donna"可知，妈妈知道这位老人和 Donna 的故事，故选 D。

52.【B】句意猜测题。根据"She normally called on Tuesdays or Thursdays around 8：00 pm. My mom made sure to be home at that time"可知，妈妈总是在老妇人打电话过来时准时在家等着，说明妈妈不想错过这位老妇人的电话，故选 B。

53.【D】细节理解题。根据"My mom felt sad when the calls stopped"可知，那位老妇人挂断电话后，妈妈感到很难过，故选 D。

54.【A】细节理解题。根据"She still thinks of that lady sometimes and wonders about her"可知，妈妈有时会怀念那位老妇人，故选 A。

55.【C】主旨大意题。根据"My mom's small act of kindness might have been a big help to someone in need"可知，作者想通过妈妈的故事告诉读者，小小的善举也能帮助别人，故选 C。

B

解析：本文主要讲述了世界上最孤独的岛屿——布韦岛。

56.【A】细节理解题。根据"one island stands alone…and huge amounts of ice"可知布韦岛很孤独，而且有大量的冰。故选 A。

57.【B】推理判断题。根据"A French man found out Bouvet Island in 1739, but the island was so difficult to reach that nobody set foot on it for nearly a hundred years."可知一个法国人在 1739 年发现了布韦岛，但该岛非常难以到达，以至于近一百年来没有人踏上它，由此可推至可

124

能在1832年有人踏上布韦岛。故选B。

58. 【D】细节理解题。根据"the government didn't allow people to catch seals and whales in the area any more"可知政府不允许人们在该地区捕捉海豹和鲸鱼。故选D。

59. 【D】主旨大意题。根据"This is Bouvet Island, the loneliest island in the world."以及全文内容可知本文主要讲述了世界上最孤独的岛屿——布韦岛，所以话题是地理和自然。故选D。

60. 【A】最佳标题题。根据"This is Bouvet Island, the loneliest island in the world."以及全文内容可知本文主要讲述了世界上最孤独的岛屿——布韦岛，以选项A"最孤独的岛屿"为标题更合适。故选A。

第二部分 （文科类职业模块考生作答，共15分）

五、单项选择题（本大题共5小题，每小题1分，共计5分）

从A、B、C、D四个选项中，选出空白处的最佳选项。

61. 【A】句意：——我能看几分钟菜单再做决定吗？——当然，慢慢来。Take your time 慢慢来；Make yourself at home 别拘束；Enjoy yourself 玩得开心；Please be in a hurry 请快一点。根据Can I look at the menu for a few minutes可知，"不着急，慢慢来"是正确答语。

62. 【C】句意：——打扰了，人民医院在哪里？——对不起，我是新来这儿的。——同样感谢你。Not at all 不客气；That's OK 没关系；Thank you all the same 同样感谢你；That's all 仅此而已；这是全部。根据语境可知对方虽然没有帮上忙，但还是要表示感谢。

63. 【A】句意：——嗨，玛丽，你看起来很累，发生了什么事？——我没赶上校车，所以今天早上不得不跑着去上学。What happened 发生了什么事；What a pain 真痛苦；You're kidding 你在开玩笑；How about you 你呢？根据语境可知，是在询问对方怎么了。

64. 【B】句意：——妈妈，这是我的朋友，Mike。——很高兴见到你，Mike。How are you 你好吗，用于熟人打招呼；Nice to meet you, Mike. Mike, 很高兴见到你；What's your name 你叫什么名字；Thanks 谢谢。根据this is my friend, Mike可知，是妈妈和Mike的第一次见面，回答应是Nice to meet you, Mike。

65. 【B】句意：——看这些云！要下雨了吗？——恐怕是这样的。收音机上说我们现在正进入雨季。I'm afraid not 恐怕不是；I'm afraid so 恐怕是这样的；Not at all 一点也不；Of course 当然不。根据语境可知，表示恐怕会下雨。

六、阅读理解（本大题共5小题，每小题2分，共计10分）

从A、B、C、D四个选项中，选出符合题目要求的最佳选项。

解析：本文主要介绍了不同国家的指路方式。

66. 【B】细节理解题。根据第二段"In Japan, most streets don't have their street names. The Japanese use landmarks(路标)to give ways."可知，日本使用路标方法来指路。故选B。

67. 【D】细节理解题。根据第三段"In the countryside of the American midwest. The land is very flat(平坦的)."可知，美国中西部地区非常平坦。故选D。

68. 【C】细节理解题。根据第三段"But in Los Angeles and California, people measure distance(测量距离)by time, not meters"可知，在加州，人们通过时间来测量距离，而不是米。故

选 C。

69.【C】词义猜测题。根据下文"use their hands to show the right or left ways"可知，是通过肢体语言来指路，body language"肢体语言"，故选 C。

70.【B】最佳标题题。根据本文内容可知，短文主要讲了在不同的地区有不同的指路方式，结合选项可知，"Different ways of giving way"符合文章大意。故选 B。

第三部分 （工科类职业模块考生作答，共 15 分）

七、单项选择题（本大题共 5 小题，每小题 1 分，共计 5 分）

从 A、B、C、D 四个选项中，选出空白处的最佳选项。

71.【A】句意：这些安全标志总是放在显著的位置，这样就可以很容易地看到它们。prominent 突出的；promotion 推广；program 计划；progress 进展。

72.【A】句意：20 比 5 等于 16 比 4。equals 等于；approximately equals 约等于；is less than 小于；is greater than 大于。

73.【B】句意：通常采用两种温度测量系统。它们是摄氏度（摄氏度）和华氏度（华氏度）。

74.【A】句意：面积的基本单位是平方米。square meter 平方米；square millimeter 平方毫米；hectare 公顷；cubic meter 立方米。

75.【A】句意：一台机器被设置成生产 18 毫米长的金属螺栓。螺栓的长度从 17.8 毫米到 18.2 毫米都是可用的，因为它们的长度误差在 0.2 毫米以内。available 可利用的；unavailable 不可用的；right 正确的；true 真正的，正确的。

八、阅读理解（本大题共 5 小题，每小题 2 分，共计 10 分）

从 A、B、C、D 四个选项中，选出符合题目要求的最佳选项。

解析：在现代社会，我们的生活变得越来越数字化。但是，花大量时间通过数字设备工作、阅读、发短信和玩游戏对我们的眼睛有害，作者给了一些保护眼睛的建议。

76.【A】推理判断题。根据"However, spending a lot of time working, reading, texting and gaming through digital devices（数码设备）is bad for our eyes."然而，花大量时间在电子设备上工作、阅读、发短信和玩游戏对我们的眼睛有害。可以推知，人们在使用数字设备后可能会有眼疾，故选 A。

77.【C】推理判断题。根据"These problems have started to increase among children. 'Children get cellphones when they're young and they are using them very often during the day.' Sarah Hinkley told USA Today."这些问题在儿童中开始增加。"孩子们在很小的时候就有手机，而且他们在白天经常使用手机。"Sarah Hinkley 告诉《今日美国》。可推知，越来越多的孩子正在经历数码眼疲劳，故选 C。

78.【C】细节理解题。根据"When you are using a cellphone, keep it at least 30 cm from your eyes and just below eye level."可知，当我们使用手机时，我们应该与眼睛保持至少 30 厘米的距离，故选 C。

79.【B】细节理解题。根据"Remember to take a 20-20-20 break：every 20 minutes, take a 20-second break and look at something 20 feet（about 6 meters）away."可知，我们每 20 分钟应休息 20 秒，故选 B。

80.【D】细节理解题。根据"When you use a computer, first sit in your chair and reach out your arm."当你使用电脑时,首先坐在椅子上,伸出手臂。"When you are using a cellphone, keep it at least 30 cm from your eyes and just below eye level. Try not to use it in the sunlight."当你使用手机时,把它放在离眼睛至少30厘米的地方,刚好低于眼睛水平线上。尽量不要在阳光下使用。"Remember to take a 20-20-20 break:every 20 minutes, take a 20-second break and look at something 20 feet (about 6 meters) away."记住,休息20-20-20:每20分钟,休息20秒,看看20英尺(约6米)远的东西。可知,A、B、C选项文中都有提到,D没有提到。故选D。

九、书面表达(15分)

Dear Christina,

  I am Li Hua. I'm writing to apologize to you for not being able to participate in the "Chinese Traditional Culture Day" activity to be held on Saturday morning with you as we planed last week.

  To be honest, I wish I could join in the activity, but I am afraid I will not be available because I was informed yesterday that I would have to go to Beijing for a contest on the morning of Saturday. That is why I fail to go with you.

  I am awfully sorry for breaking my promise and I make an apology for any inconvenience it brings to you. I sincerely hope you can accept my apology and understand my situation.

  Wish you a good time there.

Yours sincerely,
Li Hua

模拟测试卷十二

一、语音(本大题共 10 小题,每小题 1 分,共计 10 分)

从 A、B、C、D 四个选项中,选出画线部分发音不同的一项。

1. 【A】a 在 anything 中读[e],在 appear,allow,afraid 中读[ə]。
2. 【B】o 在 belong 中读[ɒ],在 become,brother,among 中读[ʌ]。
3. 【C】e 在 below 中读[i],在 better,beg,benefit 中读[e]。
4. 【A】oa 在 broad 中读[ɔː],在 road,coat,goal 中读[əʊ]。
5. 【D】ee 在 coffee 中读[i],在 free,jeep,green 中读[iː]。
6. 【C】c 在 clear 中读[k],在 center,circle,city 中读[s]。
7. 【D】th 在 either 中读[ð],在 earth,death,fifth 中读[θ]。
8. 【C】n 在 hungry 中读[ŋ],在 event,finish,hunt 中读[n]。
9. 【A】sure 在 sure 中读[ʃʊə(r)],在 measure,pleasure,treasure 中读[ʒə(r)]。
10. 【A】s 在 trials 中读[z],在 trips,weeks,sorts 中读[s]。

二、单项选择题(本大题共 25 小题,每小题 1 分,共计 25 分)

从 A、B、C、D 四个选项中,选出空白处的最佳选项。

11. 【D】句意:他过去是一名教师,但后来成了作家。第一空 teacher 是可数名词,表示泛指,需用不定冠词 a 修饰;第二空 turn 后面表示职业的单数可数名词作表语时,名词前不加冠词。故选 D。

12. 【D】句意:你似乎没有心情和我一起去看电影。所以让我们待在家里看电视吧。A. feeling 感觉;B. emotion 情感;C. attitude 态度;D. mood 心情。根据 So let's stay at home watching TV. 可知,此处表示"没有心情"去看电影,in no mood 固定短语"没有心情",故选 D。

13. 【C】句意:我要搬到乡下去,因为那里的空气比城里的新鲜很多。ones 指代可数名词复数,泛指一些;one 泛指可数名词中的一个;that 指代不可数名词,还可指代比较对象;those 是 that 的复数形式。这里指代的是比较的对象,air 是不可数名词,故选 C。

14. 【D】句意:这儿有太多的人和太多的噪声,我忍受不了。too many 用于修饰可数名词,too much 用于修饰不可数名词,题中 people 为可数名词,noise 为不可数名词,故选 D。

15. 【A】句意:Frank 由于粗心大意把票丢了。due to 固定短语,"由于,因为",作原因状语,故填 to。

16. 【D】句意:根据法律,任何一方不得向第三方泄露本合同有关内容。shall 可用于第二或第三人称表示警告、许诺、命令、威胁、规定等语气,故选 D。

17. 【A】句意:——一段长的旅行只能是一次一步地完成。——我同意。所有的小事情可以加起来变成大事情。add up 加起来;set up 建立;show up 出现;get up 起床。根据句意可知是小事情加起来变成大事情,故选 A。

18. 【C】句意:尽管这是一份报酬极少的工作,但他仍然花了很多时间和精力做它。"副词+过去分词"构成新的形容词 poorly-paid 报酬极少的。

19.【B】句意：——你什么时候去上海？——明天早上。我乘坐的飞机早上10：00起飞。此处表示在时间上已经确定好或安排好的事情，应用一般现在时表示将来，常用于come，go，leave，arrive等动词，故选B。

20.【D】句意：老师要求立刻上交作文。demand作动词后接that从句时，从句中谓语动词常用虚拟语气，即"(should+)动词原型"。

21.【C】句意：我不害怕未知的明天，因为我已经经历了昨天并且深爱着今天。so后跟结果；and表示并列关系；but表转折；for补充说明原因。

22.【A】句意：在2022年的第三季度，北欧的旅游消费稳步上升，比上一季度增长了百分之0.1。空格处作主语，故只能选名词性质的短语，故选A。

23.【C】句意：不要谈论你不懂的事情。such+名词+as+名词或从句，固定句式，as引导定语从句，代指先行词things在定语从句中做understand的宾语。

24.【C】句意：我们过去常常在那座老房子里工作，后面是一座著名的教堂。分析句子结构，第一空引导非限制性定语从句，先行词the old building，指物，位于介词后面，需用关系代词which引导；第二空位于系动词was后面，引导表语从句，引导词在从句中作地点状语，需填连接副词where。

25.【C】句意：你的支持对我们的工作是重要的，无论你能做什么事都有帮助。_____ you can do是主语从句，helps是谓语，you can do是主语成分，在主语从句中，do后缺少宾语，因此用whatever引导。

26.【D】句意：这附近有没有能吃点东西的酒吧？先行词为a bar，在定语从句中作状语，故用关系词where。

27.【A】句意：这是在我们学校唯一的一个知道如何弹钢琴的学生。当先行词被the very，the only，the same，the last等词修饰时，关系代词用that；one前有the only之类限定词，定语从句在意义上修饰的是the only one，是单数，而不是复数名词the students。

28.【C】句意：这是一个非常美丽的地方，我们很感兴趣，我们为我们的老师举办了生日聚会。第一个空是定语从句，从句中缺少主语，就用that，第二空是强调句，句中不去成分。

29.【A】句意：他一走出法庭，记者就给他提出了很多问题。Hardly had sb. done…when…——……就……。

30.【C】句意：——让我们下班后去打乒乓球，好吗？——可以啊，我迫不及待了。Forget it算了吧，不客气，没关系。Think nothing of it别放在心上。Why not表示赞同或同意，意为好的，可以啊；表示劝诱、建议或命令，意为……怎么样，为什么不……呢？Not at all根据本不。根据上句Let's play table tennis after work，shall we? 可知表示对提议的赞同。

31.【D】句意：今天是晴天，咱们去钓鱼吧，好吗？当主句是祈使句Let's时，包括说话者在内，反义疑问句使用shall we，当主句是祈使句let us的时候，不包括说话者在内，反义疑问句使用will you，本句中主句部分是Let's，故答案为D。

32.【B】句意：——您现在可以点餐了吗？——好的，请给我一些你们餐厅的特色菜。Are you OK你还好吗；May I take your order您现在可以点餐了吗；How much is it多少钱；Can you help me你能帮助我吗？

33.【B】句意：现在这么多新技术可以应用于解决工业问题。主语new technologies和谓语动词apply之间是被动关系，构成be applied to，其中to是介词，后接动名词，在情态动词

can 后用动词原形,构成情态动词的被动语态。

34.【A】句意:Jason 不时地转过身来,好像在寻找什么人。as if 似乎、好像;even if 即使;if only 要是……多好;what if 假使……会怎样。

35.【B】句意:真奇怪,他竟然没有经过主人的允许就把那些书拿走了。此处是主语从句中使用虚拟语气,should have +过去分词,表示意外的语气,意为"竟然"。

三、完型填空(本大题共 15 小题,每小题 1 分,共计 15 分)

从 A、B、C、D 四个选项中,选出空白处的最佳选项。

解析:文章大意:本文作者讲述了自己小时候经常去一家商店买东西,在店主的"刁难"下,作者学到了很多东西。

36.【A】句意:它后面是一位名叫 Miss Bee 的女士。it 它;her 她的;them 他们;us 我们。根据上文"I walked up to the counter(柜台).",结合语境,可知此处指代前面提到的"the counter",因此用 it 来代替,故选 A。

37.【D】句意:她抬起头来。called up 打电话;picked up 捡起;put up 建造、张贴;looked up 抬头看。根据上文 Excuse me 可知,当我到达柜台那里时说打扰了,因此服务员应是抬起头来看我,故选 D。

38.【B】句意:"我要买这些东西,"我继续说,举起我的购物单。held 过去式;holding 现在分词;to hold 动词不定式;holds 第三人称单数。根据题干可知,hold up 与主语 I 之间是逻辑上的主谓关系,所以用现在分词作伴随状语,故选 B。

39.【C】句意:这里除了你和我,没有人了,我不是你的仆人。anybody 任何人;somebody 某人;nobody 没有人;everybody 每个人。根据"…is here except you and me, and I am not your servant."结合上文语境,我对 Miss Bee 女士让我自己去拿那些所要购买的东西感到很惊讶,可知此处她应是说这里除了你和我,没有人了,我不是你的仆人,故选 C。

40.【D】句意:我建议你去那边拿个篮子,开始装东西。checking 检查;changing 改变;knocking 敲;filling 装满、填满。根据上文,作者要购物买东西,可知此处应是建议拿个篮子去购物,因此用 fill 符合语境,故选 D。

41.【B】句意:这对一个 7 岁的孩子来说并不容易。fair 公平的;easy 容易的;natural 天然的;safe 安全的。根据下文"I spent over an hour in the store."可知买那么多东西对一个 7 岁的孩子来说是不容易的,所以才在商店里待了一个多小时,故选 B。

42.【B】句意:她有时少找我钱。always 总是;sometimes 有时;seldom 很少;never 从不。根据下文"Other times she overcharged."可知她是有时少找我零钱,有时多收钱。故选 B。

43.【D】句意:但是在夏天结束的时候,我可以在大约 15 分钟内完成我的购物之旅。before 在……之前;for 为了;to 到;in 在……之内。根据后面的"15 minutes",结合语境,可知是经过一个夏天的锻炼,我可以在大约 15 分钟内完成我的购物之旅,in 的后面接时间时,表示的意思是"在一定时间之后或之内",故选 D。

44.【C】句意:今年夏天你学到了什么?create 创造;regret 后悔;learn 学会;complete 完成。根据下文"My job is to teach every child…",我的工作是教给每一个孩子……,可知此处是问作者这个夏天学到了什么,故选 C。

45.【A】句意:"我知道你对我的看法,"她说。what 什么;which 哪一个;who 谁;how 怎样、如何。根据上文"'That's you're mean!' I replied."结合"I know … you think of me,"可知本

句为宾语从句，这里指的是对 Miss Bee 女士的看法，what do you think of…？"你认为……怎么样？"因此用 what，故选 A。

46. 【C】句意：我的工作是教给我遇到的每一个孩子一些人生的经验。methods 方法；meanings 意思；lessons 经验、教训；results 结果。根据最后一段我的感悟可知，此处是说教给遇到的每一个孩子一些人生的经验，故选 C。

47. 【B】句意："太难了。"他说。early 早的；hard 困难的；useless 没用的；popular 受欢迎的。根据下文"Could you finish the math problem for me?"可知是数学题太难了，所以儿子才会找人寻求帮助，故选 B。

48. 【A】句意：如果我替你做了，你自己怎么学会做呢？if 如果；unless 除非；as 由于；when 何时。根据 I do it for you，结合语境，可知这是一个假设的条件，所以用 if 连接，故选 A。

49. 【D】句意：如果我替你做了，你自己怎么学会做呢？your 你的；yourselves 你们自己；you 你、你们；yourself 你自己。根据"…I do it for you, how will you ever learn to do it …?"结合语境，可知是如果我替你做了，你自己怎么学会做呢，所以这里应用反身代词"你自己"，故选 D。

50. 【C】句意：我们可能会得到一两次帮助，但运气不可能会每次都来找我们。passed 通过；shown 展示；given 给予；taken 拿、取。根据转折词 but，可知前后句之间是转折关系，结合选项及语境，可知是我们可能会得到一两次帮助，但运气不可能会每次都来找我们。give a hand"得到帮助"，这里是被动语态结构，故选 C。

四、阅读理解（本大题共 10 小题，每小题 2 分，共计 20 分）

从 A、B、C、D 四个选项中，选出符合题目要求的最佳选项。

A

解析：本文是一篇说明文。文章介绍了共享单车的优势以及目前共享单车存在的问题。

51. 【C】细节理解题。根据第一段"The bike that the service company provides has GPS or Bluetooth on it, and people can easily find them."可知，通过共享单车上的 GPS 和蓝牙，人们可以轻易找到附近的共享单车。故选 C。

52. 【B】词义猜测题。结合日常生活经验和"the QR code on the bike"可知，共享单车上的二维码是让人扫描以解锁或锁上共享单车的，所以此处 scan 应是"扫描"的意思。故选 B。

53. 【A】细节理解题。根据第二段"Before riding these bikes, you have to download such an APP on your smart phone."可知，如果要使用共享单车，最先做的事情应是拥有一台智能手机，然后在手机上下载共享单车的软件。故选 A。

54. 【D】细节理解题。根据第二段"Normally, every hour you ride, you need to pay one yuan."可知，共享单车的收费标准是每骑一个小时收费一块钱，而不是每骑一次收费一块钱，选项 D 的表述是错误的。故选 D。

55. 【B】推理判断题。通读全文可知，本文介绍了共享单车的优势以及目前共享单车存在的问题，此内容最可能在网站的新闻报道中出现。故选 B。

B

解析：本文主要讲述作者学习滑雪的难忘经历。

56. 【C】细节理解题。根据"It snows for nearly six months every year from November to April,

making it a wonderland(胜地)for winter sports."可知，Park City 成为冬季运动的圣地是因为它每年几乎会下六个月的雪。故选 C。

57.【B】细节理解题。根据"I borrowed my friend Joey's skis."可知，我借了朋友的滑雪板。B项表述错误。故选 B。

58.【D】主旨大意题。细读第四段并根据"I was touched by their kindness toward me."可知，第四段主要描述孩子们的善良使作者感动。故选 D。

59.【A】推理判断题。根据"…but also saw how sports could connect people from different places."可知，运动能让不同地方的人们聚集一起。故选 A。

60.【B】最佳标题。通读全文并根据"I will never forget that experience…"可知，文章主要讲述作者学习滑雪的难忘经历。故选 B。

第二部分 （文科类职业模块考生作答，共 15 分）

五、单项选择题(本大题共 5 小题，每小题 1 分，共计 5 分)

从 A、B、C、D 四个选项中，选出空白处的最佳选项。

61.【B】句意：——亨利，有你的电话。——我来了，谢谢你！sb. is wanted on the phone 是固定短语，意为"有某人的电话。"常用于口语交际中，根据上句 Henry, you…on the phone 可知，第二空用 I'm coming 我就来。

62.【A】句意：A 图意思是本车道仅供车辆使用，禁止骑自行车进入。B 表示禁止穿行；C 表示请勿靠近；D. 表示非公勿入。

63.【D】句意：——我们去听余先生关于中国文化的演讲，好吗？——恐怕为时已晚，我们下次可以去。Why not 为何不……（用来提建议）；That's all right 没关系；Never mind 不要紧；I'm afraid it's too late 恐怕太迟了。根据语境可知应说恐怕太迟了。

64.【C】句意：——Tom 在上周的跑步比赛中失败了。——你不是认真的吧。他是我们年级最擅长跑步的人。I know 我知道；Don't be silly 别傻了；You can't be serious 你不是认真的吧；It doesn't matter 没关系。根据句意 He is the best at running in our grade 可知，说话人不相信 Tom 失败这个消息。

65.【A】句意：——曼迪，你能送我去火车站吗？——当然，乐意效劳。with pleasure 愿意效劳；it doesn't matter 没关系；pardon me 请原谅；take it easy 别紧张。对方是在请求帮助，结合 sure 可知，乐意效劳符合语境。

六、阅读理解(本大题共 5 小题，每小题 2 分，共计 10 分)

从 A、B、C、D 四个选项中，选出符合题目要求的最佳选项。

解析：本文介绍了英国人获得他们的姓氏的方法有：根据他们家住的地方、他们的工作，或者很多人的姓氏都是由他们父亲的姓得来的。

66.【B】细节理解题。根据"Some family names come from the places of their homes.""Some family names come from a person's job."和"And many people get their family names from their fathers' family names."可知，英国人通常有三种获得姓氏的方法。故选 B。

67.【C】细节理解题。根据"Some family names come from a person's job. If a person is a cook(厨师), his family name may be Cook."可知，如果一个人是厨师，他的姓可能是库克。故

选C。

68.【D】细节理解题。根据"If you hear the name Jackson, you can know that he is the son of Jack."可知，如果你听到杰克逊这个名字，你就知道他是杰克的儿子。故选D。

69.【D】推理判断题。根据"Some family names come from the places(地方) of their homes. A man lives on or near a hill, his family name may be Hill. In England, people's names may be Wood, Lake, because they live near the wood or the lake."可知，有些家族的名字来自他们家的地方；一个人住在山上或附近，他的姓可能是Hill；在英国，人们的名字可能是Wood、Lake，因为他们住在树林或湖的附近。所以如果你听到一个名字"比尔·布什"，他可能就住在灌木丛附近。故选D。

70.【C】主旨大意题。本文介绍了英国人获得他们的姓氏的几个方法。故选C。

第三部分 （工科类职业模块考生作答，共15分）

七、单项选择题（本大题共5小题，每小题1分，共计5分）

从A、B、C、D四个选项中，选出空白处的最佳选项。

71.【A】句意：施工警示标志可以确保未经许可的人员不得靠近，并确保工人佩戴安全防护设备。unauthorized未经授权的、未经批准的；authorized经认可的、审定的、经授权的；protected受保护的；protecting保护。

72.【C】句意是：质量或重量的基本单位是克。kilogram千克；milligram毫克；gram克；tone公吨。

73.【A】句意：在焊接、研磨、处理化学品时，工人必须穿戴适当的个人防护装备。PPE个人防护装置；face shield面罩；panel控制板、仪表盘；extinguisher灭火器。

74.【A】句意：大球的大小是小球大小的三倍。

75.【B】句意：6乘以5再除以9的平方根等于10。

八、阅读理解（本大题共5小题，每小题2分，共计10分）

从A、B、C、D四个选项中，选出符合题目要求的最佳选项。
解析：本文介绍了世界各地新型冠状病毒疫情的情况。

76.【A】细节理解题。根据"The number of people who have died worldwide in the CVID-19 pandemic(新冠肺炎疫情) has passed three million, according to Johns Hopkins University(约翰斯·霍普金斯大学)."可知，根据约翰斯·霍普金斯大学的数据，全球范围内死于新冠肺炎疫情的人数已超过300万。故选A。

77.【B】细节理解题。根据"India experiencing a second wave recorded more than 230,000 new cases(病例) on Saturday alone."可知，印度也经历了第二次疫情，一天内新增病例超过23万例。故选B。

78.【C】细节理解题。根据"The US, India and Brazil, the countries with the most recorded cases, have accounted for more than a million deaths between them, according to Johns Hopkins University"可知，感染人数最多的国家有：巴西、美国和印度。故选C。

79.【D】推理判断题。根据"However, official figures worldwide(世界官方数据) may not fully reflect the true number in many countries."可知，然而，世界各地的官方数字可能不能完全

反映许多国家的真实数字，因此世界各地的官方数字可能反映许多国家的死亡人数较少，故选 D。

80.【D】标题归纳题。根据"The milestone（转折点）comes the day after the head of the WHO（世卫组织）warned the world was 'Teaching the highest rate of infection'（最高感染率）so far."和"The US, India and Brazil, the countries with the most recorded cases, have accounted for more than a million deaths between them, according to Johns Hopkins University"可知，本文主要介绍了新型冠状病毒疫情在一些国家更严重，故选 D。

九、书面表达(15分)

One possible version：

Dear Leslie,

  I'm glad to receive your email. You asked me to share with you what experienced in the epidemic situation. Here are my experiences.

  Since the outbreak of novel corona virus pneumonia in our city in March, 2022. I had been staying at the hotel. On the one hand, I paid close attention to the epidemic situation through watching CCTV news or surfing the Internet; on the other hand, I insisted on studying online. Not only did I read books, but also I had online courses given by my teachers. Besides, I took exercise every day to keep healthy. Faced with the disaster, many people including doctors, nurses and scientists acted bravely and spared no effort to fight against it. What they did impress us most and we should do all we can to study well.

  Thank you for your concern. I'm looking forward to your reply.

Yours,
Li Hua

中等职业教育课程改革教辅用书　中等职业学校对口升学考试用书

内 容 简 介

本套试卷包含根据山西省普通高等学校对口招生考试大纲及中等职业教育规划教材编写的12套单元阶段测试卷以及12套模拟测试卷。内容涵盖近年山西省对口升学考试题型与基本知识点，融入最新考试动向，练测结合，力求紧扣考纲、夯实基础，符合中等职业学校学生特点，可供学生系统复习与考前冲刺使用。

英语对口升学提升模拟测试

版权专有　侵权必究

图书在版编目(CIP)数据

英语对口升学提升模拟测试／郭洪湄，乔俊红主编. -- 北京：北京理工大学出版社，2022.9
ISBN 978-7-5763-1648-3

Ⅰ.①英… Ⅱ.①郭… ②乔… Ⅲ.①英语课-中等专业学校-升学参考资料 Ⅳ.①G634.413

中国版本图书馆 CIP 数据核字(2022)第158140号

主　编	郭洪湄　乔俊红
副主编	冯瑞金　冯变玲　高　馨
参　编	段春红　白　玉　宁惠兰

出版发行／北京理工大学出版社有限责任公司
社　　址／北京市海淀区中关村南大街5号
邮　　编／100081
电　　话／(010)68914775(总编室)
　　　　　(010)82562903(教材售后服务热线)
　　　　　(010)68944723(其他图书服务热线)
网　　址／http://www.bitpress.com.cn
经　　销／全国各地新华书店
印　　刷／定州市新华印刷有限公司
开　　本／787毫米×1092毫米　1/16
印　　张／20.75
字　　数／548千字
版　　次／2022年9月第1版　2022年9月第1次印刷
定　　价／50.00元

责任编辑／时京京
文案编辑／时京京
责任校对／刘亚男
责任印制／边心超

图书出现印装质量问题,请拨打售后服务热线,本社负责调换

前　言

为落实中共中央办公厅、国务院办公厅《关于推动现代职业教育高质量发展的意见》和《国务院关于深化考试招生制度改革的实施意见》等文件精神，促进中等职业院校学生纵向流通，同时满足山西省中等职业学校学生对于对口升学招生考试资料的需求，我们特聘请一批教学经验丰富、教学成果丰硕的一线教师共同参与，集体研究，按照普通高等学校对口招生考试基本要求和考试大纲要求，精心编写了本系列教材，供对口招生考试的广大考生复习备考使用。

本系列教材旨在着力夯实学生基础、补齐"短板"，同时帮助广大考生在较短的时间内高效、便捷、准确地把握考试脉络、熟悉考试形式。

本系列教材具有以下几点特色：

1. 编者阵容强大：编者均来自山西省重点中等职业学校，具备十五年以上教龄，均为骨干教师或学科带头人，具有丰富的对口升学复习辅导经验，并长期研究考试命题趋势与规律。

2. 内容结构合理：内容涵盖山西省普通高等学校对口招生考试基本要求和考试大纲中的内容，考查较为全面；设计单元阶段测试与综合模拟测试卷，符合学校教学规律以及复习进度。

3. 阶梯式难度设计：本教材综合模拟测试卷难易程度由低到高，适用于不同复习阶段使用。

4. 科学做题+全真模拟：本教材重在总结规律，采用阶段性测试与全真模拟测试相结合的模式，帮助学生找到自身知识点薄弱之处，使学生复习更为高效；测试题型结构、分值设置完全与高考一致，注重实战演练，适用于考前最后冲刺，有利于学生进行查漏补缺和考点巩固。

5. 详细解析：本系列丛书答案配以详解，答题思路清晰，可指导学生快速查出问题所在，灵活掌握知识。

本系列教材由郭洪湄、乔俊红担任主编，由冯瑞金、冯变玲、高馨担任副主编，由段春红、白玉、宁惠兰担任参编。在本套试卷的策划和出版过程中，得到了北京理工大学出版社和相关教师的倾心指导和鼎力支持，在此一并表示感谢。

由于编者水平有限，书中难免有不妥之处，敬请各位专家、同人及读者不吝指正。

目　录

基础模块（上册）Unit 1–Unit 3 阶段测试题一 ……………………………… 共 4 页
基础模块（上册）Unit 4–Unit 6 阶段测试题二 ……………………………… 共 4 页
基础模块（上册）Unit 7–Unit 9 阶段测试题三 ……………………………… 共 4 页
基础模块（上册）Unit 10–Unit 12 阶段测试题四 …………………………… 共 4 页
基础模块（下册）Unit 1–Unit 3 阶段测试题五 ……………………………… 共 4 页
基础模块（下册）Unit 4–Unit 6 阶段测试题六 ……………………………… 共 4 页
基础模块（下册）Unit 7–Unit 9 阶段测试题七 ……………………………… 共 4 页
基础模块（下册）Unit 10–Unit 12 阶段测试题八 …………………………… 共 4 页
拓展模块 Unit 1–Unit 3 阶段测试题九 ……………………………………… 共 4 页
拓展模块 Unit 4–Unit 6 阶段测试题十 ……………………………………… 共 4 页
拓展模块 Unit 7–Unit 9 阶段测试题十一 …………………………………… 共 4 页
拓展模块 Unit 10–Unit 12 阶段测试题十二 ………………………………… 共 4 页
模拟测试卷一 …………………………………………………………………… 共 4 页
模拟测试卷二 …………………………………………………………………… 共 4 页
模拟测试卷三 …………………………………………………………………… 共 4 页
模拟测试卷四 …………………………………………………………………… 共 4 页
模拟测试卷五 …………………………………………………………………… 共 4 页
模拟测试卷六 …………………………………………………………………… 共 4 页
模拟测试卷七 …………………………………………………………………… 共 4 页
模拟测试卷八 …………………………………………………………………… 共 4 页
模拟测试卷九 …………………………………………………………………… 共 4 页
模拟测试卷十 …………………………………………………………………… 共 4 页
模拟测试卷十一 ………………………………………………………………… 共 4 页
模拟测试卷十二 ………………………………………………………………… 共 4 页

基础模块(上册) Unit 1-Unit 3 阶段测试题一

一、语音(本大题共10小题,每小题1分,共计10分)

从A、B、C、D四个选项中,选出画线部分发音不同的一项。

1. A. l<u>a</u>rge B. h<u>a</u>rd C. st<u>a</u>r D. p<u>o</u>pular
2. A. n<u>e</u>xt B. l<u>e</u>ft C. pr<u>e</u>fer D. d<u>e</u>sk
3. A. l<u>i</u>vely B. br<u>i</u>ght C. m<u>i</u>nd D. w<u>i</u>sh
4. A. m<u>a</u>nager B. m<u>a</u>chine C. l<u>a</u>b D. <u>a</u>thlete
5. A. gr<u>ea</u>t B. l<u>ea</u>ve C. dr<u>ea</u>m D. l<u>ea</u>d
6. A. help<u>ed</u> B. need<u>ed</u> C. miss<u>ed</u> D. look<u>ed</u>
7. A. warm<u>th</u> B. grandfa<u>th</u>er C. ra<u>th</u>er D. toge<u>th</u>er
8. A. <u>u</u>ncle B. lang<u>u</u>age C. h<u>u</u>ngry D. br<u>a</u>nd
9. A. v<u>o</u>cational B. welc<u>o</u>me C. n<u>o</u>se D. z<u>e</u>ro
10. A. <u>ear</u>th B. h<u>ear</u> C. <u>ear</u>ly D. l<u>ear</u>n

二、单项选择题(本大题共30小题,每小题1分,共计30分)

从A、B、C、D四个选项中,选出空白处的最佳选项。

11. Would you please tell the way _____ Hong Xing vocational High School?
    A. at   B. to   C. in   D. for

12. Mr. White enjoys _____. He is very popular _____ his students.
    A. teaching; to   B. teaching; with
    C. to teach; with   D. to teaches; with

13. They are talking about something _____ great joy.
    A. on   B. under   C. at   D. in

14. Please write to me when you are free. I _____ to hearing from you.
    A. would like   B. am looking forward
    C. am expecting   D. want

15. I hope to be a volunteer on weekends. You should help to _____ the city parks.
    A. cheer up   B. make up   C. take up   D. clean up

16. —Kate, I'm going shopping. Anything to buy for you?
    —Yes, that will save me a _____.
    A. hand   B. trip   C. visit   D. bill

17. Thank you _____ lending me the book. It helped me a lot.
    A. for   B. in   C. to   D. at

18. There _____ only five students here, and five of them have finished their homework.
    A. is   B. are   C. am   D. /

19. It is reported that a kind of new smart phones can test the air quality around you. _____ fast the technology develops!
    A. What   B. What a   C. How   D. How a

20. There is _____ in the art exhibition. Please come and visit it.
    A. something new   B. nothing new   C. new something   D. new nothing

21. —_____ do you go to the library?
    —Four times a month.
    A. How soon   B. How often   C. How long   D. How much

22. —A latest English newspaper, please!
    —Only one copy left. Would you like to have _____, sir?
    A. it   B. one   C. this   D. That

23. —Is there a bus to the zoo?
    —I'm afraid there's _____ bus to the zoo.
    A. no   B. no a   C. some   D. none

24. —Which would you like, a cup of tea or a cup of coffee?
    —_____ is OK. I'm really thirsty.
    A. None   B. A11   C. Either   D. Neither

25. She is a beautiful lady _____ long hair and big eyes.
    A. In   B. on   C. by   D. with

26. The doctor told him _____ a balanced diet.
    A. have   B. to have   C. has   D. had

27. —Why are you standing, Alice?
    —I can't see the blackboard clearly. Two tall boys are standing _____ me.
    A. behind   B. next to   C. between   D. in front of

28. I can't _____ the teacher in class, so I often ask may classmates for help after class.
    A. listen   B. speak   C. follow   D. get

29. She works in a _____ hotel.
    A. five stars   B. five-star   C. five-stars   D. five star's

30. We should make _____ for old people in a bus.

— 1 —

A. room B. a room C. rooms D. the room
31. He is _____ as a leader but he hasn't _____ in teaching.
   A. success; many experiences   B. a success; much experience
   C. great success; an experience   D. a great success; a lot of experiences
32. —Alice, which season do you like best?
   —Autumn. The fallen _____ are like a thick blanket on the ground. What beautiful scenery it is!
   A. leaf   B. leafs   C. leaves   D. leafes
33. The market isn't far from here. It's only _____ bicycle ride.
   A. half an hours'   B. half an hour's
   C. half an hour   D. an hour and a half
34. There is usually _____ snow in the mountain area of the Northeast.
   A. a number of   B. a lot   C. many   D. a great deal of
35. _____ work has been done to improve the people's living standard.
   A. Many   B. A great many   C. A great deal of   D. A number of
36. You should do more _____. Don't always sit at your desk busy doing your _____.
   A. exercise, exercises   B. exercises, exercises
   C. exercises, exercise   D. exercise, exercise
37. —Could you please give me some _____ on how to learn English _____?
   —Sure. Practice makes perfect.
   A. advice, well   B. advice, good   C. advices, well   D. advices, good
38. The Chinese Poetry Competition quickly rose to the top television rating ranks after it was presented on CCTV. It means a growing _____ in traditional culture among China's youth.
   A. interest   B. direction   C. habit   D. dream
39. He can't hear you, because there is _____ noise here.
   A. very much   B. too much   C. much too   D. so many
40. —I hear he didn't pass the English exam.
   —_____. He is always good at it.
   A. How come?   B. So what   C. No wonder   D. No problem.

三、完型填空(本大题共15小题，每小题1分，共计15分)

从 A、B、C、D 四个选项中，选出空白处的最佳选项。

There are many reasons why students don't do well in school. Sometimes it's related to, for example, learning challenges, an __41__ to connect with an instructor, or simply being bored.

These reasons are relevant to me as a former at-risk student. In the 10th grade, I failed 6 of 7 classes because I didn't __42__ with the teacher's teaching method, and associated with students who didn't care about school. As a result, I __43__ 10th grade and was assigned to Ms. Felder's office.

Ms. Felder made it clear that my __44__ behavior wouldn't be allowed. She also provided a tough direction that I didn't want, but really needed at that time. Our ongoing conversations didn't __45__ change my behavior, although it was the first time an educator showed any concern for me.

The previous school year I didn't receive any offer of __46__ from my teachers. The difference during my second attempt at 10th grade was Ms. Felder — who was everywhere I didn't want her to be. She was always in my __47__: checking-in, providing guidance, and supporting my growth. I didn't want her __48__, but it's one of the best things that happened in my life. This seemingly __49__ year with Ms. Felder made a change in my thinking and behavior, __50__ unfortunately it would take many years before my performance and expectations for myself would slowly change.

My __51__ journey was very difficult. Part of the reason that I __52__ pushing forward was that I remember that Ms. Felder told me to do better and have higher expectations for myself. After many years of academic __53__, I graduated with my undergraduate degree from a famous university; "Ms. Felder: Thank you for being there, supporting this once __54__ youth. Please know that the lessons you taught me are now __55__ with at-risk students through my work to help them to be and do better, too."

41. A. inability   B. interest   C. indication   D. inspiration
42. A. agree   B. deal   C. connect   D. meet
43. A. feared   B. hated   C. stayed   D. repeated
44. A. violent   B. awesome   C. strange   D. bad
45. A. regularly   B. luckily   C. clearly   D. immediately
46. A. assistance   B. examination   C. scold   D. explanation
47. A. plan   B. business   C. system   D. career
48. A. introduction   B. influence   C. involvement   D. information
49. A. unbearable   B. useful   C. universal   D. unique
50. A. so   B. if   C. but   D. because

51. A. spiritual   B. educational   C. professional   D. technical
52. A. suggested   B. avoided   C. considered   D. kept
53. A. applications   B. struggles   C. performances   D. researches
54. A. absent-minded B. at-risk   C. kind-hearted   D. hard-working
55. A. shared   B. compared   C. agreed   D. combined

四、阅读理解(本大题共15小题，每小题2分，共计30分)

从 A、B、C、D 四个选项中，选出符合题目要求的最佳选项。

A

Everyone needs friends. We all like to feel close to someone. It is nice to have a friend to talk, to laugh, and to do things with. Surely, there are times when we need to be alone. We don't always want people around. But we would feel lonely if we never had a friend.

No two people are the same. Sometimes friends don't get along well. That doesn't mean they no longer like each other. Most of the time they will go on being friends.

Sometimes friends move away. Then we feel very sad. We miss them very much. But we can call them and write to them. It could be that we would never see them again. And we can make new friends. It is surprising to find out how much we like new people when we get to know them.

Families sometimes name their children after a close friend. Many places are named after men and women who have been friendly to people in a town. Some libraries are named this way. So are some schools. We think of these people when we go to these places.

When we have friends, we will be very happy. Being happy helps us stay well. Or it could be just knowing that someone cares. If someone cares about us, we take better care of ourselves.

56. The first paragraph tells us _____.
    A. no one needs friends
    B. we always need friends around us
    C. making friends is the need in people's life
    D. we need to be alone

57. In the passage the writer doesn't tell us that _____.
    A. people are unhappy when their friends leave them
    B. people will never see their friends after their friends move away
    C. people can know their friends in different ways
    D. people like their new friends very much if they get to know them

58. People will not name a _____ after friendly people.
    A. city   B. room   C. town   D. bad thing

59. When people have friends they will _____.
    A. feel happy and healthy   B. get a lot of help from their friends
    C. take better care of themselves   D. A and C

60. The main idea of this passage is _____.
    A. that people are all friends   B. that people need friends
    C. how to get to know friends   D. how to name a place

B

Do you want to live a happier, less stressful life? Try laughing for no reason at all. That's how thousands of people start their day at Laughter(笑声)Clubs around the world and many doctors now think that having a good laugh might be one of the best ways to stay healthy.

The first Laughter Club was started in Mumbai, India, in 1995 by Dr. Madan Kataria. "Young children laugh about 300 times a day. Adults laugh between 7 and 15 times a day," says Dr. Kataria. "Everyone is naturally good at laughing—it's the universal language. We want people to feel happy with their lives." There are now more than 500 Laughter Clubs in India and over 1,300 in the world.

Many doctors are also interested in the effects(效果) of laughter on our health. According to a 5-year study at the UCLA School of Medicine in California, with laughing there is less stress in the body. Laughter improves our health against illness by about 40%.

So what happens at a Laughter Club? I went along to my nearest club in South London to find out. I was quite nervous at the beginning of the class, to be honest, I wasn't interested in laughing with a group of strangers, and I was worried about looking stupid. Our laughter teacher told us to clap our hands and say "ho ho ho, ha ha ha." while looking at each other. However, our bodies can't tell the difference between real laughter and unreal laughter, so they still produce the same healthy effects.

Surprisingly, it worked! After ten minutes everybody in the room was laughing for real and some people just couldn't stop! At the end of the class I was surprised by how relaxed and comfortable I felt. So if you're under stress, then start laughing. You might be very pleased with the results!

61. The first Laughter Club was started in _____.
   A. India   B. America   C. Britain   D. China
62. How many Laughter Clubs are there in the world today?
   A. Over 300.   B. Over 500.   C. Over 800.   D. Over 1,300.
63. How did the writer feel at the beginning of the class?
   A. Surprised.   B. Pleased.   C. Nervous.   D. Tired.
64. When did the people in the club begin to laugh for real?
   A. After ten minutes.   B. After ten hours.
   C. After ten seconds.   D. After ten days.
65. The article mainly tells us _____.
   A. young children laugh much more often than adults in a day
   B. laughing is one of the best ways to stay healthy
   C. many doctors are also interested in the effects of laughter on our health
   D. real laughter and unreal laughter are both good for health

C

Do you have the experience of taking music lessons against your wishes? Perhaps you have complained about it because you thought it took you much playtime. But now you'd better thank your parents for their time and money spent on your musical training. A recent study suggests music lessons can make children have better memories than their peers (同龄人).

The Canadian study showed that after one year of musical training, children did better on a memory test than those who didn't take music lessons.

The researchers made the children aged between 4 and 6 into two groups — one group of children took music lessons outside school, and the other didn't take any musical training. In one year, they took four tests in different times. The results showed brain development changes at least every four months.

The children taking music lessons not only did better in musical listening but also made faster progress in other ways, such as reading, writing, math and IQ.

People say music is the good medicine for a broken heart. Now it seems music can also help us to improve our memories. We are sure to find more and more in the wonderful world of music.

66. You'd better thank your parents for their time and money spent on your musical training because _____.
   A. you get well after you take music lessons
   B. you will make faster progress in every way
   C. music can help you to improve your memories
   D. music lessons have taken up most of your free time
67. The researchers made one group of the children aged 4–6 take music lessons for _____.
   A. six months   B. a year   C. two years   D. four years
68. The Canadian study showed that brain development changes _____.
   A. once a week   B. twice half a year
   C. four times a year   D. at least every four months
69. According to the last paragraph, most people think music can make us _____.
   A. happy   B. worried   C. lazy   D. confident
70. What does the passage mainly tell us?
   A. How to become cleverer.
   B. Music does us much good.
   C. What to find in wonderful music.
   D. Everyone should receive music training.

五、书面表达(15分)

假设你是李华,你的英国朋友 Peter 来信向你咨询如何才能学好中文。请你根据下列要点写回信。

要点：1. 参加中文学习班；
   2. 看中文书刊、电视；
   3. 学唱中文歌曲；
   4. 交中国朋友。

注意：字数80左右,可适当增加细节,以使行文连贯。

基础模块(上册)Unit 4-Unit 6 阶段测试题二

一、语音(本大题共 10 小题,每小题 1 分,共计 10 分)

从 A、B、C、D 四个选项中,选出画线部分发音不通的一项。

1. A. n<u>ew</u>s　　　B. s<u>u</u>pper　　　C. s<u>ou</u>nd　　　D. st<u>a</u>tion
2. A. l<u>oo</u>k　　　B. g<u>oo</u>d　　　　C. c<u>oo</u>k　　　D. m<u>oo</u>d
3. A. b<u>ow</u>l　　　B. sl<u>ow</u>　　　　C. c<u>ow</u>　　　D. sh<u>ow</u>
4. A. <u>or</u>der　　　B. fav<u>or</u>　　　　C. imp<u>or</u>tant　　D. n<u>or</u>th
5. A. d<u>u</u>mplings　B. s<u>u</u>ccess　　　C. s<u>u</u>ddenly　　D. h<u>u</u>ngry
6. A. n<u>e</u>ver　　　B. r<u>e</u>ply　　　　C. m<u>e</u>mber　　D. l<u>e</u>nd
7. A. h<u>o</u>tel　　　B. h<u>o</u>pe　　　　C. c<u>o</u>ld　　　D. m<u>o</u>ney
8. A. w<u>ar</u>m　　　B. f<u>ar</u>mer　　　C. M<u>ar</u>ch　　　D. h<u>ar</u>vest
9. A. cl<u>ou</u>dy　　　B. c<u>ou</u>ple　　　C. c<u>ou</u>ntry　　D. en<u>ou</u>gh
10. A. qu<u>i</u>te　　　B. sw<u>i</u>m　　　　C. seas<u>i</u>de　　D. l<u>i</u>ne

二、单项选择题(本大题共 30 小题,每小题 1 分,共计 30 分)

从 A、B、C、D 四个选项中,选出空白处的最佳选项。

11. Farmers are very _____ with their good harvest in autumn.
    A. pleasure　　B. happy　　C. crazy　　D. fond
12. He left _____ Beijing yesterday evening.
    A. for　　B. to　　C. at　　D. in
13. I was _____ with myself for making such a stupid mistake.
    A. happy　　B. angry　　C. joyful　　D. worried
14. I _____ remember I left my book at home.
    A. quickly　　B. slowly　　C. suddenly　　D. terribly
15. —Your bike was broken. Were you late for class this morning, Linda?
    —No. Luckily, Mr. Green passed by and _____.
    A. waited for me　　B. let me down
    C. kicked me off　　D. gave me a lift
16. Don't disturb her. She is busy _____ her homework.
    A. with　　B. to　　C. for　　D. at
17. _____ fact, I don't understand what he told me just now.
    A. On　　B. For　　C. At　　D. In
18. _____ the north of China, the most popular food is dumplings.
    A. In　　B. At　　C. For　　D. With
19. Walking is a good way _____ healthy.
    A. to keep　　B. keeping　　C. to keeping　　D. kept
20. In winter, it rains _____ but never snows in Sydney.
    A. a lot　　B. a lot of　　C. lots of　　D. lot of
21. How beautifully she sings! I have never heard _____.
    A. the better voice　　B. a good voice
    C. the best voice　　　D. a better voice
22. He ran and ran, but he couldn't run _____ to catch the bus.
    A. fast enough　　B. enough quick　　C. enough fast　　D. enough quickly
23. It's time _____.
    A. to do morning exercises　　B. do morning exercises
    C. doing morning exercises　　D. done morning exercises
24. Two years ago, the 9-year-old girl set up _____ organization named Angel to help _____ homeless.
    A. the; /　　B. /; the　　C. an; a　　D. an; the
25. Lesson Five is _____ most difficult lesson, but it isn't _____ most difficult lesson in Book One.
    A. a, a　　B. a, the　　C. the, the　　D. the, a
26. Many people are still in _____ habit of writing silly things in _____ public places.
    A. the, the　　B. /, /　　C. the, /　　D. /, the
27. Shall we go to see our teacher? She is ill _____.
    A. in hospital　　B. in the hospital　　C. in a hospital　　D. in an hospital
28. —What is the woman?
    —She is _____.
    A. a dancer and a fashion designer
    B. dancer and fashion designer
    C. a dancer and fashion designer
    D. the dancer and fashion designer
29. When we speak to people, we should be _____.
    A. as polite as possible　　B. as polite as possibly
    C. as politely as possible　　D. as politely as possibly
30. _____ efforts we make, _____ happiness we may gain.
    A. The more, the most　　B. More, the most
    C. More, more　　　　　D. The more, the more
31. He often works _____ into the night, which moves us.
    A. deep, deep　　B. deeply, deep
    C. deep, deeply　　D. deeply, deeply

32. —What do you want to be when you grow up?
    —Well, _____ scientist like Yuan Longping, I think.
    A. the   B. an   C. a   D. /
33. Mr. Wu is a _____ teacher. He is always telling jokes.
    A. humorous   B. strict   C. careful   D. handsome
34. —What do you think of the 3D film last night?
    —It was _____. I enjoyed it a lot.
    A. boring   B. wonderful C. strange   D. terrible
35. A person who is _____ does not tell lies or cheat people.
    A. careless   B. stupid   C. honest   D. humorous
36. Be careful when you are driving, _____ in a rainstorm like this.
    Thanks. I will.
    A. especially B. probably C. nearly   D. hardly
37. _____, Chinese people celebrate the Mid-Autumn Festival by enjoying the full moon and eating mooncakes.
    A. Quickly   B. Suddenly C. Secretly   D. Traditionally
38. Mike hurt his back seriously and can _____ get out of bed without help.
    A. quickly   B. easily   C. nearly   D. hardly
39. Can I help you?
    _____. I want to buy some T-shirts for my children.
    A. Yes, please B. No, thanks C. It doesn't matter D. Of course I can
40. I had a good time at the charity show. Thanks for your invitation.
    _____.
    A. All right B. You are welcome C. Good luck to you D. Not too bad

三、完型填空(本大题共15小题,每小题1分,共计15分)

从A、B、C、D四个选项中,选出空白处的最佳选项。

A little boy named Harry became very ill. He had to lie in bed all day, unable to move. He spent his days feeling __41__ and blue.

There wasn't much he could do except look out of the __42__. Time passed, and his illness frustrated(使失望) him. Until one day he saw a strange __43__ in the window. It was a penguin eating a sausage sandwich. The penguin got in __44__ the open window, and said "good afternoon" to Harry, turned around, and __45__ quickly.

Of course, Harry was very __46__. He was still trying to work out what had happened. Outside his window he saw a monkey busy blowing up a balloon. At first Harry asked himself __47__ that could possibly be, but after a while, as more and more crazy-looking __48__ appeared outside the window, he couldn't help __49__ and found it hard to stop.

An elephant jumped on a stone, or a dog wore a pair of glasses and acted in a __50__ way. The little boy didn't tell anyone about this. Those strange characters ended up putting joy back in his heart, and in his body. Before long, his health had __51__ so much that he was able to go back to school again.

There he told his classmates all that he had __52__. While he was talking to his best friend, he saw __53__ coming out of his friend's school bag. Harry asked his friend what it was, and he was so insistent(坚持) that __54__ his friend had to show him what was in the bag.

There, inside, were all the things that his best friend had been using to try to __55__ the little boy!

And from that day on, Harry always did his best to make sure that no one felt sad and alone.

41. A. happy   B. sad   C. excited   D. cool
42. A. roof   B. hole   C. window   D. wall
43. A. photo   B. painting   C. sign   D. shape
44. A. above   B. below   C. over   D. through
45. A. left   B. slept   C. flew   D. drove
46. A. annoyed   B. surprised   C. bored   D. tired
47. A. what   B. which   C. when   D. where
48. A. people   B. students   C. children   D. characters
49. A. crying   B. laughing   C. running   D. coughing
50. A. funny   B. rude   C. dull   D. strict
51. A. grown   B. improved   C. increased   D. developed
52. A. acted   B. heard   C. experienced   D. dreamed
53. A. something B. anything   C. nothing   D. everything
54. A. quickly   B. Suddenly   C. immediately   D. finally
55. A. cheer up   B. give up   C. make up   D. put up

四、阅读理解(本大题共15小题,每小题2分,共计30分)

从A、B、C、D四个选项中,选出符合题目要求的最佳选项。

A

A teacher had been very annoyed by some of the boys whistling during school hours. At last he knew he would have to punish anyone who repeated the offence(过错).

The next morning, when the room was quiet, a loud whistle was heard! The students were surprised, and the teacher at once looked around to discover the offender.

The blame(指责) fell on a bad boy who was often in trouble, he strongly denied (否认) whistling. However, his words were not believed, for he was not a truthful boy. The teacher brought him up to be punished.

Seeing what was about to happen, a thin little boy, about nine years old, who had been anxiously watching the event, rose from his seat.

"Do not punish John, sir," he said to the teacher, "It was I who whistled. I was doing a long hard sum, and when I rubbed out another sum to make room for it, I rubbed out the difficult one by mistake. I spoiled it all, and before I knew what I had done, I had whistled out loud! I am very sorry, I did not mean to whistle, I cannot let John be punished for my fault." He held out his hand to be punished!

Taking his hand, the teacher said, "Charles, you have done the right thing. You were honest and spoke the truth. I believe that you did not intend to whistle. I cannot punish you, after being so honest." Charles returned to his seat with a flushed face, and even the youngest child in the school felt proud of him. Every student could see how bravely he had acted.

Charles was truly a brave boy. He had done that which he knew to be right, even though the same time he might have been punished for it.

True courage may also be shown by refusing to do that which we know is wrong, thought may get into trouble or other children may laugh at us.

56. According to the teacher, _____.
    A. Charles should be punished for the whistle
    B. John should be punished for the whistle
    C. both of them should be punished for the whistle
    D. all the boys should be punished for the whistle
57. Charles blew the whistle because _____.
    A. nobody else did it
    B. he was going to cough
    C. he rubbed out the wrong sum
    D. he was used to whistling
58. John strongly denied whistling to show that _____.
    A. he was afraid of being punished
    B. he knew who gave the whistle
    C. his words had not been believed
    D. he didn't give the whistle at all
59. The result of the event was that _____.
    A. John had been wronged and punished
    B. Charles was praised for his courage
    C. nobody cared about Charles's action
    D. the teacher made a more serious rule
60. The best title for the passage can be _____.
    A. Teacher's Mistake   B. True Courage
    C. Two Naughty Boys   D. A Sudden Whistle

B

In England recently three foreign gentlemen came to a bus stop and waited. About five minutes later, the bus they wanted came along. They were just going to get on when suddenly there was a loud noise behind them. People rushed onto the bus and tried to push them out of the way. Someone shouted at them. The bus conductor came rushing down the stairs to see what all the trouble was about. The three foreigners seem all at sea and looked embarrassed(窘迫的). No one had told them about the British custom(习惯) of lining up for a bus that the first person who arrives at the bus stop is the first person to get on the bus.

Learning the language of a country isn't enough. If you want to have a pleasant visit, find out as much as possible about the manners and customs of your host country. You will probably be surprised just how different they can be from your own. A visitor to India would do well to remember that people there consider it impolite to use the left hand for passing food at table. The left hand is supposed to be used for washing yourself. Also in India, you might see a man shaking his head at another to show that he doesn't agree. But in many parts of India a shake of the head means agreement. Nodding(点头) your head when you are given a drink in Bulgaria will most probably leave you thirsty.

In that country, you shake your head to mean "yes"— a nod means "no". At a meal in countries on the Arabic Peninsula, you will find that your glass is repeated refilled as soon as you drink up. If you think that you have had enough, you should take the cup or glasses in your hand and give it a little shake from side to side or place your hand over the top.

In Europe it quite usual to cross your legs when you are sitting talking to someone even at an important meeting. Doing this in Thailand, however, could bring about trouble. Also, you should try to avoid(避免) touching the head of an adult(成人)——it's just not done in Thailand.

61. The British people tried to push the three gentlemen out of the way, because the gentlemen _____.
    A. were foreigners   B. didn't have tickets
    C. made a loud noise   D. didn't line up for the bus

62. According to the article, if you want to have a pleasant journey in a foreign country, you should _____ .
    A. learn the language of the country
    B. understand the manners and customs of the country
    C. have enough time and money
    D. make friends with the people there

63. In India it is considered impolite _____ .
    A. to use the right hand for passing food at table.
    B. to pass food with the left hand.
    C. to eat food with your hands.
    D. to help yourself at table.

64. To cross one's legs at an important meeting in Europe is _____ .
    A. a common(平常的) habit
    B. an important manner
    C. a serious(严重的) trouble
    D. a bad manner

65. The best title(题目) for this article is _____ .
    A. People's Everyday Life
    B. Mind Your Manners
    C. Shaking and Nodding Head
    D. Taking a Bus in England

C

Have you ever used a needle(针) and thread(线) to sew(缝纫)? What did you think of it?

When I was a little boy, my mom, grandmother and I drove to my grandmother's sister's house in the next town. It was a warm summer afternoon, I went outside to play in the yard while they all sat around the kitchen table to talk.

After an hour of playing by myself, I got bored and walked inside to see what they were doing.

On the kitchen table was a large homemade quilt that was still being sewn together. Pieces of colorful cloth were everywhere. I sat in a chair and watched as my great aunt sewed a little piece of cloth onto the quilt. I looked over at one edge of the quilt and saw a piece of thread sticking out. Without thinking, I reached over to pull it.

"No!" It was my grandmother's voice. I jumped back. That was the first time I can ever remember her yelling at me. Seeing the frightened look on my face, she smiled and showed me why she had yelled. That single piece of thread wove(穿行) in and out of the different pieces of cloth.

Like a twisting road, it made its way from one end of the quilt to the other. If I pulled on it, I would have pulled the quilt apart and ruined(毁掉) hours of work.

As I look back on that moment today, I can see that each of our lives is a lot like that thread in the quilt. We are each a single piece of thread, but the other threads around us help hold everything together. That's our purpose—help and support the people around us.

66. What was the writer doing while others were talking in the kitchen?
    A. Sewing the quilt.   B. Sitting in a chair.
    C. Pulling the thread.   D. Playing in the yard.

67. What's the meaning of the underlined word "yelling"?
    A. Saying happily.   B. Shouting loudly.
    C. Crying excitedly.   D. Speaking quickly.

68. How did the writer feel after his grandma yelled at him?
    A. Funny.   B. Excited.   C. Scared.   D. Angry.

69. What would happen if the writer had pulled the thread?
    A. The quilt would be pulled apart.
    B. His mother would be happy to see that.
    C. His grandmother might praise him for doing that.
    D. The thread would weave in and out of different pieces of cloth.

70. What does the writer want to tell us?
    A. Loving the people around us.
    B. Helping the people around us.
    C. Finding out what your purpose is.
    D. Learning to work without other people.

五、书面表达(15分)

假如你叫李华，你的笔友 Ann 写信询问你家乡的气候，请用英文写一封回信，介绍你家乡的季节和天气状况。

注意：词数80词左右。

_____
_____
_____
_____
_____

基础模块(上册)Unit 7-Unit 9 阶段测试题三

一、语音(本大题共 10 小题,每小题 1 分,共计 10 分)

从 A、B、C、D 四个选项中,选出画线部分发音不同的一项。

1. A. b<u>i</u>ll   B. pr<u>i</u>ze   C. del<u>i</u>cious   D. w<u>i</u>ndow
2. A. r<u>e</u>lative   B. r<u>e</u>union   C. m<u>e</u>rry   D. t<u>e</u>nder
3. A. l<u>u</u>cky   B. c<u>u</u>stom   C. l<u>u</u>ck   D. l<u>u</u>nar
4. A. <u>Ch</u>ristmas   B. <u>ch</u>ildhood   C. Fren<u>ch</u>   D. cat<u>ch</u>
5. A. <u>ea</u>rly   B. d<u>ea</u>l   C. <u>ea</u>sy   D. m<u>ea</u>t
6. A. s<u>oo</u>n   B. m<u>oo</u>nlight   C. f<u>oo</u>d   D. bl<u>oo</u>d
7. A. <u>c</u>elebrate   B. <u>c</u>olorful   C. <u>c</u>racker   D. <u>c</u>ard
8. A. <u>ex</u>perience   B. <u>ex</u>pect   C. <u>ex</u>am   D. <u>ex</u>cuse
9. A. p<u>a</u>st   B. c<u>a</u>lendar   C. l<u>a</u>ntern   D. h<u>a</u>ppiness
10. A. p<u>are</u>nt   B. pr<u>e</u>p<u>are</u>   C. c<u>are</u>   D. r<u>are</u>

二、单项选择题(本大题共 30 小题,每小题 1 分,共计 30 分)

从 A、B、C、D 四个选项中,选出空白处的最佳选项。

11. _____ my parents help, I began to catch up _____ my classmates.
  A. with, to   B. under, with   C. with, with   D. to, to

12. Study hard, _____ you will fall behind the others.
  A. and   B. but   C. or   D. though

13. If you don't know a word, you can _____ the word in a dictionary.
  A. look up   B. look down   C. look over   D. look out

14. _____ of the teachers in our school is 118, _____ of them are women teachers.
  A. The number, first fourth   B. The number, one fourth
  C. A number, one second   D. A number, three quarters

15. The Brown flew to Kunming _____ a sunny morning.
  A. on   B. in   C. for   D. at

16. There was a big crowd waiting _____ the opening ceremony to start.
  A. by   B. from   C. for   D. with

17. The teacher asked a difficult question, but Jim managed to _____ a good answer.
  A. put up with   B. keep up with   C. come up with   D. go through with

18. Flu _____ in a small city because of the sudden change of temperature.
  A. broke out   B. broke up   C. broke into   D. broke down

19. Let Mary play with your toys as well, Jenny, you must learn to _____.
  A. support   B. care   C. spare   D. share

20. The whole society should be concerned _____ the health and growth of children.
  A. about   B. in   C. of   D. on

21. He said he was not disappointed at the score of the final exam, but the book on his face _____ himself _____.
  A. give; up   B. give; off   C. give; out   D. give; away

22. Linda and Kitty will go to Greenery Theme Park by _____ next Sunday.
  A. they   B. them   C. their   D. themselves

23. We should show respect _____ those _____ serve us.
  A. for, who   B. to, who   C. for, that   D. to, that

24. When we grow up, we cannot rely _____ our parents.
  A. in   B. on   C. for   D. with

25. Why not share the apple _____ your sister?
  A. in   B. with   C. at   D. on

26. He _____ TV at 10:00 last night.
  A. is watching   B. was watching   C. watched   D. watches

27. Can you _____ a hand to clean these windows?
  A. borrow   B. take   C. lend   D. keep

28. _____ of them are late for class.
  A. Much   B. Little   C. A little   D. A few

29. You had better _____ the teacher about this.
  A. to ask   B. ask   C. asked   D. asking

30. It took a whole day _____ my homework.
  A. finishing   B. finish   C. to finish   D. finished

31. My uncle's suddenly showing up on the deep night of a rainy day gave us _____.

   A. great surprise
   B. great surprises
   C. a great surprise
   D. the great surprise

32. His name is James but he calls _____ Jim.

   A. him   B. his   C. he   D. himself

33. He studied in _____ Beijing University.

   A. a   B. an   C. the   D. /

34. Their new assistant is _____ than the old one.

   A. more better   B. far better   C. very better   D. many better

35. We will play football _____ three o'clock.

   A. in   B. after   C. to   D. since

36. How long will it _____ you to do the job?

   A. cost   B. spend   C. pay   D. take

37. The story is too ridiculous. It _____ not be true.

   A. could   B. should   C. would   D. shall

38. A singer and dancer _____ coming.

   A. be   B. are   C. is   D. were

39. —I am thinking of the test tomorrow. I am afraid I can't pass this time.
    —_____! I am sure you will make it.

   A. Go ahead   B. Good luck   C. No problem   D. Cheer up

40. Have you ever been to that _____ bookstore.

   A. two-hand
   B. second-hand
   C. the two-hand
   D. the second-hand

三、完型填空（本大题共15小题，每小题1分，共计15分）

从 A、B、C、D 四个选项中，选出空白处的最佳选项。

There was once a rich man who __41__ his little boy very much. He wanted to try __42__ best to please him. So, he gave him a horse __43__, beautiful rooms to live in, pictures, books, toys and everything __44__ money could buy. But for all days, the little boy was still unhappy. He wore a frown __45__ he went, he always wished for something he did not have. The man did not know how to make his son __46__.

One day, a __47__ came to the man and said to him, "I can __48__ your son happy and __49__ his frowns into smiles, __50__ you must pay me a great price for __51__ him the secret."

"All right" said the man, "No matter __52__ you ask for, I will give you." The magician took the boy into a secret room. He wrote something on a piece of paper, and then give it __53__ the boy. There on the paper came the words, "Do one kind thing for someone every day." The boy __54__ the advice and became one of the happiest boys.

Only those who stop __55__ about their own happiness can be truly happy.

41. A. loves   B. loved   C. love   D. has loved
42. A. he   B. his   C. he's   D. himself
43. A. to ride   B. rode   C. ridden   D. riding
44. A. what   B. which   C. that   D. where
45. A. wherever   B. everywhere   C. somewhere   D. anywhere
46. A. happily   B. happiness   C. happy   D. unhappy
47. A. magician   B. magic   C. magical   D. magicians
48. A. make   B. take   C. keep   D. get
49. A. turn   B. to turn   C. turning   D. turned
50. A. and   B. but   C. over   D. so
51. A. telling   B. to tell   C. told   D. tell
52. A. what   B. who   C. where   D. how
53. A. to   B. with   C. for   D. on
54. A. followed   B. refused   C. thought   D. got
55. A. thinking   B. to think   C. thought   D. think

四、阅读理解（本大题共15小题，每小题2分，共计30分）

从 A、B、C、D 四个选项中，选出符合题目要求的最佳选项。

A

CaiLun improved paper around 2,000 years ago in China. It is an important invention. Before this, people had to remember lots of information or write it on stone, wood, leaves, etc.

Today everyone in the world uses paper. with paper, we can make books and print newspapers. Sharing information is a lot easier with the help of paper. People use paper every day. Students do homework and keep a diary on paper. Paper is a great invention.

Alan Turing was born in London, England, in 1912. He attended Cambridge University from 1931 to 1934. Turing was a mathematician(数学家) and a computer scientist. Many people called "Turing the father of computer science". He created the first design(设计) for a modern computer.

Turing wanted to know if a machine could think for itself and trick someone into believing they were having a conversation with another person. This became known as the Turing test. In the test, a human talked to two other people through a computer. One was a machine, and the other was person. This idea is still used today.

56. When was paper improved by Cai Lun?
   A. Around 2,000 years ago
   B. About 200 years ago.
   C. Around 1,000 years ago.
   D. About 100 years ago

57. People can do the following things with paper EXCEPT _____ .
   A. sharing information
   B. printing newspapers
   C. having the Turing test
   D. making books

58. Many people considered Alan Turing to be _____ .
   A. the inventor of printing
   B. the father of modern education
   C. the inventor of paper
   D. the father of computer science

59. In order to have the test, Turing needed _____
   A. three people, one computer and a machine
   B. two people, one computer and a machine
   C. two people, two computers and a machine
   D. one person, one computer and a machine

60. From the passage, we know Cai Lun's invention and Turning idea are _____
   A. hard to accept
   B. not used any more
   C. unknown to people
   D. still used today

B

The world's largest radio telescope was finished on Sept. 25 2017 in China. FAST is a five-hundred-meter telescope. It is called Tian-yan (The Eye of Heaven), with a dish the sire of 30 football grounds, deep in the mountains of southwest China's Guizhou Province. The <u>giant</u> dish is built on a howl-like valley.

The surrounding area has "radio silence" as there are no towns and cities within a 5-kilometers radius(半径范围) and only one country center within 25 kilometers.

FAST is made up of 4,450 panels(面板). The second largest radio telescope is in Russia. The bigger dish will be able to pick up weaker signals(信号).

The radio telescope is like an ear, listening to tell meaningful radio messages from white noise in the universe. With the help of the telescope, we can receive weaker and more radio messages far away in space. It will help us to search for intelligent life outside of the Galaxy(银河系) and explore the origins(起源) of the universe. "Any of its discoveries will lead to a Nobel Prize," said Joseph Tayor, a Nobel Prize winner.

The FAST project began in 2011. And the telescope is expected to remain the global leader for next 10 to 20 years.

61. Where was FAST developed?
   A. In China   B. In Russia   C. In America   D. In England

62. The underlined word "giant" probably means _____ in Chinese.
   A. 神秘的   B. 巨大的   C. 宽广的   D. 宏伟的

63. FAST is used to _____ .
   A. explore the origins of human beings
   B. receive messages and sounds from the Galaxy
   C. watch the beautiful scenery of the Galaxy
   D. receive distant radio messages from the universe

64. From the passage, we can know that _____
   A. FAST is the largest radio telescope all over the world so far
   B. noisy towns are around the telescope within a 5-kilometer radius
   C. the second-largest radio telescope is made up of 4,450 panels
   D. the largest radio telescope is made in Russia

65. How long did it take to finish the FAST project?
   A. About 20 years
   B. About 10 years
   C. About 6 years
   D. About 30 years

C

Many people say dolphins are very intelligent. They seem to be able to think, understand, and learn things quickly. But are they smart like humans or are they more like cats or dogs? Dolphins use their brains differently from people. But scientists say dolphin intelligence and human intelligence are similar in some ways. How?

Like humans, every dolphin has its own name. The name is a special whistle. Each dolphin chooses a specific whistle for itself, usually by its first birthday. Actually, scientists think dolphins, like people, "talk" to each other about a lot of things, such as their age, their feelings, or finding food. And, like humans, dolphins use a system of sounds and body language to communicate. But understanding their conversations is not easy for humans. No one speaks "dolphin" yet, but some scientists are trying to learn.

Dolphins are also social animals. They live in groups, and they often join others from different groups to play games and have fun—just like people. In fact, playing together is something only intelligent animals do.

Dolphins and humans are similar in another way: both <u>species</u> make plans to get something they want. In the seas of southern Brazil, for example, dolphins use an interesting strategy to get food. When fish are near a boat, dolphins show signs to the fishermen to put their nets in the water. Using this method, the men can catch a lot of fish. What is the advantage for the dolphins in doing so? They get to eat some of the fish that escape from the net.

66. What does a dolphin often use as its name?
　　A. A body language.　　　　B. A special whistle.
　　C. Its feeling.　　　　　　　D. Its age.
67. What does the underlined word "species" mean in Chinese?
　　A. 方法　　　B. 片段　　　C. 物种　　　D. 声音
68. Why do dolphins help the fishermen?
　　A. To catch a lot of fish by themselves.
　　B. To eat some fish outside the net.
　　C. To find the fish.
　　D. To show their intelligence.

69. What can we infer(推断) from the passage?
　　A. Some scientists can understand dolphin conversation.
　　B. Dolphins probably help fishermen by using their body language.
　　C. Dolphins help men because they like humans.
　　D. Dolphins can talk to humans about their age and feelings.
70. What's the main idea of the passage?
　　A. Dolphins can communicate with each other at birth.
　　B. Dolphins are social animals because they play together.
　　C. Dolphins are smart and they are like humans in some ways.
　　D. Dolphins help humans do many things like catching fish.

五、书面表达(15分)

许多学习生活中的烦恼都会使人产生压力，为了更好地发现并解决同学们存在的心理压力问题，你们班特意开展了以"Less pressure, Better Life"为题的英语演讲比赛。请你准备发言稿，谈谈你的一些缓解压力的好办法，与同学们分享，内容包括：

1. 同学们普遍存在的压力是什么；
2. 我的压力是什么；
3. 我是如何成功缓解我的压力的；

注意：文中不能出现自己的真名，词数80左右。

基础模块(上册)Unit 10-Unit 12 阶段测试题四

一、语音(本大题共 10 小题，每小题 1 分，共计 10 分)

从 A、B、C、D 四个选项中，选出画线部分发音不同的一项。

1. A. br<u>ea</u>k   B. <u>ea</u>ch   C. <u>ea</u>sy   D. <u>ea</u>st
2. A. p<u>a</u>per   B. p<u>a</u>ste   C. p<u>a</u>st   D. d<u>a</u>te
3. A. l<u>u</u>ck   B. c<u>u</u>t   C. l<u>u</u>nar   D. c<u>u</u>lture
4. A. ch<u>e</u>ss   B. r<u>e</u>ly   C. <u>u</u>pset   D. w<u>e</u>st
5. A. simpl<u>y</u>   B. <u>y</u>ear   C. angr<u>y</u>   D. apolog<u>y</u>
6. A. b<u>i</u>ll   B. hol<u>i</u>day   C. rela<u>ti</u>ve   D. th<u>i</u>nk
7. A. y<u>e</u>t   B. requ<u>i</u>re   C. s<u>e</u>t   D. dr<u>e</u>ss
8. A. w<u>i</u>ll   B. r<u>i</u>ch   C. f<u>i</u>t   D. str<u>i</u>ke
9. A. fi<u>gh</u>ting B. nei<u>gh</u>bor   C. mi<u>gh</u>t   D. cou<u>gh</u>
10. A. wi<u>s</u>e   B. noi<u>s</u>e   C. el<u>s</u>e   D. lo<u>s</u>e

二、单项选择题(本大题共 30 小题，每小题 1 分，共计 30 分)

从 A、B、C、D 四个选项中，选出空白处的最佳选项。

11. A study shows the students who are engaged in after-school activities are happier than _____ who are not.
    A. ones   B. those   C. these   D. them

12. —what are you doing these days?
    —I'm _____ with my work.
    A. please   B. busy   C. strict   D. filled

13. That restaurant is extremely popular, _____ you may have to wait to get a seat.
    A. for   B. so   C. or   D. yet

14. The quality of education in this small school is better than _____ in some larger schools.
    A. that   B. one   C. it   D. this

15. Many teenagers _____ the old and they often offer their seats to the old on buses.
    A. agree with B. worry about C. laugh at   D. care for

16. It is helpful to _____ a good habit of reading in language learning.
    A. take   B. show   C. develop   D. match

17. —What _____ do you choose, small, medium or large?
    —Large, please.
    A. color   B. size   C. price   D. kind

18. I am surprised to hear from her. _____, we last met ten years ago.
    A. On one hand   B. That is to say
    C. Believe it or not   D. In other words

19. —_____ go out for a picnic next Saturday?
    —Good idea.
    A. Why not   B. How about   C. Would you like to   D. Let's

20. She was born _____ the evening of August 8, 2008.
    A. in   B. on   C. at   D. with

21. I jumped _____ than Bill in the sports meet last year.
    A. high   B. higher   C. highest   D. the highest

22. We should take care of our belongings when taking the train, especially when we get on and _____ the train.
    A. get up   B. get in   C. get out of   D. get off

23. _____ ancient times, people in different countries wrote numbers _____ many different ways.
    A. In; in   B. On; with   C. In; of   D. On; in

24. I hope the traffic in our city will become more _____ in the future.
    A. easy   B. convenient   C. quickly   D. better

25. He would like _____ a film with his parents.
    A. sees   B. seeing   C. to see   D. see

26. —_____ the beginning of next month, we are going to have a school trip.
    —Really? Are you sure _____ that?
    A. On; about   B. In; with   C. At; to   D. At; about

27. You need to have two years' teaching _____ if you want to get the job.
    A. education   B. relationship C. experience   D. discussion

28. —Why are you so tired?
    —Drawing the picture _____ me over one and a half hours.

— 1 —

A. spends   B. costs   C. needs   D. takes

29. The new student _____ others in my class.
    A. gets on well with   B. gets in well with
    C. gets on good with   D. gets in good with

30. Life is _____ up and down, my dear.
    A. full with   B. full of   C. filled of   D. fill with

31. A friend of _____ lives in the house.
    A. my sister   B. my sisters   C. my sister's   D. my sisters's

32. Don't worry, you still have _____ time.
    A. little   B. a little   C. few   D. a few

33. _____ Chinese speak _____ Chinese.
    A. The, the   B. /, /   C. /, the   D. The, /

34. The news is _____ good to be true.
    A. so   B. much   C. too   D. very

35. This is the bus _____ the People's Park.
    A. at   B. for   C. to   D. towards

36. He is too young to _____ right from wrong.
    A. speak   B. talk   C. say   D. tell

37. I told him that he _____ use my computer wherever he wanted to.
    A. could   B. should   C. would   D. shall

38. How time flies! Ten years _____ passed.
    A. have   B. has   C. is   D. Are

39. —Do you mind my smoking here?
    —_____!
    A. No thanks.   B. No, good idea.
    C. yes, please.   D. Yes, better not.

40. 9 _____ 3 is three.
    A. divided   B. divides   C. divided by   D. is divided by

三、完型填空(本大题共15小题，每小题1分，共计15分)

从 A、B、C、D 四个选项中，选出空白处的最佳选项。

Country music __41__ very popular in America. It is a traditional kind of music __42__ the southern states of America. At first, people __43__ country music only after family parties. When people in the countryside moved __44__ towns and cities to __45__ jobs, they took their music __46__ them. __47__ country music continuing to change, it became popular throughout America. John Denver was one of __48__ country singers in America 50 years ago. His song Take Me Home, Country Roads is well-known and people still play __49__ today.

Pop music is __50__ kind of musical style. Pop music can make people __51__ happy and comfortable. Pop music __52__ since the 1950s. In China, Jay Chou is liked by a large number of __53__ of all ages. He sang many songs about the world we live in. One of them is Dao Xiang, __54__ encourages people not __55__ up even when life is difficult.

41. A. is   B. are   C. was   D. were
42. A. of   B. from   C. by   D. off
43. A. sang   B. danced   C. played   D. owned
44. A. to   B. of   C. on   D. with
45. A. find   B. discover   C. invent   D. look for
46. A. to   B. of   C. on   D. with
47. A. By   B. With   C. In   D. On
48. A. the famous   B. famous
    C. the more famous   D. the most famous
49. A. them   B. it   C. one   D. a
50. A. other   B. another   C. others   D. the other
51. A. feel   B. to feel   C. felt   D. feeling
52. A. was popular   B. is popular
    C. has been popular   D. had been popular
53. A. fans   B. fan   C. fun   D. funny
54. A. that   B. what   C. /   D. which
55. A. give   B. to give   C. giving   D. given

四、阅读理解(本大题共15小题，每小题2分，共计30分)

从 A、B、C、D 四个选项中，选出符合题目要求的最佳选项。

A

Why should you thank Ray Tomlinson? You might have never heard of his name before, but do you know that the e-mail you use every day was his "child"?

Ray Tomlinson is known as "the father of e-mail". He was born in New York in 1941. He attended college at the Renaselaer Polytechnic Institute, where he took part in a program with IBM, and in 1963 he received a bachelor(学士) of Science in electrical engineering.

In 1971, Ray created the first e-mail system, which allowed people to send messages electronically from the same computer. But he thought that there might also be a way to send messages from different computers, which led to the birth of the e-mail we know now. He chose the @ sign to separate local from global e-mails in the mailing address. "I used the '@' sign to show that the user was 'at' some other hosts rather than being local," said Ray in an interview. Person to person network e-mail was born and user @ host became the standard for e-mail addresses, as it remains today.

Ray Tomlinson died at the age of 74. Thanks Ray Tomlinson for inventing the e-mail and putting the @ sign on the map. Though he may not be famous as Mark Zuckerberg or Bill Gates, Ray Tomlinson surely has his place among the geniuses(天才) that gave us the convenience in our life.

56. Who is known as "the father of e-mail"?
    A. Bill Gates.   B. Ray Tomlinson.
    C. Steve Jobs.   D. Mark Zuckerberg.
57. When did Ray create the first e-mail system?
    A. In 1941.   B. In 1963.   C. In 1971.   D. In 2015.
58. He used the @ sign to show that _____.
    A. the user was "at" some other hosts rather than being local
    B. people could send messages from the same computer
    C. it played a key role in computer technology
    D. he took part in a program with IBM
59. Why should everybody say "thank you" to Ray Tomlinson?
    A. Because he received a bachelor of Science
    B. Because he was as famous as Mark Zuckerberg.
    C. Because he surely has his place among the geniuses.
    D. Because he invented email and put the @ sign on the map.
60. From the article, who isn't mentioned?
    A. Ray Tomlinson   B. Bill Gates
    C. Mark Zuckerberg   D. Thomas Edison

B

My mother is fifty-five years old. She retired(退休) just two months ago. After that, she was bored and didn't know what to do every day. She was kind to us before, but recently she had a chip on her shoulder. She often quarreled with my brother and me without any reason. Also, relations between my parents became difficult. My mother got into trouble and didn't know how to deal with it.

My brother thought of a good idea to solve the problem. He bought her a new smart phone and taught her how to use Wechat(微信). My mother's life changed a lot from then on. No matter where she went and whatever she did, she always used it. She took photos with her new smart phone and always shared her photos in her friend circle to express how happy she was. As a result, she often did something by mistake. She often forgot to turn off the gas and the food she was cooking usually got burnt. My father tried to stop her, but it didn't work.

This afternoon, my mother prepared to make dumplings for dinner. She took a lot of pictures in order to post them into her friend circle. After dinner, we took out our smart phones and waited to the photos she had taken. To our surprise, we didn't find any pictures of her dumplings. At last, my father couldn't help asking her, "Why don't you share your delicious dumplings in your friend circle today?" My mother looked embarrassed and said, "_____" "Oh, my God! I have to spend more money buying a new one!" cried my brother.

61. The underlined words "had a chip on her shoulder" most probably mean _____.
    A. had a pain in her shoulder
    B. got angry easily
    C. liked eating potato chips
62. My brother bought a smart phone for my mother because _____.
    A. my mother liked taking photos and sharing them in her friend circle
    B. my father retired two months ago
    C. my brother wanted to help my mother out of trouble
63. After my mother had a smart phone, _____.
    A. she liked it very much and used it all the time
    B. she often quarreled with my brother and me without any reason
    C. she was bored and didn't know what to do

64. Which of the following is TRUE according to the passage?
   A. My mother stopped my father from taking picture of food.
   B. My mother often forgot turning off the gas after she had a smart phone.
   C. After dinner, we were surprised to find no pictures of dumplings in my mother's friend circle.
65. "_____" can be the missing sentence in the passage.
   A. The dumplings were not delicious.
   B. My smart phone was boiled in the pot.
   C. I have already posted the pictures in the friend circle.

C

Traveling can be expensive. But there are some ways to save money when traveling.

Look for city tourism cards. With the card, you can pay less at restaurants and shops. You don't have to wait for a long time at busy attractions. You might even get free tickets to top tourist attractions. City tourism cards can save your money and time.

Don't get the best room. How long will you stay in your room? Will you just be sleeping there? Do you really need a bigger room with a good view(景色)?

Find a hotel outside a city. It can help you save some money by choosing a hotel away from big tourist attractions, for you are always doing the same — go to the attractions and then return to your hotel to sleep.

Book(预订) a room with a kitchen. Although some people might not like to cook while on vacation, I don't mind making breakfast in my room. We always eat at a nice restaurant on our last night of the vacation. I'd rather eat breakfast and lunch at the hotel and then spend much money on a delicious supper.

66. With _____, you can pay less at restaurants and shops.
   A. ID cards   B. tourism cards   C. bank cards   D. phone cards
67. The underlined words "tourist attractions" in Paragraph 2 mean _____.
   A. 旅游方式   B. 旅游设施   C. 旅游手册   D. 旅游景点
68. To save some money, the writer advises tourists to _____.
   A. get the best room
   B. live near big tourist attractions
   C. live away from big tourist attractions
   D. take a map with them when traveling

69. The writer prefers to make breakfast and lunch in the hotel because _____.
   A. they are healthier and more delicious
   B. he likes cookers in the hotel
   C. there are not any restaurants in the neighborhood
   D. he'd rather spend much money on a delicious supper
70. What does the passage mainly talk about?
   A. How to save money when traveling.
   B. way to get a tourism card.
   C. How to find a hotel outside a city.
   D. way to book a room on the Internet.

五、书面表达(15分)

假如你叫李华，你的美国笔友 Alice 希望你向他介绍你最好的朋友。请你根据以下信息，写一封电子邮件给 Alice，向他介绍你的好朋友。词数不少于80词。

My best friend
Name；
Age；
Birthday；
Family；parents, brother and he/she
Likes；
Favorite food；
Favorite subject(why)
Favorite sport；…

_____
_____
_____
_____
_____

基础模块(下册)Unit 1-Unit 3 阶段测试题五

一、语音(本大题共10小题,每小题1分,共计10分)

从 A、B、C、D 四个选项中,选出画线部分发音不同的一项。

1. A. m<u>a</u>gnificent   B. c<u>a</u>rry   C. c<u>a</u>pital   D. st<u>a</u>te
2. A. st<u>o</u>ne   B. sm<u>o</u>ke   C. pr<u>o</u>vince   D. l<u>o</u>cate
3. A. <u>e</u>mperor   B. <u>e</u>xcited   C. <u>e</u>xtend   D. <u>E</u>nglish
4. A. s<u>i</u>lk   B. qu<u>i</u>te   C. cred<u>i</u>t   D. s<u>i</u>t
5. A. t<u>y</u>pe   B. certainl<u>y</u>   C. lovel<u>y</u>   D. easil<u>y</u>
6. A. <u>ex</u>pensive   B. <u>ex</u>tend   C. <u>ex</u>change   D. <u>ex</u>tra
7. A. s<u>a</u>le   B. <u>a</u>ttend   C. <u>a</u>dmire   D. <u>a</u>fraid
8. A. m<u>o</u>del   B. meth<u>o</u>d   C. c<u>o</u>nfidence   D. c<u>o</u>mmodity
9. A. <u>i</u>mprove   B. d<u>i</u>ctionary   C. w<u>i</u>ll   D. w<u>i</u>fe
10. A. spee<u>ch</u>   B. tea<u>ch</u>   C. wat<u>ch</u>   D. stoma<u>ch</u>

二、单项选择题(本大题共30小题,每小题1分,共计30分)

从 A、B、C、D 四个选项中,选出空白处的最佳选项。

11. China is located _____ the north of Asia.
    A. in   B. on   C. at   D. to

12. The students in this school are made _____ uniform on Monday.
    A. to wear   B. wearing   C. wear   D. worn

13. —what do you think of the traffic accidents?
    —I think many accidents _____ by careless drivers.
    A. have caused   B. were cause   C. are caused   D. will cause

14. The ancient people built the Great Wall _____.
    A. by hand   B. by a hand   C. by the hand   D. by hands

15. The bridge is about 300 meters _____.
    A. tall   B. long   C. length   D. width

16. Every day, too much water _____ in our school. We should save it.
    A. is wasted   B. wastes   C. was wasted   D. wasted

17. The old man so _____ the good news that he couldn't say a word.
    A. interested in   B. excited about   C. afraid of   D. worried about

18. We had been stuck in heavy _____ for more than an hour and we were late.
    A. traffic   B. signal   C. alarm   D. smoke

19. Ann seems quite _____ that she will pass the exam.
    A. excited   B. sure   C. sad   D. unhappy

20. It's _____ that he will be sent to study abroad next month.
    A. say   B. to say   C. said   D. saying

21. It's dangerous for girls _____ alone at night.
    A. walk   B. walked   C. walking   D. to walk

22. Would you please tell me _____ next?
    A. how to do   B. what to do   C. what do I do   D. how should I do

23. Tom has so many exams _____. He doesn't know how to deal with the pressure.
    A. take   B. taking   C. to take   D. to taking

24. The headmaster's joke made us all _____ happily.
    A. smile   B. to smile   C. smiling   D. smiled

25. —May I help you?
    —_____.
    A. You are welcome   B. Excuse me
    C. I want a red dress   D. Don't worry

26. If the professor's research is successful, he will be the second person _____ the Nobel Prize in China.
    A. win   B. wins   C. winning   D. to win

27. Our English teacher asked us _____ a composition on how to keep healthy.
    A. write   B. to write   C. writing   D. wrote

28. —I wonder where I could find some information about our middle school.
    —Why _____ on the Internet? There is a lot of information about it.
    A. don't go   B. not to go   C. not going   D. not go

29. My sister works _____ a department store.
    A. in   B. on   C. at   D. under

— 1 —

30. —Can you help me _____ the bed into the room?
   —Certainly.
   A. move   B. moves   C. moving   D. moved

31. _____ the beginning of the party, he gave me a gift.
   A. In   B. By   C. At   D. On

32. —How much should I pay for the dresses?
   —120 dollars _____.
   A. in total   B. in style   C. in cash   D. in need

33. He decides _____ to Hong Kong on vacation.
   A. to go   B. going   C. gone   D. go

34. The bedroom is so dirty! It needs _____.
   A. to clean   B. clean   C. cleaning   D. cleaned

35. Mother made me _____ my homework carefully.
   A. do   B. doing   C. done   D. to do

36. —How would you like to pay?
   —_____ cash but not _____ credit card.
   A. With; in   B. In; by   C. With; by   D. By; in

37. _____ a hard condition, Karl got a great success.
   A. Under   B. At   C. In   D. With

38. —You were lost on your way to the lake, weren't you?
   —Yes, we were and had to stop _____ the way.
   A. asking   B. to ask   C. asked   D. to be asked

39. The man is famous _____ his works The mad man's diary.
   A. with   B. for   C. as   D. like

40. The young men put what they have learned _____ practice.
   A. into   B. in   C. to   D. at

三、完型填空(本大题共15小题,每小题1分,共计15分)

从 A、B、C、D 四个选项中,选出空白处的最佳选项。

What is language for? Some people seem to think it's for practicing grammar __41__ and learning lists of words,—the longer the words, the better. That's wrong. Language is for the exchange __42__ ideas, for communication.

The way __43__ a language is to practice speaking it as often as possible. A great man once said __44__ is necessary to drill as much as possible, and __45__ you apply it in real situations, the more natural it will become.

Learning any language __46__ a lot of effort. But don't __47__. Relax! Be patient and enjoy yourself. Learning foreign languages should be __48__. Rome wasn't built in a day. Work harder and practice more. Your hardworking will be __49__ by God one day. God is equal to everyone!

Use a dictionary and grammar guide __50__. Keep a small English dictionary with you __51__. When you see a new word, look it up __52__ the word-use it, in your mind, in a sentence.

Try to think in English whenever possible. When you see something, think of the English word of it, __53__ think about the word in a sentence.

Practice tenses as much as possible. __54__ you learn a new verb. learn its various forms.

I would also like to learn more about the __55__ behind the language. When you understand the cultural background you can better use the language.

41. A. roots   B. riddles   C. rules   D. researches
42. A. of   B. for   C. in   D. from
43. A. to learn   B. learned   C. learns   D. learning
44. A. this   B. that   C. it   D. these
45. A. the less   B. the fewer   C. the more   D. the much
46. A. takes   B. returns   C. works   D. offers
47. A. give out   B. give off   C. give in   D. give up
48. A. necessary   B. fun   C. easy   D. complete
49. A. thought   B. happened   C. rewarded   D. produced
50. A. really   B. certainly   C. differently   D. constantly
51. A. at all time   B. at times   C. at a time   D. at no time
52. A. look about   B. talk about   C. think about   D. worry about
53. A. however   B. then   C. till   D. although
54. A. Which   B. Whose   C. When   D. Why

55. A. business   B. appointment   C. importance   D. culture

四、阅读理解(本大题共 15 小题,每小题 2 分,共计 30 分)

从 A、B、C、D 四个选项中,选出符合题目要求的最佳选项。

A

Daisy needed some new clothes. Mrs. Jones took her to the department store. They went to the children's department. A saleswoman came up to them.

"Can I help you?" she asked.

"Yes." Mrs. Jones said. "My daughter needs a new blouse."

"What size is she?" the saleswoman asked.

"She was a size six last year, but she's bigger now."

"We'll try a size seven." the saleswoman said.

Daisy tried on several blouses. She didn't like any of them. Some were too big. Some were too small. Then she tried on one that was the right size.

"That one looks right." her mother said.

"No. Mom." Daisy said. "It's too heavy. I'll be hot."

At last Daisy liked one. "This is just right." she said. "It's not too heavy. It's not too thin. I like the color."

"Good." her mother said. She turned to the saleswoman.

"How much is this blouse?" she asked.

"One hundred dollars." the saleswoman said.

"That's much too expensive!" Mrs. Jones said.

Poor Daisy. She didn't get a new blouse that day.

56. What is the main idea of this passage?
  A. Mrs. Jones bought Daisy two new blouses.
  B. Daisy needed some new clothes.
  C. Daisy didn't get any new clothes that day.
  D. Daisy couldn't decide which blouse she liked.

57. What did Mrs. Jones say about Daisy's size?
  A. That Daisy was a size six now.
  B. That Daisy was a size seven now.
  C. That Daisy was the same size as last year.
  D. That Daisy was bigger than last year.

58. How many blouses did Daisy try on?
  A. Three   B. Four   C. Several   D. Seven

59. What was wrong with the blouses that Daisy tried on first?
  A. They were all too big.
  B. They were either too big or too thin.
  C. They were either too big or too small.
  D. She didn't like any of the colors.

60. Why didn't Daisy get a new blouse that day?
  A. Because she didn't like any of the blouses she tried on.
  B. Because all the blouses she tried on were too expensive.
  C. Because the only blouse she liked was too expensive.
  D. Because all the blouses she tried on were the wrong size.

B

Shopping Guide in Central Mall

Floors Articles

6　Restaurant shop/Tea/coffee house

5　Children's pleasure ground/Game center

4　Electrical equipment, clocks and watches/Writing materials and office supplies

3　Men's clothing/Bedding

2　Women's clothing/Children's clothing

1　Fruit, vegetables, meat, eggs, drinks, cooked food, etc./Kitchen ware

Business hours

Weekdays:8:30am—6:30pm

Weekends:9:00am—9:00pm

61. If you want to have a cup of coffee, you should go to the ＿＿＿＿ floor.
  A. first   B. fourth   C. fifth   D. sixth

62. If you want to buy some apples and beef, you should go to the ＿＿＿＿ floor.
  A. first   B. second   C. third   D. fourth

63. If Mr. Green wants to buy a shirt, he should go to the _____ floor.
    A. second   B. fourth   C. third   D. fifth

64. If Mrs. Green's children want to play, they should go to the _____ floor.
    A. first   B. fourth   C. fifth   D. sixth

65. If you want to do some shopping in Central Mall in the evening, you may go there on _____.
    A. Wednesday   B. Friday   C. Saturday   D. Monday

C

Traveling to every part of the world gets easier, but how well do we know and understand each other? Here's a simple test. Imagine you are planning to hold a meeting at 4 o'clock. What time should you expect your foreign business friends to arrive? If they are Germans, they will arrive on time. If they are Americans, they'll probably be 15 minutes early. If they are Englishmen, they'll be 15 minutes late, and you should allow up to an hour for the Italians.

The British seemed to think since the English language was widely used in the world, people would always understand what they do. However, they found they were completely wrong. For example, the British are happy to have a business lunch and discuss business matters and have a drink during the meal. The Japanese prefer not to work while eating. Lunch is a time for them to relax and get to know each other and they don't drink at lunchtime. The Germans like to talk business before dinner. The French like to eat first and talk afterwards. They have to be well fed and watered before they discuss anything.

66. What do the Germans prefer when they go to a meeting?
    A. They prefer to be on time   B. They prefer to arrive very early.
    C. They prefer to arrive very late.   D. They prefer to arrive a little late.

67. According to the text, if a group of Englishmen, Americans and Italians hold a meeting, who will be the last to arrive?
    A. The Englishmen.
    B. The Americans.
    C. The Italians.
    D. Both the Englishmen and the Italians.

68. What do the Japanese like to do at lunchtime?
    A. To drink.   B. To get to know each other.
    C. To talk business   D. To eat only.

69. According to the writer, the British like to _____.
    A. arrive on time and talk business during the meal
    B. arrive earliest and hate talking business at a meal
    C. arrive 15 minutes late and talk business after the meal
    D. arrive a few minutes late and discuss business during the meal.

70. By giving us the two examples, the writer means to show us that _____.
    A. different countries have different cultures in different parts of the world.
    B. the Germans are more serious and have good living habits
    C. the Italians are careless people and they are never on time for everything
    D. the French people are very lazy and they prefer eating and drinking

五、书面表达(15分)

假如你是李华, 写一封信向你的朋友 Mike 介绍自己美丽的家乡。

参考词汇: Where: in the north \ It is located... \ far from... \ near...

City or town: large; small; beautiful; mountain; hill; river; shopping center; places of interest; be famous for...

Buildings: tall \ modern buildings \ houses \ street \ road \ bridge \ hospital

People: it has a population of... \ hard working \ friendly \ living condition

要求: 语言流畅、观点正确、无语法错误。80 词左右。

_____
_____
_____
_____
_____

基础模块(下册)Unit 4-Unit 6 阶段测试题六

一、语音(本大题共 10 小题,每小题 1 分,共计 10 分)

从 A、B、C、D 四个选项中,选出画线部分发音不同的一项。

1. A. th<u>r</u>eaten   B. th<u>r</u>ow   C. t<u>r</u>uth   D. without
2. A. <u>ou</u>tside   B. nerv<u>ou</u>s   C. pr<u>ou</u>d   D. h<u>ou</u>sework
3. A. <u>c</u>lothes   B. <u>c</u>ent   C. <u>c</u>ommon   D. <u>c</u>razy
4. A. <u>a</u>ddict   B. besid<u>e</u>   C. interfer<u>e</u>   D. lift
5. A. b<u>e</u>nefit   B. <u>e</u>ntertainment   C. sp<u>e</u>nd   D. d<u>e</u>velopment
6. A. b<u>o</u>x   B. n<u>o</u>te   C. h<u>o</u>nesty   D. s<u>o</u>b
7. A. d<u>u</u>ck   B. s<u>u</u>ddenly   C. tr<u>u</u>st   D. bl<u>u</u>e
8. A. gr<u>ea</u>tly   B. w<u>ea</u>lthy   C. br<u>ea</u>th   D. inst<u>ea</u>d
9. A. <u>s</u>uppose   B. <u>s</u>uddenly   C. <u>c</u>ustomer   D. tru<u>s</u>t
10. A. d<u>r</u>ive   B. <u>r</u>emind   C. selfish   D. silent

二、单项选择题(本大题共 30 小题,每小题 1 分,共计 30 分)

从 A、B、C、D 四个选项中,选出空白处的最佳选项。

11. Last Monday, three of us _____ the meeting.
    A. stay away   B. stay from
    C. stayed away from   D. stay away from

12. He doesn't spend much time _____ his homework.
    A. in   B. on   C. at   D. with

13. She _____ everything _____ her schoolbag as soon as she got home.
    A. take; out   B. take; out of   C. took; out   D. took; out of

14. I will _____ go swimming together with you _____.
    A. Not, be more   B. not, any more
    C. not, to be   D. not, be any

15. You don't know how mother _____ about it and how it'll hurt father!
    A. take on   B. takes on   C. take care   D. find on

16. When he _____, he found everything was gone.
    A. came to himself   B. come to himself
    C. Came to him   D. came to herself

17. it _____ up _____ and came to rest on a very high branch of a big old tree.
    A. fly; with the wind   B. flew; to the wind
    C. fly; on the wind   D. flew; with the wind

18. Joe _____ but was greatly troubled.
    A. keep silent   B. kept silent
    C. keep silence   D. kept silence

19. He woke up _____ midnight and heard a loud noise.
    A. on   B. in   C. at   D. by

20. Mr. Green promised the little girl _____ back to save her.
    A. coming   B. to come   C. came   D. come

21. Could you turn _____ the bath tap for me? I want to have to bath.
    A. on   B. off   C. down   D. up

22. Don't _____ him. he looks honest but he is a snake in the grass.
    A. trust   B. wake   C. threaten   D. trouble

23. —I am feeling a bit uncomfortable.
    —I think you will go and _____ down.
    A. run   B. throw   C. sleep   D. lie

24. That night hearing Joe's words, Bill _____ realized he was so foolish.
    A. sadly   B. carefully   C. greatly   D. suddenly

25. We think he will not be addicted _____ computer games any longer.
    A. to play   B. in playing   C. to playing   D. of playing

26. We should _____ good use of the water in the lake.
    A. take   B. get   C. have   D. make

27. —What did Jim say?
    —_____.
    A. He said he was busy   B. He said I was busy
    C. He said he is busy   D. He said I am busy

28. —What did he ask you?
    —_____.
    A. He asked me what do you want   B. He asked me what do I want
    C. He asked me what I wanted   D. He asked me what you want

— 1 —

29. I find _____ necessary _____ more about other countries.
   A. this; know
   B. it; to know
   C. that; to know
   D. it; know

30. TV brings the world into our home _____ sight and _____ sound.
   A. in, through
   B. by, by
   C. in, in
   D. through, through

31. I'll tell you _____ he told me last week.
   A. all which
   B. all what
   C. that all
   D. all

32. There is no difficulty _____ can't be overcome in the world.
   A. that
   B. which
   C. who
   D. what

33. This is the last time _____ I shall come here to help you.
   A. that
   B. which
   C. when
   D. what

34. He is the only one of the three _____ got the new idea.
   A. who have
   B. whom have
   C. who has
   D. who had

35. The place _____ interested me most was the Children's Palace(少年宫).
   A. Which
   B. where
   C. what
   D. in which

36. Do you know the man _____?
   A. whom I spoke
   B. to who spoke
   C. I spoke to
   D. that I spoke

37. This is the hotel _____ last month.
   A. which they stayed
   B. at that they stayed
   C. where they stayed at
   D. where they stayed

38. Do you know the year _____ the Chinese Communist Party was founded?
   A. which
   B. that
   C. when
   D. on which

39. That is the day _____ I'll never forget.
   A. which
   B. on which
   C. in which
   D. when

40. The factory _____ we'll visit next week is not far from here.
   A. Where
   B. to which
   C. which
   D. in which

三、完型填空(本大题共 15 小题,每小题 1 分,共计 15 分)

从 A、B、C、D 四个选项中,选出空白处的最佳选项。

Alice Smith would never forget the night when she met a robber(抢劫者) many years ago.

That evening, she went to a birthday party which __41__ until two o'clock in the morning. Alice walked in the __42__ street alone. Suddenly from the back of a dark __43__ a tall man with a sharp knife in his right hand ran out at her. "Good __44__, lady," the man said in a low voice, "I don't think you wish to __45__ here!" "What do you want?" "Your earrings. Take them off!"

Alice suddenly had a __46__ idea. She tried to cover her necklace with the collar (衣领)of her overcoat while she used __47__ hand to take off both of her earrings and then quickly __48__ them on the ground.

"Take them and let me go," she said! The robber thought that the girl didn't like the ear-rings at all, only trying to __49__ the necklace. It would cost __50__, so he said, "Give me your necklace."

"Oh, sir. It doesn't __51__ much. Please let me wear it."

"I'm not that __52__. Quick!"

With shaking __53__, Alice took off her necklace. As soon as the robber left, she picked up her earrings and ran as __54__ as she could to one of her friends.

The earrings cost 480 pounds and the necklace the robber had taken away cost __55__ six pounds.

41. A. ended   B. stayed   C. stopped   D. lasted
42. A. busy   B. quiet   C. noisy   D. wide
43. A. part   B. block   C. building   D. street
44. A. morning   B. afternoon   C. evening   D. night
45. A. die   B. escape   C. fight   D. stay
46. A. funny   B. safe   C. brave   D. bright
47. A. other   B. others   C. the other   D. another
48. A. handed   B. threw   C. passed   D. put
49. A. own   B. keep   C. have   D. protect
50. A. cheap   B. expensive   C. more   D. less
51. A. weigh   B. take   C. spend   D. cost
52. A. afraid   B. angry   C. silly   D. bad
53. A. hands   B. feet   C. head   D. body
54. A. much   B. early   C. carefully   D. fast
55. A. really   B. already   C. only   D. hardly

四、阅读理解（本大题共15小题，每小题2分，共计30分）

从A、B、C、D四个选项中，选出符合题目要求的最佳选项。

A

Dear Sunday Globe,

　　I am writing to tell you about your article "Smart Phones Make Life Easier" in last Sunday's newspaper. You did an excellent job explaining the good points of smart phones, but you didn't talk about their bad points at all. So I hope you will let me give your readers some advice on smart phone etiquette(礼仪).

　　The first point I'd like to address is loudness. When you talk on your smart phone in public, please don't shout. In fact, the microphones in smart phones are very sensitive(敏感的). So, you can be heard even if you speak quietly.

　　Another point is about personal space. I don't think it is polite to make calls in small spaces full of people. This makes others uncomfortable and forces them to listen to your personal business. What's worse, it stops many face-to-face conversations from ever beginning.

　　Lastly, doing two things at the same time is dangerous. For example, making calls while driving is a bad habit. Pay attention to the road! Similarly, when staying with your friends, turn off your smart phone and enjoy their company.

Yours truly,
Amber Lily

56. Amber Lily wrote the letter to _____.
　　A. find a good job　　　　　　B. provide advice
　　C. make her life easier　　　　D. buy a smart phone

57. What does the underlined word "address" in Paragraph 2 probably mean?
　　A. 致函　　B. 称呼　　C. 陈述　　D. 选址

58. Why people cannot shout when talking on the phone in public?
　　A. It is not polite.
　　B. It is not allowed.
　　C. The microphones in smart phones are very sensitive.
　　D. It is against the law.

59. According to Paragraph 3, what makes people around you uncomfortable?
　　A. Discussing things face to face.
　　B. Speaking quietly on your phone.
　　C. Minding your own business.
　　D. Calling in small spaces full of people

60. What can we learn from the last paragraph?
　　A. It is dangerous to drive on the road.
　　B. It is easy to start a company with others.
　　C. It is bad to turn off our phones while driving.
　　D. It is important to use our smart phones properly.

B

　　A school bus is one that is used to take children to and from school. In the USA, about 450,000 school buses take more than 25 million to and from school. The yellow school bus is a US icon. Yellow became the color of school buses in the USA in 1939. Dr. Frank got the good idea. He said it was easy for people to see yellow buses and the black letters on them in early morning or the afternoon. That would made children safer.

　　There are not many school buses in Britain, and they are not yellow. They have trackers on them, so kids are being tracked while they travel to and from school by bus. The trackers let parents know where the school bus is and whether their kids are on the bus.

　　Kindergarten is difficult time for some kids. It's the first time for them to go away from their parents. To make kids love their school, Japanese kindergartens and schools have colorful buses. The buses can easily make children want to take them and then, go to school. Even some parents want to take them, too!

　　School buses are becoming more and more popular in China now. It saves a lot of time for students to take a school bus. It said that there will be 3,000 yellow school buses on the road by the end of this year in Chongqing.

61. According to Dr. Frank, _____ school buses are safer for the students.
　　A. yellow　　B. black　　C. white　　D. colorful

62. Children in Japan may easily _____ by taking the school bus.
　　A. save time　　　　　　B. love their school
　　C. play games　　　　　D. do their homework

— 3 —

63. Chinese students will save a lot of time to _____ to school.
   A. walk　　　　　　　　　　B. take a taxi
   C. ride a bike　　　　　　　D. take a school bus
64. This passage is mainly about _____.
   A. school buses　　　　　　B. school life
   C. popular colors　　　　　D. students' safety
65. According to the article, the Chinese school-buses are _____.
   A. not yellow　　B. yellow　　C. black　　D. colorful

C

　　Are you a TV lover? Can you imagine living without TV? Well, you could give it a try.

　　A group of Americans from TV-Turnoff Network(网络) have an idea. From April 19 to 25, they are asking children all over the world to turn off their TV for one week. They hope children will find more interesting things to do. Maybe they can read some books, or learn to swim, or paint a picture. Since 1995, about 24 million people in America have taken part in TV-Turnoff Week.

　　TV-Turnoff Network says watching TV too much can bring children big problems with school, health and family. They want kids to watch a lot less TV. What do you think?

　　Bad for your studies

　　American scientists did a study of 1,300 children. They watched the children for four years. They say that if children watch lots of TV, they don't do well in school.

　　Bad for your health

　　Studies show that when children watch lots of TV, they eat more unhealthy food. More children are getting overweight. Overweight children become ill more easily Watching too much TV is also bad for their eyes.

　　Bad for family life

　　About 40% of American families watch TV at dinner time. That means that they don't talk very much when they eat together.

　　Also, too many violent things

　　An American study says before a child turns 18 years old that child will see 200,000 violent things on TV. Some kids become violent in real life.

　　If you want to learn more about this unusual week, you can go to this website: www. tvturnoff. org.

66. When is TV-Turnoff Week?
   A. From April 19 to 25.　　　　B. Any week in April.
   C. The first week in April.　　 D. It doesn't tell us.
67. What do children do during that week?
   A. They watch TV much less.
   B. They go to this website: www. tyturnoff. org.
   C. They read some books, or learn to swim, or paint a picture.
   D. Both A and C.
68. The passage tells people if children watch too much TV, they may _____.
   ①be overweight　　　　　　②know more about the world
   ③be weak in study　　　　　④become violent in real life
   A. ①②③　　B. ①③④　　C. ①②④　　D. ①②③④
69. Which of the following sentences is NOT true according to the passage?
   A. Millions of people have taken part in TV-Turnoff Week since 1995.
   B. The website www. tvturnoff. org can tell you more about TV-Turnoff Week.
   C. children in America aren't allowed to see violent things on TV until they are 18.
   D. About three fifths of American families don't watch TV when they have dinner.
70. What does the underlined word "unusual" mean in the last paragraph?
   A. 通常　　B. 不同寻常的　　C. 普通的　　D. 显著的

五、书面表达(15分)

　　请以"How to Make Good Use of the Internet"为题写一篇作文，阐述你的观点。

_____
_____
_____
_____
_____

基础模块(下册) Unit 7-Unit 9 阶段测试题七

一、语音(本大题共 10 小题，每小题 1 分，共计 10 分)

从 A、B、C、D 四个选项中，选出画线部分发音不同的一项。

1. A. bl<u>oo</u>d   B. sch<u>oo</u>l   C. cart<u>oo</u>n   D. f<u>oo</u>tball
2. A. s<u>u</u>gar   B. s<u>u</u>nshine   C. p<u>u</u>blic   D. l<u>u</u>ng
3. A. d<u>ea</u>th   B. br<u>ea</u>th   C. br<u>ea</u>the   D. inst<u>ea</u>d
4. A. <u>o</u>ffice   B. p<u>o</u>lite   C. p<u>o</u>ssible   D. wr<u>o</u>ng
5. A. c<u>a</u>ncer   B. p<u>a</u>ssive   C. <u>a</u>ttack   D. h<u>a</u>bit
6. A. pr<u>e</u>ssure   B. <u>e</u>ffect   C. <u>e</u>lement   D. mov<u>e</u>ment
7. A. pol<u>i</u>te   B. <u>i</u>nspiring   C. hab<u>i</u>t   D. <u>i</u>ce
8. A. de<u>s</u>ign   B. adverti<u>s</u>e   C. fal<u>s</u>e   D. cau<u>s</u>e
9. A. e<u>x</u>hibition   B. e<u>x</u>hibitor   C. e<u>x</u>ample   D. e<u>x</u>am
10. A. occa<u>s</u>ion   B. expre<u>ss</u>ion   C. televi<u>s</u>ion   D. conclu<u>s</u>ion

二、单项选择题(本大题共 30 小题，每小题 1 分，共计 30 分)

从 A、B、C、D 四个选项中，选出空白处的最佳选项。

11. It _____ very long before smoking is not allowed anywhere in public areas.
    A. won't be   B. doesn't   C. didn't   D. be
12. If we handle our bad _____ wisely, the situation may _____.
    A. luckily; takes turns for the better   B. luck; take turns for the good
    C. luckily; take a turn for the better   D. luck; take a turn for the better
13. She has spent _____ time reading the book.
    A. a lot   B. many   C. a number of   D. a great deal of
14. Smoking makes them _____ happy and helps them _____.
    A. to feel, to relax   B. feel, relax
    C. to feel, relax   D. feels, relax
15. In many big rivers, a lot of fish die _____ water pollution.
    A. of   B. away   C. from   D. out
16. The weather is _____ hot that no one was _____ in his hot tea.
    A. so, interested   B. such; interesting
    C. so, interest   D. such, interesting
17. We have learned a lot from foreign countries _____ foreign languages.
    A. by mean of   B. on mean of
    C. by means of   D. on means of
18. The _____ story can give us some enlightenment.
    A. followed   B. follow   C. following   D. follows
19. You should apologize to your sister for _____ the truth.
    A. telling   B. not telling   C. telling not   D. not tell
20. As the ground is wet, it _____ last night.
    A. must rain   B. has rained
    C. must rain   D. must have rained
21. Brochures can contain a great deal of information if _____ well.
    A. designed   B. to be designed
    C. was designed   D. they were designed
22. _____ every one of you succeed in passing the mid-term examination!
    A. May   B. Could   C. Might   D. Would
23. Mail can be sent directly to _____ customers.
    A. select   B. selecting   C. selected   D. be selected
24. —Must I do my homework at once?
    —No, you _____ . You may do it tomorrow.
    A. needn't   B. mustn't   C. can't   D. may not
25. How can you keep the machine _____ when you are away?
    A. run   B. to run   C. being run   D. running
26. People from all the corners came to the city, _____ it very crowded.
    A. to make   B. make   C. made   D. making
27. This is the kind of atmosphere we want to _____.
    A. discover   B. invent   C. create   D. find
28. You had better learn to _____ different kinds of problems by yourself.
    A. give up   B. make up   C. play with   D. deal with
29. _____ is a good form of exercise for both young and old.
    A. Walk   B. Walking   C. To walk   D. The walk
30. He is _____ fool even though he always looks foolish.
    A. not   B. no   C. such a   D. so a
31. With the old man _____ the way, we had no trouble in _____ that cave.
    A. leads; find   B. leading; finding
    C. led; to find   D. was leading; found
32. When things go _____, we can react _____ positively or negatively.

— 1 —

A. wrong; either　　　　　　　　　B. bad; neither
C. wrongly; both　　　　　　　　　D. badly; either

33. What about _____ swimming this afternoon?
　　A. going　　　B. to go　　　C. go　　　D. having gone
34. Our teacher told us to spend some time _____ English everyday.
　　A. to practice speaking　　　　B. practicing speaking
　　C. to practice to speak　　　　D. practicing to speak
35. _____ their work, they had a rest.
　　A. Finishing　B. Finished　C. Having finished　D. Finish
36. "You can't catch me!" Janet shouted, _____ away.
　　A. run　　　B. running　　　C. to run　　　D. ran
37. While watching television, _____.
　　A. the doorbell rang　　　　　B. the doorbell rings
　　C. we heard the doorbell ring　D. we heard the doorbell rings
38. He hurried to the station only _____ that the train had left.
　　A. to find　　B. finding　　　C. found　　　D. to have found
39. —Where is my dictionary? I remember I put it here yesterday.
　　—You _____ it in the wrong place.
　　A. must put　　　　　　　　　B. should have put
　　C. might out　　　　　　　　　D. might have put
40. We _____ start before seven, or we'll be late.
　　A. would better　　　　　　　B. had better
　　C. should better　　　　　　　D. had better to

三、完型填空（本大题共 15 小题，每小题 1 分，共计 15 分）

从 A、B、C、D 四个选项中，选出空白处的最佳选项。

In many countries, people can't smoke in the office __41__ and they can't smoke even within the building. Department stores and restaurants are also becoming smoke-free. It won't be very long __42__ smoking is not allowed anywhere in public areas.

For some people, smoking __43__ a daily habit. They think that smoking makes them feel happy and helps them relax. __44__ makes things worse is that some famous actors show smoking on TV. This makes people think that smoking is cool and is a fashion of the day. Those ideas are __45__ and wrong.

In fact, smoking has many bad effects __46__ people's health. Cigarette smoking is dangerous and every cigarette one smokes __47__ one's life. A smoker usually lives a shorter life than a non-smoker. In many cases, their deaths __48__ by cancer-lung cancer or mouth cancer. Cigarette smoke can also cause tooth disease and bad breath. When smoke is breathed in, poisonous elements in the smoke __49__ the body. They __50__ blood pressure and lead to heart disease. Every year, hundreds of thousands of people in the world die __51__ smoking-related diseases.

Smoking is harmful, not only to smokers, __52__ to non-smokers. When a person smokes, people around are __53__ to breathe in the smoke, and become passive smokers. More and more people do not like to be with smokers in the same room.

Smokers should __54__ smoking as soon as possible the habit of smoking can be successfully quit as long as one has the determination to do so for those who don't smoke it is __55__ not to start smoking than it is to quit it。

41. A. any more　　B. no more　　　C. any longer　　D. no longer
42. A. after　　　　B. before　　　　C. since　　　　D. when
43. A. are becoming B. have become　C. has become　　D. become
44. A. Who　　　　B. Which　　　　C. What　　　　D. That
45. A. smart　　　 B. wise　　　　　C. exciting　　　D. foolish
46. A. in　　　　　B. on　　　　　　C. at　　　　　　D. with
47. A. short　　　　B. shortens　　　C. strengthen　　D. lengthen
48. A. excuse　　　B. is caused　　　C. are caused　　D. reason
49. A. attack　　　 B. protect　　　　C. prevent　　　D. stop
50. A. rise　　　　 B. reduce　　　　C. make　　　　D. raise
51. A. off　　　　　B. of　　　　　　C. from　　　　　D. on
52. A. but　　　　　B. and　　　　　C. or　　　　　　D. and also
53. A. allowed　　　B. decided　　　 C. forced　　　　D. made
54. A. give in　　　 B. give up　　　　C. give away　　D. give out
55. A. easy　　　　 B. more easier　　C. more easy　　D. much easier

四、阅读理解（本大题共 10 小题，每小题 2 分，共计 30 分）

从 A、B、C、D 四个选项中，选出符合题目要求的最佳选项。

A

Mobile phone has become a problem for middle schools. Some middle schools in Australia have banned students from carrying mobile phones during school hours.

Mobile phone use among children has become a problem for the school this year. Several children have got mobile phones as Christmas gifts. Teachers said mobile phone use is a distraction(分散注意力的事) to students during school hours and it also gives teachers so much trouble in their classrooms. Teachers were also saying that sometimes students might use phone messages to cheat during exams.

She said some schools had tried to ban mobile phones. Some parents felt unhappy because they couldn't get in touch with their children.

Many teachers said students should not have mobile phones at school, but if there was a good reason, they could leave their phones at school office. They also said there were many reasons why the students should not have mobile phones at school: the mobile phones were easy to lose and were a distraction from studies.

Many people say that they understand why parents would want their children to have phones, but they think schools should let the students know when they can use their mobile phones.

56. Some middle schools in Australia have banned students from carrying mobile phones _____.
    A. because they are students   B. when they are free
    C. when they are at school   D. because they are children
57. We know from the passage that some children get mobile phones from _____.
    A. the makers and sellers   B. the passers-by and strangers
    C. their parents and friends   D. some mobile phones users
58. What does the underlined word "cheat" mean in the passage? _____.
    A. 聊天   B. 核对   C. 查询   D. 作弊
59. Some parents felt unhappy because they couldn't _____ during school hours.
    A. use their mobile phones
    B. leave their mobile phones at school office
    C. help the teachers with their work
    D. get in touch with their children
60. The passage tells us that _____.
    A. students shouldn't have mobile phones at school except for some special reasons
    B. it is impossible to ban students from using mobile phones at school
    C. some parents felt unhappy because they couldn't use their phones at school
    D. parents should teach their children how to use mobile phones during school hours

B

Every day, it is easy to see advertisements in English all around us. Look at your own bags and clothes, and at the bags and clothes of your classmates. How many different advertisements can you see?

Often bags and clothes show the name of the company that made them. This is a popular form. A special picture or symbol called a logo is sometimes used. Logos appear on many different products. They are popular because when you see a logo, it is hard to forget that product or company.

It is common to see advertisements on TV and hear them on the radio. Most advertisements are very short. Sometimes the advertisers use a short sentence which is easy for people to say and remember. Nike, for example, has a simple English sentence which is used all around the world: "Just do it." Advertisements often use funny situations as well. It is simple to remember it.

All advertisements are designed to make people buy a product. An advertisement for a soft drink, for example, might show a group of young people who are having fun. The young people are all drinking the soft drink. Advertisers are saying to you, "Why don't you buy this drink and be like these people. You can be young and modern."

You might think that advertisements are not after you, but the next time you buy a soft drink, ask yourself this question: Why am I buying this particular(特别的) product?

61. From the passage, we know that _____.
    A. all the advertisements around us are written in English
    B. many bags have the name of the company that made them
    C. having soft drinks makes a person young and modern
    D. advertisements are only after young people
62. A good logo is _____.
    A. easy to remember   B. a useful product
    C. difficult to understand   D. easy to buy
63. People are most likely to remember an advertisement that is _____.
    A. in English   B. long   C. funny   D. famous
64. All advertisements are designed to _____.
    A. sell you something you don't want   B. make you young and modern
    C. make you buy the product   D. show you what you need to buy

65. The best title of this passage may be _____ .
    A. Advertisements for Bags and Clothes
    B. Advertisements on TV and Radio
    C. Advertisements About Sports
    D. Advertisements Around Us

C

Everyone has got two personalities — the one that is shown to the world and the other that is secret and real. You don't show your secret personality when you're awake because you can control your behaviour, but when you're asleep, your sleeping position shows the real you. In a normal night, of course, people frequently change their position. The important position is the one that you go to sleep in.

If you go to sleep on your back, you're a very open person. You normally trust people and you are easily influenced by fashion or new ideas. You don't like to upset people, so you never express your real feelings. You're quite shy and you aren't very confident.

If you sleep on your stomach, you are a rather secretive(不坦率的) person. You worry a lot and you're always easily upset. You're very stubborn(顽固的), but you aren't very ambitious. You usually live for today not for tomorrow. This means that you enjoy having a good time.

If you sleep curled up(卷曲), you are probably a very nervous person. You have a low opinion of yourself and so you're often defensive. You're shy and you don't normally like meeting people. You prefer to be on your own. You're easily hurt.

If you sleep on your side, you have usually got a well-balanced personality. You know your strengths and weaknesses. You're usually careful. You have a confident personality. You sometimes feel anxious, but you don't often get depressed. You always say what you think even if it annoys people.

66. According to the writer, you naturally show your secret and real personality _____ .
    A. only in a normal night
    B. only when you go to sleep
    C. only when you refuse to show yourself to the world
    D. only when you change sleeping position

67. Which is NOT mentioned in the second paragraph about a person's personality?
    A. He or she is always open with others.
    B. He or she always likes new ideas earlier than others.
    C. He or she is always easily upset.
    D. He or she tends to believe in others.

68. Point out which sentence is used to show the personality of a person who is used to sleeping on his or her stomach?
    A. He or she is careful not to offend others.
    B. He or she doesn't want to stick to his or her opinion.
    C. He or she can't be successful in any business.
    D. He or she likes to bring others happiness.

69. Maybe you don't want to make friends with a person who sleeps curled up. Why?
    A. He or she would rather be alone than communicate with you.
    B. He or she is rarely ready to help you.
    C. He or she prefers staying at home to going out.
    D. He or she wouldn't like to get help from you.

70. It appears that the writer tends to think highly of the person who sleeps on one side because _____ .
    A. he or she always shows sympathy for people
    B. he or she is confident, but not stubborn
    C. he or she has more strengths than weaknesses
    D. he or she often considers annoying people

五、书面表达(15分)

You are Wang Lin. Your friend, Liu Tao wants to sell his bike. You read a classified ad in today's newspaper. The following is the ad.

| Used bikes wanted |
| Any size & brand |
| Call after 6pm at 5624-8176 |

Write a memo to Liu Tao, telling him about the ad.

基础模块(下册)Unit 10-Unit 12 阶段测试题八

一、语音(本大题共 10 小题,每小题 1 分,共计 10 分)

从 A、B、C、D 四个选项中,选出画线部分发音不同的一项。

1. A. app<u>ly</u>   B. supp<u>ly</u>   C. summar<u>y</u>   D. fl<u>y</u>
2. A. pr<u>i</u>vate   B. dec<u>i</u>sion   C. m<u>i</u>litary   D. cont<u>i</u>nue
3. A. r<u>u</u>bbish   B. ho<u>u</u>se   C. s<u>u</u>ffer   D. s<u>u</u>pper
4. A. l<u>a</u>mp   B. r<u>a</u>t   C. b<u>a</u>nker   D. f<u>e</u>male
5. A. <u>ch</u>oose   B. <u>ch</u>aracter   C. <u>ch</u>allenge   D. <u>ch</u>at
6. A. d<u>ir</u>ty   B. b<u>ir</u>d   C. h<u>ir</u>e   D. th<u>ir</u>st
7. A. disapp<u>ear</u> B. f<u>ear</u>   C. d<u>ear</u>   D. w<u>ear</u>
8. A. <u>e</u>ducation B. <u>c</u>ontinue   C. advi<u>c</u>e   D. respe<u>c</u>t
9. A. fre<u>sh</u>   B. defen<u>s</u>e   C. reference   D. prepare
10. A. p<u>o</u>llution B. sm<u>o</u>g   C. h<u>o</u>t   D. n<u>o</u>t

二、单项选择题(本大题共 30 小题,每小题 1 分,共计 30 分)

从 A、B、C、D 四个选项中,选出空白处的最佳选项。

11. He is looking _____ the key she lost yesterday.
    A. after   B. up   C. out   D. for

12. The first consideration when looking for a job is _____ how much you can earn, _____ what you can do for the job.
    A. not; but   B. either; or
    C. neither; nor   D. not only; but also

13. The reason why I have to go is _____ if I don't.
    A. that she will be disappointed
    B. because she will be disappointed
    C. on account of her being disappointed
    D. that she will be disappointing

14. You should list your work experiences, _____ job titles, names and addresses of employers and dates of employment.
    A. included   B. including   C. includes   D. include

15. _____ your resume is completed, you can send it to prospective employers with a neat, brief "cover letter".
    A. Unless   B. When   C. Once   D. If

16. Tom has become strong and brave through practice; he is no longer _____ .
    A. what he used to be   B. what he was used to be
    C. how he used to be   D. that he used to be

17. The Smiths _____ sending e-mails _____ letters. because it is faster.
    A. prefer, to writing   B. prefer, to write
    C. prefers, to writing   D. prefers, to write

18. _____ that she has received a doctor's degree.
    A. It's an exciting news   B. This is an exciting news
    C. It's exciting news   D. This is exciting news

19. Lily _____ eat lots of desserts after supper last year, so she was very fat then.
    A. was used to   B. used to
    C. got used to   D. had been used to

20. — Why don't we take a little break?
    — Didn't we just have _____ ?
    A. it   B. that   C. one   D. this

21. _____ the time table, the train for I London leaves at seven o'clock in the evening.
    A. Thanks to   B. As for   C. With the help of   D. According to

22. The room is a little small; _____ it is so hot.
    A. in addition   B. in addition to   C. additional   D. adding

23. Everyone except Bill and Jim _____ there when the meeting began.
    A. was   B. is   C. are   D. were

24. I hate _____ when my mother asks me to eat eggs.
    A. that   B. it   C. these   D. them

25. Most parents are not _____ the danger of their babies, eating jelly, which causes most unfortunate incidents to happen.
    A. well aware to   B. very aware of
    C. aware that   D. well aware of

26. . His mother is satisfied with _____ he has done.
    A. that   B. what   C. how   D. when

27. Florence also wrote home _____ the soldiers.
    A. on behalf of   B. instead of   C. because of   D. in behalf of

28. _____ is kind _____ you to have taken good care of your classmates.
    A. this, to   B. it, for   C. that, it   D. it, of

29. He was always ready to help others; _____ , he was liked by others.
    A. in addition   B. in return   C. in response   D. in case

30. We each _____ strong points and each of us on the other hand _____ weak points.
    A. have; have   B. has; have

— 1 —

C. has; has D. have; has

31. It is known _____ us that Nightingale is best known _____ the founder of the modern profession of nursing.
    A. for; to   B. for; as   C. to; as   D. as; for

32. Since 2016, Hangzhou has become a new city. Everything _____ .
    A. are changed   B. was changed
    C. has changed   D. had changed

33. _____ I accept the gift or refuse it is none of your business.
    A. If   B. Whether
    C. Even if   D. No matter when

34. _____ that there will be another good harvest this autumn.
    A. He is said   B. It is said   C. It says   D. It was said

35. By making efforts, we can all _____ no matter _____ we are in the world.
    A. take a difference; where   B. make a difference; where
    C. make a difference; how   D. take a difference; how

36. _____ you don't like him is none of my business.
    A. Whether   B. Who   C. That   D. what

37. —I drove to Zhuhai for the air show last week.
    —Is that _____ you had a few days off?
    A. why   B. when   C. that   D. where

38. The photographs will show you _____ .
    A. what does our village look like
    B. what our village looks like
    C. how does our village look like
    D. how our village looks like

39. You as well as he _____ to blame for the accident.
    A. are   B. is   C. have   D. has

40. "All _____ present and all _____ going on well," our manager said.
    A. is; is   B. are; are   C. are; is   D. is; are

三、完型填空(本大题共 15 小题，每小题 1 分，共计 15 分)

从 A、B、C、D 四个选项中，选出空白处的最佳选项。

Florence Nightingale was born in Italy on 12 May 1820 and was named Florence __41__ her birthplace. Florence and her sister were educated by their father and private teachers. She __42__ in her studies, When she grew up she decided to become a nurse. This decision greatly __43__ her family, because at that time nurses in England were __44__ by people But she was determined, and began caring for the sick in hospitals.

In 1854, England was fighting a war with Russia in Turkey At the front many British soldiers were __45__ or sick. The wounded soldiers lay on the hard floors of a dirty army hospital. In the evening they tried to sleep, but rats ran over their bodies. The conditions for them were __46__ .

Reports of the __47__ of the wounded at the front created anger in Britain. In __48__ , the government appointed Florence to hire female nurses to work in the military hospital at the front. Nightingale arrived in Crimea with thirty-eight nurses. At first the doctors did not believe that women could __49__ . But in fact, the nurses did make a difference. By day nurses cleaned the wards and cared for the soldiers. At night, Nightingale took a lamp and walked around the hospital __50__ the patients. The soldiers began to call Florence "The Lady With the Lamp".

Nightingale and the nurses worked __51__ the clock tending the sick and the wounded. Thanks __52__ their hard work, many wounded soldiers survived.

Florence returned to Britain as a heroine. __53__ her excellent work she was given many awards. With the funds she received, Florence set up a nursing school to train professional nurses. She continued __54__ her advice on hospital reform. In 1910, at the age of 90, Nightingale closed her eyes forever. Every year the International Red Cross __55__ the Nightingale Medal to dedicated nurses of the world.

41. A. in   B. after   C. with   D. for
42. A. excelled   B. skilled   C. good   D. bad
43. A. anger   B. please   C. satisfy   D. upset
44. A. looked down upon   B. looked up to
    C. looked forward to   D. looked after
45. A. injured   B. hurt   C. wounded   D. damaged
46. A. afraid   B. terrible   C. frightening   D. interesting
47. A. sufferings   B. experiences   C. punishments   D. hardships
48. A. response   B. return   C. reply   D. answer
49. A. participate   B. appoint   C. tend   D. help
50. A. to attend   B. attending   C. attended   D. attend
51. A. all   B. for   C. around   D. throughout
52. A. to   B. for   C. of   D. in
53. A. Because   B. Because of   C. For   D. As
54. A. offer   B. offering   C. offered   D. to offer
55. A. awards   B. rewards   C. prizes   D. gifts

四、阅读理解（本大题共 10 小题，每小题 2 分，共计 30 分）

从 A、B、C、D 四个选项中，选出符合题目要求的最佳选项。

A

Facing the Smart Phone Age
Wed. May 11, 10:00am-12:30pm;
Shores Building, Room 206

If you find it hard to imagine life without your smart phone, you are not alone. Mobile communication technology become an important part of life and has changed the world in many important ways.

Health Care

Mobile communication has helped spread medical treatment information. For example, smart phones are used to send people medical information, disease-treatment information and other information to some places short of care workers.

Environmental Protections

Smart phones are often used to watch the movements and habits of animals in danger, helping with their protection. Environmental groups have sent text messages to tell people about their work and need. And they get better results than emails.

News Reporting

Smart phones has changed how news is covered and reported. Making anyone who owns a smart phone anywhere in the world a news reporter. Smart phone video cameras allow people to record news events. As they happen and smart phone communication allows them to get the video out the rest of the world.

Guest speakers

Dr. Levi Tbile and Dr. Erin Lasiter of the Midwest Center of Information Technology.

Free talks but only ticket holders are allowed in.

A light lunch reception will follow in the Goldstein Library.

56. The talks will last _____.
 A. 1.5 hours B. 2.5 hours C. 9.5 hours D. 14.5 hours

57. Smart phones help people _____ in area where care workers are not enough.
 A. do more sports to keep fit
 B. know more medical knowledge
 C. know more medical care workers
 D. get immediate medical treatment

58. The underlined word "their" refers to _____.
 A. the animals' B. the smart phones'
 C. the environmental groups' D. the people's

59. Which of the following is NOT true?
 A. These two talks are given by Dr. Levi Tbile and Dr. Erin Lasiter.
 B. People can use smart phone video cameras to record news events.
 C. You have to pay for your ticket before the talk.
 D. A light lunch will be served in the library after the talks.

60. The above information is about _____.
 A. the increase of smart phone sales
 B. the new ways of spreading information
 C. health care and environmental protection around the world
 D. the changes mobile communication has brought to our life

B

Collecting coins can be an interesting hobby for kids. Collecting coins from all over the world can make you learn about different cultures.

It's easy to start collecting coins. The first place to look at is your piggy bank(储钱罐). Next ask your parents for cool and interesting coins. It's also great to get coins from your grandparents. They may have some from a trip or maybe they have an old coin collection. Don't be sorry if they don't want to give them to you, but it's OK to ask.

You'll want to get a good magnifier(放大镜) to see your coins clearly. You'll also need to get a good book about coins. The book will give you some information about coins, such as dates, prices and types.

Also you'll need a place to store your coins. If you have very dear coins, you can store them in special boxes. Maybe this is the easiest way to store your coins. Another way is to buy albums(相册) where you can store your coins. This is an easy way to see your coins and look through them.

61. What's the advantage of collecting coins according to the passage?
 A. You can get a lot of money.
 B. You can meet interesting people.
 C. You can travel to different places.
 D. You can learn about different cultures.

62. The easiest way to store your coins is to _____.
 A. buy albums where you can store coins
 B. put them in your piggy bank
 C. put them in special boxes
 D. take them with you every day

63. You'll need all the following things in order to collect coins EXCEPT _____.

A. an album	B. a ruler
C. a magnifier	D. a book about coins

64. What's the meaning of the underlined word "store"?
   A. To make something bad happen.
   B. To make sure that something is safe.
   C. To bring things from different people or places together.
   D. To put something somewhere and keep in there to use later.
65. What does the passage mainly tell us?
   A. Some suggestions on collecting coins.
   B. The information about dear coins.
   C. Who can give us coins.
   D. Where to find coins.

C

Almost every Chinese person can recite the two lines of the famous poem, "Every grain on the plate comes from hard work(谁知盘中餐，粒粒皆辛苦)." But sadly, many of us don't actually get the real meaning of these lines: Don't waste food.

A CCTV program, News One Plus One, reported that the food Chinese people throw away every year is enough to feed 200 million people for a year.

Do we have too much food? Of course not. According to the UN World Food Program, there were 925 million hungry people around the world, especially in developing countries. Six million children die of hunger every year.

Chinese people are well known for being hospitable and generous. Many even feel that they lose face if their guests have eaten all the food on the table.

Luckily, a number of people have realized the importance of saving food. Last November, Li Hong, a waitress in a restaurant in Nanjing, got fired because she took some leftover food home for her son. Many people stood by her side and criticized the waste of food.

What should we do in our daily lives to waste less food? Here are some tips:

1. Do not order too much in a restaurant. Only order as much as you want to eat. If you cannot eat all the food you ordered, take the rest of it home.

2. Don't be too picky about food. Some food may not taste great, but your body needs it.

3. Keep an eye on what food you have at home. don't buy too much, especially for vegetables and fruit.

66. What does the writer want to show us through Li Hong's story?
   A. Many Chinese restaurants waste a large amount of food.
   B. Many Chinese people are kind-hearted and ready to help the weak.
   C. Many Chinese people don't agree with the behavior of wasting food.
   D. Chinese people feel that they lose face if their guests eat all the food.
67. From the third paragraph, we know that _____.
   A. we have too much food to feed people in the world
   B. there were 925 million people in developing countries
   C. there are only a few people getting hungry every year
   D. because of hunger, six million children die every year
68. According to the passage, we shouldn't waste food because _____.
   A. there is enough food to feed all the people
   B. six million children die of hunger every day
   C. food comes from very hard work
   D. Chinese are hospitable and generous
69. Which of the following is a good way to save food?
   A. Taking home restaurant leftovers.
   B. Ordering more than you need at a restaurant.
   C. Not knowing what you already have at home when shopping.
   D. Not eating the food you don't like even if it's healthy.
70. What's the main idea of the passage?
   A. Many people die of hunger.
   B. Don't waste food.
   C. Don't be picky about food.
   D. Eat all the food you order.

五、书面表达(15分)

假如你是李华，得知某美国餐厅要招聘一名兼职服务员，你对该职位很感兴趣，写一封申请信。要点如下：

1. 具有丰富的工作经验；
2. 周末拥有大量的闲余时间；
3. 拥有能够胜任工作的语言能力；
4. 期待面试。

注意：不得出现真实的校名和姓名；词数60~80词。

_____
_____
_____
_____

拓展模块 Unit 1-Unit 3 阶段测试题九

一、语音（本大题共 10 小题，每小题 1 分，共计 10 分）

从 A、B、C、D 四个选项中，选出画线部分发音不同的一项。

1. A. m<u>ea</u>ns B. rep<u>ea</u>t C. pl<u>ea</u>sant D. br<u>ea</u>the
2. A. h<u>u</u>man B. r<u>u</u>de C. <u>u</u>niform D. <u>u</u>sual
3. A. r<u>a</u>ther B. t<u>a</u>ste C. h<u>a</u>ndshake D. eng<u>a</u>ge
4. A. d<u>o</u>llar B. <u>o</u>ptimistic C. l<u>o</u>bby D. st<u>o</u>mach
5. A. w<u>a</u>nder B. <u>a</u>ttract C. gl<u>a</u>dly D. l<u>a</u>p
6. A. r<u>e</u>turn B. g<u>e</u>neral C. <u>e</u>mpty D. c<u>o</u>llect
7. A. hi<u>gh</u> B. cou<u>gh</u> C. enou<u>gh</u> D. rou<u>gh</u>
8. A. g<u>o</u>ld B. c<u>o</u>la C. s<u>o</u>cial D. m<u>o</u>vement
9. A. crou<u>ch</u> B. s<u>ch</u>ool C. crot<u>ch</u> D. wat<u>ch</u>
10. A. w<u>a</u>ke B. m<u>a</u>ke C. n<u>a</u>tive D. c<u>a</u>nvas

二、单项选择题（本大题共 30 小题，每小题 1 分，共计 30 分）

从 A、B、C、D 四个选项中，选出空白处的最佳选项。

11. He is always tolerant _____ different opinions.
    A. to B. of C. from D. at
12. He grew up in America, which is known as a rich and _____ country.
    A. developing B. developed C. develop D. to develop
13. The window is _____. Who broke it?
    A. break B. broke C. broken D. to break
14. When _____ who was on duty, Billy said he was.
    A. asked B. asking C. to ask D. ask
15. When Miss Williams went into the meeting room, she found all the windows _____.
    A. close B. closed C. closing D. to close
16. People sometimes feel _____ when they are interrupted in a conversation.
    A. annoying B. annoyed C. annoy D. annoys
17. We were extremely _____ when we heard the news.
    A. depress B. / C. depressing D. depressed
18. Mr. Crisp had his wallet _____ on a bus last week.
    A. steal B. stole C. stolen D. to steal
19. Although he had failed several times, Franklin finally succeeded in _____ lightning rod. (避雷针)
    A. invent B. to invent C. inventing D. invented
20. _____ you've studied this quick overview of manners in the US, you're ready to be polite in English.
    A. So B. Now that C. That D. But
21. I need _____ water. Would you give me _____?
    A. any, any B. some, any C. any, some D. some, some
22. I do not care _____ it rains or not.
    A. if B. unless C. until D. whether
23. The man was poor, she thought, but _____ he was honest.
    A. at least B. at once C. at times D. at noon
24. Thoughts are expressed _____ means of words.
    A. in B. by C. with D. on
25. _____ I have a cold, I get a nosebleed.
    A. Wherever B. Whenever C. Whoever D. However
26. _____ he's old, he can still carry this heavy bag.
    A. Though B. Since C. For D. So
27. All women want to keep _____ their weight freely.
    A. down B. up C. from D. off
28. It is _____ that we'd like to go out for a walk.
    A. a lovely day B. too lovely a day C. so lovely a day D. such lovely a day
29. Do you know a girl _____ Yang Mei?
    A. name B. named C. call D. calling

30. He walked down the hills, _____ softly to himself.
   A. sing   B. singing   C. sung   D. to sing
31. The ground is _____ with _____ leaves.
   A. covering, falling   B. covered, falling
   C. covered, fallen   D. covering, fallen
32. _____ many times, he still couldn't understand.
   A. Having been told   B. Having told
   C. He having been told   D. Telling
33. The child sat in the dentist's chair _____.
   A. tremble   B. trembling   C. trembled   D. to trembled
34. When I came in, I saw Dr. Li _____ a patient.
   A. examine   B. to examine   C. examining   D. examined
35. I have some trouble _____ the silk dress.
   A. washing   B. wash   C. to wash   D. washed
36. The graduating students are busy _____ material for their reports.
   A. collect   B. to collect   C. collected   D. collecting
37. Were you _____ when you saw that wild animal?
   A. fright   B. frightening   C. frightened   D. frighten
38. A person _____ a foreign language must be able to use the foreign language, _____ all about his own.
   A. to learn, to forget   B. learning, to forget
   C. to learn, forgetting   D. learning, forgetting
39. We must choose a good attitude _____ life.
   A. out   B. for   C. in   D. towards
40. _____ a post office, I stopped _____ some stamps.
   A. Passed, buying   B. Passing, to buy
   C. Having passed, buy   D. Pass, to buy

三、完型填空(本大题共15小题，每小题1分，共计15分)

从 A、B、C、D 四个选项中，选出空白处的最佳选项。

When you write a letter or make a telephone call, your words __41__ a message. People communicate with words. Do you think you can communicate __42__ words? A smile __43__ your face shows you are happy and friendly. Tears in your eyes tell __44__ that you are sad. When you __45__ your hand in class, the teacher knows you want to say something __46__ ask questions. You shake your head, and people know you are saying no. You nod and people know you are saying __47__.

Other things can also give some information. For example, a sign at the bus stop helps you to know which bus __48__. A sign on the wall of your school helps you to find the library. Signs on doors tell you __49__ to go in or out. __50__ you ever noticed that there are a lot of signs around you and that you receive messages __51__ them all the time? People can communicate __52__ many other ways. __53__ artist can use his drawings to tell about beautiful mountains, about the blue sea and many other things. Books __54__ to tell you about all wonderful things in the world and also about people and their ideas. Books, magazines, TV and radio and films all help us to communicate with other people. They all help us to know __55__ is going on in the world.

41. A. take   B. bring   C. carry   D. gives
42. A. by   B. with   C. use   D. without
43. A. in   B. on   C. at   D. over
44. A. others   B. the others   C. other   D. the other
45. A. put on   B. put out   C. put up   D. put down
46. A. when   B. or   C. but   D. if
47. A. no   B. hello   C. yes   D. nothing
48. A. to get   B. to choose   C. to have   D. to take
49. A. which   B. where   C. how   D. what
50. A. Do   B. Did   C. Had   D. Have
51. A. from   B. of   C. about   D. for
52. A. with   B. by   C. without   D. in
53. A. The   B. An   C. A   D. Some
54. A. write   B. wrote   C. is written   D. are written
55. A. what   B. which   C. that   D. who

四、阅读理解(本大题共15小题，每小题2分，共计30分)

从 A、B、C、D 四个选项中，选出符合题目要求的最佳选项。

A

A farmer was put in prison(监狱). One day, he got a letter from his wife. "I am worried about out farm," she wrote. "It's time to plant potatoes, but I can't do all the digging(挖) by myself." The farmer thought over and then had an idea. He wrote to his wife, "Don't dig the fields. This is where my gold(金子) is. Don't plant potatoes until I come home." A few days later, the farmer got another letter from his wife. It said, "Two days ago, about ten prison guards(监狱看守) came to our fields. It looked as if they were looking for something. They have dug our field." The farmer wrote to his wife at once. "Now you can plant our potatoes," he wrote.

56. The farmer was put in prison _____ .
 A. because he had done something wrong
 B. because he had a lot of gold in the fields
 C. The writer didn't say anything about why the farmer was put in prison
 D. For nothing

57. The farmer's wife was much worried about _____ .
 A. her husband　　　　　　B. their farm
 C. planting potatoes　　　　D. herself

58. The farmer told his wife _____ first.
 A. not to dig the fields　　　B. to dig the fields
 C. to ask the prison guards for help　　D. to find the gold in the fields

59. Why did the prison guards dig the farmer's fields?
 A. They wanted to help the farmer.
 B. Their leader ordered them to do so.
 C. The farmer asked them to do so.
 D. They wanted to find out the gold.

60. Why did the farmer ask his wife to plant potatoes at once?
 Because _____ .
 A. their fields had been dug
 B. the gold was found out
 C. the prison guards asked him to do so

B

When you visit a European family in winter, you'd better not take off your coat as soon as you enter the house. Because that means you will stay for a long time, which will make the host feel nervous. So you should wait until the host asks, "May I take your coat?"

If you are lucky enough to be invited to a formal dinner party in Paris, you should mind your manners. Even your "finest manners" may not be correct by French custom.

For example, it is not polite to arrive with a gift of flowers in hand, because the hostess will deal with finding a vase, when she is too busy to do that.

Though the French love wine, you must never bring a bottle of wine to a dinner party. Why? It's as if you feared your hosts would not have enough wine on hand, and that's an insult(侮辱). You may, however, offer a box of chocolate which the hostess will pass after dinner with coffee.

Another thing you should remember: it is not polite to use the bathroom in a private house. Once seated at the table, guests must never get up and leave the table—not to go to the bathroom, not to help the hostess in the kitchen, and not to serve or clear.

61. You shouldn't take off your coat on arriving at a French house, because _____ .
 A. the coat will make the house dirty
 B. you will catch a cold
 C. it will make the host nervous
 D. it will bring bad luck to the host

62. The finest manners in China will _____ in France.
 A. help you a lot　　　　　B. not be accepted
 C. be the same　　　　　　D. be the worst manners

63. Why is it not polite to bring a gift of flowers in hand to a dinner party in France?
 A. Because flowers mean bad luck in France.

B. Because no one like flowers in France.

C. Because the hostess will be too busy to find a vase for them.

D. Because there is no vase in France.

64. What should you bring to the dinner party as a gift?

　　A. A box of chocolate.　　　　B. Some flowers.

　　C. A bottle of wine.　　　　　D. A cup of coffee.

65. Which of the following statements is not true?

　　A. French people like wine.

　　B. You should not use the bathroom in a private house.

　　C. In France, people usually have coffee after a dinner.

　　D. You should help the hostess in the kitchen.

C

April 27 is a special day in Britain. It's called Take our Daughter to Work Day. It was brought to Britain in 1994 from America. On that day, thousands of girls take a day off school and go with one of their parents to their work places. By doing this, it can teach girls more about the society where they live.

Now the girls can have a close look at what their parents are doing. This may help them to be calmer when they have to choose a job. Mary experienced a day of work at her mother's office. This helped her understand her mother's work better. She said that this made her feel more confident about her future.

Schools and many companies support the activity, too. Some schools even make the day a necessary part of school life.

Experts think that girls with more self-confidence are more likely to be successful than common girls. If parents can set good examples both at work and at home for them, they will do better than others. Take Our Daughter to Work Day is surely a step in the right direction.

66. Where was Take Our Daughter to Work Day brought?

　　A. From America.　　　　　B. From China.

　　C. From Canada.　　　　　　D. From Australia.

67. On Take Our Daughter to Work Day, thousands of girls _____.

　　A. go on a journey with their parents

　　B. have a party with their friends at home

　　C. go to the work places of one of their parents

　　D. take part in a school activity freely

68. What's the advantage by doing such an activity?

　　A. It can help girls understand their parents' work better.

　　B. It can teach girls more about the society.

　　C. It can make girls feel more confident about their future.

　　D. All of the above.

69. Which of the following is NOT true about Take Our Daughter to Work Day?

　　A. It is a special activity on April 27 in Britain.

　　B. Schools and many companies support this activity.

　　C. Many girls like this day because they won't go to school.

　　D. Some schools even make the day a necessary part of school life.

70. According to the experts, being _____ is the most important to girls in their future.

　　A. smart and careful　　　　B. confident

　　C. hard-working　　　　　　D. friendly

五、书面表达(15分)

假如你是Susan，你的生日快到了，请用英语写一份简短的邀请函。做到时间、地点清楚。内容简明扼要。80词左右。

_____

_____

_____

_____

_____

拓展模块 Unit 4–Unit 6 阶段测试题十

一、语音(本大题共 10 小题，每小题 1 分，共计 10 分)

从 A、B、C、D 四个选项中，选出画线部分发音不同的一项。

1. A. ribbon   B. connection   C. policeman   D. object
2. A. opposite   B. associate   C. particularly D. fine
3. A. vest   B. steal   C. guest   D. presence
4. A. shape   B. lane   C. announce   D. ashamed
5. A. blood   B. cool   C. pool   D. choosy
6. A. source   B. disaster   C. costume   D. instrument
7. A. achieve   B. blue-chip   C. character   D. choosy
8. A. apologize   B. apology   C. somewhat   D. contrary
9. A. future   B. center   C. dormitory   D. debt
10. A. hardship   B. honest   C. humorous   D. heritage

二、单项选择题(本大题共 30 小题，每小题 1 分，共计 30 分)

从 A、B、C、D 四个选项中，选出空白处的最佳选项。

11. Snowman is often associated _____ a snowy winter.
    A. for   B. to   C. about   D. with

12. I used to _____ very late, but now I'm used to _____ at 6 o'clock every morning.
    A. get up; get up   B. getting up; getting up
    C. getting up; get up   D. get up; getting up

13. The thief was caught _____ last night.
    A. red-hand   B. red-handed   C. black-hand   D. black-handed

14. _____ is a pleasant color because it has a meaning of life and hope.
    A. Green   B. Blue   C. Yellow   D. Red

15. When people expect their _____ one to come back home, they pin a yellow ribbon on the door.
    A. love   B. loving   C. loved   D. lovely

16. Policemen wear yellow color vest to warn people _____ their presence.
    A. that   B. of   C. about   D. what

17. When people became very angry, we say they _____.
    A. see green   B. see red   C. see blue   D. see red-handed

18. The picture reminded me _____ my hometown.
    A. for   B. in   C. of   D. to

19. When someone is _____, we say that he or she feels blue.
    A. with low spirits   B. in low spirits
    C. in high spirits   D. with high spirits

20. He prefers bright colors, _____, his wife likes dark colors.
    A. on the contrary   B. on the whole
    C. believe it or not   D. at the same time

21. —Will you go home this weekend?
    —No, and _____.
    A. neither Li Ming will   B. Li Ming won't too
    C. neither will Li Ming   D. so won't Li Ming

22. Only in this way _____ improve our written English.
    A. we can   B. can we   C. we do   D. do we

23. Seldom _____ warn them not to do so.
    A. did we   B. we   C. we did   D. did

24. Not until all the fish died in the river _____ how serious the pollution was.
    A. did the villagers realize   B. the villagers realized
    C. the villagers did realized D. didn't the villagers realize

25. Little _____ about his own safety, though he was in great danger himself.
    A. does he care B. did he care C. he cares   D. he cared

26. —David has made great progress recently.
    —_____, and _____.
    A. So he has; so you have   B. So he has; so have you
    C. So has he; so have   D. So has he; so you have

27. —It was careless of you to have left your clothes outside all night.
    —My God! _____.
    A. So did I   B. So I did   C. So were you D. So did you

— 1 —

28. Not a single song _____ at yesterday's party.
    A. she sang   B. sang she   C. did she sing   D. she did sing
29. Not only _____ difficult to understand, but it was too long.
    A. it was   B. it made   C. did it make   D. was it
30. _____ had I finished my translation when the class was over.
    A. Never   B. No sooner   C. Hardly   D. How
31. I am terribly sorry for that, please accept my _____ apology.
    A. good   B. since   C. sincerely   D. sincere
32. When you realize that you were wrong for losing your temper, you may say, "I apologize for my poor _____".
    A. act   B. thing   C. attitude   D. temper
33. When someone apologizes to you, you may say, "_____".
    A. I'm sorry   B. It's all right   C. Excuse me   D. pardon
34. He apologized not for having done something wrong, but for the inconvenience he _____.
    A. had caused   B. had been caused   C. would take   D. has done
35. Chinese people and Japanese people usually feel ashamed _____ making apologies.
    A. by   B. of   C. with   D. for
36. If you are not sure whether the person would accept your apology, you may avoid a _____ situation.
    A. back-to-back   B. teeth-to-teeth   C. face-to-face   D. hand-to-hand
37. I'd rather ride a bike as bike riding has _____ of the trouble of taking buses.
    A. much   B. all   C. neither   D. none
38. I am familiar _____ computer very much.
    A. with   B. to   C. at   D. for
39. —May I help you with some trousers, sir?
    —Yes, I'd like to try those blue _____.
    A. one   B. ones   C. pair   D. two
40. We couldn't eat in a restaurant because _____ of us had _____ money on us.
    A. all; no   B. any; no   C. none; any   D. no one; any

三、完型填空(本大题共15小题，每小题1分，共计15分)

从 A、B、C、D 四个选项中，选出空白处的最佳选项。

Different things usually stand for different feelings. Red, for example, is the color of fire, heat, blood and life. People say red is an exciting and active color. They associate(使发生联系) red with a strong feeling like __41__. Red is used for signs of __42__, such as STOP signs and fire engines. Orange is the bright, warm color of __43__ in autumn. People say orange is a __44__ color. They associate orange with happiness. Yellow is the color of __45__. People say it is a cheerful color. They associate yellow too, with happiness. Green is the cool color of grass in __46__. People say it is a refreshing color. In general, people __47__ two groups of colors: warm colors and cool colors. The warm colors are red, orange and __48__. Where there are warm color and a lot of light, people usually want to be __49__. Those who like to be with __50__ like red. The cool colors are __51__ and blue. Where are these colors, people are usually worried. Some scientists say that time seems to __52__ more slowly in a room with warm colors. They suggest that a warm color is a good __53__ for a living room or a __54__. People who are having a rest or are eating do not want time to pass quickly. __55__ colors are better for some offices if the people working there want time to pass quickly.

41. A. sadness   B. anger   C. administration   D. smile
42. A. roads   B. ways   C. danger   D. places
43. A. land   B. leaves   C. grass   D. mountains
44. A. lively   B. dark   C. noisy   D. frightening
45. A. moonlight   B. light   C. sunlight   D. stars
46. A. summer   B. spring   C. autumn   D. winter
47. A. speak   B. say   C. talk about   D. tell
48. A. green   B. yellow   C. white   D. gray
49. A. calm   B. sleepy   C. active   D. helpful
50. A. the other   B. another   C. other one   D. others
51. A. black   B. green   C. golden   D. yellow
52. A. go round   B. go by   C. go off   D. go along

53. A. one   B. way   C. fact   D. matter
54. A. factory   B. classroom   C. restaurant   D. hospital
55. A. Different   B. Cool   C. Warm   D. All

四、阅读理解（本大题共 15 小题，每小题 2 分，共计 30 分）

从 A、B、C、D 四个选项中，选出符合题目要求的最佳选项。

A

Happiness is for everyone. You don't need to care about those people who have beautiful houses with large gardens and swimming pools or those who have nice cars and a lot of money and so on. Why? Because those who have big houses may often feel lonely and those who have cars may want to walk on the country roads at their free time.

In fact, happiness is always around you if you put your heart into it. When you are in trouble at school, your friends will help you; when you study hard at your lessons, your parents are always taking good care of your life and your health; when you get success, your friends will say congratulations to you; when you do something wrong, people around you will help you to correct it. And when you do something good to others, you will feel happy, too. All these are your happiness. If you notice them, you can see that happiness is always around you.

Happiness is not the same as money. It is a feeling of your heart. When you are poor, you can also say you are very happy, because you have something else that can't be bought with money. When you meet with difficulties, you can say loudly you are very happy, because you have more chances to challenge yourself. So you cannot always say you are poor and you have bad luck. As the saying goes, life is like a revolving（旋转）door. When it closes, it also opens. If you take every chance you get, you can be a happy and lucky person.

56. Happiness is for _____ .
    A. those who have large and beautiful houses
    B. those who have cars
    C. all people

57. When you do something wrong, _____ .
    A. you may correct it
    B. you will have no chance to challenge yourself
    C. anybody will laugh at you

58. Which is TRUE according to the passage?
    A. When you get success, your friends will be very proud of you.
    B. You can get help from others when you make mistakes.
    C. All the above.

59. Why do we say "Happiness is not the same as money"? Because _____ .
    A. money always brings happiness
    B. money doesn't always bring happiness
    C. everything can be bought with money

60. Which is the title of the passage?
    A. Do Something Good to Others
    B. Happy and Lucky
    C. Happiness

B

We each have a memory. That's why we can still remember things after a long time. Some people have very good memories and they can easily learn many things by heart, but some people can only remember things when they say or do them again and again.

A good memory is a great help in learning a language. Everybody learns his mother language when he is a small child. He hears the sounds, remember them and then he learns to speak. Some children are living with their parents in foreign countries. They can learn two languages as easily as one because they hear, remember and speak two languages every day. In school it is not so easy to learn a foreign language because the students have so little time for it, and they are busy with other subjects, too.

But a man's memory is quite improvable. Your memory will become better and better when you do more and more exercises. If we want to learn a foreign language well, we must do a lot of listening and speaking. And this can improve our memories. Memory is a diary, and we all carry it with us.

61. We can still remember things after a long time because _____ .
    A. we often talk about them
    B. we often take photos
    C. we have memories

62. People _____ can't easily remember things.
   A. who have few friends
   B. who are too busy
   C. who have poor memories
63. A good memory helps people _____ .
   A. know if their friends are true.
   B. learn languages easily
   C. find light jobs
64. Some children are living with their parents in foreign countries, so _____ .
   A. they can easily learn two languages
   B. they can forget their mother language.
   C. they can't talk with the people around them
65. _____ can help people improve their memories.
   A. Books
   B. TV programs
   C. More and more exercises

C

Surtsey was born in 1963. Scientists saw the birth of this island. It began at 7:30 a.m. on 14th November. A fishing boat was near Iceland. The boat moved under the captain's (船长) feet. He noticed a strange smell. He saw some black smoke. A volcano (火山) was breaking out. Red-hot rocks, fire and smoke were rushing up from the bottom (底部) of the sea. The island grew quickly. It was 10 meters high the next day and 60 meters high on 18th November. Scientists flew there to watch. It was exciting. Smoke and fire were still rushing up. Pieces of red-hot rock were flying into the air and falling into the sea. The sea was boiling and there was a strange light in the sky. Surtsey grew and grew. Then it stopped in June 1967. It was 175 meters high and 2 kilometers long. And life was already coming to Surtsey. Plants grew. Birds came. Some scientists built a house. They want to learn about this young island. A new island is like a new world.

66. Surtsey is _____ .
   A. an island not far from Iceland
   B. a new volcano
   C. a fishing boat

67. Scientists flew there _____ .
   A. to watch the birth of the island
   B. to save the fishing boat
   C. to learn about the island
68. When did scientist fly there to watch?
   A. Before the volcano broke out.
   B. As soon as the volcano broke out.
   C. About four days after the volcano broke out.
69. Put the following sentences in correct order.
   a. The captain found the boat was moving.
   b. A new island appeared in the sea.
   c. Fire, smoke and rocks were seen rushing up.
   d. A fishing boat was near Iceland.
   e. The island grew quickly.
   A. d-a-c-b-e
   B. a-b-c-d-e
   C. a-b-e-c-d
70. The best title of this article is _____ .
   A. A new island
   B. The birth of an island
   C. A new world

五、书面表达(15分)

Talk about traffic nowadays
要求：遵守交通规则；孩子们不在街道上玩耍和踢球；成年人不能酒后驾车。80词左右。

_____
_____
_____
_____
_____

拓展模块 Unit 7–Unit 9 阶段测试题十一

一、语音（本大题共 10 小题，每小题 1 分，共计 10 分）

从 A、B、C、D 四个选项中，选出画线部分发音不同的一项。

1. A. ch<u>a</u>rm   B. dem<u>a</u>nd   C. f<u>a</u>me   D. d<u>a</u>rk
2. A. <u>r</u>esidence   B. <u>r</u>epresent   C. <u>r</u>egister   D. <u>r</u>eplace
3. A. <u>th</u>is   B. <u>th</u>at   C. <u>th</u>ough   D. <u>th</u>ree
4. A. c<u>a</u>se   B. m<u>a</u>ke   C. m<u>a</u>p   D. c<u>a</u>pable
5. A. prov<u>i</u>ding   B. l<u>i</u>ke   C. l<u>i</u>ttle   D. l<u>i</u>vely
6. A. acr<u>o</u>ss   B. v<u>o</u>lt   C. ag<u>o</u>   D. c<u>o</u>mpose
7. A. c<u>u</u>rrent   B. d<u>u</u>ck   C. <u>u</u>mbrella   D. form<u>u</u>la
8. A. <u>g</u>eneral   B. <u>g</u>rasp   C. <u>g</u>roup   D. <u>g</u>arage
9. A. i<u>n</u>k   B. tha<u>n</u>k   C. a<u>n</u>nounce   D. hu<u>n</u>gry
10. A. d<u>ou</u>bt   B. m<u>ou</u>th   C. d<u>ou</u>ble   D. m<u>ou</u>ntain

二、单项选择题（本大题共 30 小题，每小题 1 分，共计 30 分）

从 A、B、C、D 四个选项中，选出空白处的最佳选项。

11. His family have been a very positive influence _____ him.
    A. about   B. with   C. in   D. on
12. The film was boring to an unbelievable _____.
    A. level   B. degree   C. extent   D. extant
13. American pop music _____ in the twentieth century.
    A. transmitted   B. produced   C. exposed   D. accelerated
14. _____ it was getting very late, we soon turned back.
    A. As   B. While   C. So   D. However
15. After lunch they went on _____ for three hours.
    A. talk   B. to talk   C. talking   D. having talked
16. She promised _____ her mother in the hospital.
    A. look after   B. looking after   C. looked after   D. to look after
17. Keeping silence was the necessary _____ of the conference.
    A. idea   B. demand   C. question   D. meaning
18. The people who _____ Net worms are those who are addicted to the Internet.
    A. referred to as   B. called   C. are known as   D. are known for
19. He'd rather _____ in the countryside.
    A. work   B. to work   C. working   D. having worked
20. —It's late. I'd like to say goodbye.
    —_____.
    A. Please stay more a while.
    B. That's all right.
    C. Hope you had a good time. See you tomorrow.
    D. I'll miss you.
21. —Lucy failed to _____ her mid-term exam.
    —What a pity! No wonder she is in low spirits.
    A. get over   B. get through   C. get across   D. get round
22. In cold winter, the temperature in Harbin often remains _____ zero all day.
    A. above   B. below   C. over   D. under
23. _____ of them has an English dictionary.
    A. Every   B. All   C. Both   D. Each
24. I shall go _____ it doesn't rain.
    A. although   B. unless   C. providing   D. because
25. We expect you _____ here for a long time.
    A. staying   B. stay   C. to stay   D. stayed
26. It's hard to convey _____, but you'll see what we're talking about in the video.
    A. in words   B. in need   C. in detail   D. in order
27. You can also _____ knowledge through practice.
    A. calculate   B. obtain   C. push   D. multiply
28. He drove at a _____ speed.
    A. constant   B. content   C. conscious   D. continue
29. The cost of the party will _____ the number of people invited.
    A. respond to   B. the same as   C. proportion to   D. be proportional to
30. It's difficult for him to _____ the maths problem.
    A. count out   B. calculate out   C. work out   D. work

31. Eight _____ two is four.
    A. plus   B. minus   C. times   D. divided by
32. My watch doesn't work. I have to _____ it _____ right now.
    A. make; repair   B. have; repair
    C. make; to repair   D. have; repaired
33. I don't think he's ever been to the Monkey Island, _____?
    A. has he   B. hasn't he   C. is it   D. isn't he
34. This shirt is _____ for my brother, I am afraid.
    A. much too big   B. much too bigger
    C. too much big   D. too much bigger
35. It's been over two weeks _____ he left home.
    A. for   B. before   C. since   D. Because
36. We don't know the woman _____ wants to see you.
    A. she   B. which   C. whom   D. who
37. —Must I finish all this work in an hour?
    —No, you _____.
    A. must   B. need not   C. should not   D. won't
38. —Do you want to come with us?
    —If Mary wants to go, _____.
    A. I also go   B. so do I   C. so will I   D. so I will
39. When they saw so many high buildings in Pudong, they couldn't help _____, "Great!".
    A. cry   B. crying   C. cries   D. cried
40. —Stop _____. Let's begin our class.
    —OK, we will stop _____ to you.
    A. to talk; to listen   B. to talk; listening
    C. talking; to listen   D. talking; listening

三、完型填空(本大题共15小题，每小题1分，共计15分)

从 A、B、C、D 四个选项中，选出空白处的最佳选项。

My father and I are moving gracefully(优雅地) across the floor. Around and around we go, __41__ and nodding to the other dancers. My father holds my hand. All the years that I __42__ to dance with him disappear now. And those __43__ times come back.

I remember when I was almost three and my father came home from work, he pulled me into his __44__ and began to dance me around the table. We danced through the years. One night when I was fifteen, I was __45__ in some painful feelings. My father asked me to dance with him. "Come on," he said, "let's get the __46__ on the run." When I turned away from him, my father put his hand on my shoulder, and I __47__ out of the chair shouting, "Don't touch me! I am sick and __48__ of dancing with you!" I saw the __49__ on his face, but words were out and I could not call them back. I ran to my room crying __50__. We did not dance together after that night. My father waited up for me through my high school and college years when I danced my way out of his __51__.

Many years later, soon after his __52__ picked up from a heart problem, my mother wrote that they had __53__ a dance club. "You remember how your father loves to dance." Yes, I remembered. My eyes filled up with __54__. I knew he was waiting for a(an) __55__ from me.

41. A. laughing   B. crying   C. speaking   D. joking
42. A. refused   B. hated   C. used   D. hid
43. A. happy   B. hard   C. early   D. unhappy
44. A. head   B. hands   C. arms   D. face
45. A. covered   B. settled   C. stopped   D. lost
46. A. feelings   B. unhappiness   C. pains   D. regret
47. A. ran   B. waved   C. walked   D. jumped
48. A. tired   B. concerned   C. uninterested   D. frightened
49. A. disappointment B. hurt   C. attitude   D. anger
50. A. formally   B. incorrectly   C. loudly   D. hardly
51. A. control   B. floor   C. life   D. field
52. A. speed   B. heart   C. body   D. health
53. A. joined   B. left   C. started   D. trained
54. A. loving   B. remembering   C. worrying   D. dancing
55. A. answer   B. change   C. apology   D. praise

四、阅读理解(本大题共 15 小题，每小题 2 分，共计 30 分)

从 A、B、C、D 四个选项中，选出符合题目要求的最佳选项。

A

A young man once went into town and bought himself a pair of trousers. When he got home, he went upstairs to his bedroom and put them on. He found that they were about two inches too long.

He came downstairs, where his mother and his two sisters were washing up tea things in the kitchen. "These new trousers are too long." He said. "They need shortening(缩短) by about two inches. Would one of you mind doing this for me, please?" His mother and sisters were busy and none of them said anything.

But as soon as his mother had finished washing up, she went quietly upstairs to her son's bedroom and shortened the trousers by two inches. She came downstairs without saying anything to her daughters.

Later on, after supper, the elder sister remembered her brother's trousers. She was a kind-hearted girl, so she went quietly upstairs without saying anything to anyone, and shortened the trousers by two inches.

The younger sister went to the cinema, but when she came back, she, too, remembered what her brother had said. So she ran upstairs and took two inches off the legs of the new trousers.

56. The young man bought the new trousers _____ his size.
    A. as long as
    B. two inches longer than
    C. as big as
    D. two inches shorter than

57. He asked _____ to shorten his new trousers.
    A. his mother and sisters
    B. his two sisters
    C. his elder sister
    D. his mother and one of his sisters

58. His mother and sisters _____.
    A. agreed to do that
    B. didn't want to do that
    C. said nothing to him
    D. said something to him

59. His elder sister shortened the trousers _____.
    A. after finished washing
    B. before she went to bed
    C. when she came back from the cinema
    D. after having supper

60. The next morning the young man would find the trousers were _____.
    A. two inches shorter
    B. four inches shorter
    C. six inches shorter
    D. eight inches shorter

B

When you are learning English, you find it not clever to put an English sentence, word for word, into your own language. Take the sentence "How do you do?" as an example. If you look up each word in the dictionary, one at a time, what is your translation? It must be a wrong sentence in your own language.

Languages do not just have different sounds, they are different in many ways. It's important to master(掌握) the rules(规则) for word order in the study of English, too. If the speaker puts words in a wrong order, the listener can't understand the speaker's sentence easily. Sometimes when the order of words in an English sentence is changed, the meaning of the sentence changes. But sometimes the order is changed, the meaning of the sentence doesn't change. Let's see the difference between the two pairs of sentences.

"She only likes apples."
"Only she likes apples."
"I have seen the film already."
"I have already seen the film."

When you are learning English, you must do your best to get the spirit(精神实质) of the language and use it as the English speaker does.

61. From the passage we know that _____ when we are learning English.
    A. we shouldn't put every word into our own language
    B. we should look up every word in the dictionary
    C. we need to put every word into our own language
    D. we must read word by word

62. The writer thinks it is _____ in learning English.
    A. difficult to understand different sounds
    B. possible to remember the word order
    C. important to master the rules in different ways
    D. easy to master the rules for word order

63. We can learn from the passage that _____.
   A. the meaning of an English sentence always changes with the order of the words
   B. The order of words can never change the meaning of an English sentence
   C. sometimes different order of words has a different meaning
   D. if the order of words is different, the meaning of the sentence must be different

64. "She only likes apples." _____.
   A. is the same as "Only she likes apples."
   B. is different from "Only she likes apples."
   C. means "She likes fruit except apples."
   D. means "She doesn't like apples."

65. Which is the best title(标题)for this passage?
   A. Different Orders, Different Meanings
   B. How to Speak English
   C. How to Put English into Our Own Language
   D. How to Learn English

C

If you look at the sky one night and see something moving and shining that you have never seen before, it might be a comet(彗星).

A comet sometimes looks like a star. Like a planet, a comet has no light of its own. It shines from the sunlight it reflects(反射). Like the earth, a comet goes round the sun, but on a much longer path(轨道)than the earth travels.

If a comet isn't a star, what is it then?

Some scientists think that a large part of a comet is water frozen into pieces of ice and mixed with iron and rock dust and perhaps a few big pieces of rock. When sunshine melts(融化)the ice in the comet, great clouds of gas go trailing after it. These clouds, together with the dust, form a long tail.

Many people perhaps have seen a comet. However no one knows how many comets there are. There may be millions of comets, but only a few come close enough for us to see.

An Englishman named Edmund Halley, who lived from 1656 to 1742, found out a lot about the paths that comets take through the sky. Some comets move out of our sight and never come back. Others keep coming back at regular times. A big comet that keeps coming back was named after Halley because he was the one who worked out when it would come back again. Maybe you have ever seen Halley's Comets because the last time it came close to the sun and the earth was in the year 1986. Then people all over the world were outside at night to look at it. You will probably be able to see Halley's Comets when it comes near the earth again.

66. A comet is like _____.
   A. sun   B. moon   C. sunlight   D. the earth

67. A large part of a comet is _____.
   A. water and rock
   B. water frozen into pieces of ice and mixed with iron
   C. ice, iron and rock dust
   D. only a few big pieces of rock

68. Maybe many people _____.
   A. haven't seen any comets   B. have seen all comets
   C. have seen a comet at daytime   D. have seen a comet

69. Some comets keep coming back _____.
   A. at any time   B. at noon
   C. at regular times   D. at daytime

70. Halley's Comets came back _____.
   A. in 1990   B. in 1980   C. in 1986   D. in 1989

五、书面表达(15分)

健康对每个人来说都是很重要的,我们应该怎么做才能保持身体健康呢? 请写一篇短文来描述。

内容包括：健康饮食；多运动,多锻炼；不熬夜,拥有充足睡眠。

注意：文中不能出现自己的真名,词数80左右。

拓展模块 Unit 10-Unit 12 阶段测试题十二

一、语音(本大题共 10 小题,每小题 1 分,共计 10 分)

从 A、B、C、D 四个选项中,选出画线部分发音不同的一项。

1. A. wisd<u>o</u>m　　B. g<u>o</u>lden　　C. c<u>o</u>ld　　D. p<u>o</u>tato
2. A. daugh<u>t</u>er　　B. p<u>er</u>suade　　C. p<u>er</u>cent　　D. p<u>er</u>fect
3. A. <u>s</u>ix　　B. hou<u>s</u>es　　C. exi<u>s</u>t　　D. boxe<u>s</u>
4. A. <u>u</u>nless　　B. <u>u</u>ncle　　C. h<u>u</u>ge　　D. <u>u</u>nusual
5. A. <u>a</u>pple　　B. cr<u>a</u>zy　　C. tr<u>a</u>nslate　　D. n<u>a</u>rrow
6. A. <u>o</u>ffice　　B. <u>o</u>ffer　　C. <u>o</u>bey　　D. <u>o</u>peration
7. A. w<u>ou</u>nd　　B. s<u>ou</u>p　　C. r<u>ou</u>te　　D. th<u>ou</u>ght
8. A. b<u>ear</u>　　B. s<u>ear</u>ch　　C. sw<u>ear</u>　　D. w<u>ear</u>
9. A. fl<u>ow</u>er　　B. yell<u>ow</u>　　C. sparr<u>ow</u>　　D. tomorr<u>ow</u>
10. A. ques<u>tion</u>　　B. genera<u>tion</u>　　C. reflec<u>tion</u>　　D. illustra<u>tion</u>

二、单项选择题(本大题共 30 小题,每小题 1 分,共计 30 分)

从 A、B、C、D 四个选项中,选出空白处的最佳选项。

11. It's _____ of Li Lei to save the boy who fell into the river.
　　A. cruel　　B. energetic　　C. kind　　D. confident
12. You will be late for school _____ you don't get up early.
　　A. but　　B. if　　C. and　　D. or
13. —Where are you going this month?
　　—We _____ go to Beijing, but we're not sure.
　　A. must　　B. mustn't　　C. needn't　　D. might
14. Between the two mountains _____ .
　　A. lies a tower　　B. a tower lies
　　C. a tower lays　　D. does a tower lie
15. —Dad, I've got the first prize in the speech contest.
　　—_____!
　　A. Not at all　　B. Good luck.
　　C. Good idea　　D. Congratulations
16. The teacher said that the dictionary would help _____ his grades.
　　A. improved　　B. to improve
　　C. improving　　D. having improved
17. Tom and Mike play football very well. We hope _____ of them can join our team.
　　A. both　　B. all　　C. every　　D. same
18. Try to protect your skin _____ by the sun.
　　A. from burnt　　B. from being burn
　　C. away from burning　　D. away from burnt
19. We should pay attention to _____ our planet.
　　A. protect　　B. protecting　　C. protects　　D. protected
20. It was not until near the end of the letter _____ she mentioned her plan.
　　A. that　　B. where　　C. why　　D. when
21. Bob can speak English, he can speak French _____ .
　　A. neither　　B. also　　C. either　　D. as well
22. It's hard to _____ when driverless cars will be everywhere in our city.
　　A. addict　　B. predict　　C. indict　　D. contradict
23. We can't agree with you. _____ , thank you for putting it.
　　A. nevertheless　　B. since　　C. as　　D. till
24. Have you ordered tickets _____ ?
　　A. on time　　B. in advance　　C. in a row　　D. time after time
25. —That's a nice coat. You look beautiful in it.
　　—Thank you a lot. I bought it yesterday, but I don't _____ the color.
　　A. afraid of　　B. concentrate on　　C. worry about　　D. concern about
26. What else has she done _____ washing the dishes?
　　A. beside　　B. except　　C. besides　　D. expect
27. They recognize him _____ one of the best singers.
　　A. as　　B. to　　C. on　　D. in
28. She was invited, but didn't _____ .
　　A. show off　　B. show through　　C. show up　　D. show around
29. It's no use _____ .
　　A. quarrel　　B. quarreling
　　C. quarreled　　D. having quarreled

— 1 —

30. Look! _____ beautiful that picture is!
   A. How   B. What   C. What a   D. How a
31. If I _____ the film, I would have told you about it.
   A. see   B. saw   C. seen   D. had seen
32. I wish that you _____ again.
   A. try   B. trying   C. could try   D. having tried
33. —Thank you for your wonderful dinner.
   —_____.
   A. Don't say that   B. It's nothing
   C. I don't think so   D. I'm glad you enjoyed it
34. Your body will soon recover if you _____ the medicine on time.
   A. take   B. drink   C. eat   D. get
35. The song reminded me _____ the days with my classmates.
   A. with   B. of   C. to   D. on
36. —The cake looks _____.
   —Yes, and it tastes even _____.
   A. well; good   B. nice; better
   C. good; worse   D. better; best
37. The beautiful paper flowers _____ the whole store.
   A. were used to decorating   B. used to decorate
   C. were used to decorate   D. used to be decorate
38. —_____ will you come back? I feel so helpless.
   —In an hour.
   A. How soon   B. How often   C. How far   D. How long
39. He insisted that I _____ abroad for education.
   A. go   B. went   C. will go   D. gone
40. I really can't see anything. His head is _____ of my view.
   A. on my way   B. by the way   C. in the way   D. out of the way

三、完型填空(本大题共15小题，每小题1分，共计15分)

从A、B、C、D四个选项中，选出空白处的最佳选项。

My head was so full of digital noise that my brain was about to explode. As a writer, I was __41__ to admit my love of books had been replaced by a brain that simply could not sit still. So, this year I __42__ to return to books before the Internet broke my brain.

My goal was 52 books. It seemed like an impossible __43__. A 400-page book will take the __44__ person around eight hours to read. Finding the time to read was a challenge but I __45__ it anyway. I treated my mind like a misbehaving child who needs some rules laid down. Then I read for an hour or two at a time without __46__ each day. It was something I hadn't done in years.

In The Distracted Mind, Larry Rosen says that the more we __47__ spending time away from our electronic devices, the __48__ and more focused we become. And this is what I found. Again, I would __49__ bring myself back to the page, __50__ the urge to reach for that screen. For me, finding that quiet time __51__ finding time just to read. It was a __52__ moment between me and my book when I ordinarily would have reached for my __53__. I read on the tram, in bed at night and on lunch __54__. In our fast-paced world, reading for the sake of reading is not selfish but a powerful way to __55__ and be ourselves.

41. A. wise   B. ashamed   C. cautious   D. numb
42. A. determined   B. happened   C. seemed   D. hesitated
43. A. standard   B. choice   C. expectation   D. task
44. A. intelligent   B. diligent   C. average   D. gifted
45. A. received   B. made   C. refused   D. got
46. A. delay   B. hesitation   C. permission   D. disturbance
47. A. avoid   B. practice   C. admit   D. imagine
48. A. calmer   B. stronger   C. tougher   D. luckier
49. A. hardly   B. violently   C. easily   D. difficultly
50. A. expressing   B. possessing   C. accepting   D. resisting
51. A. required   B. suggested   C. meant   D. differed
52. A. critical   B. delightful   C. special   D. busy
53. A. wallet   B. book   C. phone   D. pen
54. A. program   B. menu   C. option   D. break
55. A. slow down   B. speed up   C. cheer up   D. feel down

四、阅读理解(本大题共 15 小题,每小题 2 分,共计 30 分)

从 A、B、C、D 四个选项中,选出符合题目要求的最佳选项。

A

If you get into the forest with your friends, stay with them always. If you don't, you may get lost. If you really get lost, this is what you should do. Sit down and stay where you are. Don't try to find your friends—let them find you by staying in one place.

There is another way to help your friends or other nearby people to find you. Give them a signal(信号) by shouting or whistling(吹口哨) three times. Any signal given three times is a call for help.

Keep up shouting or whistling always three times together. When people hear you, they will know that you are not just making noise for fun. They will let you know that they have heard your signal. They give you two shouts, two whistles, or two gun-shots(枪声). When someone gives you a signal, it is an answer to a call for help. If you don't think that you will get help before night comes, try to make a little house—cover up to the holes with branches(树枝) with lots of leaves. Make yourself a soft bed with leaves and grass.

What should you do if you get hungry or need drinking water? You would have to leave your little house to look for a river. Don't just walk away. Pick off small branches and drop them as you walk so that you can find your way back. The most important thing to do when you are lost is—stay in one place.

56. If you lost in the forest, you should _____.
    A. stay where you are and give signals three times
    B. walk around the forest and shout so that your friends could hear you
    C. try to find your friends as soon as possible
    D. try to get out of the forest and shout for help

57. If you want to let people believe that you are not just making noise for fun, you should _____.
    A. tell people that you are lost   B. keep up shouting or whistling
    C. shout at the top of your voice   D. shout or whistle three times

58. When you hear two shouts, or whistles, or gunshots, _____.
    A. you should shout more loudly
    B. you can whistle three times
    C. it is an answer to your call for help
    D. you should try to run to them

59. When you want to leave your place to get drinking water, you should _____.
    A. just go to the river
    B. find some glasses or bottles before you go
    C. make a fire so that you can have some tea
    D. leave marks so that you can find your way back

60. This passage mainly tells you _____.
    A. when you hear a signal always three times, it is a call for help
    B. What you should do if you get lost in a forest
    C. any signal given twice means an answer to a call for help
    D. how you can live longer in a forest

B

A young man once went into town and bought himself a pair of trousers. When he got home, he went upstairs to his bedroom and put them on. He found that they were about two inches too long. He came downstairs, where his mother and his two sisters were washing up tea things in the kitchen. "These new trousers are too long." He said. "They need shortening(缩短) by about two inches. Would one of you mind doing this for me, please?" His mother and sisters were busy and none of them said anything.

But as soon as his mother had finished washing up, she went quietly upstairs to her son's bedroom and shortened the trousers by two inches. She came downstairs without saying anything to her daughters. Later on, after supper, the elder sister remembered her brother's trousers. She was a kind-hearted girl, so she went quietly upstairs without saying anything to anyone, and shortened the trousers by two inches. The younger sister went to the cinema, but when she came back, she, too, remembered what her brother had said. So she ran upstairs and took two inches off the legs of the new trousers.

61. The young man bought the new trousers _____ his size.
    A. as long as   B. two inches longer than
    C. as big as   D. two inches shorter than

62. He asked _____ to shorten his new trousers.

A. his mother and sisters   B. his two sisters
C. his elder sister   D. his mother and one of his sisters

63. His mother and sisters _____.
    A. agreed to do that   B. didn't want to do that
    C. said nothing to him   D. said something to him

64. His elder sister shortened the trousers _____.
    A. after finished washing
    B. before she went to bed
    C. when she came back from the cinema
    D. after having supper

65. The next morning the young man would find the trousers were _____.
    A. two inches shorter   B. four inches shorter
    C. six inches shorter   D. eight inches shorter

C

Artificial (假的) flowers are used for scientific as well as for decorative purposes. They are made from a variety of materials, such as wax and glass, so skillfully that they can scarcely be distinguished from natural flowers. In making such models, painstaking and artistry are called for, as well as thorough knowledge of plant structure. The collection of glass flowers in the Botanical Museum of Harvard University is the most famous in North America and is widely known throughout the scientific world. In all, there are several thousand models in colored glass, the work of two artist-naturalists, Leopold Blaschka and his son Rudolph?

The intention was to have the collection represent at least one member of each flower family native to the United States. Although it was never completed. It contains more than seven hundred species representing 164 families of flowering plants, a group of fruits showing the effect of fungus diseases, and thousands of flower parts and magnified details. Every detail of these is accurately reproduced in color and structure. The models are kept in locked cases as they are too valuable and fragile for classroom use?

66. Which of the following is the best title for the passage?
    A. An Extensive Collection of Glass Flowers
    B. The Lives of Leopold and Rudolph
    C. Flowers Native to the United States
    D. Material Used for Artificial Flowers

67. It can be inferred from the passage that the goal of Leopold and Rudolph was to _____.
    A. create a botanical garden where only exotic flowers grew
    B. do a thorough study of plant structure
    C. make a copy of one member of each United States flower family
    D. show that glass are more realistic than wax flowers

68. The underlined word "it" refers to _____?
    A. the intention   B. the collection
    C. one member   D. each flower family

69. Which of the following is NOT included in the display at the Botanical Museum of Harvard University?
    A. Models of 164 families of flowering plants
    B. Magnified details of flower parts
    C. Several species of native birds
    D. A group of diseased fruits

70. Which of the following statements is true of the flowers at Harvard University?
    A. They form a completed collection.
    B. They have a marvelous fragrance.
    C. They are loaned to schools for classroom use.
    D. They use authentic representations.

五、书面表达(15分)

阅读是运用语言文字来获取信息,认识世界,发展思维,并获得审美体验的活动。请你就阅读写一篇英语作文。

内容包括:增长知识;提高写作能力;拓宽视野。

注意:文中不能出现自己的真名,词数80左右。

_____
_____
_____
_____
_____

模拟测试卷一

说明：
1. 本试卷分选择题和非选择题两部分。满分100分，考试时间90分钟。
2. 选择题分三部分，第一部分为共答题，所有考生作答；第二部分由文科类职业模块考生作答；第三部分由工科类职业模块考生作答。
3. 考生必须且只能在下列其中一个职业模块后的空格内"√"，确定本人作答部分，在确定范围以外作答一律不计分。
4. 考试结束后，将本试卷和答题卡一并交回。

选择题

注意事项：
1. 选择题答案必须填涂在答题卡上，写在试卷上一律不计分。
2. 答题前，考生务必将自己的姓名、准考证号、座位号、考试科目涂写在答题卡上。
3. 考生须按规定要求正确涂卡，否则后果自负。

第一部分 共答题（所有考生作答，共70分）

一、语音（本大题共10小题，每小题1分，共计10分）

从A、B、C、D四个选项中，选出画线部分发音不同的一项。

1. A. n<u>e</u>t　　　B. s<u>e</u>ll　　　C. g<u>e</u>t　　　D. m<u>a</u>nage
2. A. scr<u>ee</u>n　　B. <u>o</u>ffice　　C. c<u>o</u>ffee　　D. cl<u>ea</u>r
3. A. b<u>oo</u>k　　B. f<u>oo</u>t　　C. childh<u>oo</u>d　　D. ch<u>oo</u>se
4. A. birthd<u>ay</u>　　B. with<u>ou</u>t　　C. wh<u>e</u>ther　　D. <u>ei</u>ther
5. A. sh<u>ou</u>ld　　B. tr<u>ou</u>ble　　C. c<u>ou</u>plet　　D. c<u>ou</u>ple
6. A. <u>ex</u>press　　B. <u>ex</u>cuse　　C. <u>ex</u>hausted　　D. <u>ex</u>pect
7. A. <u>ea</u>st　　B. tr<u>ea</u>sure　　C. <u>ea</u>ch　　D. <u>ea</u>sy
8. A. p<u>er</u>son　　B. ang<u>er</u>　　C. <u>ea</u>ger　　D. c<u>or</u>ner
9. A. ha<u>ng</u>　　B. spe<u>nd</u>　　C. ri<u>ng</u>　　D. dri<u>nk</u>
10. A. <u>a</u>ble　　B. <u>a</u>pologize　　C. <u>a</u>ncient　　D. r<u>a</u>ce

二、单项选择题（本大题共25小题，每小题1分，共计25分）

从A、B、C、D四个选项中，选出空白处的最佳选项。

11. You can save money _____ you buy cheaper things.
    A. before　　B. unless　　C. if　　D. until

12. I am looking _____ a flat _____ a bathroom.
    A. for, with　　B. at, of　　C. after, of　　D. at, with

13. I was looking for a birthday gift for my mother, but I could not find _____ suitable.
    A. something　　B. anything　　C. nothing　　D. everything

14. —Would you like some coffee?
    —Yes, and please get me some milk, too. I prefer coffee _____ milk.
    A. to　　B. with　　C. than　　D. of

15. —Would you like _____ some wine?
    —No, thanks. I don't feel like _____ anything now?
    A. having, drinking　　　C. to have, to drink
    B. having, to drink　　　D. to have, drinking

16. The little boy was afraid to _____.
    A. examine　　B. examining　　C. exam　　D. be examined

17. It is possible for LiMing to _____ the first prize in a coming speech contest.
    A. beat　　B. win　　C. make　　D. receive

18. —_____ brave ZhangHua is!
    —Yes, he helped his neighbor, Mrs Du out of the fire.
    A. What a　　B. How　　C. how a　　D. what

19. _____ the old man spoke, _____ he became.
    A. The more, the angry　　　B. The more, the more angrily
    C. The more, the angrier　　　D. The most, the angrier

20. Mr. Green and Mr. Brown are neighbors of _____.
    A. my　　B. mine　　C. I　　D. me

21. Study hard, _____ you will catch up with your friends.
    A. but　　B. and　　C. or　　D. so

22. Although we have learned English for three years, we still have trouble _____ the new words.
    A. learn　　B. to learn　　C. learning　　D. of learning

23. Now people have more free time. Square dancing is becoming more and more _____.
    A. comfortable　　B. difficult　　C. different　　D. popular

24. Don't be late. No one would like _____.
    A. to be kept waiting　　　B. being kept waiting
    C. to be kept to wait　　　D. being kept to wait

25. _____ efforts we make, _____ happiness we may gain.
    A. The more, the most　　　B. More than, most
    C. More, more　　　D. The more, the more

26. He is very tired. He does not want to do _____.
    A. something　　B. nothing　　C. everything　　D. anything

27. He lost his _____ and fell off his bicycle.
    A. balance　　B. strength　　C. power　　D. way

28. _____ apple fell from the tree and hit him on _____ head.
    A. An, the　　B. The, the　　C. An, the　　D. The, /

29. The meeting room is _____ to hold 600 people.
    A. large enough　　B. very large　　C. so large　　D. too large

30. This picture reminds me _____ my childhood.
    A. in　　B. from　　C. of　　D. off

— 1 —

31. We were made _____ for two hours.
　　A. to wait　　　　B. wait　　　　　　C. waiting　　　　　D. waited
32. The number of people who _____ cars _____ increasing.
　　A. owns, are　　　B. own, is　　　　 C. own, are　　　　 D. own, is
33. It _____ both rain and sunshine to create a rainbow.
　　A. spends　　　　B. need　　　　　　C. takes　　　　　　D. costs
34. —_____ will you come back, Mum?
　　—In ten minutes.
　　A. How long　　　B. How soon　　　　C. How often　　　　D. How far
35. He passed by me without _____ any notice of me.
　　A. paying　　　　B. taking　　　　　　C. making　　　　　D. putting

三、完形填空(本大题共15小题,每小题1分,共计15分)

从A、B、C、D四个选项中,选出空白处的最佳选项。

An old man lived in a nice house with a large garden. He took care of his __36__ all the time, watering and fertilizing them.

One day a young man went by the __37__. He looked at the beautiful flowers, imagining how happy he could be __38__ he lived in such a beautiful place. Then, suddenly he found the old gardener was __39__. He was very surprised about this and asked, "You can't see these flowers. __40__ are you busy taking care of them every day?"

The old man smiled and said, "I can tell you four __41__. First, I was a gardener when I was young, and I really like this job. Second, __42__ I can't see these flowers, I can touch them. __43__, I can smell the sweetness of them. As to the last one, that's __44__."

"Me? But you don't know me," said the young man.

"yeah, it's __45__ that I don't know you. But I know that flowers are angels that everybody __46__. We enjoy the happiness these flowers have brought us."

The blind man's work opened our eyes, and __47__ our hearts, which also made his life __48__. It was just like Beethoven, who became deaf in his later life wrote many great musical works. Beethoven himself couldn't __49__ his wonderful music, but his music has __50__ millions of people to face their difficulties bravely. Isn't it one kind of happiness?

36. A. flowers　　　B. trees　　　　　C. vegetables　　　D. grass
37. A. balcony　　　B. kitchen　　　　C. garden　　　　　D. study
38. A. after　　　　B. as　　　　　　　C. before　　　　　D. if
39. A. blind　　　　B. famous　　　　 C. smart　　　　　 D. friendly
40. A. What　　　　B. Who　　　　　　C. Why　　　　　　D. Which
41. A. stories　　　B. reasons　　　　C. excuses　　　　D. conclusions
42. A. although　　 B. since　　　　　 C. because　　　　D. unless
43. A. First　　　　B. Second　　　　 C. Third　　　　　D. Fourth
44. A. me　　　　　 B. you　　　　　　 C. my mother　　　D. my son
45. A. true　　　　 B. hard　　　　　　C. cool　　　　　　D. fair
46. A. greets　　　 B. doubts　　　　　C. meets　　　　　 D. knows
47. A. broke　　　　B. hurt　　　　　　C. pleased　　　　 D. treated
48. A. emptier　　　B. busier　　　　　C. luckier　　　　 D. happier
49. A. write　　　　B. hear　　　　　　C. play　　　　　　D. believe
50. A. changed　　　B. affected　　　　C. discovered　　　D. encouraged

四、阅读理解(本大题共10小题,每小题2分,共计20分)

从A、B、C、D四个选项中,选出符合题目要求的最佳选项。

A

Fights at school sometimes happen. But how can you keep away from a fight? Here's something you can do.

Be calm(冷静). Sometimes, you feel so angry that you really want to teach somebody a lesson. But being angry can't solve problems. Neither can a fight. Instead, it may bring you more problems. In the school, everyone involved(卷入) in a fight will be punished, no matter who started it. There are winners in a fight.

Shout loudly. If you know someone is coming up behind you to <u>attack</u>, turn toward the person with your hands up in front of your body and loudly say "stop" before walking away. Loud voice can usually make the attacker calm down. If the person doesn't stop, cry for help by calling out the name of a teacher whose office is nearby.

_____ Your friend may ask you to join in a fight. Learn to say no. Helping him fight is not really helpful to him. If you really want to give him a hand, try to ask him to give it up. Also, you can tell him if he gets involved in a fight, he may get hurt and be punished. Then, try to learn why he wants a fight and help him find a right way to deal with the problem.

51. The underlined word "attack" in Paragraph 3 means "_____" in Chinese.
　　A. 抱　　　　　 B. 攻击　　　　　 C. 阻止　　　　　 D. 吸引
52. Which of the following sentences can be put in the _____ ?
　　A. Face bravely.　　　　　　　　　　B. Join in a fight.
　　C. Learn to refuse.　　　　　　　　　D. Talk to someone.
53. The passage is written to _____.
　　A. help students keep away from fights
　　B. warn students not to fight
　　C. advise students to help each other
　　D. encourage students to work hard
54. The passage is written in a/an _____ tone(气).
　　A. sad　　　　　B. angry　　　　　C. serious　　　　D. crazy
55. Where may the passage come from?
　　A. A travel guide.　　　　　　　　　 B. A newspaper.
　　C. A storybook　　　　　　　　　　　 D. A weather report.

— 2 —

B

Two weeks after the Second World War(战争) began, Peter wanted to join the army(军队), but he was only 16 years old, and boys were allowed to join only if they were over 18. So when the army doctor examined him, he said that he was 18. But Peter's brother Bill had joined the army a few days before, and the same doctor had examined him, too. This doctor remembered Bill's family name, so when he saw Peter's papers, he was surprised.

"How old are you?" he said.

"Eighteen, Sir." Said Peter.

"But your brother was eighteen, too." said the doctor, "Are you twins?"

"Oh, no, Sir," said Peter, and his face went red, "My brother is five months older than me."

56. When did the story happen?
   A. Before the Second World War.
   B. During the Second World War.
   C. Before the First World War.
   D. During the First World War.

57. In fact, how old was Peter?
   A. 18   B. 17   C. 16   D. 15

58. What did Bill do at that time?
   A. He was a doctor.   B. He was a soldier.
   C. He was a student.   D. He was a teacher.

59. How did the doctor feel when he saw Peter's papers?
   A. He was surprised.   B. He was mad.
   C. He was excited.   D. He was disappointed.

60. What is the Chinese meaning of "examined" in the passage?
   A. 考试   B. 照顾   C. 训练   D. 检查

第二部分 （文科类职业模块考生作答，共 15 分）

五、单项选择题(本大题共 5 小题，每小题 1 分，共计 5 分)

从 A、B、C、D 四个选项中，选出空白处的最佳选项。

61. —Tony said he could fix my bicycle, but I really doubt it.
    —_____. He is very good at his sort of thing.
    A. Don't worry   B. I could not agree more
    C. of course   D. a piece of cake

62. —Jenny, I think I will just have some coffee for a change.
    —_____. The coffee I bought yesterday is in the cupboard.
    A. Change it, please   B. Never mind
    C. With pleasure   D. Help yourself

63. —I will never found a better job.
    —_____.
    A. I don't think so   B. too bad
    C. congratulations   D. Don't worry

64. —Nowadays children are bearing too heavy a learning burden.
    —_____.
    A. So what?   B. It can't be better.
    C. Good idea!   D. I cannot agree more.

65. —I think you should phone Jenny and say sorry to her.
    —_____. It was her fault.
    A. No way   B. Not possible   C. No chance   D. Not at all

六、阅读理解(本大题共 5 小题，每小题 2 分，共计 10 分)

A farmer had a cow. He took very good care of this cow and one day when it was ill. He was very worried. He telephoned the vet.

"What's the problem?" The vet asked him when he arrived.

"My cow is ill." the farmer said. "I don't know what's the matter with her. She's lying down and won't eat. She's making a strange noise."

The vet looked over the cow. "She's certainly ill," he said, "and she needs to take some very strong medicine."

He took a bottle out of his box, put two pills into his hand and said, "The pills should make her better."

"How should I give them to her?" the farmer asked.

The vet gave him a tube(管子) and said, "Put this tube in her mouth, then put the pills in the tube and blow. That'll make it."

The next day the vet came to the farm again. The farmer was sitting outside his house and looked more worried.

"How's your cow?" the vet asked.

"No change," the farmer said. "and I'm feeling very strange myself."

"Oh?" the vet said. "Why?"

"I did what you said," the farmer answered. "I put the tube in the cow's mouth and then put two pills down it."

"And?" the vet asked.

"The cow blew first." the farmer said.

66. In the story, the vet must be _____.
    A. the farmer's friend   B. a milk factory
    C. a hospital for cows   D. a doctor for animals

67. The farmer asked the vet for help when his cow _____.
    A. was ill   B. didn't eat the pills
    C. couldn't make any noise D. couldn't lie down

68. What medicine did the vet give the farmer?
    A. Two pills.   B. A long tube.
    C. Bottle of pills.   D. A small box.

69. The vet taught the farmer how _____ .
   A. to blow the tube
   B. to make the cow take the pills
   C. to take the medicine
   D. to put the tube in his mouth
70. Which of the following is true?
   A. The farmer ate the pills himself.
   B. The cow got better after taking the medicine.
   C. The vet came to help farmer change the cow the next day.
   D. The farmer waited for me vet outside his house the next day.

第三部分 （工科类职业模块考生作答，共 15 分）

七、单项选择题（本大题共 5 小题，每小题 1 分，共计 5 分）

71. The cube root of twenty-seven plus the cube root of eight equals _____ 。
   A. five   B. thirty-six   C. six   D. eighteen
72. _____ is the basic unit of capacity or volume.
   A. Newton   B. Square meter   C. Cubic meter   D. Metric ton
73. The basic unit of mass or weight is _____ .
   A. kilogram   B. gram   C. milligram   D. metric ton
74. Mary had a fever. Her temperature is 100.4°F, that is, her temperature is _____ ℃
   A. 37   B. 37.5   C. 37.4   D. 38
75. "The screwdriver is 25 centimeters long" can also be written "_____"
   A. The screwdriver is 25 centimeters in depth.
   B. The screwdriver is 25 centimeters in height.
   C. The screwdriver is 25 centimeters in weight.
   D. The screwdriver is 25 centimeters in length.

八、阅读理解（本大题共 5 小题，每小题 2 分，共计 10 分）

从 A、B、C、D 四个选项中，选出符合题目要求的最佳选项。

The world is not hungry, but it is thirsty. It seems strange that nearly 3/4 of the earth is covered with water while we say we are short of (短缺) water. Why? Because about 97% of water on the earth is sea water which we can't drink or use for watering plants directly (直接地). Man can only drink and use the 3% — the water that comes from rivers and lakes. And we can't even use all of that, because some of it has been polluted (污染).

Now more water is needed. The problem is: Can we avoid (避免) a serious water shortage later on? First, we should all learn how to save water. Secondly, we should find out the ways to reuse it. Scientists have always been making studies in the field. Today, in most large cities water is used only once and then runs to the sea or rivers. But it can be used again. Even if (即使) every large city reused its water, still there would not be enough. What could people turn to next?

The sea seems to have the best answer. There is a lot of water in the sea. All that needs to be done is to get the salt out of the sea water. This is expensive, but it's already used in many parts of the world. Scientists are trying to find a cheaper way of doing it. So you see, if we can find a way out, we'll be in no danger of drying up.

76. The world is thirsty because _____ .
   A. 3/4 of the earth is covered with water
   B. We have enough sea water to use directly
   C. We haven't used all the water in rivers and lakes
   D. About 97% of water on the earth can't be drunk or used for watering plants directly
77. Which of the following is true?
   A. 3% of water on the earth is in rivers and lakes.
   B. 75% of water on the earth is the sea.
   C. 97% of the earth is covered with water.
   D. 3% of water on the earth is sea water.
78. From the passage we learn _____ .
   A. If every city reuses its water, we'll be in no danger of drying up
   B. Man can only drink and use about 25% of water on the earth
   C. Today, in most large cities water is used only once
   D. Water can be used only once
79. To avoid the serious water shortage, which of the following is the most important?
   A. Save water and try to make good use of the water in rivers and lakes.
   B. Don't pollute water and keep all rivers and lakes clean.
   C. Make dirty water clean and then reuse it.
   D. Try to find a cheaper way to get the salt out of the sea water.
80. The name of the passage would be _____
   A. The Sea Water   B. How to Save Water
   C. The Thirsty World   D. The Polluted Water

非选择题

九、书面表达（15 分）

请以介绍你的学校生活为主题，写一篇文章。
   要求：1. 80 字左右；
   　　　2. 不能出现真名。

_____
_____
_____
_____
_____

模拟测试卷二

说明：

1. 本试卷分选择题和非选择题两部分。满分100分，考试时间90分钟。
2. 选择题分三部分，第一部分为共答题，所有考生作答；第二部分由文科类职业模块考生作答；第三部分由工科类职业模块考生作答。
3. 考生必须且只能在下列其中一个职业模块后的空格内"v"，确定本人作答部分，在确定范围以外作答一律不计分。
4. 考试结束后，将本试卷和答题卡一并交回。

选择题

注意事项：

1. 选择题答案必须填涂在答题卡上，写在试卷上一律不计分。
2. 答题前，考生务必将自己的姓名、准考证号、座位号、考试科目涂写在答题卡上。
3. 考生须按规定要求正确涂卡，否则后果自负。

第一部分　共答题（所有考生作答，共70分）

一、语音（本大题共10小题，每小题1分，共计10分）

从A、B、C、D四个选项中，选出画线部分发音不同的一项。

1. A. n<u>ei</u>ghbor　　B. <u>e</u>nough　　C. m<u>i</u>dnight　　D. m<u>i</u>ght
2. A. sta<u>tion</u>　　B. ques<u>tion</u>　　C. educa<u>tion</u>　　D. tradi<u>tion</u>
3. A. sorr<u>ow</u>　　B. wind<u>ow</u>　　C. sl<u>ow</u>ly　　D. all<u>ow</u>
4. A. p<u>u</u>ll　　B. s<u>u</u>ccess　　C. f<u>u</u>ll　　D. b<u>u</u>tcher
5. A. r<u>ea</u>lly　　B. cl<u>ea</u>rly　　C. m<u>ea</u>n　　D. h<u>ea</u>r
6. A. clo<u>th</u>es　　B. <u>Th</u>ursday　　C. streng<u>th</u>　　D. <u>th</u>ought
7. A. <u>s</u>ilent　　B. be<u>s</u>ide　　C. willing　　D. <u>s</u>ide
8. A. <u>a</u>board　　B. <u>a</u>way　　C. <u>a</u>ctive　　D. <u>a</u>gain
9. A. ba<u>g</u>　　B. apolo<u>g</u>ize　　C. an<u>g</u>er　　D. <u>g</u>lory
10. A. ex<u>h</u>austed　　B. <u>h</u>onest　　C. <u>h</u>our　　D. <u>h</u>oliday

二、单项选择题（本大题共25小题，每小题1分，共计25分）

从A、B、C、D四个选项中，选出空白处的最佳选项。

11. When someone says "yes" to your idea, plan or suggestion, you have got his/her _____.
    A. improvement　　B. agreement　　C. doubt　　D. sentiment
12. It's _____ that the Earth moves around the sun.
    A. practical　　B. certain　　C. funny　　D. sorrow
13. —Will you help me _____ this puzzle?
    —Certainly. It's a piece of cake.
    A. prevent　　B. control　　C. solve　　D. make
14. Sweetie, walk slowly or the water in the cup will _____.
    A. run over　　B. act out　　C. dry up　　D. rely on
15. The healthy lifestyle she is used to _____ her look much more energetic.
    A. makes　　B. make　　C. be made　　D. making
16. Some people died _____ hunger, so the scientist began research _____ hybrid rice.
    A. of; from　　B. into; into　　C. of; into　　D. from; of
17. Don't forget to take your passport with you _____ you leave for the airport.
    A. After　　B. before　　C. while　　D. until
18. Do you know _____ my mail will be received by my friend in New York?
    A. how long　　B. how soon　　C. how often　　D. how far
19. —Would you like me to show you the way to operate the new camera?
    —_____.
    A. That's very kind of you　　B. Yes, I'd like to
    C. No problem　　D. Not at all
20. —_____.
    —Sorry, but I cannot make it today.
    A. I often go to the concert at weekends　　B. Thanks a lot for your support
    C. Make yourself at home　　D. Let's go out for dinner tonight
21. The train _____ for twenty minutes.
    A. left　　B. has left　　C. is leaving　　D. has been away
22. Which is the way to the _____?
    A. shoe factory　　B. shoes factory
    C. shoe's factory　　D. shoes' factory
23. This class _____ now. Miss Gao teaches them.
    A. are studying　　B. is studying
    C. be studying　　D. studying
24. We will have a _____ holiday after the exam.
    A. two month　　B. two-month
    C. two month's　　D. two-months
25. There is no enough _____ on the corner to put the table.
    A. place　　B. room　　C. floor　　D. ground
26. We can have _____ blue sky if we create _____ less polluted world.
    A. a; a　　B. a; the　　C. the; a　　D. the; the
27. You like playing basketball, and he likes running, _____?
    A. don't you　　B. doesn't he
    C. do you　　D. does he
28. —When shall we meet again next week?
    —_____ day is possible. It's no problem with me.
    A. Either　　B. Neither　　C. Every　　D. Any
29. Robert has gone to _____ city and he'll be back in a week.
    A. other　　B. the other　　C. Another　　D. any other
30. Mrs. Lee teaches _____ math. We all like her.
    A. we　　B. us　　C. our　　D. ours

— 1 —

31. There are many trees on _____ side of the street.
     A. either   B. any   C. all   D. both
32. _____ is the population of the city?
     A. How many   B. What
     C. How many people   D. How much
33. About _____ the fans are waiting here. They want to see the great singer.
     A. two thousand of   B. two thousand
     C. thousand of   D. two thousands of
34. The postman shouted, "Mr Green, here is a letter _____ you."
     A. to   B. from   C. for   D. of
35. He hasn't heard from his friend _____ last month.
     A. since   B. by the end of   C. for   D. until

三、完形填空(本大题共15小题，每小题1分，共计15分)

从A、B、C、D四个选项中，选出空白处的最佳选项。

Trees are one of the oldest "citizens(公民)" of our Earth. They keep our air __36__, reduce noise pollution, improve water quality(质量) and __37__ food and building materials. At 1 to 3 years old, young trees learn how to protect __38__. Most young trees have large, deep green leaves __39__ they can catch enough sunlight and change it __40__ their food and energy.

When trees are 4 years old, they begin __41__ very rapidly and become __42__ to face challenges later in life. __43__ the age of 15, trees become young adults. It is not until the tree is 20 to 25 years old __44__ it becomes a real adult. Gradually trees begin to grow __45__ and even die. When a tree becomes hollow or part of it becomes dead it provides a home to small animals' and is a __46__ of food for many __47__ animals.

In many ways, the life of a tree is __48__ to our own life experience. When we are __49__ the life of a tree, we learn __50__ that each period of life brings its own form of joy and challenge. Enjoy every minute of the life of the trees and take care of the trees!

36. A. clean   B. cleaning   C. cleaned   D. cleanly
37. A. create   B. produce   C. provide   D. give
38. A. they   B. them   C. themselves   D. theirselves
39. A. so as to   B. so that   C. such that   D. in order to
40. A. for   B. to   C. of   D. into
41. A. grow   B. to grow   C. growed   D. grew
42. A. strongly enough   B. enough strongly   C. enough strong   D. strong enough
43. A. At   B. In   C. During   D. On
44. A. when   B. which   C. that   D. while
45. A. old   B. older   C. older and older   D. elder
46. A. source   B. route   C. race   D. sauce
47. A. another   B. other   C. the other   D. others
48. A. same   B. similar   C. seem   D. different
49. A. looking at to   B. looking   C. watching   D. seeing
50. A. of   B. from   C. for   D. about

四、阅读理解(本大题共10小题，每小题2分，共计20分)

从A、B、C、D四个选项中，选出符合题目要求的最佳选项。

A

What can be both red or green, round or sharp, big or small, and more importantly, loved or hated by someone? Yes, the answer is chilies(辣椒).

Many of us in China enjoy adding chilies to our food, but did you know that this spicy vegetable could also be dangerous? A 34-year-old US man recently ended up in hospital after eating a Carolina Reaper, the spiciest chili people have known so far. After taking just a single bite of one, the man suffered from serious headaches in the following days, reported BBC News.

In fact, eating spicy food causes stomachache and headache. But if chilies are harmful, why do people like to eat this vegetable? So what makes people love chilies so much? The human body is influenced by natural chemicals that produce "a sense of happiness", noted BBC news.

And chilies do good to people in another way. Scientists found that the death rate of those who eat spicy food once or twice a week is 10 percent lower than those who eat it less than once a week. The death rate is 14 percent lower for those who eat spicy food six to seven times a week. This encourages people to eat more spicy food to improve health and bring less death risk at an early age.

51. What is the main idea of the second paragraph?
     A. Eating chilies can be dangerous.
     B. The US man died in hospital.
     C. The US man of ten had headaches.
     D. The Chinese enjoy eating chilies.
52. People like to eat chilies because.
     A. chilies do no harm to people
     B. the chili is a kind of vegetable
     C. they can get personal enjoyment
     D. chemicals in chilies make them mad
53. What is true about the last paragraph?
     A. The more chilies you eat, the longer you must live.
     B. Scientists encourage us to add chilies to our food.
     C. We should eat spicy food six times a week.
     D. Proper spicy food may improve our health.
54. Which of the following can be the best title?
     A. Eating Chilies, A Healthy Lifestyle
     B. A Loved and Hated Vegetable
     C. Chili—A Harmful Vegetable
     D. Causes of Stomachache

55. What's the meaning of the word "spicy" in the article?
   A. 下流的   B. 香的   C. 辛辣的   D. 猥亵的

B

AI(人工智能) makes our lives easier and better. Let's see the amazing AI.

Cool driverless bus

A bus door opens and you get on. Wait! Where is the driver? Here is a new kind of driverless bus called Apolong. It has 14 seats and doesn't need a driver. The bus follows traffic rules. It will stop as soon as it sees stoplight.

Your close friend

Hi, everyone. I'm Xiaobing, a chatbot(聊天机器人). I speak like a 17-year-old girl. If you feel lonely, you can talk with me. I'm talented at singing, writing poems and telling stories. I want to be your friend!

World's first AI anchor(主播)

Hey, look! The famous Chinese anchor Qiu Hao is reporting the news for us. But, is "he" really Qiu Hao? The answer is "no". This is the world's first AI anchor. It looks and speaks just like a real person. It can work 24 hours and doesn't make any mistakes. You might see it on TV soon.

Popular AI artist

This beautiful painting was at an auction(拍卖) in 2020. The painting is worth about 3,000,000 yuan! But it is not a work by a famous painter, such as Vincent van Gogh. It was painted by an AI artist. Three Frenchmen created the AI artist. It studied over 15,000 paintings. In this way, it learned to paint.

56. The fact about Apolong is that _____
   A. the bus door can't open itself
   B. it will stop as soon as it sees a stop light
   C. there are 24 seats in it
   D. it doesn't follow the traffic rules

57. Xiaobing can NOT _____
   A. go out to play with you   B. talk with you if you feel lonely
   C. sing   D. be your friend

58. The painting _____
   A. was at an auction in 2019
   B. is worth about 3,000,000 yuan at an auction
   C. is a work painted by Vincent van Gogh
   D. was studied by three French artists over 15,000 times

59. Which of the following is TRUE according to the passage?
   A. AI makes our lives harder and worse.
   B. This new kind of driverless bus also needs a driver to control it.
   C. Xiaobing is a 17-year-old girl.
   D. The AI anchor can work 24 hours and doesn't make any mistakes.

60. We can probably read the passage in _____
   A. a storybook   B. a notice   C. a newspaper   D. a novel

第二部分 （文科类职业模块考生作答，共15分）

五、单项选择题（本大题共5小题，每小题1分，共计5分）

从 A、B、C、D 四个选项中，选出空白处的最佳选项。

61. —I am going to Hawaii with my aunt this month for my holiday.
    —_____!
    A. Have a good time   B. Best wishes to them
    C. Thank you very much   D. It's OK

62. —Bill, can I get you anything to drink?
    —_____.
    A. You are welcome   B. No problem
    C. I wouldn't mind a coffee D. It doesn't matter

63. —I prefer to eat cakes that have cream on top.
    —_____! They are delicious.
    A. Good luck   B. Me too
    C. I hope so   D. You are kidding

64. —The radio says there will be a rainstorm this weekend, so we have to cancel the hiking to Nanshan.
    —_____ I am looking forward to it.
    A. Never mind.   B. What a pity!
    C. My pleasure.   D. No problem

65. —I am sure you will do better next time. Cheer up!
    —_____
    A. I will try.   B. Cheer up!   C. Congratulations   D. Thanks.

六、阅读理解（本大题共5小题，每小题2分，共计10分）

Do you want a job in the holiday? Just go for it. First, you need to know what kind of job is suitable for your age and interest.

If you're 13 to 15.

It seems that you can't work almost anywhere, but you're probably allowed to clean your neighbours' cars or walk their dogs. There is no lowest wage(工资) for children under 16. By law, you can't work more than 35 hours each week during school holidays. And you can't work before 7 a.m. or after 7 p.m.

If you're 16 or 17.

The lowest wage for 16-17 years old teenagers should be no less than 7 dollars per hour. You can't work in a pub or bar, but you can work in many other places. By law, you can't work more than 40 hours each week.

What jobs are out there?

Obviously your choices are limited(限制) by the fact that you can only work during school holidays, but the following situations are fine.

At Christmas, most shops are short of hands, so you may find something to do there. In autumn, there's always fruit picking. It can be pretty hard work, but it pays really well.

  If you're mad about football, you can choose to work in a sports shop or help out at a local football club. No matter how much you are paid, you are doing what you like.

66. In the school holidays, 14-year-old kids _____.
  A. can work anywhere they want   B. are not allowed to work alone
  C. can't go to work at night   D. can work as long as 14 hours a day
67. How much can a 16-year-old kid be paid at least in two hours?
  A. 21 dollars.   B. 17 dollars.   C. 14 dollars.   D. 7 dollars.
68. If you want to clean cars for others, you should at least be _____.
  A. 16   B. 15   C. 14   D. 13
69. According to the passage, which statement is true?
  A. not right for children   B. tiring but pays well
  C. better than other jobs   D. more interesting to girls
70. According to the passage, which statement is true?
  A. If you are 17 years old, you're not allowed to walk the dog for your neighbour.
  B. Teenagers can choose their jobs according to their interest.
  C. Fruit picking pays well because there are fewer people to pick it.
  D. Only football fan is allowed to work in a football club.

第三部分 （工科类职业模块考生作答，共 15 分）

七、单项选择题（本大题共 5 小题，每小题 1 分，共计 5 分）

71. About _____ of the engineers in my company seem to be in their _____.
  A. second-nines; forties   B. two-ninths; forties
  C. second-ninths; fortieth   D. two-ninths; fortieth
72. The new flat is _____ as the old one.
  A. twice larger   B. larger twice
  C. twice as large   D. as twice large
73. The cube root of sixty-four minus three is _____.
  A. six   B. nine   C. one   D. zero
74. 50 degrees Fahrenheit is _____ degrees centigrade.
  A. 8   B. 10   C. 18   D. 20
75. Which of the following is the least?
  A. 0.406   B. 0.064   C. 0.604   D. 0.46

八、阅读理解（本大题共 5 小题，每小题 2 分，共计 10 分）

从 A、B、C、D 四个选项中，选出符合题目要求的最佳选项。

  Mr. and Mrs. Smith have two children, Kevin and Jenny. The whole family are all busy, so they often leave notes to each other. Here are these four notes of today.

3:30 pm To Kevin, Mr. King rang, telling there is no football practice today, and he asked you to get ready for the football match tomorrow and play with him after school. Jeny	4:00 pm To Jenny, It's your turn to walk our pet dog Teddy Kevin
6:45 pm To all, Has anyone found my tennis shoes? I'm doing my homework in my bedroom. Kevin	9:00 pm To Kevin, I saw your shoes this morning. They smelt terrible, so I put them outside the back door. Good night, dear! Mum

76. _____ was asked to walk the pet dog after school.
  A. Mum   B. Kevin   C. Jenny
77. Kevin was doing his homework in the _____.
  A. bedroom   B. garden   C. living room
78. Kevin could find his tennis shoes _____ at 6:45 pm.
  A. under the desk   B. outside the back door
  C. in the bag
79. What will Kevin probably do tomorrow?
  A. Play with Teddy.   B. Play tennis.
  C. Play in a football match.
80. What can we learn from the notes?
  A. Teddy doesn't like to stay at home.
  B. Mr. King may be a coach.
  C. Mum washed Kevin's shoes.

非选择题

九、书面表达（15 分）

  幸福的家庭是我们一生最宝贵的财富。请以 My family 为题，介绍一下你的家庭吧。（80 词）

_____
_____
_____
_____

模拟测试卷三

说明：
1. 本试卷分选择题和非选择题两部分。满分100分，考试时间90分钟。
2. 选择题分三部分，第一部分为共答题，所有考生作答；第二部分由文科类职业模块考生作答；第三部分由工科类职业模块考生作答。
3. 考生必须且只能在下列其中一个职业模块后的空格内"√"，确定本人作答部分，在确定范围以外作答一律不计分。
4. 考试结束后，将本试卷和答题卡一并交回。

选择题

注意事项：
1. 选择题答案必须填涂在答题卡上，写在试卷上一律不计分。
2. 答题前，考生务必将自己的姓名、准考证号、座位号、考试科目涂写在答题卡上。
3. 考生须按规定要求正确涂卡，否则后果自负。

第一部分 共答题（所有考生作答，共70分）

一、语音（本大题共10小题，每小题1分，共计10分）

从A、B、C、D四个选项中，选出画线部分发音不同的一项。

1. A. hammer　　　B. vehicle　　　C. exhausted　　　D. hour
2. A. wealth　　　B. treasure　　　C. cheap　　　D. pleasant
3. A. gate　　　B. crazy　　　C. after　　　D. take
4. A. teach　　　B. meat　　　C. peach　　　D. great
5. A. cloudy　　　B. reply　　　C. really　　　D. heavy
6. A. standard　　　B. language　　　C. plan　　　D. extend
7. A. windy　　　B. rice　　　C. climate　　　D. mild
8. A. morning　　　B. horse　　　C. short　　　D. doctor
9. A. cloth　　　B. clothes　　　C. clothing　　　D. weather
10. A. speech　　　B. chemistry　　　C. church　　　D. charge

二、单项选择题（本大题共25小题，每小题1分，共计25分）

从A、B、C、D四个选项中，选出空白处的最佳选项。

11. The foreign guests, were government officials, _____ were warmly welcomed at the airport.
    A. most of them　　　B. most of that
    C. most of whom　　　D. most of those

12. Studying Wendy's menu, I found that many of the items are similar to _____ of McDonald's.
    A. those　　　B. ones　　　C. any　　　D. all

13. She was _____ because she had been listening to their _____ conversations.
    A. boring, bored　　　B. bored, boring
    C. boring, boring　　　D. bored, bored

14. —Aha, I got first place in the English competition again!
    —Peter! You are _____ again.
    A. giving off　　　B. putting off　　　C. taking off　　　D. showing off

15. The new policy will come into _____ on the day when it is passed.
    A. use　　　B. effect　　　C. service　　　D. existence

16. —Of the two apples, which one do you prefer?
    —_____ bigger one. It's _____ most delicious one, I think.
    A. The, a　　　B. A, /　　　C. The, the　　　D. A, the

17. _____ he gave us on how to keep a healthy habit!
    A. What a good advice　　　B. How a good advice
    C. How good advice　　　D. What good advice

18. Not until he went through real hardship _____ the love we have for our families is important.
    A. had he realized　　　B. did he realize
    C. he realized　　　D. he had realized

19. Eye doctors suggest that a child's first eye exam _____ at the age of six months old.
    A. was　　　B. is　　　C. were　　　D. be

20. _____ the new computer, people car in now buy their air tickets much faster.
    A. Because　　　B. Thanks for　　　C. Thanks to　　　D. Since

21. The increase of the number of the students makes the limited computers not _____ to each student.
    A. available　　　B. affordable　　　C. helpful　　　D. acceptable

22. —Who's in the gym?
    —The trainer together with two trainees _____ in the gym.
    A. is　　　B. are　　　C. am　　　D. be

23. Novel Coronavirus _____ in China in 2019 but now everything is fine.
    A. brokedown　　　B. broke up　　　C. broke into　　　D. broke out

24. _____ work has been done to improve the people's living standard.
    A. A great many　　　B. Many
    C. A great deal of　　　D. A number of

25. I wonder if it _____ tomorrow. If it _____, I will go shopping with my friends tomorrow.
    A. rains, doesn't rain　　　B. rains, won't rain
    C. will rain, won't rain　　　D. will rain, doesn't rain

26. —Must I hand in my homework by this afternoon?
    —No, you _____, but you _____ hand it in before the day after tomorrow.
    A. mustn't, must　　　B. needn't to, must
    C. can't, must　　　D. don't have to, must

27. You left very early last night, but I wish I _____ so early.
    A. didn't leave　　　B. hadn't left
    C. haven't left　　　D. couldn't leave

28. His father _____ the Party since 1978.
    A. joined　　　B. has joined　　　C. has been in　　　D. was in

29. It was such a funny show that people couldn't help _____ again and again.
    A. laugh	B. to laugh	C. laughing	D. laughed
30. With a lot of difficult problems _____, the newly-elected president is having a hard time.
    A. settled	B. settling	C. being settled	D. to settle
31. My mother often says, "Stand tall like the sunflower and be proud _____ who you are."
    A. of	B. with	C. at	D. in
32. —Why are you leaving your job?
    —I can't stand it any longer. I _____ always _____ to work overtime.
    A. am, asking	B. am, asked
    C. was, asking	D. was, asked
33. It was the second time that we _____ in holding such important parties.
    A. succeed	B. had succeeded
    C. succeeded	D. have succeeded
34. Everyone is different and that is _____ makes our world so much better.
    A. that	B. which	C. what	D. who
35. There were _____ many people there _____ I wasn't able to pick her out.
    A. such; that	B. very; that
    C. such; who	D. so; that

三、完形填空(本大题共 15 小题,每小题 1 分,共计 15 分)

从 A、B、C、D 四个选项中,选出空白处的最佳选项。

Amy did not have any friends. All the girls in her class were __36__ with a best friend or in groups, and she always felt left out. So, Amy often walked around __37__. She wanted to seesaw(跷跷板), __38__ she needed to do it with a friend. She liked to swing(荡秋千) and __39__ someone would push her.

One day, Mrs Gibbs walked up and put __40__ arm around Amy. "What's the matter, Amy? Why don't you __41__ with others?" she asked kindly.

Amy replied, "Everyone has a __42__ except me. I have no one." The teacher smiled and said, "Amy, the __43__ to get a friend is to be a friend." Amy asked, "How do I do that?"

She answered, "__44__ around the playground. There are some students out here during this break time. __45__ someone who is alone and then go to ask them to play." Amy wanted to do so, but she was __46__ to be refused.

The next day, Amy noticed a girl all alone on the playground. She worked up her __47__ and walked to her. "Hi! I'm Amy. Do you want to play with me?"

"Okay," the girl said shyly. As they took turns pushing each other on the __48__, Amy found out that the girl's family had just moved from Japan and she also __49__ a friend.

"Want to seesaw?" Amy asked. Ming smiled and nodded. Paired up with each other, they played so __50__.

36. A. broken up	B. come up	C. built up	D. paired up
37. A. alone	B. again	C. gladly	D. quickly
38. A. and	B. so	C. but	D. because
39. A. decided	B. wished	C. explained	D. suggested
40. A. my	B. your	C. his	D. her
41. A. write	B. study	C. agree	D. play
42. A. friend	B. classmate	C. sister	D. parent
43. A. plan	B. way	C. lesson	D. reason
44. A. Turn	B. Look	C. Jump	D. Sit
45. A. Stop	B. Hide	C. Find	D. Lead
46. A. afraid	B. proud	C. pleased	D. surprised
47. A. interest	B. skill	C. courage	D. attention
48. A. seesaw	B. chair	C. swing	D. bike
49. A. needed	B. chose	C. shared	D. trusted
50. A. carefully	B. quietly	C. simply	D. happily

四、阅读理解(本大题共 10 小题,每小题 2 分,共计 20 分)

从 A、B、C、D 四个选项中,选出符合题目要求的最佳选项。

A

On February 9th, 2013, Sarah Darling was walking along the street when she met a homeless man named Billy Ray Harris. She reached into her change purse, emptied out all the coins she had and gave them to the homeless man. Neither of them realized that this small generous act would change their lives.

Sarah didn't realize that she had given Billy not only all her change but also her diamond ring that she had put in her change purse earlier until the next morning. She and her husband, Bill Krejci, rushed to see if they could find Billy. The homeless man was not only in the same place, but also immediately returned the ring. The grateful couple paid him back for his honesty by emptying out their pockets of all the money they had.

Bill Krejci, a web designer, felt that he needed to do something more for this amazingly honest man. So on February 18th, he set up a special page to raise money for him. In just four days, Billy received over $85,000 and there seems to be no end yet.

That is not enough. Billy is living with a person who is generous instead of living in the streets. And that's not all—Thanks to the news report, he got together again with his elder brother, Edwin Harris who he had been unable to find for 27 years.

All the good luck is just because Billy did the right thing—returning something that didn't belong to him.

51. When did Sarah realize that she had also given Billy her diamond ring?
    A. On February 9th, 2013.	B. On February 10th, 2013.
    C. On February 18th, 2013.	D. On February 22nd, 2013.
52. Which of the following is NOT mentioned in the passage?
    A. Billy is living with a generous person.
    B. Billy has found his brother.
    C. Billy bought a diamond ring.
    D. Billy appeared in the news report.
53. The underlined word "That" in Paragraph 4 refers to(指代) "_____".
    A. returning the ring	B. setting up a page

C. living in the streets D. receiving money
54. What's the main idea of the passage?
   A. A generous woman changed her own life.
   B. A kind man set up a special page.
   C. A homeless man returned diamond ring.
   D. Many people donated much money.
55. From this story, we know that _____.
   A. helping others is helping ourselves
   B. helping those in trouble is sometimes not necessary
   C. life is not that easy
   D. we should always help old people

B

It's reported that more than 450 million Chinese have myopia(近视). Around 30 percent for primary school students, 60 percent for junior high students and 80 percent for senior high students are nearsighted. Maybe this is because students spend a lot of time reading books and using electronic products.

Parents might have tried to do something to fix it, such as having their children get eye massages(按摩), take medicine or even get surgery. People who offer these services or products often promise that they can reduce or even cure myopia.

However, you will no longer see advertisements like this before long. The government has made a notice to ban this kind of advertisements. The notice bans businesses from using words like "recovery" and "myopia cure" in their advertisements. The notice says that myopia cannot be completely cured with medical technology now. As a result, these advertisements could mislead children and their parents.

To reduce myopia among young people, the government made a new plan last August. The plan limits not only the time children play video games but also the production of new video games.

Young people can prevent and control myopia by spending more time outside and less time in front of books or computers. People who have eyesight problems should go to a hospital and let a doctor decide what to do.

56. What's the myopia rate of junior high students according to the passage?
   A. 30%.   B. 45%.   C. 60%.   D. 80%.
57. Parents might do the following EXCEPT _____ to fix myopia according to Paragraph 2.
   A. have their children get eye massages
   B. buy them special glasses
   C. make their children take medicine
   D. get their children to do surgery
58. You won't see advertisements on myopia with the word "_____" in the near future.
   A. recovery   B. eyesight   C. medical   D. reduce
59. Which sentence is True according to Paragraph 4 and 5?
   A. Students in lower grades are easy to get myopia.
   B. Production of new video games has been limited.
   C. Spending less time outdoors is good for children's eyesight.
   D. The notice gives advice on protecting the eyesight of elderly people.
60. What can we learn from the passage?
   A. Don't believe the advertisements.
   B. Students shouldn't be allowed to play video games.
   C. The government and people are saving children's eyesight.
   D. Myopia can be cured with the medical technology at present.

第二部分 （文科类职业模块考生作答，共15分）

五、单项选择题(本大题共5小题，每小题1分，共计5分)

从A、B、C、D四个选项中，选出空白处的最佳选项。

61. —Thank you for the delicious dinner.
    —_____.
    A. Don't say that   B. It's nothing Billy
    C. I don't think it's good D. I'm glad you enjoyed it
62. All of the following are traffic sign except _____.
    A. SAVE WATER   B. STOP
    C. NO PARKING   D. DANGER ICE ON ROAD
63. —Could you be so kind as to close the window?
    —_____.
    A. With pleasure B. Go ahead   C. Yes, please   D. That's OK
64. —How I can get to the nearest park?
    —_____.
    A. The flowers there are beautiful B. The park is very large
    C. It's not far from here   D. Go down this street and turn left.
65. —I'm feeling terrible and lonely all the time. What should I do? —_____. Try to talk to your friends, and take care of your health.
    A. Don't mention it   B. That's right
    C. Take it easy   D. It's OK.

六、阅读理解(本大题共5小题，每小题2分，共计10分)

Paper is one of the most important products ever invented by man. The invention of paper meant that more people could be educated because more books could be printed. Paper provided an important way to communicate with knowledge

Paper was first made in China about 2,000 years ago. In Egypt and the West, paper was not very commonly used before the year 1400. Paper was not made in southern Europe until about the year 1100. After that the forestry countries of Canada. Sweden, Norway, Finland, and the United States because the most important in paper-making. Today Finland makes the best paper in the world. And it has the biggest paper industry in the world.

When we think of paper, we think of newspapers, books, letters, envelopes, and writing paper. So paper plays an important role in our lives.

Paper is very good for keeping you warm. Houses are often insulated(隔热)with paper. You perhaps seen homeless men sleep on a large number of newspapers. They are insulating themselves from the cold.

In Finland, in winter it is sometimes 40 degrees below zero. The farmers wear paper boots in the snow. Nothing could be warmer.

66. What did the invention of paper mean? It meant _____.
   A. more people could be educated
   B. more books could be printed
   C. paper is one of the most important products
   D. Paper was invented by man.
67. When was paper made in southern Europe?
   A. Before 1100.   B. After 1400.   C. After 1100.   D. Before 1400.
68. Which country makes the best paper?
   A. Norway.   B. Canada.   C. The United States.   D. Finland.
69. What's the meaning of the sentence "Nothing could be warmer."?
   A. Books are warmer.   B. Newspapers are warmer.
   C. Paper is the warmest.   D. Houses are the warmest.
70. What's the main idea of the passage?
   A. The invention of paper.   B. The best paper.
   C. The paper-making.   D. The uses of paper.

第三部分 （工科类职业模块考生作答，共 15 分）

七、单项选择题（本大题共 5 小题，每小题 1 分，共计 5 分）

71. This summer we'll have a _____ holiday, I'm taking my daughter along.
   A. two month's   B. two months   C. two-month   D. two-months
72. What is the sign of the picture?
   A. Fire extinguishers safety signs.   B. Construction warning signs.
   C. Chemicals safety signs.   D. Electrical warning signs.
73. When you study the local map, you'll find this town is _____.
   A. twice the size of that one   B. twice as a large town as that
   C. twice as larger as that one   D. twice as larger a town as that
74. The basic unit of time is _____.
   A. hour   B. second   C. minute   D. millisecond
75. The cube root of sixty-four times the square of three is _____.
   A. 36   B. 27   C. 4   D. 64

八、阅读理解（本大题共 5 小题，每小题 2 分，共计 10 分）

从 A、B、C、D 四个选项中，选出符合题目要求的最佳选项。

About 750 years ago, a man named Marco Polo went to China. He started in Europe and traveled more than 5,000 miles. He crossed some large deserts. The journey took almost three years. There were no planes or trains then. So how did Polo make the trip? He rode a camel.

Like horses, camels can work as pack animals. They can carry many pounds of cargo(货物), such as food and supplies. That is very helpful for a long trip. They act as "ships of the desert".

Camels do well in the desert. They can go for several days without water. They can survive a long time without food, too.

There are two kinds of camels. One kind has one hump. The other has two. These humps store fat. If needed, the fat turns into water.

Camels have other special ways to deal with desert life. They have a thick coat. This keeps them warm at night and cool in the day. They have long eyelashes and an extra eyelid. These help protect their eyes. Camels also have thick lips. They can eat all kinds of plants, even thorny ones.

They are not picky about food. That is good because few plants grow in deserts. They also have very large feet. These help camels walk on sand. Camels can run on sand, too. They can go about 25 miles per hour. That's about as fast as a racing bicycle.

Camels have carried people and things for thousands of years. Today they play other roles in the modern world, too.

76. According to the passage, how did Marco Polo make his trip to China?
   A. By horse.   B. By camel.   C. On foot.   D. By ship.
77. The underlined word "survive" in paragraph 3 means _____.
   A. live   B. start   C. sleep   D. leave
78. What can help camels deal with the desert life?
   ①They have a thick coat. ②They only eat thorny plants.
   ③They have short eyelashes. ④They have an extra eyelid.
   A. ①③   B. ②③   C. ②④   D. ①④
79. What can we know about camels from the passage?
   A. Camels can carry few pounds of supplies.
   B. Camels store fat and water in their stomachs.
   C. Camels can run fast on sand with large feet.
   D. Camels have been used for transportation for hundreds of years.
80. Which is the best title of the passage?
   A. Habits of Camels.   B. Marco Polo's Trip to China.
   C. Life in the Desert.   D. Camels — Ships of the Desert.

非选择题

九、书面表达（15 分）

以 "Saying No to smoking" 为题写一篇文章，词数在 100 左右。

模拟测试卷四

说明：
1. 本试卷分选择题和非选择题两部分。满分100分，考试时间90分钟。
2. 选择题分三部分，第一部分为共答题，所有考生作答；第二部分由文科类职业模块考生作答；第三部分由工科类职业模块考生作答。
3. 考生必须且只能在下列其中一个职业模块后的空格内"√"，确定本人作答部分，在确定范围以外作答一律不计分。
4. 考试结束后，将本试卷和答题卡一并交回。

选择题
注意事项：
1. 选择题答案必须填涂在答题卡上，写在试卷上一律不计分。
2. 答题前，考生务必将自己的姓名、准考证号、座位号、考试科目涂写在答题卡上。
3. 考生须按规定要求正确涂卡，否则后果自负。

第一部分 共答题（所有考生作答，共70分）

一、语音（本大题共10小题，每小题1分，共计10分）

从A、B、C、D四个选项中，选出画线部分发音不同的一项。

1. A. bay   B. say   C. Monday   D. day
2. A. suggestion   B. infection   C. emotion   D. location
3. A. tasks   B. photos   C. names   D. legs
4. A. comb   B. climb   C. doubt   D. trouble
5. A. selected   B. reacted   C. interested   D. noticed
6. A. publish   B. sunshine   C. summary   D. sugar
7. A. near   B. hear   C. early   D. dear
8. A. amazing   B. adapt   C. agriculture D. admit
9. A. colorful   B. monkey   C. another   D. cold
10. A. known   B. power   C. how   D. down

二、单项选择题（本大题共25小题，每小题1分，共计25分）

从A、B、C、D四个选项中，选出空白处的最佳选项。

11. As we all know, _____ Great Wall is _____ longest wall in the world.
    A. A, a   B. A, the   C. The, a   D. The, the
12. He lives in a hotel, _____ is only five minutes' walk from here.
    A. that   B. which   C. in which   D. where
13. Dear student, please read every sentence carefully. _____ you are, _____ mistakes you'll make.
    A. The more carefully; the few   B. The more careful; the less
    C. The more carefully; the less   D. The more careful, the fewer
14. Guan Dong saved an old lady out of the Yangtze River. _____ great courage he showed!
    A. What a   B. What   C. How a   D. How
15. He said he wasn't disappointed at the score of the final exam, but the look on his face _____ himself _____.
    A. gave, up   B. gave, off   C. gave, out   D. gave, away
16. —Are you going out with Jade tonight?
    —That's my _____. Mind your own!
    A. offer   B. question   C. business   D. chance
17. There _____ a dolphin show in the zoo tomorrow evening.
    A. is going to have   B. will have
    C. is going to be   D. is be
18. —I don't care what people think of me.
    —Well, you _____. You're not alone in this world.
    A. can   B. may   C. should   D. will
19. He found _____ impossible to learn a foreign language well in such a short time.
    A. that   B. this   C. one   D. it
20. After the war, a new school library was put up _____ there once had been a swimming pool.
    A. that   B. where   C. which   D. when
21. No matter how much money you have, it cannot _____ a healthy body.
    A. compare   B. fit   C. defeat   D. match
22. _____ the beautiful scenery, he recited a poem all of a sudden.
    A. Seeing   B. Seen   C. Saw   D. See
23. Scarcely _____ entered the university _____ she dyed her hair red.
    A. had she, than   B. she had, when
    C. had she, when   D. did she, when
24. Do you know any other foreign language _____ English?
    A. except   B. except for   C. beside   D. besides
25. _____ get the low price on "Black Friday", shoppers stand in a line in the early morning.
    A. In order that B. So that   C. In order to   D. So as to
26. It was at five o'clock yesterday afternoon _____ the policeman came to himself.
    A. when   B. that   C. in which   D. until
27. —Which of the shirts do you like better?
    —I'll take _____. They are expensive and out of fashion.
    A. neither   B. either   C. none   D. both
28. —Do you think George has passed the driving test
    —No. If so, he _____ his car to our college yesterday.
    A. would drive   B. drove
    C. would have driven   D. had driven
29. All the factors _____, we decided to offer the job to Li Wei, a man of rich experience.
    A. considered   B. being g considered

C. considering D. having considered
30. He can hardly stay awake because he is so tired. _____?
    A. does he B. isn't he C. can't he D. can he
31. No one except Jack and Tom _____ the answer.
    A. know B. knows C. is knowing D. are known
32. I prefer _____ TV at home rather than _____ out on Sundays.
    A. to watch; to go B. to watch; go
    C. watching; to go D. watching, going
33. There is a lake _____ the foot _____ the mountain.
    A. on, of B. of, of C. at, of D. to, of
34. The reason why he was late is _____ his bike was broken on the way to school.
    A. because B. why C. that D. because of
35. Could you tell me _____ the radio without help?
    A. how did he mend B. what did he mend
    C. how he mended D. what he mended

三、完形填空(本大题共15小题，每小题1分，共计15分)

从A、B、C、D四个选项中，选出空白处的最佳选项。

Wishing to encourage her young son's progress on the piano, a mother took her boy to a pianist's concert in a evening. After they found their __36__, the mother saw two friends in the hall and walked to __37__ them.

It was the boy's first time to come to the hall. He thought it was a good __38__ for him to explore the wonders of the concert hall. He __39__ and walked around. He walked __40__ a door marked "NO Entry".

When the hall lights dimmed(变暗), the __41__ would begin. The mother returned and discovered that her son was __42__. The mother was __43__ worried that tears were in her eyes.

The concert began, and the lights became bright on stage. The mother was __44__ to see her little boy sitting at the keyboard, playing the song Twinkle, Twinkle Little Star __45__ he did at home.

At that moment, the great pianist came, quickly moved to the piano and __46__ in the boys ear, "Don't stop. Keep playing." He leaned over and began playing with his left __47__. They played the piano together __48__. The old pianist and the young beginner changed a frightening situation into a wonderful creative experience. The audience stood up and __49__ them.

An artist's achievements and charm depend on not only his perfect skills __50__ his good qualities.

36. A. desks B. stage C. seats D. piano
37. A. greet B. feed C. notice D. search
38. A. use B. chance C. season D. cultural
39. A. flew B. sat C. fell D. rose
40. A. through B. across C. above D. over
41. A. film B. concert C. conversation D. meeting
42. A. sleepy B. missing C. tired D. excited
43. A. so B. very C. much D. such
44. A. serious B. sad C. patient D. surprised
45. A. when B. if C. as D. before
46. A. called B. shouted C. whispered D. cried
47. A. hand B. shoulder C. foot D. leg
48. A. badly B. carelessly C. terribly D. happily
49. A. fought with B. laughed at C. shouted at D. cheered for
50. A. or B. but C. and D. so

四、阅读理解(本大题共10小题，每小题2分，共计20分)

从A、B、C、D四个选项中，选出符合题目要求的最佳选项。

A

The health code(健康码) is a kind of OR code based on the real data, which needs to get online. The health code works as an electronic credential(电子证明) for people to show they have a healthy body when they need to get in and out of the public area. The aim of creating health code is to make the society safer. Here are the <u>characteristics</u>:

Quick and safe

You just need three steps to get a health code. First, search the health OR code in Alipay on Wechat; then fill in a form with your information; after examination, you will get a health OR code The process takes only twenty seconds. It can also keep your personal information from theft by others.

Cost-free

You can download the code from Alipay without paying anything. A green code holder with normal body temperature is allowed to enter and leave public places and take public transportation vehicles such as buses, trains and planes. But yellow and red code holders are not.

Convenient

Widely used Internet can cover almost all cities in China. A health code can show this code to them without going back to your own city.

Environmentally friendly

The new health code builds a highly reliable connection between government and online information. Everything is done on the mobile phone without using any paper, thus saving many resources.

51. In what case do we have to show our health code?
    A. Surfing the Internet in the offices.
    B. Paying for the things we buy.
    C. Staying at home.
    D. Getting in and out of public places.
52. What does the underlined word "characteristics" mean?
    A. 特点 B. 建议 C. 用途 D. 关键
53. What kinds of code holder are not allowed to move around?
    A. Green and yellow code holders. B. Yellow and red code holders.

C. Only red code holders.   D. Green and red code holders.
54. How can the health code help to protect the environment?
   A. By selling more mobile phones.   B. By getting more information.
   C. By using less mobile phones.   D. By using less paper.
55. What is the purpose of this article?
   A. To tell us the advantages of the health code.
   B. To understand why we don't like Alipay.
   C. To use health code through mobile phone.
   D. To protect the environment.

B

The weather is getting hotter and you'll be getting thirstier playing basketball or riding home from school. A cold drink may be just the thing. But be careful what you pour down your throat. Something that looks cool may not be good for your health.

There are plenty of so-called energy drinks on the market. Most of them have an attractive colour and cool name. Their nutrition list also contains various things from vitamins to ginseng. Sounds great!

But after a careful check you may find that most energy drinks contain high levels of caffeine. These drinks are typically aimed at young people, students, busy people and sports players.

Makers sometimes say their drinks make you better at sports and can keep you awake. But be careful not to drink too much.

Caffeine raises your heartbeat. Because of this, the International Olympic Committee has limited their use. The amount of caffeine in most energy drinks is at least as high as in a strong cup of coffee or strong tea.

Research by Australian scientists has found that many teenagers are affected by caffeine. The results of their survey show that 27 percent of boys aged 8-12 take in more caffeine than their parents.

There are potential health risks linked to energy drinks. Just one can of energy drink can make you nervous, have difficulty sleeping and can even cause heart attacks.

Teenagers should be discouraged from consuming drinks with a lot of caffeine in them, an expert from the Australia Nutrition Foundation said.

56. Have a cold drink after a basketball game is _____.
   A. very cool thing for boys   B. one's own idea
   C. cool but it may hurt you   D. just OK
57. Most energy drinks that contain high levels of caffeine are aimed at _____.
   (Which one is FALSE?)
   A. young people, busy people   B. sports players
   C. students   D. women and girls
58. What should be the young's attitude towards energy drinks?
   A. Drink them as much as possible
   B. Throw and never drink them again
   C. Drink less energy drinks with lots of caffeine
   D. Try to make new drinks

59. It is said that energy drinks can _____. (Which one is FALSE?)
   A. make people better at sports   B. keep people awake
   C. raise people's heartbeat   D. make people die
60. What's the main idea of the whole passage?
   A. A cold drink after a game is not so good.
   B. Drinking energy drinks may be cool, but it also brings some harm.
   C. People shouldn't drink energy drinks.
   D. Energy drinks are harmful, so we should get rid of them.

第二部分 （文科类职业模块考生作答，共15分）

五、单项选择题（本大题共5小题，每小题1分，共计5分）

从A、B、C、D四个选项中，选出空白处的最佳选项。

61. —I got that job I wanted at the public library.
    —_____! That's good news.
    A. Go ahead   B. Cheers   C. Congratulations   D. Come on
62. —Hey, can I ask you a favor?
    —Sure, _____.
    A. what can I do for you?   B. just as I thought.
    C. how is it going?   D. here you are.
63. —Who's that speaking?
    —_____.
    A. This is Jack speaking   B. I am speaking
    C. Jack is me   D. I am Jack.
64. —May I put my car here?
    —Sorry, you mustn't. Look at the sign, it says "_____"
    A. DANGEROUS   B. NO RIGHT TURN
    C. NO PHOTOS   D. NO PARKING
65. —Daddy, do you like it if I buy a wallet for my mom's birthday?
    —_____.
    A. Don't bother   B. That all depends
    C. It couldn't be better   D. It's a good deal

六、阅读理解（本大题共5小题，每小题2分，共计10分）

从A、B、C、D四个选项中，选出符合题目要求的最佳选项。

Want to stay away from colds? Put on a happy face.

Compared to unhappy people, those who are cheerful and relaxed are less likely to suffer from colds, according to a new study. It's possible that being happy helps the body fight illnesses, say the researchers from New York University.

"It seems that positive feelings may reduce the danger of illness," said the study's chief researcher Sheldon Cohen.

In an earlier study, Cohen found that people who were cheerful and lively caught coughs and colds less often. People who showed feelings were also less likely to tell their doctors that they felt ill.

In this study, Cohen's interviewed 193 adults every day for two weeks. During the interviews, the people told researchers about were given colds by doctors and had to stay alone in a room for six days.

The results showed that everyone in the study was equally likely to get ill. But for people who said they felt happy during the research period, their illness are less serious and lasted for a shorter time.

Cohen believes that when people experience positive feelings, their body may produce a chemical that helps fight illness and disease. So if you are worried abut your health, look on the bright side more often.

66. Which of the following was NOT a part of the study?
    A. People talked about their feelings every day.
    B. People were kept alone for six days.
    C. People were made to feel unhappy.
    D. People were given colds by doctors.
67. What did the study find?
    A. People who felt happy never got ill.
    B. People's feelings didn't influence their health.
    C. People with good feelings became ill more easily.
    D. People with positive feelings had less serious illnesses.
68. According to Cohen, which of the following may help fight illness?
    A. Eating.   B. Crying.   C. Sleeping.   D. Laughing.
69. This passage is a/an _____.
    A. advertisement   B. story
    C. newspaper report   D. scientist's diary
70. What is the best title for this passage?
    A. Smiles can fight colds   B. Cause of colds found
    C. The danger of colds   D. How people get sick

第三部分 (工科类职业模块考生作答，共15分)

七、单项选择题(本大题共5小题，每小题1分，共计5分)

从 A、B、C、D 四个选项中，选出空白处的最佳选项。

71. He joined the army in _____ when he was in _____.
    A. 1940's, his twenties   B. the 1940's, his twenties
    C. 1940's, the twenties   D. the 1940's, the twenties
72. _____ people in the world are sending information by email every day.
    A. Several million   B. Many millions
    C. Several millions   D. Many million
73. Which of the following is the meaning "禁止通行"?
    A. Notice: wear hard hats   B. Warning: high voltage
    C. Fire hose   D. Warning: restricted area
74. Our ordinary temperature is 36.5℃. It equals _____ °F.
    A. 96.5   B. 106.5   C. 97.7   D. 36.5
75. About _____ of the books in our school library are written in English.
    A. four-fifth   B. four-fifths   C. fourth-fifths   D. fourths-fifth

八、阅读理解(本大题共5小题，每小题2分，共计10分)

从 A、B、C、D 四个选项中，选出符合题目要求的最佳选项。

NOTICES		
DANCE & MUSIC Jazz and hiphop music to Time: 6-8p.m. Every Tuesday and Saturday. Place: Sally's Dance club, 32 Admiral Road. All ages welcome. $15 each class.	A GREEN CITY Help make the city greener by planting trees. Time: 10-11:30 a.m. every Saturday. Place: Foxdale Park. All ages welcome.	SWEET THINGS Learn make cakes with Anne Time: 3-5 pm. every Sunday. Place: Sunnyside Kitchen, 3A Baker' Street (Behind Sunnyside Hall). All ages welcome. $5 for ingredients. (原材料)

76. If Harry only has 4 dance classes, he should pay _____ dollars.
    A. 15   B. 30   C. 45   D. 60
77. On Saturday morning, people in Foxdale Park can _____.
    A. take a dance class   B. plant trees
    C. learn to make cakes   D. do exercise
78. Where can people make cakes?
    A. At Sally's Dance Club.   B. In Foxdale Park.
    C. At Sunnyside Kitchen.   D. On 32 Admiral Road.
79. Which of the following is TRUE?
    A. All ages are welcomed to exercise at Sally's Dance Club.
    B. Ingredients are free for people at Sunnyside Kitchen.
    C. People can make the city greener every Saturday in Foxdale Park.
    D. Teenagers can dance with music for about 3 hours at Sally's Dance Club.
80. You may see these notices _____.
    A. in a newspaper   B. in a book
    C. on a magazine   D. on a bus

九、书面表达(15分)

每个人都有不同的休闲娱乐方式，请以 My Hobby 为题，写一篇文章，字数不少于80字。

模拟测试卷五

说明：
1. 本试卷分选择题和非选择题两部分。满分100分，考试时间90分钟。
2. 选择题分三部分，第一部分为共答题，所有考生作答；第二部分由文科类职业模块考生作答；第三部分由工科类职业模块考生作答。
3. 考生必须且只能在下列其中一个职业模块后的空格内"√"，确定本人作答部分，在确定范围以外作答一律不计分。
4. 考试结束后，将本试卷和答题卡一并交回。

选择题
注意事项：
1. 选择题答案必须填涂在答题卡上，写在试卷上一律不计分。
2. 答题前，考生务必将自己的姓名、准考证号、座位号、考试科目涂写在答题卡上。
3. 考生须按规定要求正确涂卡，否则后果自负。

第一部分 共答题（所有考生作答，共70分）

一、语音（本大题共10小题，每小题1分，共计10分）

从A、B、C、D四个选项中，选出画线部分发音不同的一项。

1. A. b<u>a</u>sic   B. <u>a</u>wake   C. pl<u>a</u>ne   D. dr<u>a</u>g
2. A. d<u>e</u>ssert   B. d<u>e</u>sign   C. <u>e</u>ffect   D. <u>e</u>xercise
3. A. g<u>oo</u>d   B. f<u>oo</u>t   C. fl<u>oo</u>d   D. t<u>oo</u>k
4. A. f<u>u</u>ture   B. g<u>u</u>ard   C. am<u>u</u>sement   D. arg<u>u</u>e
5. A. <u>au</u>dience   B. <u>Au</u>gust   C. l<u>au</u>gh   D. c<u>au</u>se
6. A. kn<u>ow</u>   B. narr<u>ow</u>   C. n<u>ow</u>   D. <u>ow</u>e
7. A. on<u>c</u>e   B. perfe<u>c</u>t   C. proje<u>c</u>t   D. produ<u>c</u>t
8. A. <u>th</u>emselves   B. clo<u>th</u>es   C. toma<u>t</u>oes   D. teac<u>h</u>es
9. A. <u>al</u>so   B. w<u>al</u>k   C. b<u>al</u>l   D. t<u>al</u>k
10. A. com<u>b</u>   B. <u>b</u>ell   C. <u>b</u>eside   D. <u>b</u>ank

二、单项选择题（本大题共25小题，每小题1分，共计25分）

从A、B、C、D四个选项中，选出空白处的最佳选项。

11. We can't make a sandwich without _____.
    A. bread   B. onions   C. yogurt   D. tomatoes

12. Write it _____ possible and try not to make any mistakes.
    A. as careful as   B. as carefully as   C. more careful   D. less careful

13. _____ can we help victims after a natural disaster?
    A. Who   B. How   C. Where   D. When

14. —What do you think of your Junior Middle School life?
    —I think it is colorful, _____ I am always busy.
    A. if   B. though   C. while   D. until

15. New York is a good place to visit _____ May or December.
    A. on   B. at   C. in   D. of

16. _____ I have a word with you? It won't take long.
    A. Can   B. Must   C. Shall   D. Should

17. —I want to be a teacher when I grow up.
    —Work hard, _____ your dream will come true.
    A. or   B. but   C. though   D. and

18. Tom _____ an interesting question in yesterday's class meeting.
    A. rose   B. raised   C. rise   D. raise

19. I've been trying to phone Mom all evening, but I can't seem to _____.
    A. get in   B. get off   C. get through   D. get along

20. Tim Cook called his mother every week even while he _____ around the world.
    A. was traveling   B. is traveling   C. traveled   D. travels

21. At school, some students are active _____ some are shy, yet they can be good friends with one another.
    A. while   B. although   C. so   D. as

22. I'll have to push the car to the side of the road because we _____ if we leave it here.
    A. will fine   B. will be fined   C. fine   D. are fined

23. The teacher knows _____ the mobile phone you brought to school today.
    A. how he will do with   B. what he will deal with
    C. how to deal with   D. what to deal with

24. —You look rather tired. _____ stop to take a rest?
    —All right. But I'll have to work for a few more minutes.
    A. Do you   B. Why not   C. What about   D. How about

25. Bill suggested _____ early so that we could watch the sunrise at the beach.
    A. get up   B. getting up   C. to get up   D. to getting up

26. —_____ goldfish you keep!
    —Yes. They are my good friends.
    A. How lovely   B. What lovely   C. What a lovely   D. How a lovely

27. —Listen! _____
    —Oh, let's go to the classroom.
    A. There goes the bell.   B. There is a bell.
    C. There the bell go.   D. There a bell is.

28. It was not until I told him _____ he knew about it.
    A. that   B. when   C. while   D. as

29. On the top of the hill _____ the old man once lived.
    A. a temple stands there in which   B. a temple standing on which
    C. does a temple stand where   D. stands a temple where

30. I'm so glad that I have found the same modern computer _____ I am working on.
    A. which   B. as   C. that   D. where

31. I am not sure _____ I am going to Tom's birthday party or not. I may go to the concert _____.
    A. whether; instead of   B. if; instead of
    C. whether; instead   D. if; instead

32. I don't think _____ he said is right.

A. that what   B. what what   C. whether how   D. when how
33. If I _____ harder when I was young, I _____ a university and lived a different life.
   A. worked; would entered   B. had worked; would have entered
   C. would worked; had entered   D. have worked; will have entered
34. —How much _____ the apples?
   —Five dollars _____ enough.
   A. is; is   B. is; are   C. are; are   D. are; is
35. "Do you go to school by bus or by bike?" → He _____ me _____ _____ to school by bus or by bike.
   A. ask; if; go   B. asked; if; went
   C. say; if; go   D. said; if; went

三、完型填空(本大题共 15 小题，每小题 1 分，共计 15 分)

从 A、B、C、D 四个选项中，选出空白处的最佳选项。

Tea to some people in eastern countries is like air or water. It's something that they can't live __36__.

When I was 22 years old, I experienced(经历) a __37__ deep and warm kindness. I was very sad __38__ my loved grandma died. My neighbor __39__ me to have tea at her home one evening.

That night, she placed a beautiful tea set(茶具). She __40__ me all about her life story. She came to America because she __41__ her husband. She told me, over that cup of tea, that her sad feeling was gone. She advised that I should make a __42__ about how to go forward. We __43__ our evening tea at 2 a.m. It was __44__ a heartwarming and unforgettable cup of tea.

When I was 38 years old, I was teaching English in Japan. During the __45__ lesson, one young woman brought her tea set—a lovely box with all the things needed for a Japanese tea to thank me. She quietly knelt(跪) at my coffee table, __46__ green tea powder(粉末) into a bowl, added hot water, whisked(搅拌) it gently with a brush, and then placed some small pieces of gold leaf on top! She quietly held it out to me to drink with both hands, __47__ sweetly. I was __48__ at the beauty of her gift and at her kind heart. It was so much __49__ a cup of tea!

When you feel upset, why not have a cup of tea and enjoy __50__ happy and calm it makes you feel? Drinking tea is always a good way to make you feel good and relax you.

36. A. with   B. without   C. beside   D. through
37. A. mother's   B. teacher's   C. friend's   D. neighbor's
38. A. after   B. but   C. before   D. and
39. A. taught   B. needed   C. invited   D. agreed
40. A. told   B. talked   C. said   D. spoke
41. A. gave   B. helped   C. lost   D. left
42. A. fire   B. idea   C. life   D. plan
43. A. started   B. drank   C. made   D. ended
44. A. badly   B. really   C. even   D. never
45. A. last   B. first   C. different   D. same
46. A. prepared   B. painted   C. planted   D. poured
47. A. smiling   B. whispering   C. answering   D. crying
48. A. excited   B. surprised   C. angry   D. sad
49. A. more   B. more than   C. less than   D. less
50. A. where   B. when   C. how   D. why

四、阅读理解(本大题共 10 小题，每小题 2 分，共计 20 分)

从 A、B、C、D 四个选项中，选出符合题目要求的最佳选项。

A

With the development of China, many traditional ink paintings(水墨画) show the changes in southern Chinese villages. Shang Xinzhou, a painter from the Guangxi Arts University, has been creating traditional ink paintings for many years. His paintings show the life in poor areas.

"Thanks to my experience in Duomai Village, I can make the paintings much lovelier," said the 36-year-old painter, who has spent two and a half years working there.

Shang's paintings show the progress in the fight against poverty. His works show changes from difficult local conditions and people's hard times to better conditions and happy lives.

"I like drawing people's real lives, and paintings can be a bridge for communication between the local people and me." said Shang.

During his stay, he put his paintings about the local life on the Internet to help villagers sell their products. To make the nightlife there richer, he sold paintings to buy streetlights, so people could enjoy square dancing in the evening.

Shang's excellent works were popular in the village. "I love his paintings and they show great changes in our village," said a farmer.

In recent years, more artists have traveled to mountain villages to record the development of China's poor areas, telling stories of the country's fight against <u>poverty</u>. "I've seen the local poverty alleviation. I want to record the changes of the poor areas and create more works about people," said Shang.

51. What made Shang's paintings lovelier?
   A. His happy life.   B. His stay in a city.
   C. His experience in a village.   D. His experience in a university.
52. What does the underlined word "poverty" mean in Chinese?
   A. 沉默   B. 交流   C. 富有   D. 贫穷
53. What did Shang do for the people in Duomai Village?
   ①he taught them to dance.
   ②He bought them streetlights.
   ③He helped them sell their products.
   ④He taught them to create paintings.
   A. ①④   B. ②③   C. ①③   D. ②④
54. What can we learn from the last paragraph?
   A. Why Shang created the paintings.   B. When Shang started to paint.
   C. How Shang's life was in the village.   D. Where Shang will work in the future.
55. What's the main idea of the passage?

— 2 —

A. A painter spent his whole life fighting against poverty in his city.
B. A painter tried to show the world Chinese traditional ink paintings.
C. A painter used his paintings to record the changes in poor areas.
D. A painter found the easiest way to make himself famous in his country.

B

A report on hundreds of research studies says plastic pollution at sea is reaching worrying levels. The report warned that pollution will continue to grow even if immediate (立即的) action is taken to stop such waste from reaching the world's oceans.

The report, by Germany's Alfred Wegener Institute, examined almost 2,600 research studies on plastic pollution.

Some areas, such as the Mediterranean, East China and Yellow Seas, already have dangerous levels of plastic. Other bodies of water will become more polluted in the future, the report found.

The writers reported that almost every kind of ocean animal has been <u>affected</u> by plastic pollution. That pollution is harming important environmental systems.

As plastic breaks down into smaller pieces, it is eaten by many different sea creatures. It is harmful to them and those who eat them.

Melanie Bergmann, one of the report's writers, said getting that plastic out of the water again is nearly impossible. She added that policymakers (政策制定者) should make an effort to prevent any more pollution from entering the oceans.

Heike Vesper is with the World Wildlife Fund. She said people can help reduce plastic pollution by changing their behavior. But she added that governments must help in dealing with the problem.

The United Nations Environment Assembly is expected to meet and discuss the plastic pollution problem.

56. The report found that _____ already have dangerous levels of plastic.
   A. East China   B. the Mediterranean
   C. Yellow Seas   D. all above
57. What does the underlined word "affected" in Paragraph4 mean in Chinese?
   A. 分开   B. 重视   C. 影响   D. 限制
58. How can people help reduce plastic pollution according to Heike Vesper?
   A. By stopping using plastic bags.   B. By writing more research reports.
   C. By having more discussions.   D. By changing their behavior.
59. In which part of a newspaper can we read the passage?
   A. Technology.   B. Business.   C. Environment.   D. Travel.
60. What's the main idea of the passage?
   A. Plastic pollution at sea is reaching worrying level.
   B. It is nearly impossible to get that plastic out of the water.
   C. Governments must help in dealing with the plastic pollution problem.
   D. Policymakers should try their best to stop more pollution from entering the seas.

第二部分 （文科类职业模块考生作答，共15分）

五、单项选择题（本大题共5小题，每小题1分，共计5分）

从A、B、C、D四个选项中，选出空白处的最佳选项。

61. —Hello, this is Jim speaking. May I speak to Tom?
    —_____ He is in the study.
    A. Go ahead   B. That's all right
    C. Hold the line, please. D. Hurry up
62. —_____
    —Sure, I'd like a bowl of rice and a bottle of beer.
    A. May I have the bill?   B. May I take your order?
    C. Could you please help me? D. May I help you?
63. —Hello, Ben _____?
    —I have a really bad stomachache. I feel terrible.
    A. Can you help me   B. How do you do
    C. What seems to be the problem   D. How long have you felt like this
64. —Shall we meet at the park gate at 8 o'clock tomorrow morning?
    —_____. How about 9 o'clock?
    A. It's not a big deal   B. I can't make it
    C. I can't agree more   D. It's a good idea
65. Which of the following means "Mind your head. The ceiling is too low. There's not much room left."
    A. WARNING: NO TRESPASSING   B. CAUTION: LOW HEADROOM
    C. CAUTION: DEEP WATER   D. CAUTION: MIND YOUR HEAD

六、阅读理解（本大题共5小题，每小题2分，共计10分）

从A、B、C、D四个选项中，选出符合题目要求的最佳选项。

"Can I have a glass of hot water?" This is a very common question in a restaurant. For many Chinese people, nothing is more common than drinking hot water every day. However, the simple habit is like a mystery to people from other countries.

For many Westerners, the idea of drinking hot water is very strange. However, most Chinese people think the Americans' habit of drinking ice water is also strange and even unhealthy. Some old people take a tea kettle (茶壶) when they travel. Chinese doctors are encouraging more people to take on the habit of drinking hot water, especially for women.

But in Western countries, drinking hot water isn't common. Westerners often have drinks with ice, not just on hot days but almost every day.

There is a story online about a British man, who has been in Beijing for over five years. He visited a local cafe when going back to England. He asked for a glass of hot water in a British accent. But this request surprised the waitress, "To...to...to drink?" she doubted. Finally, the man received the hot water <u>but felt cold stares from every corner of the cafe</u>.

Westerners wonder why Chinese people drink hot water as Chinese are wondering why Westerners drink cold water. This cultural difference is not a simple problem, but related to history, culture and science.

As a matter of fact, many teenagers now depend on bottled water for daily drinking. With the younger generation growing up, will drinking hot water become a less popular life habit? Who knows?

66. What do most Chinese think of drinking icy water from the passage?
   A. Normal and healthy.   B. Strange but healthy.
   C. Normal but unhealthy.   D. Strange and unhealthy.
67. Who are especially advised to drink hot water by Chinese doctors?
   A. Women.   B. Students.   C. Westerners.   D. The elderly.
68. What's the meaning of the underlined part in the fourth paragraph?
   A. Other people in the restaurant were angry at the man's request.
   B. Other people in the restaurant laughed at the man.
   C. Other people in the restaurant thought the man's request was strange.
   D. Other people in the restaurant were interested in the man's request.
69. What's the purpose of the fourth paragraph?
   A. To introduce a British man.
   B. To prove the westerners love drinking hot water.
   C. To show that it is uncommon to drink hot water in Britain.
   D. To show that the waitress is impolite to the British man.
70. What can be inferred from the passage?
   A. Drinking hot water is very good for health.
   B. Drinking cold water is very harmful to health.
   C. Different drinking habits are probably related to different countries.
   D. More and more people will take a tea kettle for daily drinking.

第三部分 (工科类职业模块考生作答，共15分)

七、单项选择题(本大题共5小题，每小题1分，共计5分)

从A、B、C、D四个选项中，选出空白处的最佳选项。

71. Two cube minus the cube root of sixty-four equals _____.
    A. 1   B. 2   C. 3   D. 4
72. _____ is the basic unit of length.
    A. Newton   B. Square meter   C. meter   D. kilometer
73. "The hole is 100 mm deep." can also be written _____.
    A. The hole is 100 mm in length.   B. The hole is 100 mm in width.
    C. The hole is 100 mm in depth.   D. The hole is 100 mm in weight.
74. 1,000 liters is equal to _____ cm^3.
    A. 1,000   B. 1,000,000,000
    C. 1   D. 1,000,000
75. "A set of strict and complete supervisory system" means _____.
    A. 一套严格和完善的监管制度   B. 一套严格和完善的管理制度
    C. 一系列严格和完善的监管制度   D. 一系列严格和完善的管理制度

八、阅读理解(本大题共5小题，每小题2分，共计10分)

从A、B、C、D四个选项中，选出符合题目要求的最佳选项。

There are 365 days in a year. We sleep 8 hours a day, so we have 122 days for sleeping. Then our work time has 243 days left. But there are 52 weekends in a year. Each weekend has two days. We lose another 104 days a year for work. It takes us about one hour to have breakfast and supper. This comes to 15 days over a year. But we can't work all that time.

We need a holiday. Let's say we have three weeks' holiday. We don't work all day. For free hours each evening takes up 61 days. We have to remember that we get 2 days' holiday at Easter(复活节), 3 at Christmas and we have 32 days for work. But then we have one and a half hours' lunch every day, and half an hour's coffee break. That comes to 30 days a year. This means(意味着) that we have only a few days left for work every year!

76. How many days do we sleep in a year? _____.
    A. 365 days   B. 122 days   C. 8 days   D. 52 days
77. We spend 15 days on _____.
    A. rest   B. the coffee break
    C. lunch   D. breakfast and supper
78. Which of the following is true?
    A. Each weekend has one day   B. We have 61 days for free time
    C. We get 3 days' holidays at Easter.   D. The coffee break takes us one hour
79. According to the passage, the word That refers to _____.
    A. time for work   B. time for sleep
    C. time for holiday   D. time for lunch and coffee break
80. The main idea of the passage is _____.
    A. we should know the numbers.
    B. time is important and we'd better not waste it
    C. we need more holidays.
    D. a few days for work is enough

九、书面表达(15分)

每年6月5日是世界环境日，我们周围的环境正变得越来越糟糕，污染越来越严重。假如你是John，你校要进行以"如何保护我们的环境"为主题的演讲比赛。请你根据以下要点，写一篇演讲稿。词数80词左右。

要点：1. 列举1~3个现存的环境问题；
　　　2. 应采取怎样的措施来保护环境；
　　　3. 提出倡议。

模拟测试卷六

说明：
1. 本试卷分选择题和非选择题两部分。满分100分，考试时间90分钟。
2. 选择题分三部分，第一部分为共答题，所有考生作答；第二部分由文科类职业模块考生作答；第三部分由工科类职业模块考生作答。
3. 考生必须且只能在下列其中一个职业模块后的空格内"√"，确定本人作答部分，在确定范围以外作答一律不计分。
4. 考试结束后，将本试卷和答题卡一并交回。

选择题
注意事项：
1. 选择题答案必须填涂在答题卡上，写在试卷上一律不计分。
2. 答题前，考生务必将自己的姓名、准考证号、座位号、考试科目涂写在答题卡上。
3. 考生须按规定要求正确涂卡，否则后果自负。

第一部分　共答题（所有考生作答，共70分）

一、语音（本大题共10小题，每小题1分，共计10分）

从A、B、C、D四个选项中，选出画线部分发音不同的一项。

1. A. age B. page C. danger D. fact
2. A. debt B. deck C. elect D. fetch
3. A. engine B. exit C. fill D. idea
4. A. few B. flew C. brew D. jewelry
5. A. piece B. quiet C. relieve D. thief
6. A. courage B. four C. pour D. your
7. A. ability B. angry C. apology D. cry
8. A. each B. hatch C. machine D. lunch
9. A. mix B. next C. exact D. except
10. A. here B. interest C. reference D. difference

二、单项选择题（本大题共25小题，每小题1分，共计25分）

从A、B、C、D四个选项中，选出空白处的最佳选项。

11. —Who is she?
—She is _____.
A. a woman B. Mrs Wang C. a driver D. a worker
12. Life is changeable. No one knows what _____ happen in the future.
A. should B. need C. have to D. might
13. After the vacation, I'm _____ heavier than before.
A. a few B. a little C. more D. very
14. They usually watch cartoons at home _____ doing outdoor activities.
A. instead of B. instead C. instead to D. instead with
15. My school is _____ the east of the museum. It's five kilometers _____ from the museum.
A. in; far B. to; far C. in; away D. to; away
16. —Goodbye, John, Come back again sometime.
—Sure. _____.
A. I did B. I do C. I shall D. I will
17. My arm is still painful, _____ I'm going to see a doctor.
A. so B. for C. but D. or
18. Welcome to our restaurant. We'll _____ you _____ delicious food.
A. provide; of B. give; of C. provide; with D. give; with
19. Could you ring me up as soon as Lily _____ in Beijing?
A. arrived B. arrives C. will arrive D. would arrive
20. —Excuse me sir. When can we have a swim in the pool?
—Not until it _____ next month.
A. will repair B. repairs
C. is repaired D. will be repaired
21. It is in Shanghai _____ I met my classmate.
A. who B. what C. that D. where
22. _____ good time we had yesterday in the park!
A. How B. What C. What a D. What an
23. —I'd like to order a cappuccino with extra cinnamon and a piece of cheese cake.
—I'm sorry but I _____ quite _____ you. What _____ you order just now?
A. don't...catch; did B. didn't...catch; was
C. wasn't...catch; did D. didn't...catch; is
24. I have a stomachache today. I don't _____ eating anything.
A. feel like B. would like C. want to D. want
25. _____ where the hospital was, he asked a stranger the way.
A. Knowing B. Not knowing C. Known D. Not known
26. During the holiday, a lot of people are attracted to Chengdu _____ has got a long history and beautiful scenery.
A. where B. what C. which D. whose
27. Mary would like to be a secretary. That's _____ she wants to be.
A. which B. what C. how D. when
28. _____ in order to sit for the college entrance exam?
A. What did she suggest he read B. What did she suggest he reads
C. Did she suggest for him to read D. Did she suggest what he read
29. Here _____ some books for you, Tom.
A. am B. is C. are D. be
30. _____ of the information _____ translated into German by the _____.
A. Two three; is; Germany B. Two thirds; is; Germans
C. Two third; are; Germen D. Two three; are; Germen
31. —_____ there were only three solders left at the front, _____ they went on fighting.

— 1 —

—How brave they are!
  A. If; and   B. Though; but   C. Though; /   D. Because; so
32. It is no use _____ your past mistakes.
  A. regret   B. regretted   C. regretting   D. to regret
33. You _____ cut your hair during the Spring Festival month.
  A. had not better   B. had better not
  C. could not better   D. could better not
34. The motto of the modern Olympics is "_____".
  A. Fast, high, strong   B. Faster, Higher, Stronger
  C. Faster; high; strong   D. Fastest, Highest, Strongest
35. Don't make noise in the hospital, _____?
  A. do you   B. will you   C. won't you   D. don't you

三、完型填空(本大题共 15 小题,每小题 1 分,共计 15 分)

从 A、B、C、D 四个选项中,选出空白处的最佳选项。

Dogs are our friends. They work with the police and help fight against bad men. They also save people in __36__. As guide dogs, they __37__ the blind(盲人). In some hospitals, some patients(病人) are too weak, so the dogs can even open the doors, __38__ or off the lights for them. They are __39__ helpers to make sick people feel __40__. But do you know how people train dogs to help protect __41__ and animals?

Dogs use their __42__ to find out the harmful insects(有害的昆虫) in the trees. For example, in May every year, a kind of insects kill ash trees(白蜡树) by __43__ their branches and roots(树枝和树根). These insects lay eggs(产卵) in the trees. When the eggs grow in insects, they begin to eat part __44__ the trees. But the eggs of the insects are so small that people can __45__ see them. With dog's sniffing (嗅觉), scientists can find the __46__ and take action(采取行动).

Dogs also help protect animals in their ways. Every year, some people catch, or even __47__ animals for things they need, from shark's fin to the tiger's skin. Then they make products like clothes and sell them illegally(非法的). Dogs special smelling helps the __48__ find out products and __49__ the selling. If there is no selling, there will be no killing.

Dogs certainly become not only man's best friends, but __50__ the environment's best friends.

36. A. half   B. the river   C. danger   D. the rain
37. A. look for   B. look after   C. look up   D. look like
38. A. turn into   B. turn up   C. turn to   D. turn on
39. A. friendly   B. friends   C. friend   D. friend's
40. A. warm   B. cool   C. sad   D. scary
41. A. blind   B. police   C. plants   D. dogs
42. A. mouths   B. noses   C. eyes   D. heads
43. A. eat   B. ate   C. eatting   D. eating
44. A. of   B. at   C. to   D. with
45. A. often   B. hardly   C. sometimes   D. usually
46. A. eggs   B. insects   C. trees   D. people
47. A. help   B. protect   C. kill   D. eat
48. A. policewomen   B. polices   C. policeman   D. police
49. A. get   B. stop   C. need   D. where
50. A. also   B. always   C. either   D. too

四、阅读理解(本大题共 10 小题,每小题 2 分,共计 20 分)

从 A、B、C、D 四个选项中,选出符合题目要求的最佳选项。

A

Today, roller skating(滑旱冰) is easy and fun. But many years ago, it wasn't easy at all. Before 1750, people never tried skating on wheels. That changed because of a man named Hoseph Merlin. Merlin's work was making instruments. In his free time he liked to play the violin. Merlin was a man with many ideas and many dreams. People called him a dreamer.

One day Merlin received an invitation to go to an important party. He was very pleased and a little excited. As the day of the party came near, Merlin began to think. He wanted to find a way to make a wonderful entrance at the party. Merlin had an idea. He thought that he would attract a lot of attention if he could skate into the room.

Merlin tried different ways to make himself roll. Finally, he decided to put two wheels under each shoe. These were the first roller skate shoes. Merlin was very proud of them. He dreamed of arriving at the party and skating into the room while playing the violin. He was sure that everyone would be very surprised.

On the night of the party Merlin rolled into the room, playing his violin. Everyone was really surprised to see him. There was just one problem. Merlin had no way to stop his roller skating. He rolled on, playing the violin. Then, with all eyes on him, Merlin hit into a huge mirror on the wall. The mirror broke into many pieces with a very loud noise. But nobody forgot Merlin's wonderful entrance after that.

51. What's Merlin's job?
  A. Making instruments.   B. Playing the violin.
  C. Roller skating.   D. Making roller skate shoes.
52. People called Merlin a dreamer because _____.
  A. he slept and dreamed a lot
  B. he always made people's dreams come true
  C. he invented the first roller skate shoes
  D. he was full of many different ideas
53. Why did Merlin think of skating on wheels?
  A. Because he loved his work.
  B. Because he wanted to make a wonderful entrance at a party.
  C. Because he wanted to play the violin better.
  D. Because there was a huge mirror.

54. What was Merlin's problem after he rolled into the room?
    A. He couldn't stop his roller-skating.
    B. He couldn't attract a lot of attention.
    C. Everyone was surprised at him.
    D. He couldn't play the violin while rolling.
55. What does the passage talk about?
    A. How to use the roller skate shoes.
    B. How people enjoyed themselves in the 18th century.
    C. How the roller skating was invented.
    D. How people made instruments.

B

Li Haoqin is an 8th-grader in Mianyang, Sichuan. The 14-year-old girl studies hard in her English class. Every day, she listens carefully in class and does many exercises after class. However, she can't get good grades, so she is very sad. "Why doesn't my hard work pay off(回报)?" Li Haoqin asks.

Lots of middle school students are now facing this problem: They try their best at something but can't make it. "They don't have effective (有效的) learning methods. This is the main reason of their difficulties," says BiQin. She is a well-known English teacher in Beijing No. 4 High School.

Bi Qin thinks that hard work is not enough for middle school students. She says, "Students have more subjects now. They should learn in many different ways. The more you use new words, the better you can remember them. For example, making sentences with new words is an effective way to learn."

Chen Xiping, 13, of Shandong, has his own ways of learning English. "I study hard in school, and I also like watching CCTV-9. On this TV channel, I always see the English words from my textbook," says Chen Xiping. "It's really useful." Lin Pingyi, 13, of Shanghai, has a habit of reading. "I like English novels like The Old Man and the Sea(《老人与海》). And I write notes in my diary," says Lin Pingyi. "In this way, I can remember more words, and make my reading and writing better."

56. Li Haoqin studies hard at English but she can't get good grades because she doesn't _____.
    A. listen carefully in class   B. have effective learning methods
    C. do many exercises   D. play sports after class
57. Bi Qin is a _____.
    A. writer   B. student   C. teacher   D. reporter
58. The underlined phrase "make it" means "_____" in Chinese.
    A. 按时到达   B. 获得成功   C. 能够出席   D. 事倍功半
59. In Bi Qin's opinion, students should remember new words effectively by _____.
    A. listening to them   B. using them more
    C. writing them often   D. reading them aloud
60. From the passage, we know that _____.
    A. Li Haoqin is a student in Grade 9
    B. Bi Qin asks students to learn different subjects in the same way
    C. Chen Xiping doesn't like watching CCTV-9
    D. Lin Pingyi has a habit of reading English novels

第二部分 （文科类职业模块考生作答，共15分）

五、单项选择题（本大题共5小题，每小题1分，共计5分）

从 A、B、C、D 四个选项中，选出空白处的最佳选项。

61. Which of the following means "Please do not step on the grass."
    A. Please Keep Off Grass   B. STOP
    C. CLEAN OUT   D. STAY CLEAR
62. —Amy, I haven't been to Kuanhouli. What about you?
    —_____ . Let's go there this weekend.
    A. Me, too.   B. Me neither.   C. I agree   D. I'd love to
63. —What about meeting here at six o'clock tomorrow morning?
    —_____ . Will seven be OK?
    A. Sure, it's up to you   B. Sure, no problem
    C. Sorry, I can't make it   D. Sorry, I'm not free now.
64. —Don't forget to keep a safe distance at least one meter, John!
    —_____ .
    A. Thanks, I will   B. No, I can't do it
    C. Not at all   D. I don't think so
65. —Sorry, it's already 6 o'clock. I have to be off for an important dinner.
    —OK. _____ .
    A. It couldn't be better   B. You really have me there
    C. Take your time   D. Let's call it a day

六、阅读理解（本大题共5小题，每小题2分，共计10分）

从 A、B、C、D 四个选项中，选出符合题目要求的最佳选项。

For the British, the home is a private(私密的) place where he or she goes to hide away from the troubles of life. It is not very common that one would be invited to a British person's home. It is rude to knock on a person's door if you are not invited. If you are invited, don't ask to see more than the downstairs that your British host invites you into. Never ask how much the house or any of the things in it costs.

To the American, most of them want their home to be a place where they can entertain(款待) and share their lives with their friends. They may be happy to give you a full tour of their houses. They may also be pleased when you show your interest in their houses.

Both British and American people will engage in quite a bit of talk and a drink or two before meals. After the first mouthful, you should say how delicious the food is and ask something about it. Remember, never eat with your mouth open and make very little noise while eating. It would be nice of you to help your host in any way. Maybe offer to pour(倒) some drinks or clear up after the meal.

66. British people _____ invite friends to their home.
   A. often   B. always   C. not very often   D. never
67. If your British friend invites you to his home, you can _____.
   A. see anything you like
   B. ask how much his house is
   C. ask the cost of any of the items in it
   D. only see the downstairs that you are invited into
68. When you show your interest and pleasure in American people's house, they may be _____.
   A. angry   B. happy   C. sad   D. worried
69. What does the underlined phrase "engage in" mean in Chinese?
   A. 陷入   B. 参与   C. 回避   D. 限制
70. What's the main idea of the passage?
   A. Some manners on visiting the British and American home.
   B. Different table manners between the British and Americans.
   C. Different ideas about the home between the British and Americans.
   D. Different ideas about getting along with the British and American neighbors.

第三部分 （工科类职业模块考生作答，共15分）

七、单项选择题（本大题共5小题，每小题1分，共计5分）

从A、B、C、D四个选项中，选出空白处的最佳选项。

71. In the USA, the emergency number is _____.
   A. 110   B. 120   C. 119   D. 911
72. 1.8t equals _____.
   A. 1,800kg   B. 1,800g   C. 1,800cm   D. 1,800km
73. "national specialty safety organization" means _____.
   A. 国家专业安全机构   B. 国家特殊安全组织
   C. 国家特殊安全机构   D. 国家专业安全组织
74. 100℃ is as warm as _____℉.
   A. 212   B. 210   C. 220   D. 222
75. Sixteen divided by four is _____.
   A. 3   B. 4   C. 5   D. 6

八、阅读理解（本大题共5小题，每小题2分，共计10分）

从A、B、C、D四个选项中，选出符合题目要求的最佳选项。

You may know about "junk food" like French fries. But do you know about "junk sleep"? Recently, a British survey(调查) shows that there are many electronic products in teenagers' bedrooms. They are influencing teenagers' sleep badly.

The survey was done among 1,000 British kids from 12 to 16. It found that 50% of them got just 4 to 7 hours' sleep every day. But doctors say they need 8 to 9 hours.

Almost 25% of the kids said they often fell asleep while they were watching TV, listening to music or using other electronic products.

"This is very worrying," said Dr. Chris, a British professor(教授). "We call it 'junk sleep'. It means you don't get enough sleep and the quality(质量) of the sleep is low, too. If you don't get a good rest, you won't do well in school the next day."

The survey found that quite a few of the kids felt tired each day because of the junk sleep, especially girls between 13 and 16 feeling the worst. Nearly all the teenagers have a phone, MP5 or TV in their bedrooms. And lots of them even have all the three.

Dr. Chris suggested that parents should help their children keep away from electronic products, and teenagers should spend less time on the electronic products.

76. What does this passage mainly talk about?
   A. Junk food.   B. Junk sleep.
   C. Electronic products.   D. The importance of sleep.
77. How many of the children sleep only 4 to 7 hours a day in the survey?
   A. 200.   B. 250.   C. 500.   D. 1,000.
78. "Junk food" and "junk sleep" are similar to each other because _____.
   A. they are both low in quality
   B. they are both needed in our life
   C. they are both enjoyed at weekends
   D. they are both necessary for people's health
79. Which of the following is TRUE according to the passage?
   A. Teenagers of 12 to 16 only need 4 to 7 hours' sleep each day.
   B. Few of the teenagers have electronic products in their bedrooms.
   C. Teenagers spend too much time on electronic products.
   D. Girls between 13 and 16 spend the least time on electronic products.
80. Which of the following should be the best way to solve the problem?
   A. Parents must take the electronic products away from their children.
   B. Parents stop the teenagers from using any electronic product.
   C. Teenagers should decide not to use the electronic products.
   D. Teenagers should spend less time on the electronic products.

九、书面表达（15分）

夏初是疾病多发季节，提前做好预防非常重要。请根据以下提示，以"How to protect ourselves from the illness"为题写一篇有关疾病预防的英语短文。

提示：1. 有积极的心态；
2. 养成良好的生活习惯，如健康饮食、适度活动；
3. 劳逸结合。

要求：1. 包含以上要点，可适当发挥；
2. 80词左右。

模拟测试卷七

说明：
1. 本试卷分选择题和非选择题两部分。满分100分，考试时间90分钟。
2. 选择题分三部分，第一部分为共答题，所有考生作答；第二部分由文科类职业模块考生作答；第三部分由工科类职业模块考生作答。
3. 考生必须且只能在下列其中一个职业模块后的空格内"√"，确定本人作答部分，在确定范围以外作答一律不计分。
4. 考试结束后，将本试卷和答题卡一并交回。

选择题
注意事项：
1. 选择题答案必须填涂在答题卡上，写在试卷上一律不计分。
2. 答题前，考生务必将自己的姓名、准考证号、座位号、考试科目涂写在答题卡上。
3. 考生须按规定要求正确涂卡，否则后果自负。

第一部分　共答题（所有考生作答，共70分）

一、语音（本大题共10小题，每小题1分，共计10分）

从A、B、C、D四个选项中，选出画线部分发音不同的一项。

1. A. fan　　　　B. range　　　　C. calculate　　　　D. rapidly
2. A. butter　　　B. bubble　　　　C. ruler　　　　　　D. cup
3. A. box　　　　B. nod　　　　　 C. topic　　　　　　D. correct
4. A. half　　　　B. talk　　　　　C. small　　　　　　D. wall
5. A. sea　　　　B. meat　　　　　C. instead　　　　　D. east
6. A. book　　　B. cook　　　　　C. foot　　　　　　D. broom
7. A. course　　 B. your　　　　　C. four　　　　　　D. hour
8. A. science　　B. lie　　　　　　C. society　　　　　D. diet
9. A. light　　　 B. daughter　　　C. cough　　　　　D. high
10. A. style　　　B. beautify　　　　C. satisfy　　　　　D. busy

二、单项选择题（本大题共25小题，每小题1分，共计25分）

从A、B、C、D四个选项中，选出空白处的最佳选项。

11. My mother persuaded me _____ again.
    A. try　　　B. to try　　　C. trying　　　D. have tried
12. This area of the country is rich _____ coal.
    A. on　　　B. to　　　　C. in　　　　　D. of
13. We can improve our math _____ practicing more.
    A. in　　　B. with　　　C. of　　　　　D. by
14. There are lots of Chinese books here, and _____ of them is easy to understand.
    A. both　　B. all　　　　C. every　　　　D. each
15. In summer, there is always _____ rain.
    A. many　　B. many a　　C. a great number of　　D. a great deal of
16. Lily and I are _____ workmates. We are close friends.
    A. more than　B. no more than　C. not more than　D. no more
17. I _____ take a taxi home _____ drive a car during the rush hours.
    A. would rather; than　　　　B. would like; to
    C. would rather; to　　　　　D. would like; than
18. _____ I you, I would go to work.
    A. be　　　B. am　　　　C. is　　　　D. were
19. _____ he worked hard, he would have finished the task.
    A. Have　　B. Had　　　C. Having　　D. To have
20. I wish I _____ everything in the world.
    A. know　　B. knew　　C. having known　　D. had known
21. I wish that the experiment _____ a success.
    A. be　　　B. am　　　　C. is　　　　D. were
22. He is not a rich man but he _____ he were.
    A. wishes　B. hopes　　C. longs　　D. believes
23. Can you guess _____ at this moment?
    A. how far is it　　　　　B. where he went
    C. when did he go　　　　D. what he is doing
24. —Your father hasn't given up smoking, has he?
    —_____, he smokes _____ now.
    A. Yes; no more　B. No; no more　C. Yes; any more　D. No; any more
25. —How often do you have history lessons?
    —_____, Monday, Wednesday and Friday.
    A. Every day　　　　　　B. Every other day
    C. Every three days　　　D. Every few days
26. —The cake looks _____.
    —Yes, and it tastes even _____.
    A. well; good　　　B. nice; better
    C. good; worse　　D. better; best
27. You should _____ the bad habit instead of getting into it.
    A. break away　　B. keep away
    C. get on　　　　　D. get rid of
28. She saw _____ boy playing with his dog.
    A. eight-year-old　　　　B. an eight-years-old
    C. an eight-year-old　　　D. a eight-years-old
29. John told me to _____ the pictures _____ tomorrow.
    A. take; here　　　B. bring; there
    C. taking; there　　D. bring; here
30. It is very hot today, please keep the window _____.
    A. opening　　B. open　　C. opens　　D. to open
31. —May I play with my dog?

— 1 —

—I am afraid not. You can't play with it _____ you finish your homework.
A. when   B. until   C. after   D. Because

32. —Must I clean the cage today?
—No, you _____.
A. must not   B. can not   C. need not   D. may not

33. Kate has a cat _____ Mimi.
A. called   B. call   C. to call   D. Calling

34. —How often do you clean the fish tank?
—_____.
A. this afternoon   B. only once
C. once a month   D. for two days

35. All the students in my class did their homework except _____.
A. Jane and I   B. Jane and mine
C. I and Jane   D. Jane and me

三、完形填空(本大题共 15 小题，每小题 1 分，共计 15 分)

从 A、B、C、D 四个选项中，选出空白处的最佳选项。

It started four years ago. My wife would see a __36__ man near where she worked. It was the week before Christmas and she said she wanted to purchase a new coat for him because his coat was __37__. We don't have a lot of __38__. We are really a step step away from being homeless in rags most months but we try to __39__ when we can. We talked and found a way to get some money together to __40__ him a coat. I __41__ that since we were giving a coat to him, we should look at what else he might __42__. We decided to fill a __43__ with some useful __44__ things—a toothbrush, soap, clothes, a hat, gloves and some food. A small gift and Christmas card was put in it as well. We haven't had money to exchange __45__ for birthdays or Christmas for many years, too. It feels wonderful to have someone __46__ you at Christmas but I've always been a little __47__ when friends ask "What did you get for Christmas?" It always makes my wife feel bad that she can't __48__ to give me anything and I feel the same. So I would __49__ and say she bought me this thing or that. But that year we could say we __50__ something to others instead and that's exactly what happened.

36. A. sick   B. homeless   C. generous   D. energetic
37. A. loose   B. large   C. shabby   D. tight
38. A. money   B. power   C. time   D. trouble
39. A. recover   B. bargain   C. escape   D. help
40. A. buy   B. make   C. show   D. lend
41. A. commanded   B. warned   C. regretted   D. insisted
42. A. ignore   B. need   C. dislike   D. store
43. A. backpack   B. room   C. suitcase   D. car
44. A. left   B. external   C. daily   D. cheap
45. A. principles   B. gifts   C. opinions   D. congratulations
46. A. rely on   B. turn to   C. think of   D. stand for
47. A. embarrassed   B. contradictory   C. pleased   D. content
48. A. expect   B. reject   C. wait   D. afford
49. A. admit   B. lie   C. debate   D. disagree
50. A. compared   B. exposed   C. presented   D. sold

四、阅读理解(本大题共 10 小题，每小题 2 分，共计 20 分)

从 A、B、C、D 四个选项中，选出符合题目要求的最佳选项。

A

On the afternoon of the day that we arrived in Xingcheng, we left for Qinhuangdao. It was raining heavily while we were on the highway. I kept the speed less than 100 kilometres per hour. We got to Qinhuangdao in the late afternoon. We booked in a hotel a normal room with a large bed, an air conditioner, a TV and a toilet. 150 yuan more or less is worthy of that.

The next morning, it only took us less than 30 minutes to get to the beach. Policemen were everywhere, and they guided our traffic. The bill of the parking was 20 yuan. I paid some money for life buoys because none of us could swim. The water was not too deep near the beach and with a life buoy I could float on the water in order not to get drowned. I taught my wife how to use the life buoy, although it was also the first time that I used it. But my daughter was fascinated by the sand. She played with the sand with all her attention, which made us laugh. The environment in Beidaihe was fine, although it was not very clean, and we had a good time.

By the way, in the evening we visited the shopping street in the central city. We visited a shopping street near Beidaihe. There were a lot of people, shopping and dining. Of course, we had some seafood there too.

51. The writer went to Beidaihe _____.
A. by train   B. by bus   C. by car   D. by plane

52. What do the underlined words "life buoys" mean in Chinese?
A. 防晒霜   B. 救生圈   C. 游泳衣   D. 游艇

53. What was the writer's daughter doing while they were swimming?
A. Taking a walk along the beach.   B. Having a picnic.
C. Lying in the sun.   D. Playing with the sand.

54. Which of the following is TRUE according to the passage?
A. The writer booked a room with 300 yuan a night.
B. The writer's wife is very good at swimming.
C. The environment is very clean in Beidaihe.
D. The writer had some seafood that evening.

55. What's the best title for the passage?
A. The trip to Beidaihe   B. The sea in Beidaihe
C. The weather in Beidaihe   D. The food in Beidaihe

B

Dear friend, do you know the boy Wang Yuan? He is a member of the Chinese boy band, TFBOYS. Do you want to know more about him? Follow me, please.

Wang Yuan was born November 8th, 2000 in Chongqing. His English name is Roy. He is good at singing, dancing and playing the piano. He can also write songs alone. He and two other boys formed the boy band TFBOYS in 2013. They are very popular with the young girls and boys in China now.

In January, 2017, Wang Yuan made a speech on good quality education(优质教育) in English at the United Nations in front of 500 people from, around the world. It's great. As for middle school students, we should learn from Wang Yuan, and put our hearts into what we are doing to make a difference in our daily lives.

56. Wang Yuan was born _____.
  A. on November 18th, 2013 B. on November 18th, 2001
  C. on November 8th, 2000   D. on November 8th, 2013
57. Wang Yuan's English name is _____.
  A. Jay B. Roy C. Lay D. Kay
58. Wang Yuan is a talented boy, he can _____, sing and play the piano.
  A. play the drums B. drive
  C. paint   D. dance
59. Wang Yuan made a speech in _____ in 2017.
  A. Chongqing B. Beijing
  C. Shanghai   D. the United Nations
60. What can you learn from the passage?
  A. Working hard can make a difference.
  B. Being a star can make a lot of money.
  C. Wang Yuan sings well but can't write songs.
  D. Four people are in the band.

第二部分　（文科类职业模块考生作答，共15分）

五、单项选择题(本大题共5小题，每小题1分，共计5分)

从A、B、C、D四个选项中，选出空白处的最佳选项。

61. —People should stop using their cars and start using public transport.
  —_____. The roads are too crowded as it is.
  A. All right C. Exactly B. Go ahead D. Fine
62. —Shall I give you a ride as you live so far away.
  —Thank you. _____.
  A. It couldn't be better. B. Of course you can.
  C. If you like   D. It's up to you.
63. —You had better not eat too much salt.
  —_____.
  A. Not at all B. You are welcome
  C. I am thirsty now D. Thank you for you advice
64. —How could you say that?
  —_____. I didn't mean to hurt you.
  A. Excuse me B. I won't regret
  C. I'm really sorry D. That's all right
65. —Don't smoke here, please.
  —_____.
  A. I don't B. Sorry, I won't
  C. No way D. I will

六、阅读理解(本大题共5小题，每小题2分，共计10分)

从A、B、C、D四个选项中，选出符合题目要求的最佳选项。

When his mum fainted(昏厥) and knocked herself out, unconscious, four year old Henry Davies knew just what to do — thanks to a storybook.

He calmly dialled 999 and told the <u>emergency services</u> how to get to his home and then phoned his father.

The boy told the doctors what had happened and directed them to the house in Coundon, Coventry, and even offered the doctors a drink.

When they arrived. Henry also offered to look after his 12 — month old brother Noah.

His father, Iran, 35, said, "Chloe has been unwell with a high fever which has made her feel quite poorly. I left for work early at about 7:30 am and as she got up after I left she felt quite dizzy and faint. The next thing she remembers is fainting down on the floor and hearing Henry talking to someone. He had seen her fall and hit her head on the table, but he couldn't wake her up. So he picked up the phone and dialled 999 for an ambulance."

Chloe said, "Henry has a storybook, Ambulance Crew, on what to do in an emergency, which we've read a few times. He even put a blanket over me. The ambulance crew were amazed. We're very proud of him."

66. How old was Henry?
  A. 1. B. 2. C. 3. D. 4.
67. What was the matter with Henry's mother?
  A. She fainted on the floor. B. She was shot by a gun.
  C. She was badly ill.   D. She was hurt badly.
68. How did Henry know the knowledge of saving his mother?
  A. By watching TV.   B. By reading a book.
  C. His teacher taught him. D. By WeChat.
69. The underlined words "emergency services" mean "_____" in Chinese.
  A. 紧急应变机构 B. 突发事件
  C. 急诊室   D. 医疗室
70. Which of the following is NOT true according to the passage?
  A. There are 4 people in Henry's family.

B. Henry prepared a drink for the doctors.
C. Henry's father is very proud of Henry.
D. His father is 29 years old.

第三部分　(工科类职业模块考生作答，共15分)

七、单项选择题(本大题共5小题，每小题1分，共计5分)

71. Which of the following is not a unit of capacity or volume? _____.
    A. milliliter   B. hectare   C. cubic centimeter   D. cubic meter
72. Our ordinary temperature is 36.5℃. It equals _____ °F.
    A. 96.5   B. 106.5   C. 97.7   D. 36.5
73. The second power of four minus four is _____.
    A. ten   B. eleven   C. twelve   D. thirteen
74. In China, the emergency number is _____.
    A. 110   B. 114   C. 123   D. 911
75. 1.5t equals _____.
    A. 1,500 kg   B. 1,500 g   C. 1,500 cm   D. 1,500 km

八、阅读理解(本大题共5小题，每小题2分，共10分)

从 A、B、C、D 四个选项中，选出符合题目要求的最佳选项。

　　The British National Health Service(NHS) was set up in 1948 and was designed to provide equal basic health care, free of charge, for everybody in the country. Before this time health care had to be paid for by individuals.

　　Nowadays central government is directly responsible for the NHS although it is administered by local health authorities. About 83 percent of the cost of the health service is paid for by general taxation and the rest is met from the National Insurance contributions paid by those in work. There are charges for prescription and dental care but many people, such as children, pregnant women, pensioners, and those on Income Support, are <u>exempt</u> from pament. Most people are registered with a local doctor(a GP, or General Practitioner) who is increasingly likely to be part of a health centre which serves the community.

　　As the population of Britain gets older, the hospital service now treats more patients than before, although patients spend less time in hospital. NHS hospitals—many of which were built in the nineteenth century — provide nearly half a million beds and have over 480,000 medical staff. The NHS is the biggest employer in Europe although Britain actually spends less per person on health care than most of her European neighbours.

　　During the 1980s there was considerable restructuring of the Health Service with an increased emphasis on managerial efficiency and the privatization of some services (for example, cleaning). At the end of the 1980s the government introduced proposals for further reform of the NHS, including allowing some hospitals to be self-governing, and encouraging GPs to compete for patients. Patients would be able to choose and change their family doctor more easily and GPs would have more financial responsibility. The political questions continue of how much money should be provided to support the NHS and where it should come from.

76. We can know from the first paragraph that _____.
    A. the original aim of the NHS was to provide equal basic health care for everybody
    B. people didn't have to pay for health care since the NHS was set up
    C. patients were charged for receiving health care before 1948
    D. the NHS was an organization which gave free advice to villagers
77. What do we know about the NHS?
    A. It's managed by the central government.
    B. Its cost is mainly paid for by the National Insurance contributions.
    C. It hires more people than any other unit in Europe.
    D. Fewer patients go to its hospitals than before because they spend less on health care.
78. All the following statements about GPs are true except that they _____.
    A. take care of the local people's health
    B. often take part in competitions to see who is the best
    C. work under high pressure nowadays
    D. have more responsibilities than before
79. What does the underlined word "exempt" probably mean?
    A. suffering   B. different   C. prevented   D. free
80. The biggest problem for the NHS is _____.
    A. many hospitals are too old to be used
    B. some services are in the charge of individuals
    C. more and more patients go to GPS for treatment
    D. there is not enough money for further reform

非选择题

九、书面表达(15分)

　　最近，绿色出行的话题展开了广泛的讨论，请你以绿色出行(Green Travel)为主题，写一篇文章。
　　要求：1. 80 词左右；
　　　　　2. 不能出现真名。

_____
_____
_____
_____

模拟测试卷八

说明：
1. 本试卷分选择题和非选择题两部分。满分100分，考试时间90分钟。
2. 选择题分三部分，第一部分为共答题，所有考生作答；第二部分由文科类职业模块考生作答；第三部分由工科类职业模块考生作答。
3. 考生必须且只能在下列其中一个职业模块后的空格内"√"，确定本人作答部分，在确定范围以外作答一律不计分。
4. 考试结束后，将本试卷和答题卡一并交回。

选择题

注意事项：
1. 选择题答案必须填涂在答题卡上，写在试卷上一律不计分。
2. 答题前，考生务必将自己的姓名、准考证号、座位号、考试科目涂写在答题卡上。
3. 考生须按规定要求正确涂卡，否则后果自负。

第一部分　共答题（所有考生作答，共70分）

一、语音（本大题共10小题，每小题1分，共计10分）

从A、B、C、D四个选项中，选出画线部分发音不同的一项。

1. A. with　　　　B. think　　　　C. thank　　　　D. third
2. A. mend　　　　B. every　　　　C. evening　　　D. twelve
3. A. for　　　　　B. worker　　　 C. morning　　　D. forty
4. A. China　　　 B. chair　　　　C. machine　　　D. teacher
5. A. put　　　　 B. uncle　　　　C. jump　　　　 D. run
6. A. what　　　　B. who　　　　　C. which　　　　D. where
7. A. coat　　　　B. now　　　　　C. know　　　　 D. soap
8. A. told　　　　B. soda　　　　 C. cola　　　　 D. not
9. A. house　　　 B. honor　　　　C. heritage　　　D. huge
10. A. mouse　　　B. cloud　　　　C. pound　　　　D. touch

二、单项选择题（本大题共25小题，每小题1分，共计25分）

从A、B、C、D四个选项中，选出空白处的最佳选项。

11. Miss Li is _____ our teacher _____ our friend.
    A. neither; or　　B. either; or　　C. not only; but also　　D. either; nor
12. He began learning English. _____ the age of five.
    A. for　　B. on　　C. in　　D. At
13. His job is _____ cars.
    A. to repair　　B. repaired　　C. repairs　　D. Repair
14. We should protect our eyes _____ sunglasses.
    A. in wear　　B. by wearing　　C. with wearing　　D. to wear
15. You must have left your glasses _____.
    A. somewhere else　　B. anywhere else　　C. somewhere other　　D. some other where
16. I will talk with you about it _____ time.
    A. the other　　B. others　　C. another　　D. the others
17. All the students like the teachers who _____ their lessons interesting.
    A. makes　　B. make　　C. making　　D. to make
18. We can watch the TV programmers from other countries _____ the satellites.
    A. because　　B. because of　　C. if　　D. That
19. The teacher told us not _____ our dictionaries to school the next day.
    A. to bring　　B. to take　　C. bring　　D. Take
20. I will go to visit my uncle _____ next week.
    A. sometimes　　B. some times　　C. some time　　D. sometime
21. Will you _____ come tomorrow?
    A. be able to　　B. can　　C. must　　D. be able
22. The used car is _____ 500 dollars.
    A. cost　　B. pay　　C. worth　　D. Spend
23. —Will you go shopping tonight?
    —If you go, _____.
    A. so do I　　B. so will I　　C. so I go　　D. that I will go
24. —Do you still remember _____ me somewhere in Shanghai?
    —yes, of course, two years ago.
    A. seeing　　B. see　　C. to see　　D. Saw
25. _____ is really hard _____ them to climb Mount Qomolangma.
    A. This; is　　B. It; for　　C. This; for　　D. It; to
26. _____ cloudy day it is!
    A. how　　B. what　　C. how a　　D. what a
27. The flood killed _____ people
    A. thousands of　　B. thousand of　　C. thousands　　D. Thousand
28. This math problem is not easy. I can't work it out _____.
    A. without he　　B. with him　　C. without him　　D. with he
29. I don't know _____ the computer.
    A. what to use　　B. how use　　C. how to use　　D. how can use
30. Billy didn't come to school this morning. What happened _____ him?
    A. with　　B. for　　C. to　　D. In
31. I don't know if she _____ tomorrow. If it _____, perhaps she'll come.
    A. will come; stops raining　　B. comes; will stop raining
    C. will come; won't rain　　　 D. comes; doesn't rain
32. My father can't come to parents' meeting. He _____ to Beijing on business this morning.
    A. has gone　　B. has been　　C. went　　D. would go
33. I _____ to answer the question in English. But as you know, I'm not so good at English.

— 1 —

A. told   B. was told   C. have told   D. was telling
34. There is no _____ in the boat, so we have to wait for another one.
　　A. seats   B. room   C. rooms   D. A seat
35. These foreign friends have already _____ Nanjing for about two days.
　　A. reached   B. arrived in   C. got to   D. been in

三、完形填空(本大题共 15 小题，每小题 1 分，共计 15 分)

从 A、B、C、D 四个选项中，选出空白处的最佳选项。

At my heaviest I weighed 370 pounds. I had a very poor relationship with food. Worried about my health, I tried many different kinds of __36__ but nothing worked. I came to believe that I could do nothing about my __37__. When I was 50, my weight problem began to affect me __38__. I didn't want to live the rest of my life with this __39__ weight any more. That year, I __40__ a seminar where we were asked to create a project that would touch the world. A seminar leader shared her __41__ story —she had not only 125 pounds, but also raised ＄25,000 for homeless children. __42__ by her story, I created the As We Heal(痊愈), the World Heals __43__. My goal was to lose 150 pounds in one year and raise ＄50,000 __44__ a movement founded 30 years ago to end hunger. This combination of healing myself and healing the world __45__ me as the perfect solution. __46__ I began my own personal weight program, I was filled with the fear that I would __47__ the same difficulties that beat me before. I hired a fitness coach, and I began to eat small and __48__ meals. A year later, I __49__ my goal: I lost 150 pounds and raised ＄50,000! I feel that I've been given a second life to devote to something that is __50__ and enormous.

36. A. diets   B. drinks   C. fruits   D. dishes
37. A. height   B. ability   C. wisdom   D. weight
38. A. temporarily   B. recently   C. seriously   D. secretly
39. A. ideal   B. extra   C. normal   D. low
40. A. attended   B. organized   C. recommended   D. mentioned
41. A. folk   B. success   C. adventure   D. science
42. A. Surprised   B. Amused   C. Influenced   D. Disturbed
43. A. project   B. business   C. system   D. custom
44. A. in search of   B. in need of   C. in place of   D. in support of
45. A. scared   B. considered   C. confused   D. struck
46. A. As   B. Until   C. If   D. Unless
47. A. get over   B. run into   C. look for   D. put aside
48. A. regularly   B. limitlessly   C. suddenly   D. randomly
49. A. set   B. reached   C. missed   D. dropped
50. A. stressful   B. painful   C. meaningful   D. peaceful

四、阅读理解(本大题共 10 小题，每小题 2 分，共计 20 分)

从 A、B、C、D 四个选项中，选出符合题目要求的最佳选项。

A

Parents have to do much less for their children today than they used to do, and home has become much less of a workshop. Clothes can be bought ready made; washing can go to the laundry; food can be bought; cooked, canned or preserved; bread is baked and delivered by the baker; milk arrives on the doorstep; meats can be had at the restaurant, the work's canteen, and the school dining-room.

It is unusual now for father to pursue his trade or other employment at home, and his children rarely, if ever, see him at his place of work. Boys are therefore seldom trained to follow their father's occupation, and in many towns they have a fairly wide choice of employment and so do girls. The young wage-earner often earns good money, and soon acquires a feeling of economic independence. In textile areas it has long been customary for mothers to go out to work, but this practice has become so widespread that the working mother is now a not unusual factor in a child's home life, the number of married women in employment having more than doubled in the last twenty-five years. With mother earning and his older children drawing substantial wages father is seldom the dominant figure that he still was at the beginning of the century. When mother works, economic advantages accrue, but children lose something of great value if mother's employment prevents her from being home to greet them when they return from school.

51. The writer mentions home as workshop because _____.
　　A. fathers often pursue employment at home
　　B. parents had to make food and necessity themselves for their daily-life
　　C. many families produce goods at home for sale
　　D. both fathers and mothers and mothers in most families are workers
52. The writer says that home has become much less of a workshop. He means _____.
　　A. in the past, home was more like a workshop
　　B. home is much more of a workshop now
　　C. home-workshops are becoming fewer and fewer
　　D. home was less like a workshop in the past
53. The word "accrue" in the sentence "When mother... accrue," is closest in meaning to _____.
　　A. change   B. dwindle   C. double   D. increase
54. The chief reason that boys are seldom trained to follow their father's occupation is _____.
　　A. that children nowadays rarely see their fathers at their place of work
　　B. that fathers do not like to pursue employment at home any more
　　C. that there is a wide choice of employment for children
　　D. that children also like to have jobs outside

55. What makes father no longer the only dominant person in a family?
    A. With their earning, mother and children do not need to depend on father for their life.
    B. There are many choice of employment for mothers and children.
    C. Father does much less for his children today than he used to.
    D. The number of married women in employment has increased greatly now.

B

People all have problems. If we don't deal with these problems, we can easily become unhappy. Worrying about our problems can affect how we do at school. It can also influence the way we behave with our families. So how do we deal with our problems? There are many ways and here is one of them

Most of us have probably been angry with our friends, parents or teachers. Perhaps they said something you didn't like, or you felt they were unfair. Sometimes people can stay angry for years about a small problem. Time goes by, and good friendship may be lost.

When we are angry, however, we are usually the ones affected. Perhaps we have seen young children playing together. Sometimes they have disagreements, and decide not to talk to each other. However, this usually does not last for long. This is an important lesson for us to learn.

56. What is the writer?
    A. A shopkeeper.   B. A doctor.
    C. A student.   D. A dentist.
57. What is the main idea of the passage?
    A. How to deal with problems.   B. How to do at school.
    C. How to behave with families.   D. How to talk to each other.
58. What will happen if people stay angry for long according to the text?
    A. They feel unfair.   B. They may get sick.
    C. Good friendship may be lost.   D. They may miss each other.
59. Children decide not to talk to each other probably because _____.
    A. they become unhappy   B. thay have different ideas
    C. they worry about a small problem D. they want disagreements
60. From the passage, we know an important lesson for us is
    A. playing together   B. learning to forget
    C. staying angry   D. feeling unfair

第二部分 （文科类职业模块考生作答，共15分）

五、单项选择题(本大题共 5 小题，每小题 1 分，共计 5 分)

从 A、B、C、D 四个选项中，选出空白处的最佳选项。

61. —I would like you to meet my new friend, Lily.
    —_____.
    A. Hello, there   B. How do you do, Lily?
    C. Nice to meet you, Lily D. How are you
62. —Thank you for your help.
    —_____.
    A. You're welcome.   B. Never mind
    C. That's all right   D. Help yourself
63. —I have won the first prize in the competition.
    —_____.
    A. Good luck   B. Too bad   C. Congratulations   D. Don't worry
64. —I will take a test tomorrow.
    —_____.
    A. So what   B. Good Luck
    C. Good idea   D. I cannot agree more
65. —I am going to go on a vocation next month.
    —_____.
    A. Have a good time   B. Good Luck
    C. Congratulations   D. Best wishes

六、阅读理解(本大题共 5 小题，每小题 2 分，共计 10 分)

从 A、B、C、D 四个选项中，选出符合题目要求的最佳选项。

It's 10 am on a school day morning in Shanghai and students are standing in lines on the playground, doing their morning exercises. As a teacher at the front calls out, "Yi, er, san, si…" the students extend their arms, then bring them to their chests; bend their knees, then straighten up. Many of the students seem bored.

Meanwhile, in a primary school in Xiangyang, Hubei Province, students are dancing to pop music. Which would you rather do?

Since 1951, morning calisthenics(健身操) have been a part of Chinese life. The school in Xiangyang wanted to make morning exercises more fun, so it looked to a group of people who seemed to really enjoy exercising damas (大妈)! These "aunties" dance on public squares each evening, often driving neighbours crazy with their loud music. But it is good exercise and they are having fun. So, why shouldn't students be allowed to follow their example?

Well, on the Internet, most posters said dancing in the primary school in Xiangyang looked funny. One poster said that calisthenics were old-fashioned and that "the organized movements leave no room for personal freedom".

Fitness is essential for young people. Too much study and too much computer time are making many young Chinese fat and unfit, so it's important that they become more active. And being active is the key, even if that means doing away with calisthenics and, instead, dancing like dramas.

66. The first paragraph mainly tells us that _____.
    A. students' school life is colourful in Shanghai
    B. morning exercises are helpful to students' health
    C. many students feel bored about morning exercises

D. PE is important to school students

67. The underlined word "Meanwhile" means"_____" in Chinese.
   A. 反之　　　B. 同时　　　C. 总之　　　D. 幸运的是
68. How long have morning calisthenics been in Chinese schools?
   A. For 20 years.　　　B. For over 60 years.
   C. Since last year.　　　D. Since 1951 years ago.
69. What do most people think of dancing in the primary school in Xiangyang?
   A. Funny.　　　B. Helpful　　　C. Boring　　　D. Hard
70. What is the best title for the passage?
   A. After-class activities　　　B. Colourful school life
   C. A history of morning exercises　　　D. Dancing like dramas

第三部分 （工科类职业模块考生作答，共15分）

七、单项选择题（本大题共5小题，每小题1分，共计5分）

从A、B、C、D四个选项中，选出空白处的最佳选项。

71. Ten to the fourth power is _____.
   A. 10　　　B. 100　　　C. 1,000　　　D. 10,000
72. My sister paid _____ for the map.
   A. three times so much　　　B. three times the usual price
   C. three times more　　　D. three times as much as ever
73. The new students is in _____.
   A. Class 2　　　B. Class second　　　C. 2 Class　　　D. class 2
74. It's twenty to ten. We can also read it _____.
   A. nine forty　　　B. nine fourteen
   C. ten past twenty　　　D. ten ten
75. The cube root of twenty-seven times five makes _____.
   A. one hundred and thirty-five　　　B. thirty-two
   C. twenty-two　　　D. fifteen

八、阅读理解（本大题共5小题，每小题2分，共计10分）

从A、B、C、D四个选项中，选出符合题目要求的最佳选项。

What should we do if one of our classmates suddenly falls ill or gets hurt? Here are some steps you should follow. But always remember to look for medical care after first aid(急救) if the wound is serious.

Broken bones (骨头): Take away clothing from the wound, Use an ice pack. Don't move the hurt body part while waiting for the doctor to arrive.

Animal bites(咬伤): Wash the bite area with soap and water. Pack the wound with a clean cloth if it is bleeding. If the bleeding has stopped, cover the area with a bandage and take the person to hospital. Make sure you remember what kind of animal it is, so the doctor can find the right way to treat him or her at once.

Fainting(昏厥): Have him or her lie with feet lifted a little. Don't move the body if you think there might be wounds from the fall, Make sure he or she can breathe and let in fresh air. Clean the person's face with a cool cloth.

Nosebleeds: Have the person sit up with his or her head tilted(倾斜) forward a little, Do not have the person tilt his or her head back because this may cause heavy breathing or coughing. Pinch(捏)the lower part of the nose for at least 10 minutes.

76. What should we do first when an animal bite happens?
   A. Put an ice pack on the wound.
   B. Wash the bite area with soap and water.
   C. Try to stop the bleeding with a clean cloth.
   D. Take the injured person to the hospital.
77. When dealing with the problems of _____, we shouldn't move the hurt.
   A. broken bones and animal bites　　　B. animal bites and nosebleeds
   C. broken bones and fainting　　　D. fainting and nosebleeds
78. Which of the following is NOT right when a boy's nose bleeds?
   A. Let his head not tilt back.
   B. Let his head tilt forward a little.
   C. Let him sit up.
   D. Pinch his nose for less than 10 minutes.
79. Which part of a magazine may the passage come from?
   A. Lifestyle.　　B. Health.　　C. Sports.　　D. Education.
80. What's the main idea of the passage?
   A. First aid for some accidental wounds.
   B. Steps of looking for medical care.
   C. Advice on ways not to get hurt.
   D. Ways to ask for help in getting hurt.

非选择题

九、书面表达（15分）

请你介绍科技与生活（Science and Technology）为主题，写一篇文章。

要求：1. 80词左右；
　　　2. 不能出现真名。
内容提示：1. 科学与技术发挥着重要作用。
　　　　　2. 科技是一把双刃剑。
　　　　　3. 滥用科技会造成危害。

模拟测试卷九

说明：
1. 本试卷分选择题和非选择题两部分。满分100分，考试时间90分钟。
2. 选择题分三部分，第一部分为共答题，所有考生作答；第二部分由文科类职业模块考生作答；第三部分由工科类职业模块考生作答。
3. 考生必须且只能在下列其中一个职业模块后的空格内"v"，确定本人作答部分，在确定范围以外作答一律不计分。
4. 考试结束后，将本试卷和答题卡一并交回。

选择题
注意事项：
1. 选择题答案必须填涂在答题卡上，写在试卷上一律不计分。
2. 答题前，考生务必将自己的姓名、准考证号、座位号、考试科目涂写在答题卡上。
3. 考生须按规定要求正确涂卡，否则后果自负。

第一部分 共答题（所有考生作答，共70分）

一、语音（本大题共10小题，每小题1分，共计10分）

从 A、B、C、D 四个选项中，选出画线部分发音不同的一项。

1. A. arr<u>a</u>nge   B. br<u>a</u>ve   C. c<u>a</u>stle   D. r<u>a</u>dio
2. A. r<u>e</u>gion   B. r<u>e</u>spond   C. r<u>e</u>quest   D. r<u>e</u>place
3. A. f<u>ie</u>ld   B. sc<u>ie</u>nce   C. var<u>ie</u>ty   D. d<u>ie</u>t
4. A. f<u>ear</u>   B. h<u>ear</u>t   C. n<u>ear</u>   D. y<u>ear</u>
5. A. dialo<u>gu</u>e   B. fi<u>gu</u>re   C. <u>gu</u>ard   D. lan<u>gu</u>age
6. A. h<u>o</u>tel   B. dev<u>o</u>te   C. c<u>o</u>st   D. c<u>o</u>mb
7. A. t<u>oo</u>th   B. g<u>oo</u>d   C. sch<u>oo</u>l   D. f<u>oo</u>d
8. A. p<u>e</u>rhaps   B. y<u>e</u>ah   C. h<u>a</u>ppy   D. h<u>a</u>bit
9. A. h<u>o</u>rse   B. h<u>o</u>st   C. <u>i</u>ncrease   D. <u>i</u>ndoors
10. A. me<u>th</u>od   B. mon<u>th</u>   C. nor<u>th</u>ern   D. nor<u>th</u>ward

二、单项选择题（本大题共25小题，每小题1分，共计25分）

从 A、B、C、D 四个选项中，选出空白处的最佳选项。

11. You made the same mistake for _____ second time, dropping _____ "n" in the word "government".
    A. a; the   B. a; a   C. the; a   D. a; an

12. —Which of the two films did you prefer?
    —Actually I didn't like _____.
    A. either of them   B. both of them
    C. none of them   D. neither of them

13. We read $10 as _____.
    A. ten dollar   B. ten dollars   C. dollar ten   D. dollars ten

14. Meals are very boring. He _____ has the same things to eat every day.
    A. never   B. every   C. usually   D. sometimes

15. —How do you improve your pronunciation, Li Lei?
    —I learn it _____ listening to CCTV News _____ the radio.
    A. in; on   B. in; in   C. by; on   D. by; in

16. I _____ a new pair of shoes. I need to buy a new shirt instead.
    A. don't need   B. needn't   C. don't need to   D. need

17. It _____ that the road will be closed tomorrow for repairs.
    A. was announced   B. has been announced
    C. had been announce   D. would be announced

18. The pupils in our school like reading after lunch, most of _____ seated on the grass unless it rains.
    A. them   B. whom   C. that   D. who

19. The matter _____ our study surely requires _____ carefully.
    A. related to; dealing with   B. relating to; deal with
    C. related to; being dealt with   D. relating to; having dealt with

20. Jennifer was not _____ in the study, which made her mum worried.
    A. involved   B. responded   C. inspired   D. persuaded

21. The mother saw her baby fall to the ground, _____ brought her heart to her mouth.
    A. it   B. and that   C. and which   D. that

22. Tom's new watch _____ hands are made of gold is quite expensive.
    A. that   B. which   C. whose   D. of which

23. _____ Li Bai, a great Chinese poet, was born is known to the public, but some won't accept it.
    A. That   B. Why   C. Where   D. How

24. If you miss this chance, it may be years _____ you get another one.
    A. As   B. before   C. since   D. after

25. Don't call me at the office _____ it is necessary.
    A. before   B. unless   C. although   D. till

26. "_____ polite to the guests." said my father.
    A. Please   B. Do be   C. Are   D. Should

27. Nothing but several glasses _____ bought by my father the day before yesterday.
    A. have been   B. were   C. was   D. would be

28. It was the training _____ he had as a young man _____ made him such a good engineer.
    A. what; that   B. that; what
    C. that; which   D. which; that

29. Try _____ she might, Sue couldn't get the door open.
    A. if   B. when   C. since   D. as

30. The boy want to ride his bicycle in the street, but his mother told him _____.
    A. not to   B. not to do   C. not do it   D. do not to

31. It was the first time that she _____ such a heavy rain.
    A. had witnessed   B. has witnessed
    C. should witness   D. witnessed

— 1 —

32. Many of your classmates dislike having to stay up late doing their lessons, _____?
   A. do they   B. have they   C. don't they   D. haven't they
33. _____ is known to us that the Amber Room belongs to the Russians.
   A. As   B. Which   C. It   D. What
34. It is strongly recommended that the machines _____ every year.
   A. check   B. be checked   C. checked   D. checking
35. Being rejected and told "no" for too many times made him feel _____.
   A. value   B. invaluable   C. valueless   D. valuable

三、完形填空(本大题共 15 小题，每小题 1 分，共计 15 分)
从 A、B、C、D 四个选项中，选出空白处的最佳选项。

Many years ago in a village, Harlem, Holland, there lived a young boy. His name was Hans and he was eight years old. One __36__ day, Hans went across the reservoir(水库) to visit an old blind man. He took the man some biscuits and stayed there for a while. Then, Hans decided to __37__ his home.

"The water in the reservoir usually gets __38__ in autumn," said the old man. "Be __39__ Hans." On his way home, Hans sang a song, watched the rabbits run around and picked some flowers for his mother. __40__, the sky got dark and heavy rain began to fall. Hans felt afraid and started to __41__. Just then, he heard the sound of water running away. He looked around carefully, and then __42__ a very small hole in the dam(水坝).

Hans felt scared __43__ he knew what could happen. The __44__ could get bigger and bigger. Then the dam could break and the whole Harlem would be covered by the water. Hans knew what to do. He put his finger into the hole, __45__ no more water could come through it. "Please, someone, help me!" Hans __46__. But there was no one to help him. After some time, he began to feel very cold and tired, but he could not __47__ the dam. All night long, Hans waited and waited…

The next morning, a farmer walked by and heard Han's cries. "I am trying to stop the __48__," the boy said. "Can you help me?" The farmer called some other people and they quickly __49__ the hole. Then, they took Hans home. Everyone was very proud of that __50__ boy.

36. A. spring   B. summer   C. autumn   D. winter
37. A. clean   B. find out   C. return to   D. draw
38. A. dirtier   B. colder   C. quieter   D. higher
39. A. careful   B. kind   C. clever   D. helpful
40. A. Surely   B. Suddenly   C. Finally   D. Normally
41. A. jump   B. wait   C. run   D. work
42. A. made   B. noticed   C. dug   D. felt
43. A. because   B. even if   C. before   D. so that
44. A. rain   B. dam   C. finger   D. hole
45. A. unless   B. when   C. so   D. but
46. A. regretted   B. expected   C. imagined   D. shouted
47. A. leave   B. believe   C. see   D. build
48. A. rabbits   B. people   C. water   D. river
49. A. discovered   B. repaired   C. developed   D. protected
50. A. brave   B. patient   C. active   D. cute

四、阅读理解(本大题共 10 小题，每小题 2 分，共计 20 分)
从 A、B、C、D 四个选项中，选出符合题目要求的最佳选项。

A

Five years is a rather short time in the long history of China. But for digital(数字的) development, a lot of changes have taken place in many aspects of our life.

Nowadays, it's normal for people to communicate on WeChat, the most popular mobile social media platform in China. People take less cash(现金) with them because most of the stores and hotels accept WeChat Pay and Alipay.

In China, holding a mobile phone means having the world in your hands. You can shop, travel, communicate, have fun by using a mobile phone, and all of these tasks can be completed with a few finger taps. Without mobile phones, life would seem dull.

By the end of 2016, there were 695 million mobile phone users in China, an increase of 12 percent on year-on-year basis. The average mobile Internet data traffic reached 172 megabytes per month, which was far more than the global average.

At the two sessions(两会), Premier Li Keqiang pointed out that in 2017 the speed of mobile network would be increased and the cost would be reduced greatly. Mobile rates for domestic roaming(国内漫游) and long distance calls would be canceled.

Meanwhile, the TD-LTE 4G communication technology developed mainly in China has been accepted and widely used across the world.

In 2020, China's 5G network is in service. It helps China's mobile telecommunication overtake(反超) the international community's.

51. People take less cash with them because _____.
   A. cash isn't useful any more
   B. it's easier to use online pay by mobile phone
   C. many stores refuse cash
   D. online pay is used in all stores and hotels
52. By using a mobile phone, you can do many things EXCEPT _____.
   A. ordering something to eat   B. chatting with friends
   C. playing games   D. cooking something delicious
53. What does the underlined word "dull" mean in Paragraph 3?
   A. Interesting.   B. Amazing.   C. Boring.   D. Exciting.
54. According to the passage, we know that _____.
   A. The cost of using mobile phones is lower
   B. the speed of mobile network slowed down
   C. Chinese users will make phone calls for free in the future
   D. the using of mobile phones was canceled
55. Which one is true according to the passage?
   A. People can't live without mobile phones.
   B. The speed of mobile network and the cost would be increased greatly.
   C. The TD—LTE 4G communication technology is only used in China.

D. China's 5G network has already been in service.

B

The Boston Marathon(马拉松) is one of the world's oldest and most famous races. It has a 125-year history. Nearly half the players who take part in the 26.2-mile race are women. But for most of the time in the past, only men were allowed to enter the race.

A woman named Gibb helped change that in 1966. That year she took part in the Boston Marathon and finished faster than most of the men.

Gibb first saw and got to know the Boston Marathon in 1964. And she wanted to run the race herself. For nearly two years, Gibb trained hard to prepare for the race. But when she sent in an application(申请) for the 1966 race, it was refused.

At the time, the longest official(官方的) races for women were only 1.5 miles. Many people didn't think women were able to run longer than that. But the 23-year-old Gibb refused to give up her dream. She came up with a plan to run the race anyway. On 19th April, she showed up at the marathon. She wore her brother's shorts and a shirt to disguise that she was a woman.

Gibb hid near the starting line. When the race began, she jumped into the crowd. Shortly into the race, Gibb took off her shirt. To her surprise, the crowd cheered when they realised she was a woman. Gibb finished the race in 3 hours and 21 minutes —faster than two thirds of the men.

In the following years, she and other women ran in the Boston Marathon, even though the rules still stopped women from running in the race. Finally, in 1972, the marathon was opened to women.

56. When did the first Boston Marathon begin?
   A. In 1853.   B. In 1897.   C. In 1905.   D. In 1964.
57. What does the underlined word "disguise" mean in Chinese?
   A. 炫耀   B. 证明   C. 宣布   D. 掩盖
58. As for Gibb's first Boston Marathon, she finished _____.
   A. first
   B. last
   C. faster than most of the men
   D. more slowly than most of the man
59. How long did it take Gibb to train for her first marathon?
   A. For only one year.   B. For about eight years.
   C. For about two years.   D. For nearly six years.
60. What does the passage mainly tell us?
   A. The standard of the Boston Marathon.
   B. Some famous Boston Marathon runners.
   C. How to prepare for the Boston Marathon.
   D. The first woman to run the Boston Marathon.

第二部分 (文科类职业模块考生作答，共15分)

五、单项选择题(本大题共5小题，每小题1分，共计5分)

从 A、B、C、D 四个选项中，选出空白处的最佳选项。

61. —Hello, who's that speaking?
   —_____.
   A. That's Jane   B. She is Mary
   C. I'm Mike   D. This is William speaking
62. —I didn't find the way to the post office.
   —_____ I told you about it this morning.
   A. No problem.   B. Not really.
   C. How come?   D. That's for sure.
63. —I am not feeling well these days. Is there anything wrong with me, doctor?
   —_____. Nothing serious.
   A. Don't mention it.   B. You are kind.
   C. No problem.   D. Don't worry.
64. —Why not go out for dinner? My treat this time.
   —_____. But I'm busy with my homework.
   A. That's all right.   B. Sounds great.
   C. With pleasure.   D. No problem
65. _____ means You can make a U turn here.

   A.   B.   C.   D.

六、阅读理解(本大题共5小题，每小题2分，共计10分)

从 A、B、C、D 四个选项中，选出符合题目要求的最佳选项。

Most English people have a first name, a middle name and the family name. Their family name comes last. For example, my full name is Jim Allen Green. Green is my family name. My parents gave me both of my other names.

People don't use their middle names very much. So "John Henry Brown" is usually called "John Brown". People never use Mr., Mrs. or Miss before their first names. So you can say John Brown or Mr. Brown, but you should never(从不) say Mr. John. They use Mr., Mrs. or Miss with the family name but never with the first name.

Sometimes people ask me about my name. "When you were born, why did your parents call you Jim?" They ask, "Why did they choose that name?" The answer is they didn't call me Jim.

They called me James. James was the name of my grandfather. In England, people usually call me Jim for short. That's because it is shorter and easier than(比) James.

66. How many names do most English people have?
   A. One.   B. Two.   C. Three.   D. Four.
67. What names are given by parents?
   A. The first name.   B. The middle name.
   C. The family name.   D. The first name and middle name.
68. English people use Mr., Mrs. or Miss with _____.
   A. the family name   B. the first name
   C. the middle name   D. the first name and middle name

69. Why do people usually call James Jim?
   A. To remember his grandfather.
   B. Because his parents gave him that name.
   C. Because it is fun.
   D. Because Jim is shorter and easier than James.
70. What's the best title of this passage?
   A. Jim's family.
   B. Names in England.
   C. How to use the family name correctly(正确地)?
   D. Why do people call me Jim?

第三部分 （工科类职业模块考生作答，共15分）

七、单项选择题(本大题共5小题，每小题1分，共计5分)

从A、B、C、D四个选项中，选出空白处的最佳选项。

71. _____ is not a unit of area.
   A. square millimeter   B. hectare
   C. square kilometer   D. centimeter
72. _____ means "危险：地下埋有电缆".
   A. WARNING：MEN WORKING ABOVE
   B. DANGER：BURIED CABLE
   C. CAUTION：OPEN PIT
   D. EMERGENCY：911，FIRE RESCUE POLICE
73. 53.273 reads _____.
   A. fifty-three point two seven three
   B. fifty-three point two hundred and seventy-three
   C. fifty three point two seven three
   D. fifty three point two hundred and seventy three
74. Rated power means _____.
   A. 额定功率   B. 电源   C. 交流电   D. 电动工具
75. The cube root of one hundred twenty-five plus the square of 3 equals _____.
   A. 12   B. 13   C. 14   D. 15

八、阅读理解(本大题共5小题，每小题2分，共计10分)

从A、B、C、D四个选项中，选出符合题目要求的最佳选项。

In old Tibet(西藏), about 5 percent of the population owned almost all of the land, forests, mountains and rivers. Most people there were very poor. Thanks to the leadership of the Chinese government, Tibet is catching up with other parts of the country. Over the past 70 years, the Chinese government has introduced many good ideas for Tibet including education, health and environmental protection.

In 1951, Tibet's GDP was 129 million yuan. Last year, its GDP reached 190 billion yuan. Since its peaceful liberation(解放), Tibet has set up a network of highways, railways and air ways. 118,800 km highways have been built in Tibet. It has also made great progress in improving its environment, spending 81.4 billion yuan on the area by the end of last year. In 2020, the forest covered 12.3 percent.

By the end of 2019, all poor people in Tibet had shaken off poverty(脱贫) for the first time in history. Before 1951, more than 90 percent of Tibetan people did not have their own houses. In 2020, the living space of farmers reached 41.46 square meters, and that of city people reached 33.4 square meters. People's life has risen from 35.5 years in 1951 to 71.1 years in 2019. Education has also made great progress. In old Tibet there was not a proper school. 95 percent of the people could not go to school. From 1951 to 2020, the central government spent 224 billion yuan on Tiber's education. Today's Tibet has a really good development.

76. How many people owned the land in old Tibet?
   A. 95 percent of the population.   B. 5 percent of the population.
   C. 70 percent of the population.   D. 30 percent of the population.
77. Why is Tibet catching up with other parts of the country?
   A. Because of the leadership of the Chinese government.
   B. Because of the poor people in old Tibet.
   C. Because the 5 percent of the population owned most of the land.
   D. Because of the help of other countries.
78. How much was spent on the environment in Tibet by the end of last year?
   A. 81.4 billion yuan.   B. 129 million yuan.
   C. 190 billion yuan.   D. 224 billion yuan.
79. When did all poor people in Tibet shake off poverty?
   A. By the end of last year. B. From 1951 to 2020.
   C. By the end of 2019.   D. In 2019.
80. How many years longer of people's life in 2019 than in 1951?
   A. 35.5 years.   B. 71.1 years.   C. 33.4 years.   D. 35.6 years.

九、书面表达(15分)

端午节(Dragon Boat Festival)是中国的传统节日之一，蕴含着厚重的历史和美好的祝愿，假如你是Li Hua，你的外国朋友Steve想了解你和你的家人如何过这一节日，请你写一封邮件，向他介绍你们家的过节传统。

要求：词数80词左右。

Dear Steve,

_____

_____

_____

_____

_____

Yours,
Li Hua

模拟测试卷十

说明：
1. 本试卷分选择题和非选择题两部分。满分100分，考试时间90分钟。
2. 选择题分三部分，第一部分为共答题，所有考生作答；第二部分由文科类职业模块考生作答；第三部分由工科类职业模块考生作答。
3. 考生必须且只能在下列其中一个职业模块后的空格内"v"，确定本人作答部分，在确定范围以外作答一律不计分。
4. 考试结束后，将本试卷和答题卡一并交回。

选择题

注意事项：
1. 选择题答案必须填涂在答题卡上，写在试卷上一律不计分。
2. 答题前，考生务必将自己的姓名、准考证号、座位号、考试科目涂写在答题卡上。
3. 考生须按规定要求正确涂卡，否则后果自负。

第一部分 共答题（所有考生作答，共70分）

一、语音（本大题共10小题，每小题1分，共计10分）

从A、B、C、D四个选项中，选出画线部分发音不同的一项。

1. A. medal　　　　B. lecture　　　　C. helicopter　　　D. depend
2. A. pollute　　　B. public　　　　 C. result　　　　　D. rubber
3. A. remove　　　 B. slope　　　　　C. stone　　　　　 D. stove
4. A. sort　　　　　B. sport　　　　 C. sorry　　　　　D. storm
5. A. tomorrow　　 B. toward　　　　C. unknown　　　　D. widow
6. A. wheat　　　　B. wheel　　　　 C. whistle　　　　 D. who
7. A. bicycle　　　 B. broadcast　　　C. cellar　　　　　D. cart
8. A. climb　　　　B. comb　　　　 C. debt　　　　　　D. blame
9. A. coach　　　　B. headache　　　C. kitchen　　　　 D. match
10. A. matters　　　B. markets　　　　C. numbers　　　　D. times

二、单项选择题（本大题共25小题，每小题1分，共计25分）

从A、B、C、D四个选项中，选出空白处的最佳选项。

11. World Reading Day is _____ April 23. It's _____ special day that was founded in 1995 by the UN.
    A. on; a　　　　B. in; a　　　　C. on; an　　　　D. in; an
12. You should be honest and not copy _____ answers in the exam.
    A. nobody else　　　　　　　　B. somebody elses'
    C. anybody else　　　　　　　　D. anybody else's
13. —What do you think of her teaching English?
    —Great! No one teaches _____ in our school.
    A. good　　　　B. worse　　　　C. best　　　　D. better
14. _____ of the area _____ covered by trees.
    A. Two-third; is　　　　　　　 B. Two thirds; is
    C. Two-third; are　　　　　　　D. Two thirds; are
15. They built a big statue _____ the hero in the centre of the town.
    A. in memory of　　B. in memory　　C. from memory　　D. with memory
16. There is no bridge _____ the river, so we _____ the river by boat.
    A. cross; cross　　　　　　　　B. cross; across
    C. across; cross　　　　　　　　D. across; across
17. His _____ English is very good, because he is from Australia, an _____ country.
    A. spoken; English-spoken　　　B. speaking; English-speaking
    C. spoken; English-speaking　　D. speaking; English-speaking
18. The poor girl has to see the doctor because she _____ a lot lately.
    A. coughed　　　　　　　　　　B. coughs
    C. had coughed　　　　　　　　D. has been coughing
19. In any unsafe situation, simply _____ the button and a highly-trained agent will get you the help you need.
    A. press　　　B. to press　　　C. pressing　　　D. pressed
20. _____ in English, he joined a club to practice _____ well.
    A. Interested; speaking　　　　B. Interested; speak
    C. Interested; to speak　　　　D. Interesting; speaking
21. _____ no bus, we had to walk home.
    A. There was　　　　　　　　　B. There being
    C. Because there being　　　　　D. There were
22. I will _____ Peking University with a master's degree in June of this year.
    A. come up with　　　　　　　　B. graduate from
    C. graduates from　　　　　　　D. comes up with
23. My telephone is out of order. Can you tell me the _____ news about the COVID-19 pandemic?
    A. lately　　　B. latest　　　C. later　　　D. latter
24. Is this the only reason _____ at the meeting for his carelessness in his work?
    A. why he explained　　　　　　B. what he explained
    C. that he explained　　　　　　D. which he explained
25. Is this hotel _____ you said we were to stay in your letter?
    A. in which　　　B. what　　　C. that　　　D. where
26. He said that he had visited his teachers in the junior middle school _____.
    A. two weeks before　　　　　　B. last week
    C. a week ago　　　　　　　　　D. before two weeks
27. This is a very interesting book. I'll buy it _____.
    A. no matter how it may cost　　B. how may it cost
    C. how much may it cost　　　　D. however much it may cost
28. The committee _____ made up of 20 members, who _____ experts in medicine.
    A. is; are　　B. is; is　　C. are; is　　D. are; are
29. You are waiting at a wrong place. It is at the hotel _____ the coach picks up tourists.
    A. where　　B. who　　C. which　　D. that
30. So much of interest _____ that most visitors simply run out of time before seeing it all.
    A. offers Beijing　　　　　　　　B. Beijing offer
    C. does Beijing offer　　　　　　D. Beijing does offer
31. _____ no modern telecommunications, we would have to wait for weeks to get

— 1 —

news from around the world.
A. Were there   B. Had there been   C. If there are   D. If there have been

32. —What's the matter with Della?
—Well, her parents wouldn't allow her to go to the party, but she still _____.
A. hopes to   B. hopes so   C. hopes not   D. hopes for

33. —How about going out for a walk this evening?
—_____ good.
A. Sound   B. Sounded   C. Sounding   D. Sounds

34. I don't think he could have done such a stupid thing last night, _____?
A. did he   B. could he   C. do I   D. hasn't he

35. —Is Dongting Lake the largest Lake in China?
—No, it's the second _____ one _____ all the lakes in China.
A. large; in   B. largest; of
C. larger; of   D. the largest; in

三、完型填空(本大题共15小题，每小题1分，共计15分)

从A、B、C、D四个选项中，选出空白处的最佳选项。

A little boy once found a jar(罐子) of nuts(果仁) on the table. "I'd like some of these nuts," he thought. "I'm sure mother will give them to me __36__ she is here. I want some to eat now." So he __37__ the jar. As he was very hungry, he grabbed as __38__ as he could hold.

But when he tried to pull his __39__ out, he found the neck of the jar was too __40__. His hand was held fast, but he did not want to __41__ any of the nuts. He __42__ again and again, but he couldn't get the whole handful out all the time. __43__ he began to cry.

Just then his mother came into the room. "What's the matter?" she asked. "I can't take this handful of nuts __44__ the jar," sobbed the boy. "Well, don't be so greedy," his mother replied. "Just take two or three, and you'll have no trouble __45__ your hand out." "How __46__ that was," said the boy as he moved his hand off __47__. "I might have thought of that __48__."

The story tells us that a man can't be so greedy, maybe thing will go to a/an __49__ side if we want to finish a thing in one time. Do thing step by step! This is the best __50__ to success. Only like that can we go further.

36. A. while   B. because   C. if   D. whether
37. A. put into   B. took out   C. push into   D. reached into
38. A. many   B. much   C. some   D. few
39. A. hand   B. head   C. mouth   D. legs
40. A. big   B. small   C. large   D. tiny
41. A. to drop   B. drop   C. dropping   D. dropped
42. A. tried   B. did   C. thought   D. threw
43. A. Recently   B. Luckily   C. Finally   D. Simply
44. A. in   B. off   C. out of   D. into
45. A. to give   B. giving   C. to get   D. getting
46. A. easy   B. difficult   C. interesting   D. boring
47. A. the jar   B. the room   C. his mother   D. his neck
48. A. itself   B. myself   C. yourself   D. herself
49. A. right   B. opposite   C. possible   D. same
50. A. answer   B. way   C. information   D. example

四、阅读理解(本大题共10小题，每小题2分，共计20分)

从A、B、C、D四个选项中，选出符合题目要求的最佳选项。

A

Shashiyu was once a poor village in Hebei Province, but now it has changed into a rich and livable place.

In the 1940s, villagers in Shashiyu had little food and few clothes, but they had a strong wish for a better life. Zhang Guishun, the Party secretary of Shashiyu, encouraged his villagers to do their best to pull themselves out of poverty. "In the ancient Chinese story, Yu Gong could move mountains with his strong will and hard work, why can't we? Nobody was born to be poor?" Hearing his words, the villagers decided to make a difference.

Led by the Communist Party of China(中国共产党), the villagers carried water and soil to their village from faraway places to improve their land. From 1966 to 1971, they reclaimed(开垦) lots of land and greatly improved their life.

However, the village encountered a new problem two decades later as the environment became heavily polluted by chemical plants and mine refineries built in 1990s.

The polluting factories were shut down in 2004, and villagers started grape cultivation, which soon became a main industry in Shashiyu.

In 2009, the city-level government invested over 1 million yuan($152,723) to change the village's exhibition hall into a museum in memory of development efforts made by earlier generations.

After 10 years, the village was called "National Forest Village".

Zhang said that the village started a yearly tourism festival in 2015 to attract travelers to pick grapes. "The grapes could be sold at a better price once Shashiyu becomes famous through this festival. Our villagers can then live even better lives," he said.

51. Why did Zhang Guishun use the story of Yu Gong to encourage the villagers?
A. Because Yu Gong had strong will and hard work.
B. Because Yu Gong was born poor too.
C. Because the villagers worshiped Yu Gong.
D. Because Yu Gong became rich at last.

52. From 1966 to 1971, what did the villagers do to improve their living situation?
A. They planted grapes to earn money.
B. They carried water and soil to their village to improve their lands.
C. They moved to another place to live a better life.
D. They built a lot of factories.

53. Which word can be used to describe the villagers?
A. Hard-working.   B. Lazy.
C. Kind-hearted.   D. Stupid.

54. When was Shashiyu called "National Forest Village"?
A. In 2009.   B. In 2004.   C. In 2015.   D. In 2019.

55. Where can you probably read the passage?
A. In a storybook.   B. In a newspaper.

C. In a sports magazine.   D. In a science book

B

Climate change is a global challenge. One way to fight it is by reducing the amount of carbon dioxide in the air. New research shows that trees planted in China have helped in this fight.

A recent study in the journal *Nature* shows that the amount of carbon dioxide absorbed(吸收) by new forests in two parts of China is more than we thought. These areas are in the northeastern Heilongjiang and Jilin provinces and the southwestern Yunnan and Guizhou provinces and Guangxi Zhuang autonomous region. They make up about 35 percent of China's land-based(基于陆地的) carbon sinks(碳汇). A carbon sink is a natural area like a forest or ocean that absorbs more carbon dioxide than it emits (排放). Carbon sinks help to reduce the amount of CO_2 in the atmosphere.

China's goal is to peak(达到峰值) its CO_2 emissions(排放) before 2030 and reach carbon neutrality(中和) by 2060, Xinhua reported. Carbon neutrality refers to removing as much CO_2 as one puts into the air.

According to study co-author Yi Liu at the Chinese Academy of Sciences, "the afforestation(植树造林) activities described in our Nature paper will play a role in reaching that goal."

56. A recent study in *Nature* shows that _____.
   A. China has serious air pollution
   B. China has planted the most trees in the world
   C. China has fewer CO_2 emissions(排放) now
   D. China has planted fewer trees

57. Carbon sinks will _____.
   A. absorb more CO_2 than they emit   B. give off CO_2 emissions more quickly
   C. release less CO_2 into the air   D. have no CO_2 in their air

58. According to Xinhua, China _____.
   A. is the world's largest emitter of CO_2
   B. will bring CO_2 emissions down after 2030
   C. will not release CO_2 in the future
   D. will reach carbon neutrality by 2030

59. Which of the following is NOT TRUE in the passage?
   A. One way to fight climate is by reducing the amount of carbon dioxide in the air.
   B. Trees planted in China have helped fight against climate change.
   C. New forests in two parts of China absorbed more carbon dioxide than we thought.
   D. 35 percent of China's land has been affected by CO_2 emission.

60. What do we know from the story?
   A. It takes a long time for carbon sinks to form.
   B. Climate change is no longer a serious problem.
   C. More trees will be planted in China in the future.
   D. China has beaten climate change.

第二部分 （文科类职业模块考生作答，共15分）

五、单项选择题（本大题共5小题，每小题1分，共计5分）

从 A、B、C、D 四个选项中，选出空白处的最佳选项。

61. —Hello! _____
    —I'm just looking, thanks.
    A. May I speak to Alice?   B. What can I do for you?
    C. May I take your order?   D. Could you tell me your name?

62. —How was your trip to Mount Huangshan last year?
    —_____. I hope to go there again.
    A. We drove there   B. It took me two hours
    C. It was really great   D. People there were friendly

63. —It is a fantastic trip. So, which city do you like best, Hangzhou, Suzhou or Yangzhou?
    —_____. There are good things and bad things about them.
    A. No problem   B. It is hard to say
    C. Enjoy yourself   D. You must be joking

64. —The train is going to move, I have to go.
    —_____! I will miss you so much.
    A. Let it go   B. Take care
    C. Come on   D. Don't mention it.

65. —The shoes are 20 dollars.
    —OK. _____
    A. You're welcome.   B. Here you are
    C. I'll take them.   D. Yes, you are right.

六、阅读理解（本大题共5小题，每小题2分，共计10分）

从 A、B、C、D 四个选项中，选出符合题目要求的最佳选项。

New Year's Day is a traditional(传统的) festival in the world. On this day, people in different countries eat different food.

In the USA, people eat herrings(鲱鱼). Americans like herrings because herrings always swim fast together in the water. They are the symbol of happiness and richness for a family.

In Spain, families like to get together, listen to music and play games. And when it is twelve o'clock at night and the New Year begins, people will eat twelve grapes. They think the grapes can bring good luck in the next twelve months.

As we all know, dumplings are the best food for Chinese. They mean tuanyuan. And many families make one or two dumplings with coins(硬币) inside. People who eat dumplings with coins will get happiness.

Different people eat different food on New Year's Day, but they all want health and happiness.

66. In the USA, herrings are the symbol of _____ for a family.
    A. happiness and richness   B. good luck
    C. tuanyuan   D. health and happiness

67. Which of the following is NOT true?
    A. Chinese put some coins in their dumplings.

— 3 —

B. Different people eat different food on New Year's Day.
C. Americans eat herrings when the New Year begins.
D. The Spanish eat twenty grapes when the New Year begins.

68. Who likes to eat grapes on New Year's Day?
   A. People in the USA.   B. People in Spain.
   C. People in China.   D. People in England.
69. Why do Chinese like to eat dumplings on New Year's Day?
   A. Because they mean tuanyuan in China.
   B. Because there are coins in the dumplings.
   C. Because it is easy to make dumplings.
   D. Because dumplings may bring them happiness.
70. This passage mainly tells us _____ on New Year's Day.
   A. different people   B. different food
   C. different countries   D. different cities

第三部分 （工科类职业模块考生作答，共15分）

七、单项选择题（本大题共5小题，每小题1分，共计5分）

从 A、B、C、D 四个选项中，选出空白处的最佳选项。

71. The third power of three minus five is equal to _____.
   A. twenty-one   B. twenty-two   C. nine   D. eleven
72. Five degrees Centigrade below zero can be written _____.
   A. -5℃   B. 5℃   C. -5℉   D. 5℉
73. _____ is not a unit of capacity or volume.
   A. milliliter
   B. hectare
   C. cubic centimeter
   D. cubic meter
74. _____ clearly mark the machines that are out of order, under repair or out of service.
   A. Bold signs   B. Construction warning signs
   C. Chemicals safety signs D. Electrical equipment warning signs
75. As an employer or employee, the importance of basic safety cannot be _____.
   A. overstressed   B. overworked   C. overnight   D. overtime

八、阅读理解（本大题共5小题，每小题2分，共计10分）

从 A、B、C、D 四个选项中，选出符合题目要求的最佳选项。

Nowadays, we use digital devices in many ways, such as waking us up in the morning, listening to music, communicating with friends and so on. But studies have found that overuse of electronics can affect our sleep, our study and work.

To help people take a break from their always-on lifestyles, America set the National Day of Unplugging in 2010 to encourage people to put away their electronics for 24 hours, which is on the second Friday of March every year.

Without any doubt, many people find that the unplugged day seems longer than a typical day. "Without my phone, my breakfast was too short and I did not know what to do next," one participant of last year's unplugging experiment wrote. Another shared his grief at not being able to look at his phone during bus and train rides, calling the day "the longest time of my life".

But others see the experiment as a way to experience what life was like before the rise of electronics. "My friend and i has dinner in the evening, and we both discussed about how much more present we felt—how we could hear what each other was saying," one participant wrote.

Although living without electronics seems impossible in today's world, unplugging from time to time allows people to slow down and reflect on life. "At the end of the day, I was missing neither social media nor having a digital connection," one participant noted. "I note. "I was happy for the opportunity to challenge my unhealthy daily habits, because this gave me the opportunity to discover a slower, clearer way of life."

76. Using digital devices too often might _____.
   A. help us study better   B. keep us away from music
   C. help us communicate easily D. bring us some sleep problems
77. The National Day of Unplugging was set _____.
   A. in many countries in 2010
   B. on the second day of March every year
   C. to help people take a break from busy work
   D. to make people away from their electronics for a day
78. What is the meaning of the underlined word "grief"?
   A. Rudeness   B. Sadness   C. Happiness   D. Coldness
79. Some participants of the experiment _____.
   A. thought that it was impossible for them to slow down
   B. didn't know what to eat for breakfast without phones
   C. felt exited during bus and train rides without phones
   D. enjoyed hearing each other by discussing face to face
80. What is the best title for this passage?
   A. Get Back to Real Life.   B. Unhealthy Daily Habits.
   C. The Digital Connection.   D. The Longest Time of Life.

九、书面表达（15分）

假设你是李华，你校英语协会招聘志愿者，接待来访的外国中学生。请你写一封信应聘，内容包括：
1. 口语能力；
2. 相关经验；
3. 应聘目的。
注意：1. 词数80词左右；
　　　2. 开头和结尾已给出，不计入词数；
　　　3. 可以适当增加细节，以使行文连贯。

Dear Sir/Madam,

_____

_____

_____

_____

_____

　　　　　　　　　　　　　　　　　　　　Yours,
　　　　　　　　　　　　　　　　　　　　Li Hua

模拟测试卷十一

说明：
1. 本试卷分选择题和非选择题两部分。满分100分，考试时间90分钟。
2. 选择题分三部分，第一部分为共答题，所有考生作答；第二部分由文科类职业模块考生作答；第三部分由工科类职业模块考生作答。
3. 考生必须且只能在下列其中一个职业模块后的空格内"√"，确定本人作答部分，在确定范围以外作答一律不计分。
4. 考试结束后，将本试卷和答题卡一并交回。

选择题

注意事项：
1. 选择题答案必须填涂在答题卡上，写在试卷上一律不计分。
2. 答题前，考生务必将自己的姓名、准考证号、座位号、考试科目涂写在答题卡上。
3. 考生须按规定要求正确涂卡，否则后果自负。

第一部分 共答题（所有考生作答，共70分）

一、语音（本大题共10小题，每小题1分，共计10分）

从A、B、C、D四个选项中，选出画线部分发音不同的一项。

1. A. st<u>u</u>dy   B. s<u>u</u>bway   C. s<u>u</u>gar   D. s<u>u</u>n
2. A. c<u>ow</u>   B. fl<u>ow</u>   C. d<u>ow</u>n   D. t<u>ow</u>n
3. A. fr<u>ui</u>t   B. g<u>ui</u>de   C. j<u>ui</u>ce   D. s<u>ui</u>t
4. A. st<u>o</u>ve   B. st<u>o</u>ne   C. sm<u>o</u>ke   D. pr<u>o</u>ve
5. A. sw<u>ea</u>t   B. st<u>ea</u>l   C. sp<u>ea</u>k   D. st<u>ea</u>m
6. A. c<u>h</u>eque   B. frequently   C. quarter   D. queen (画线为qu/ch处)
7. A. f<u>o</u>nd   B. h<u>o</u>nor   C. h<u>o</u>t   D. s<u>o</u>n
8. A. hou<u>s</u>e   B. ju<u>s</u>t   C. pea<u>s</u>ant   D. mou<u>s</u>e
9. A. pla<u>y</u>er   B. serious   C. shipper   D. whoever
10. A. although   B. daughter   C. cough   D. delight

二、单项选择题（本大题共25小题，每小题1分，共计25分）

从A、B、C、D四个选项中，选出空白处的最佳选项。

11. —Her concert was _____ big success last night.
    —I think it surely makes _____ difference for a new talent.
    A. /; /   B. a; a   C. a; the   D. a; /

12. The round moon cake is a _____ of reunion and happiness in Chinese culture.
    A. symbol   B. signal   C. sign   D. symptom

13. My brother rather than my parents is fond of new energy vehicles. _____ of us have a positive attitude to this trend.
    A. Both   B. All   C. Not all   D. Not any

14. In the future, robots may think _____ themselves, just as people use their brains and act _____ themselves.
    A. of; for   B. for; for   C. about; of   D. for; of

15. At the meeting, the old man _____ some good advice and all the people there agreed with them.
    A. came about   B. came up   C. came out   D. came up with

16. The law _____ back to the 17th century is still in use today.
    A. dates   B. dated   C. was dated   D. dating

17. Mary _____ the job he offered to her but she didn't.
    A. can't take   B. ought to have taken
    C. should take   D. must have taken

18. Each of the _____ students on the stage _____ help from their teachers and parents.
    A. frightening; need   B. frightened; needs to
    C. frightening; needs to   D. frightened; needs

19. The river _____ such heavy pollution already, so it may now be too late to clean it up.
    A. has suffered   B. has happened
    C. has offered   D. has filled

20. —So what is the procedure?
    —All the applicants _____ before a final decision is made by the authority.
    A. interview   B. are interviewing
    C. are interviewed   D. are being interviewed

21. _____ a beautiful singing voice, so she was encouraged to apply for the program of vocal music(声乐).
    A. Born in   B. Having born in
    C. Being born with   D. She was born with

22. Though a typhoon is on the way, people are still looking forward _____ the outdoor concert by the pop singer.
    A. to canceling   B. not to canceling
    C. not to cancel   D. to not canceling

23. I can still remember the very sitting-room _____ my mother and I used to sit in the evening.
    A. which   B. what   C. that   D. where

24. Anyone _____ has a dog as a pet will tell you _____ a dog means to a family.
    A. who; what   B. who; why
    C. which; what   D. which; why

25. I really enjoy listening to music _____ it helps me relax and takes my mind away from other cases of the day.
    A. because   B. before   C. unless   D. until

26. _____ tool the computer is!
    A. What important   B. How important
    C. What important a   D. How important a

27. As you can see, the number of cars on our roads _____ rising these days.
    A. was keeping   B. keep   C. keeps   D. were keeping

28. If you have a job, _____ yourself to it and finally you'll succeed.
    A. do devote   B. don't devote   C. devoting   D. not devoting

29. It might have saved me some trouble _____ the schedule.
    A. did I know   B. have I know   C. do I know   D. had I know

— 1 —

30. Something will have to be done about the air pollution, _____?
    A. won't it   B. will it   C. won't they   D. will they
31. —I'm sorry I lost your notebook.
    —_____.
    A. You're welcome   B. That's right
    C. That's all right   D. Not at all
32. You _____ feel all the training a waste of time, but I'm a hundred percent sure later you'll be grateful you did it.
    A. should   B. need   C. shall   D. may
33. I don't like math _____ it's difficult for me.
    A. because   B. but   C. in   D. and
34. —What's your plan for the coming weekend?
    —There's going to be a horse show. If you go there, _____.
    A. I do so   B. so I will   C. so do I   D. so will I
35. The fruit shop is 200 metres _____ my house, _____ the bus station.
    A. to; next
    B. far from; next to
    C. away from; next to
    D. from; next

三、完型填空(本大题共15小题，每小题1分，共计15分)

从 A、B、C、D 四个选项中，选出空白处的最佳选项。

I was feeling a little blue because my mother had lost her job.

One day, while I was __36__ in the street, I heard the piano music and singing rising above the noise of the people. I walked more slowly to __37__ where it was coming from. Then I saw a young lady siting at a piano.

She was singing songs about love, __38__ yourself and keeping on trying. The way she was singing made me a little comfortable. I stood there __39__, watching her playing on such a crowded square. I thought that she must be __40__ enough to perform in front of so many people. She noticed me. I walked over and told her how good her __41__ sounded. "Thank you," she said.

"I have been going through a hard time recently, __42__ you've made me hopeful again," I said to her.

"I'm glad that I could help," she replied. "Why are you so __43__?"

"Well, my mum has lost her job, and I'm not sure what to do…"

"Did you notice the __44__ you were walking? Your head was down," she said. "Don't be upset, because __45__ comes in different ways and if your head is down, you might not see it. You should __46__ more, and lift your head up."

I looked __47__ her, amazed at how she was encouraging me. "__48__ are you playing the piano here?" I asked her with a smile. She __49__ that she saw a lot of unhappy people in the world and she tried to cheer __50__ up by playing music.

I smiled a little wider, realizing that no difficulties could stop me from going on.

36. A. driving   B. riding   C. running   D. walking
37. A. find out   B. send out   C. take out   D. get out
38. A. dressing   B. believing   C. hurting   D. losing
39. A. nervously   B. rudely   C. angrily   D. quietly
40. A. brave   B. shy   C. bored   D. honest
41. A. advice   B. idea   C. music   D. interest
42. A. or   B. but   C. so   D. and
43. A. dirty   B. busy   C. sad   D. lazy
44. A. way   B. time   C. reason   D. station
45. A. opportunity B. health   C. pain   D. life
46. A. complain   B. rest   C. smile   D. pay
47. A. like   B. after   C. for   D. at
48. A. How   B. Why   C. When   D. Where
49. A. dreamed   B. hoped   C. guessed   D. explained
50. A. us   B. them   C. me   D. her

四、阅读理解(本大题共10小题，每小题2分，共计20分)

从 A、B、C、D 四个选项中，选出符合题目要求的最佳选项。

A

What would people in ancient times do when they missed someone very much? What do you think of the invention of cellphones?

My mom told me that when she and my dad were newly married, before people had cellphones, she'd get phone calls from an elderly lady. The lady wanted to speak to someone named Donna. She was very friendly. My mom told her that she was not Donna, but the lady would still say my mom was Donna.

At least once a week this old lady would call for Donna—sometimes more! Every call started with, "Hello, Donna! How are you?" She never cared if it was the wrong number.

My mom never learned who that lady was. The lady only ever said her first name. She talked about her daily life, her cat, her garden, and the newspaper. Sometimes she'd talk about memories of Donna. She could only talk for 10 or 15 minutes before getting tired and saying goodbye.

<u>She normally called on Tuesdays or Thursdays around 8:00 pm. My mom made sure to be home at that time.</u>

The whole thing lasted for about a year. Then the calls just stopped. My mom thinks the old woman was lonely. From her stories, my mom guessed that Donna was a childhood friend of the lady.

Why did she call? Why did she stop? My mom felt sad when the calls stopped. She still thinks of that lady sometimes and wonders about her. Maybe that woman knew there was no Donna. Maybe she just had nobody else to talk to. My mom's small act of kindness might have been a big help to someone in need.

51. What did the mom know about the lady?
    A. Her cellphone number.   B. Her home address.
    C. Her family name.   D. Her stories with Donna.
52. The underlined sentence shows that _____.
    A. the mom was busy on Tuesdays or Thursdays
    B. the mom didn't want to miss the lady's calls
    C. the mom didn't want to chat with the lady
    D. the mom hoped to see the lady in person
53. From the story, we can learn that _____.
    A. the lady called the mom for years

— 2 —

B. the mom was also very lonely
C. the lady found the real Donna in the end
D. the mom felt sad after the lady stopped calling

54. The mom _____ the old lady.
    A. missed   B. never talked about
    C. forgot   D. tried to save

55. What does the writer want to express in this story?
    A. Everyone should respect the elderly.   B. True friendship will never end.
    C. A small, kind act helps others.   D. Life is hard for the elderly.

B

In the middle of the South Atlantic Ocean, one island stands alone. It is near Antarctica. But it is far away that people had difficulty finding it. At about 6.4 km long, the island is covered in glaciers(冰川). It is home to an inactive volcano(死火山) and huge amounts of ice. The sharp and high rocks around the island make sea landings almost impossible. This is Bouvet Island, the loneliest island in the world.

A French man found out Bouvet Island in 1739, but the island was so difficult to reach that nobody set foot on it for nearly a hundred years. No people live on Bouvet Island, and few plants grow there. Seals(海狮) come and go, but they haven't seen people since the government didn't allow people to catch seals and whales in the area any more. The island is cold all year round, with an average(平均的) temperature of about −1.7℃.

In recent years, Bouvet Island has been known a little more by the world. Norway, which claimed(宣称拥有) the island in 1928, set up an unmanned weather station there in 1977. Today, this quiet island near the South Pole sends weather data to a satellite(卫星), which passes the information to researchers in Norway. Scientists learn more every day about the island and its environment. Anyhow, Bouvet Island stands strong and silent in the cold weather condition.

56. What is Bouvet Island like?
    A. It's lonely and icy.   B. It is full of volcanoes.
    C. It's about 4.6 km long.   D. It's far from Antarctica.

57. When might humans first arrive on the island?
    A. In 1739.   B. In 1832.   C. In 1928.   D. In 1977.

58. What can we learn from the text?
    A. Bouvet Island is close to the North Pole.
    B. There are many plants in the Bouvet island.
    C. Bouvet Island belongs to the United States.
    D. Catching whales isn't allowed in the island.

59. What is the topic of the text mainly about?
    A. Sports and health.   B. Music and art.
    C. Problems and advice.   D. Geography and nature.

60. What's the best title of the text?
    A. The Loneliest Island   B. The Best Weather Station
    C. The Newest Research   D. The Hardest Weather Condition

第二部分 (文科类职业模块考生作答,共15分)

五、单项选择题(本大题共5小题,每小题1分,共计5分)
从A、B、C、D四个选项中,选出空白处的最佳选项。

61. —Can I look at the menu for a few minute before I decide?
    —Of course. _____
    A. Take your time   B. Make yourself at home
    C. Enjoy yourself   D. Please be in a hurry

62. —Excuse me, where is Renmin Hospital?
    —Sorry, I'm new here.
    —_____.
    A. Not at all   B. That's OK
    C. Thank you all the same.   D. That's all.

63. —Hi, Mary. You look tired. _____
    —I missed the school bus so I had to run to school this morning.
    A. What happened   B. What a pain!
    C. You're kidding   D. How about you?

64. —Mom, this is my friend, Mike.
    —_____
    A. How are you?   B. Nice to meet you, Mike.
    C. What's your name   D. Thanks.

65. —Look at the clouds! Is it going to rain?
    —_____. The radio says that we're getting into the rainy season now.
    A. I'm afraid not   B. I'm afraid so
    C. Not at all   D. Of course not

六、阅读理解(本大题共5小题,每小题2分,共计10分)
从A、B、C、D四个选项中,选出符合题目要求的最佳选项。

Do you often carry maps when you travel to other countries? Maps can show you the right ways. But if you don't bring maps with you, what should you do? I'm afraid that you need to ask the way. Here are some tips(建议) for you, because there are different ways to give ways in the world.

In Japan, most streets don't have their street names. The Japanese use landmarks(路标) to give ways. So when you ask, "Excuse me, could you tell me how to get to the nearest post office?" They often say, "Go along the road, turn left on the second street and go past a supermarket. The post office is opposite the hospital."

In the countryside of the American midwest. The land is very flat(平坦的). So if you have the same question, people will say to you, "Go east 3 kilometers, turn north and then walk another kilometer." But in Los Angeles and California, people measure distance(测量距离) by time, not meters. So when you ask, "How far is the nearest post office?", they will tell you, "It's about 10 minutes' walk from here".

People in Greece often use body language to help you. They will use their hands to show the right or left ways, or they will simply say, "follow me." Because they

can't speak English and the tourists couldn't understand the language there.
66. If you are in Japan, _____.
   A. the street name will help you find the way easily
   B. the Japanese use landmarks to help you find the ways
   C. you need to use body language to ask the way
   D. you can see some street names in Japanese
67. Which part of America is flat?
   A. Northwest.   B. Southwest.   C. Northeast.   D. Midwest.
68. How do the people in California show the way?
   A. They use the landmarks.   B. They use body language.
   C. They measure distance by time. D. They usually say "follow me".
69. What's the Chinese meaning of the underlined words "body language"?
   A. 指示路牌   B. 当地方言   C. 肢体语言   D. 翻译机器
70. What's the best title of the passage?
   A. Asking the way   B. Different ways of giving way
   C. Funny things in the world   D. The important language—English

第三部分 （工科类职业模块考生作答，共15分）

七、单项选择题（本大题共5小题，每小题1分，共计5分）

从A、B、C、D四个选项中，选出空白处的最佳选项。

71. These safety signs are always placed in a _____ position so they can easily be seen.
   A. prominent   B. promotion   C. program   D. progress
72. The ratio of 20 to 5 _____ the ratio of 16 to 4
   A. equals   B. approximately equals
   C. is less than   D. is greater than
73. There are two measuring systems of _____ commonly adopted. They are Celsius (Centigrade) degrees(℃) and Fahrenheit degrees(℉).
   A. angle   B. temperature   C. weight   D. length
74. The basic unit of area is _____.
   A. square meter   B. square millimeter
   C. hectare   D. cubic meter
75. A machine is set to produce metal bolts which are 18 mm in length. The bolts whose length are from 17.8 mm to 18.2 mm are _____ all because their error of length is within(*)0.2 mm.
   A. available   B. unavailable   C. right   D. true

八、阅读理解（本大题共5小题，每小题2分，共计10分）

从A、B、C、D四个选项中，选出符合题目要求的最佳选项。

Our lives have become more digital(数码的) in the modern world. We can study, find information and communicate with friends through computers and cellphones. However, spending a lot of time working, reading, texting and gaming through digital devices(数码设备) is bad for our eyes.

Digital eyestrain(眼睛疲劳) is one of the problems. People with digital eyestrain may get headaches, dry and red eyes, eye pain, and other problems.

These problems have started to increase among children. "Children get cellphones when they're young and they are using them very often during the day." Sarah Hinkley told *USA Today*.

There are many things you can do to reduce digital eyestrain.

When you use a computer, first sit in your chair and reach out your arm. Your hand should rest comfortably on the screen, as if you're high-fiving(击掌) the screen. Increase text size until your eyes feel comfortable.

When you are using a cellphone, keep it at least 30 cm from your eyes and just below eye level. Try not to use it in the sunlight.

Remember to take a 20-20-20 break：every 20 minutes, take a 20-second break and look at something 20 feet(about 6 meters) away.

76. According to the passage, people may have _____ after using digital devices.
   A. eye problems   B. back pain   C. stomach ache   D. dry mouths
77. What do we know from Sara Hinkley?
   A. Children can easily get eyestrain.
   B. Children shouldn't use cellphones.
   C. More children are experiencing digital eyestrain.
   D. Using cell phones may not cause so many problems.
78. When we use phones, we should keep at least _____ from our eyes.
   A. 10 cm   B. 20 cm   C. 30 cm   D. 40 cm
79. How long should we take for a break every 20 minutes?
   A. 20 minutes.   B. 20 seconds.   C. 40 minutes.   D. 40 seconds.
80. The passage gives suggestions about _____.
   a. how to use computers safely
   b. how to use phones safely
   c. when to take breaks from digital devices
   d. how to clean your eyes
   A. abd   B. bcd   C. acd   D. abc

九、书面表达（15分）

假定你是李华，你和Christina原定于本周六上午一起参加"中国传统文化日(Chinese Traditional Culture Day)"活动；但因故你不能赴约，请根据下面的写作提示，用英语给她发一封电子邮件，内容包括：
1. 告诉她你不能赴约；
2. 解释爽约的原因；
3. 希望她谅解。
注意：1. 词数80词左右；
      2. 可适当增加细节，以使行文连贯。

Dear Christina,

_____

Yours sincerely,
Li Hua

模拟测试卷十二

说明：
1. 本试卷分选择题和非选择题两部分。满分100分，考试时间90分钟。
2. 选择题分三部分，第一部分为共答题，所有考生作答；第二部分由文科类职业模块考生作答；第三部分由工科类职业模块考生作答。
3. 考生必须且只能在下列其中一个职业模块后的空格内"v"，确定本人作答部分，在确定范围以外作答一律不计分。
4. 考试结束后，将本试卷和答题卡一并交回。

选择题
注意事项：
1. 选择题答案必须填涂在答题卡上，写在试卷上一律不计分。
2. 答题前，考生务必将自己的姓名、准考证号、座位号、考试科目涂写在答题卡上。
3. 考生须按规定要求正确涂卡，否则后果自负。

第一部分 共答题(所有考生作答，共70分)

一、语音(本大题共10小题，每小题1分，共计10分)

从A、B、C、D四个选项中，选出画线部分发音不同的一项。

1. A. anything   B. appear   C. allow   D. afraid
2. A. become   B. belong   C. brother   D. among
3. A. better   B. beg   C. below   D. benefit
4. A. broad   B. road   C. coat   D. goal
5. A. free   B. jeep   C. green   D. coffee
6. A. center   B. circle   C. clear   D. city
7. A. earth   B. death   C. fifth   D. either
8. A. event   B. finish   C. hungry   D. hunt
9. A. sure   B. measure   C. pleasure   D. treasure
10. A. trials   B. trips   C. weeks   D. sorts

二、单项选择题(本大题共25小题，每小题1分，共计25分)

从A、B、C、D四个选项中，选出空白处的最佳选项。

11. He used to be _____ teacher but later he turned _____ writer.
    A. a; a   B. the; /   C. a; a   D. a; /

12. You seem to be in no _____ to go to the cinema with me. So let's stay at home watching TV.
    A. feeling   B. emotion   C. attitude   D. mood

13. I'm moving to the countryside because the air there is much fresher than _____ in the city.
    A. ones   B. one   C. that   D. those

14. There are _____ people and _____ noise here. I can't stand it.
    A. too much; too many   B. too; too
    C. much; many   D. too many; too much

15. Frank lost his ticket due _____ his carelessness.
    A. to   B. for   C. in   D. from

16. By law, no party _____ give away the contents of the contract to the third party.
    A. may   B. can   C. need   D. shall

17. —A long journey can be covered only by taking one step at a time.
    —I agree. All small thing can _____ and become big things.
    A. add up   B. set up   C. show up   D. get up

18. Though it is a _____ job, he still devotes much time and energy to it.
    A. poor-paying   B. poorly-paying   C. poorly-paid   D. poor-paid

19. —When are you leaving for Shanghai?
    —Tomorrow morning. My plane _____ at 10：00 am.
    A. is left   B. leaves   C. was leaving   D. has left

20. The teacher demanded that the composition _____ immediately.
    A. must be submitted   B. would be submitted
    C. submits   D. be submitted

21. I am not afraid of tomorrow, _____ I have seen yesterday and I love today.
    A. so   B. and   C. for   D. but

22. _____ in Northern Europe rose steadily in the third quarter of 2022, following a 0.1 percent increase in the previous quarter.
    A. Tourist spending   B. Tourist spent
    C. Tourist spend   D. Tourist spends

23. Do not talk about such things _____ you do not understand.
    A. that   B. which   C. as   D. where

24. The old building behind _____ was a famous church, was _____ we used to work.
    A. that; the place   B. it; the place
    C. which; where   D. what; where

25. Your support is important to our work. _____ you can do helps.
    A. However   B. Whoever   C. Whatever   D. Wherever

26. Is there a bar around _____ I can have something to eat?
    A. that   B. what   C. which   D. where

27. This is the only one of the students _____ how to play the piano in our school.
    A. that knows   B. that know   C. who know   D. which knows

28. It was a very beautiful place _____ interested us a lot _____ we held a birthday party for our teacher.
    A. where; which   B. that; which
    C. that; that   D. /; that

29. Hardly _____ he got out of the court _____ the reporters raised a lot of questions to him.
    A. had; when   B. had; than   C. did; when   D. has; that

30. —Let's play table tennis after work, shall we?
    —_____ I can't wait to do that.
    A. Forget it!   B. Think nothing of it
    C. Why not   D. Not at all

31. It's a fine day. Let's go fishing, _____?
    A. won't you   B. will you   C. don't we   D. shall we

32. —_____?
    —Yes. Some specials in your restaurant, please.
    A. Are you OK   B. May I take your order

— 1 —

C. How much is is
D. Can you help me
33. Now a lot of new technologies can _____ problems in industry.
　　A. be applied to solve　　　　B. be applied to solving
　　C. apply to solve　　　　　　D. apply to solving
34. From time to time Jason turned around, _____ he was searching for someone.
　　A. as if　　B. even if　　C. if only　　D. what if
35. It's strange that he _____ have taken the books without the owner's permission.
　　A. would　　B. should　　C. could　　D. might

三、完型填空(本大题共 15 小题，每小题 1 分，共计 15 分)

从 A、B、C、D 四个选项中，选出空白处的最佳选项。

When I spent the summer with my grandmother, she sent me down to the grocery store with a list. I walked up to the counter(柜台). Behind __36__ was a lady named Miss Bee.

"Excuse me," I said. She __37__. "I need to get these," I continued, __38__ up my list.

"So? Go get them," Miss Bee said, "__39__ is here except you and me, and I am not your servant. I suggest you get yourself a basket over there and start __40__." It was not __41__ for a 7-year-old child, there were so many different kinds of things. I spent over an hour in the store.

I visited Miss Bee twice a week that summer. She __42__ short-changed(少找零钱) me. Other times she overcharged. Going to the store was like going into a war. But by the end of the summer, I could finish my shopping trip __43__ around 15 minutes. The morning I was to return home, I stopped in the store again to buy something.

"All right," Miss Bee said. "What did you __44__ this summer?"

"That's you're mean!" I replied.

Miss Bee just laughed. "I know __45__ you think of me," she said. "Well, I don't care! My job is to teach every child I meet some life __46__. When you get older you'll be glad that you met me!" Glad I met Miss Bee? Ha! How could it be?

It sounded funny until one day my son came to me with his homework. "It's too __47__." he said. "Could you finish the math problem for me?"

"__48__ I do it for you, how will you ever learn to do it __49__?" I said. Suddenly, I was back in that store where I had learned to and add up my bill by myself. Had I ever been overcharged since?

Life is full of difficulties. We may be __50__ a hand once or twice, but luck may not find us every time. So we should work them out by ourselves.

36. A. it　　　　B. her　　　　C. them　　　　D. us
37. A. called up　B. picked up　C. put up　　　D. looked up
38. A. held　　　B. holding　　C. to hold　　　D. holds
39. A. Anybody　B. Somebody　C. Nobody　　　D. Everybody
40. A. checking　B. changing　C. knocking　　D. filling
41. A. fair　　　B. easy　　　　C. natural　　　D. safe
42. A. always　　B. sometimes　C. seldom　　　D. never
43. A. before　　B. for　　　　C. to　　　　　D. in
44. A. create　　B. regret　　　C. learn　　　　D. complete
45. A. what　　　B. which　　　C. who　　　　D. how
46. A. methods　B. meanings　　C. lessons　　　D. results
47. A. early　　　B. hard　　　　C. useless　　　D. popular
48. A. If　　　　B. Unless　　　C. As　　　　　D. When
49. A. your　　　B. yourselves　C. you　　　　D. yourself
50. A. passed　　B. shown　　　C. given　　　　D. taken

四、阅读理解(本大题共 10 小题，每小题 2 分，共计 20 分)

从 A、B、C、D 四个选项中，选出符合题目要求的最佳选项。

A

Bike-sharing has swept across China, with an increasing number of people choosing bike riding instead of driving. The bike that the service company provides has GPS or Bluetooth on it, and people can easily find them. Those bikes can be easily unlocked with a smart phone and left anywhere in public. Bike-sharing allows people to borrow a bike from one place and return it at another place easily.

In some cities, we can see more and more people riding this kind of sharing-bikes. It's very convenient to use the bikes if you have a smart phone. Before riding these bikes, you have to download such an APP on your smart phone. Then what you need to do is to find a nearest bike through the APP, scan the QR code on the bike or connect your phone with the bike over a Bluetooth wireless connection. You will find the bike can be unlocked itself. Then you can enjoy your trip. What's more, the greatest advantage of bike-sharing is that you can easily find one and never worry about where to park it. The cost of riding depends on the time that you spend. Normally, every hour you ride, you need to pay one yuan. It doesn't cost so much, does it?

At the same time, some people park the bikes in their own homes. Besides, some people don't value the bikes. Hundreds of bikes are found destroyed every month. Now service companies are trying to solve the problem like being stolen.

Technology and science have changed our social lifestyles. We have to say bike-sharing brings us more convenience without doubt. And we also hope that people can not only enjoy it but also put it to good use.

51. _____ makes it possible for people to know where there is a sharing-bike nearby.
　　A. The APPs　　　　　　　　B. The smart phones
　　C. The GPS and Bluetooth　　D. The service company
52. The underlined word "scan" in Paragraph 2 probably means "_____" in Chinese.
　　A. 浏览　　B. 扫描　　C. 审视　　D. 细查
53. If you want to use a sharing-bike, you must _____ first.
　　A. have a smart phone and download an APP
　　B. download an APP and pay for the trip
　　C. unlock the bike and download an APP
　　D. find a nearest bike and borrow it from anyone
54. Which of the following is NOT true according to the passage?
　　A. Bike-sharing makes it easy for some people to go out.
　　B. Sharing-bikes may be stolen.
　　C. We can return the sharing-bike in a different place.
　　D. We pay 1 yuan each time when we use the sharing-bike.

55. The passage probably comes from a _____.
    A. science textbook   B. website news report
    C. tourist guide   D. dictionary

B

Park City is the best-known ski(滑雪) town in Utah, the U.S. It snows for nearly six months every year from November to April, making it a wonderland(胜地) for winter sports. Many of the people who live there are professional athletes. Over time, snow has become a symbol of the city and its people.

When I lived in the US, my friends and my family went on a trip to Park City together. After arriving, I made up my mind to learn how to ski.

The ski lessons were expensive. Luckily, my friend's mom, Vicky, could teach me. I borrowed my friend Joey's skis(滑雪板). They were so heavy that I couldn't lift my feet! I tried going down a hill and fell face down into the snow. Vicky helped me up. She taught me two important things—keep my skis parallel(平行的) and look ahead, not down.

As I practiced, I fell down over and over again. Sometimes other children would come and help me up. They said most of the children here learned how to ski at a young age, and it was their responsibility to help others. I was touched by their kindness toward me.

At the end of the day, I could ski down a gentle slope(斜坡) with no problems. I will never forget that experience because I not only realized my dream of learning to ski, but also saw how sports could connect people from different places.

56. Why is Park City a wonderland for winter sports?
    A. Because Park City is the most beautiful city in Utah.
    B. Because many athletes often train there.
    C. Because it snows nearly six months every year.
    D. Because people there are kind and helpful.

57. Which of the following statements is NOT true according to the passage?
    A. A large number of people in town are professional athletes.
    B. The writer borrowed skis from his friend's mother.
    C. The skis were too heavy for the writer to lift his feet.
    D. The writer was told to keep his skis parallel and look ahead.

58. What does Paragraph 4 mainly talk about?
    A. The writer had so many falls as he practiced.
    B. Some of the children were really talented in skiing.
    C. The children learned how to ski when they were very young.
    D. The writer was moved by the children's kindness.

59. What can we learn from the passage?
    A. Sports could bring people from different places together.
    B. The writer used to live in Park City.
    C. Learning to ski is important.
    D. The writer finally became a professional athlete.

60. What's the best title for the passage?
    A. An Interesting Sport   B. An Unforgettable Experience
    C. A Useful Skill   D. A Wonderland for Skiing

第二部分 （文科类职业模块考生作答，共15分）

五、单项选择题（本大题共5小题，每小题1分，共计5分）

从A、B、C、D四个选项中，选出空白处的最佳选项。

61. —Henry, you _____ on the phone.
    —Oh, _____ Thank you.
    A. are wanted; I come   B. are wanted; I'm coming
    C. are being wanted; I come D. are wanting; I'm coming

62. _____ means this lane is for vehicles only. No bike allowed on this lane.
    A.   B.   C.   D.

63. —Let's go to Mr. Yu's speech on Chinese culture, shall we?
    —_____ We can go next time.
    A. Why not?   B. That's all right
    C. Never mind   D. I'm afraid it's too late

64. —Tom failed in the running competition last week.
    —_____! He is the best at running in our grade.
    A. I know   B. Don't be silly
    C. You can't be serious D. It doesn't matter.

65. —Mandy, could you please give me a lift to the train station?
    —Sure. _____.
    A. with pleasure   B. it doesn't matter
    C. pardon me   D. take it easy

六、阅读理解（本大题共5小题，每小题2分，共计10分）

从A、B、C、D四个选项中，选出符合题目要求的最佳选项。

Everyone has a family name. In English countries(国家), the family name is the last name. Do you know how English people get their family names? And what do they mean? English people usually get their family names in these ways(方式).

Some family names come from the places(地方) of their homes. A man lives on or near a hill, his family name may be Hill. In England, people's names may be Wood, Lake, because they live near the wood or the lake.

Some family names come from a person's job. If a person is a cook(厨师), his family name may be Cook.

And many people get their family names from their fathers' family names. If you hear the name "Jackson", you can know that he is the son of Jack.

Do you know more interesting stories about English names?

66. In the passage, English people usually have _____ ways to get their family names.
    A. two   B. three   C. four   D. five

67. Jack's family name is Cook. His family name may come from the _____ place.
    A. place   B. hobby   C. job   D. country

68. A boy's family name is Jackson because he is _____.
    A. Jack's father   B. Jack's best friend
    C. the grandfather of Jack D. the son of Jack

69. According to the passage, which sentence is true?
    A. English people put their family names first.
    B. Many people get their family names from their mother's family names.
    C. A man live on or near a hill, his family name must be Lake.
    D. If you hear a name "Bill Bush", his family may live near the bush.
70. The passage mainly talks about _____ in English countries.
    A. hills and lakes   B. English people
    C. family names   D. jobs and homes

第三部分 （工科类职业模块考生作答，共15分）

七、单项选择题（本大题共5小题，每小题1分，共计5分）

从 A、B、C、D 四个选项中，选出空白处的最佳选项。

71. Construction warning signs can make sure that _____ people keep away and that workers wear safety protection equipment.
    A. unauthorized   B. authorized   C. protected   D. protecting
72. The basic unit of mass or weight is _____.
    A. kilogram   B. milligram   C. gram   D. tonne
73. When welding, grinding, handling chemicals, the workers have to wear _____.
    A. PPE   B. face shield   C. panel   D. extinguisher
74. The big ball is _____ the small ball.
    A. three times the size of   B. three times big than
    C. as three times big as   D. three times bigger then
75. Six times five divided by the square root of nine is _____.
    A. 9   B. 10   C. 11   D. 12

八、阅读理解（本大题共5小题，每小题2分，共计10分）

从 A、B、C、D 四个选项中，选出符合题目要求的最佳选项。

The number of people who have died worldwide in the CVID-19 pandemic(新冠肺炎疫情) has passed three million, according to Johns Hopkins University(约翰霍普金斯大学). The milestone(转折点) comes the day after the head of the WHO(世卫组织) warned the world was "Reaching the highest rate of infection"(最高感染率) so far. India experiencing a second wave recorded more than 230,000 new cases(病例) on Saturday alone.

More than 140 million cases have been recorded all over the world since the pandemic began.

WHO chief Dr. Tedros warned on Friday that "cases and deaths are continuing to increase at worrying speeds". He added that "All over the world, the number of new cases every week has nearly doubled over the past two months".

The US, India and Brazil, the countries with the most recorded cases, have accounted for more than a million deaths between them, according to Johns Hopkins University.

Last week, an average(平均) of 12,000 deaths a day reported around the world, according to news agency AFP. However, official figures worldwide(世界官方数据) may not fully reflect the true number in many countries.

76. How many people have died all over the world according to Johns Hopkins University?
    A. More than 3,000,000.   B. Less than 3,000,000.
    C. More than 30,000,000.   D. Less than 30,000,000.
77. Which of the following statements is RIGHT?
    A. According to Johns Hopkins University, the world was reaching the highest rate of infection.
    B. India experiencing a second wave recorded more than 230,000 new cases only in one day.
    C. More than 140 million cases have been recorded all over India since the pandemic began.
    D. Dr. Tedros is the head of Johns Hopkins University.
78. Which countries has the most infections?
    A. The UK, the US. and India.   B. Brazil, the UK. and India.
    C. Brazil, the US. and India.   D. Britain, the US and Brazil.
79. The last paragraph mainly tells us that _____.
    A. there will be the most deaths all over the world soon
    B. there were the most deaths last week all over the world
    C. official figures worldwide may reflect lager number of deaths in many countries
    D. official figures worldwide may reflect smaller number of deaths in many countries
80. Which should be the best title of the passage?
    A. The COVID-19 pandemic is in control all over the word.
    B. How to poet ourselves in the COVID 19 pandemic.
    C. The cause of the COVID-19 pandemic.
    D. The COVID-19 pandemic is still serious in some countries.

九、书面表达（15分）

假定你是李华，你的英语朋友 Leslie 听说你所在的城市暴发新型冠状病毒肺炎疫情，给你发邮件询问你在此期间是怎么度过的，请你根据下列要点写一封邮件回复她。

1. 暴发时间；
2. 怎么度过；
3. 你的感受。

注意：1. 词数80词左右，给出的部分不计入词数；
　　　2. 可以适当增加细节，以使行文连贯。

参考词汇：疫情 epidemic situation；新冠肺炎：novel corona virus pneumonia

Dear Leslie,

　　I'm glad to receive your email. You asked me to share with you what experienced in the epidemic situation. Here are my experiences.

_____

_____

_____

_____

Thank you for your concern. I'm looking forward to your reply.

Yours,
Li Hua